TRAVELS

IN

CEYLON AND CONTINENTAL INDIA

TRAVELS

IN

CEYLON AND CONTINENTAL INDIA;

INCLUDING

NEPAL AND OTHER PARTS OF THE HIMALAYAS,

TO THE BORDERS OF THIBET,

WITH SOME NOTICES OF THE OVERLAND ROUTE.

BY

DR. W. HOFFMEISTER

GYAN

Published by

Gyan Publishing House
5, Ansari Road
Daryaganj, New Delhi-110002
Phone: 011-47034999, 9811692060
E-mail: books@gyanbooks.com

Distribution Network
gyanbooks.com
India, USA, Canada, UK, Australia, France

ISBN: 978-81-212-8296-3 (PB)
First Published, 1848

2nd Impression 2023

Printed at: Gyan Press, Delhi.

TRAVELS IN CEYLON AND CONTINENTAL INDIA
Author: W. HOFFMEISTER

TRAVELS

IN

CEYLON AND CONTINENTAL INDIA;

INCLUDING

NEPAL AND OTHER PARTS OF THE HIMALAYAS, TO THE BORDERS OF THIBET,

WITH SOME NOTICES OF THE OVERLAND ROUTE.

APPENDICES,

I.

ADDRESSED TO BARON VON HUMBOLDT,

ON THE GEOGRAPHICAL DISTRIBUTION OF CONIFERÆ ON THE HIMALAYAN MOUNTAINS.

II.

ON THE VEGETATION OF THE HIMALAYAN MOUNTAINS.

III.

THE BIRDS OF THE HIMALAYAN MOUNTAINS.

BY

DR W. HOFFMEISTER,

TRAVELLING PHYSICIAN TO HIS ROYAL HIGHNESS

PRINCE WALDEMAR OF PRUSSIA.

Translated from the German.

EDINBURGH:

WILLIAM P. KENNEDY, ST ANDREW STREET.

LONDON: HAMILTON, ADAMS, AND CO.

MDCCCXLVIII.

PREFACE.

THE following Letters and descriptive sketches are the legacy of a traveller in the distant lands of the East;—one who may be said to have reached the summit of that peculiar happiness attainable by those only who are of enthusiastic temperament, and inquisitive in the pursuit of natural science. Ever true to the duties of his own calling,—still, even in war, beside that Prince whom he had accompanied as medical attendant through all the dangers of a most arduous journey, as far as the banks of the Sutlej in the territory of the Sikhs,—himself a lover of peace, he was snatched away by a violent death on a battle-field. The fragments now presented to the public, must be considered as the relics of a mind, imbued with the living freshness of youth, cultivated by a scientific education, full of susceptibility to impression in a world new to him, of unwearied activity in comprehending the ever-changing phases of nature in her most varied and most gorgeous forms, and of human society in its manifold relations, and withal, animated by a lively desire to communicate without delay to friends at home what he had recently witnessed. These are but scattered pages, which could only have been moulded into their proper shape after the author's return. His brothers and relatives, painfully deprived of that hope, have deemed it a fitting tribute of love and respect to the deceased, to collect these fragments, in order that even what is merely touched on, or hinted at, in them, may not sink, useless, into oblivion.

And we must acknowledge our obligation to them in this matter; for even the few pages, printed formerly in the journals of the day, excited a universal interest, which may now, it is hoped, be increased by more connected details.

If a rapid journey does not afford time or opportunity for thorough investigation and deep scientific research, because one picture too quickly supplants another; it has, on the other hand, the advantage of affording facilities for the more lively apprehension of every remarkable position of affairs, every salient object, every striking appearance,—viewed in the boldest outlines, the most marked contrasts, the most pleasing aspects.

Such advantages will not fail to be noticed among

the letters and papers now collected, especially as they present before us scenes from the most celebrated, most lovely, and most magnificent countries of the East, enlivened by a foreground which the suite of a Prince can alone furnish.

As these are the communications of a travelling companion of the first German Prince who ever visited Ceylon, Bengal, and the courts of Cathmandoo and Oude, we thus obtain a new point-de-vue, from which we may become acquainted with the mode of life of the nations that inhabit the lands of the Ganges and of the Sutlej, with that also of the people of Ceylon and of the elevated valleys of the Himalayas.

Natural History and Topography have not been without their share of benefit; as new paths have been forced through the wonderful mountain-range of the Himalayan chain, over rocky heights and snowy peaks, by the enterprising courage of these travellers; and as the productions of animal creation, as well as those of the most luxuriant vegetation, in valleys and on mountains, have afforded much new matter and many curious surveys to the naturalist.

In conclusion,—the many characteristic and well-combined touches, describing the manners and customs of society among the most various races, nations, classes, religious and political communities, and grades of civilization, in the East, add not a little to the agreeable and exciting interest which pervades the following pages, compensating to the reader for the want of those finishing strokes which the destroying hand of Fate rendered it impossible to supply.

C. RITTER.

BERLIN, 14th March 1847.

MEMOIR OF THE AUTHOR.

OWING to the very scanty amount of information hitherto obtained by natives of Germany on the subject of India and Indian affairs, the oriental journey of His Royal Highness Prince Waldemar of Prussia excited a universal interest, as giving rise to the hope that the observations made on the regions traversed by him,—some of them as yet but rarely visited,—would be made the property of the public at large. A few detached epistolary communications from Dr Hoffmeister, who accompanied the Prince as travelling physician, were favourably received in numerous circles, on account of the peculiarly comprehensive and graphic descriptions contained in them; and they led to the expectation that, on the traveller's return, these short fragments might be collected and presented in an entire form.

The death of the Author put an end to that hope. It appeared, therefore, to the surviving relatives, to be a sacred duty to collect those posthumous fragments,—which indeed could have been arranged in a regular, scientific manner by his hands only,—and to commit them to the press. In taking this step, they were favoured by the gracious approval of his Royal Highness.

This origin of the publication accounts for its present form. It contains only those letters which were written for his own immediate circle of relatives and friends, usually penned amid the engrossing occupations of a rapid and fatiguing journey, under the oppressive influence of a tropical climate. Yet not only are their contents unaltered, but their original form is likewise preserved, because it alone could afford sufficient freedom in the connection and communication of the diversified matter of which they treat. The gaps have been, as far as possible, filled up from the journals; several shorter letters have been united to form one longer one, and placed in chronological order, so as to furnish a distinct survey of the whole route. The fragments of botanical and zoological information, which were scattered through the posthumous papers, and could not well be introduced into the series of letters, have been appended separately.

Thus much it was necessary to say regarding the origin and form of the book. As to the value of the matter now laid before the public, it behoved not the Editor to form any opinion; nothing, therefore, could give him greater satisfaction, than to be enabled to preface it with the favourable judgment pronounced upon it by Professor Dr Carl Ritter.

Many readers, who may turn with closer interest to the personal character of the Author, as displayed in these letters, may wish to find here a short sketch of his life, and of his scientific pursuits.

Werner Hoffmeister was born in Brunswick on the 14th of March 1819. His parents resided in that place till the year 1827, when his father, who hitherto had been minister of the parish of St Peter's, was transferred to Wolfenbuttel, in the capacity of member of the Consistorial Council. Werner's cloudless childhood was passed in the untroubled domestic circle of his parents' house, till his father's death, in the year 1832. The joyous nature of the boy soon got the better of the painful impression of that event.

From his early childhood, it was the fresh life of nature which, above all else, attracted and occupied him. He delighted in roaming, with his youthful companions, over the surrounding hills and forests, to collect plants and insects; or, at other times, his hours were spent in watching, and taking care of, a number of animals of various kinds, with which he peopled the house and the court-yard. Sometimes sparrows or tit-mice,*—sometimes a pair of young jack-daws or owls, from the neighbouring church-steeple,—or again, mice or bats, formed his ménagerie. His first surgical experiments were performed on an owl, which had had its legs broken by the roughness of the keeper of the tower; and the sufferings then endured by the poor animal, had well-nigh caused him to waver in the inclination which he had already manifested towards the medical profession.

Amidst these occupations, the scientific education, which his great abilities made it requsite that he should receive at an early age, was by no means neglected. The classical languages, and still more, mathematics and geography, excited a vivid interest in his mind; still, however, his passion for the study of natural science continued to predominate; and it was nourished and strengthened by meeting with similar tastes in an elder brother, and by the scientific instruction he received from a friend. The diligent reading of books of travels, and frequent excursions among the neighbouring Harz mountains, enlarged, with his advancing years, the circle of his obser-

* The Penduline Titmouse,—one of Nature's most ingenious architects,—is a bird well known in Germany, Poland, Lithuania, and Northern Italy. The young naturalist could not fail to admire its exquisitely-formed nest of closely woven down, which is suspended, like a bag, from some pliant bough, and carefully sheltered from cold, having none but a side aperture, and that defended by a projecting brim; but the structure is looked on with a somo what different feeling by the peasantry, who regard it with superstitious veneration. In some parts of Germany, one of these nests is suspended near the door of each cottage, and the possessors look upon it as a protector from thunder, and its little architect as a sacred bird.—Tr.

vations, and increased his desire of becoming acquainted with remoter regions, and with nature in the peculiar forms there displayed. Even in those days, he was occasionally pained by reflecting how little prospect his future life appeared to offer of the possibility of satisfying this craving.

During his last year at school, he had finally determined to study medicine; and after his mother's death, he removed, with a view to preparing for the university, to the "Collegium Carolinum" at Brunswick, where, in quiet retirement, he devoted his time to anatomical, botanical, and mineralogical studies. In the spring of 1839 he quitted Brunswick, to commence his academic course at Berlin, attracted thither not merely by the distinguished fame of its university, but by the privilege there offered him, of enjoying the scientific aid and the advice of his uncle, Professor Lichtenstein, to whom, more than to any one else, he was indebted for the guidance of his studies. He availed himself, with unremitting diligence, of the means of improvement afforded him in the lectures of Muller, Mitscherlich, Kunth, and Weiss; and as his insight into that science which was his chosen portion grew deeper, his affection for it still increased.

On leaving Berlin, he betook himself to the University of Bonn, where his cheerful lively character was developed in all its vigour and energy, under the influence of academic life, and of a numerous circle of friends. Various tours, both in the immediate vicinity of the valley of the Rhine, and in Switzerland, the South of France, and Holland, tended, in some measure, to satisfy that desire,—as intense as ever in his mind,—of penetrating into distant parts; and at the same time they were far from being fruitless, in point of scientific improvement; as he profited diligently by every advantage he met with in visiting the various learned institutions, museums, hospitals, and clinical lecture-rooms; and also, while at Montpelier, by his acquaintance with Marcel de Serres, Lallemand, and Kuinolz. His medical knowledge was enlarged and more deeply fixed, while at Bonn, by his academical and personal intercourse with Nasse, Harless, and Von Ibell, by repeated experiments, and by his own medical practice.

In a similar manner he passed the latter years of his course at the Berlin University, to which he returned at Michaelmas, 1841; but his hitherto joyous spirit was overwhelmed with sadness by the sudden death of a younger sister, to whom he was tenderly attached. For a considerable time, his energy was so much crushed, and such a deep and settled melancholy had taken possession of his soul, that, withdrawing himself from everything in the shape of recreation, and remaining in close retirement, he pursued, from a principle of duty alone, the course of study which he had begun. The medical practice in which he was employed, both in Busch's clinical hospital, and in Dr Behrendt's Orthopædic Institution, was little fitted to restore his wonted cheerfulness; yet he continued to attend to it with great diligence, and with much self-devotion. Besides this, he bestowed much time upon a scientific work,—a treatise on earthworms,—which he commenced with a view to the examination for his doctor's degree, and which he subsequently enlarged, and printed in a separate form. The lectures of Schönlein, Wagner, and Hecker, gave a fresh impulse to his love of science, and completed his academic course.

Possessed of a degree of cultivation which fully qualified him for the medical profession, and of a rich store of knowledge in the various branches of natural science, he quitted Berlin in the autumn of 1843, after having taken his doctor's degree, with the intention of visiting London and Paris. During the three months he spent in London, he not only enlarged his scientific acquirements, but sought an opening for going out to India as ship-surgeon. He met with no situation such as he desired; and another plan, for going out from Paris as superintendent and physician of a colony to Malacca, which was nearly carried into execution, also failed. Discouraged and cast down, he returned to his "fatherland." There, fortune, which he thought had for ever forsaken him, unexpectedly smiled upon him. His Royal Highness Prince Waldemar of Prussia was making preparations for his journeyings in the East. Dr Hoffmeister was recommended for the situation of travelling physician, by Humboldt, Schönlein and Lichtenstein, and was accepted by His Royal Highness. In this situation, no less honourable than enjoyable, the cherished dreams of his early days were abundantly realized. The varied cultivation of his intellect, the youthful freshness of his mind and spirit, and the healthful vigour of his bodily frame, seemed to ensure the happiest and most valuable results to his journey. Thus, with the brightest prospects both for nearer and more distant futurity, he quitted his native land, to find, after dangers escaped and difficulties overcome during a long wandering, an early grave in a distant clime!

DR. A. HOFFMEISTER.

BERLIN, 7TH OF APRIL, 1847.

LETTERS FROM THE EAST.

FIRST LETTER.

DEPARTURE FROM TRIESTE—ANCONA—CHURCH OF ST CYRIACUS—CORFU—ITS INHABITANTS—CAFE DEL CLUB—PRINCE GEORGE OF CAMBRIDGE—EXCURSION TO THE MOUNTAINS—DEPARTURE—BAY OF PATRAS—PATRAS—CASTLE—CAFE—CORINTH—THE ACRO-CORINTHUS—DEPARTURE FROM KENKRES—ATHENS—ACROPOLIS—DESCRIPTION OF THE CITY—THE GREEK COURT—FETE CHAMPETRE—MARKET AT ATHENS—MUSEUM—VILLAGE OF KALAKI—GROTTO OF THE NYMPHS—BOTANIC GARDEN—DEPARTURE.

ATHENS, *Sept.* 21, 1844.

EVERYTHING apparently conspires to render this journey one of the most agreeable that can be imagined. The weather is incomparably beautiful; the sun and moon alternate in ever gladdening brightness, the sea is smooth as a mirror, of a deep sapphire-blue, the heat not excessive, the society agreeable in the extreme; in short, we have all that heart can desire.

We sailed from Trieste on the afternoon of the 16th of September, and arrived next morning at eight o'clock at Ancona, where we were received by the Consul. Under his guidance we visited every thing worthy of any notice in that small shabby town. The dirty white houses, with their flat, whitewashed roofs of hollow tiles, appeared tolerably neat when viewed from above; and the sea, to whose shore I longed to betake myself, lay at our feet, clear as crystal and of an azure hue. Our principal object was the Church of St Cyriacus, said to have been built out of the ruins of a temple of Venus. The exterior appears like a building of Venetian architecture, with numerous small pillars supported by lions, at the principal entrance, and many variegated marble ornaments inserted in the grey limestone. The interior corresponds exactly with my idea of a Moorish mosque, with broad arched ceilings of many-coloured cloth. The monuments and antiquities which it contains are of no particular interest.

After having partaken of a tolerable dinner in a dirty hotel,—the best, however, in the place,—we rambled through some streets of the town, all swarming with filthy, ragged creatures,—and speedily re-embarked in the steamer, which, leaving Ancona, followed the coast of Istria. As far as Corfu we kept always within view of the shore, which became even more parched and arid than it had been at Ancona and at Trieste. Olive groves, in which were trees of great age and wonderful size, and vineyards, were the only traces of cultivation discernible even by the aid of a spy-glass, on the bare limestone rock. Here and there peeped forth a group of small white limestone cottages, or a wreath of curling smoke,—not a man was to be seen,—not another sign of life. At length appeared the island of Corcyra, now called Corfu,—to its right the island of Tano, on which the nymph Calypso is said to have dwelt, and the rocks of the Cyclops. These rocks are not few in number round Corfu, and at least a dozen of them may be distinctly noticed. How enchanting, once more to rest one's eyes on a green isle! The lofty Albanian hills too, on the opposite coast, have a bolder and more picturesque appearance, as seen from this point. Above them again tower the

Ceraunian mountains, to the height of seven thousand feet. Corresponding to them, on the island itself, rises the noble San Salvador, about four thousand feet in height.

The town of Corfu has a bright and pleasing aspect; flags of many colours, and multitudes of fishermen and of sailors, Greeks and Turks, in varied and motley costumes, (chiefly however quite white, or with red or blue jackets, and white *fustanelle*,) crowd the shores. The castle occupies the projecting eminence; of equal strength are the fortifications of the adjacent island of Vido, from which the English,—the present possessors of Corfu,—may command the harbour. At last the longed-for permission to land arrived. At three o'clock in the afternoon, an elegant little bark, lined throughout with linen, fetched us from our ship. What a crush upon the quay,—what a multitude of strange, wild-looking faces! On our right, a large depôt of melons, cactus-fruit, and grapes;—on our left, the filthy office of the board of health, over the door of which was inscribed "Υγιεῖον καταστήρων." Amid the crowd of sun-burnt faces, and the tattered Greek costumes, which had once been white, the multitude of Greek priests, all in black, with high four-cornered caps, produces a striking effect.

The natives of the island are still, for the most part, distinguished by the mixed colours of their attire, and by their blue *bag-stockings*, which, the Greek name having escaped me, I am unable to designate by any other expression. They consist of a large folded bag, in which a hole is cut on either side to admit the foot. The Palikari of the Morea, on the other hand, wear the white *fustanella*, a cotton petticoat, laid in innumerable folds, and scarcely reaching over the knee;—and, with it, the beautifully ornamented "calza," of red cloth, or morocco-leather, a sort of gaiter, stretching from below the knee to the instep, and hooked round the calf of the leg. All

Greeks wear the red *fez*, with blue or silver tassel,—a covering for the head, which appears to me marvellously unsuited to the frightful glow of their scorching sun. The red or blue jacket, without sleeves, embroidered in gold or silver, worn by persons of distinction, is a magnificent dress;—the sleeves form a separate piece and leave open all the inner side of the arm, from which hangs forth a full and very white shirt-sleeve. The belt round the waist is broad, and beautifully adorned with embroidery of gold and silver. But of such persons we met with very few in Corfu; the people we saw were, generally, exceedingly ragged and filthy-looking, with the exception of the countless priests, on whose black or dark-blue long gowns dirt may have passed unperceived. The chief qualification for the priesthood here appears to be a long black beard, with corresponding whiskers: to me it is inconceivable how such roguish-looking beings can be ecclesiastics. The dark-brown complexion of the lower classes struck me as pleasing; it results rather from their custom of being always half-naked, than from their having Moorish or Gipsy blood in their veins. Most of these people were very ugly, more especially the dark, chesnut-coloured hucksters, with heads half-shorn, and the remaining tuft of hair tied in a tail behind, who offer, at a cheap rate, prickly pears, oranges, jujube and love-apples.

On our way to the hotel, to which we were led through narrow lanes, stinking, and full of dirty rubbish, we were assailed by beggars of every description. A house, fully as dirty on the outside as all the others, was pointed out as the hotel. On the steps, at the door of entrance, lay a filthy Moor, playing at dice with five other ragged fellows;—while all around them were strewn the well-gnawed rinds of the water-melons, which had served them for breakfast. With some trouble we forced our way through, and scrambled up a steep wooden stair, covered with a thick coating of dirt. Our whole party were unanimous in thinking that we had hit upon the wrong house, and that this pig-sty could not possibly be the first-rate hotel, described in all our guide-books as a capital house. Our cicerones were therefore compelled to turn to the right about, to make search for another hotel, which, it was supposed, must exist. We had scarcely however reached the door, when the whole party of our English friends met us, a sure sign that our guides had led us right. A few words passed, among which the English word "*dirty*" repeatedly caught my ear. Unfortunately, this had been heard and understood by the landlord, a half-civilized Albanian, who now poured forth a volley of curses, accompanied by most furious looks.

The dice-playing public, and many other folk, to whom such a scene appeared highly delectable, gathered around us, and we were forced hastily to retreat. The other hotel had remarkably pleasant apartments, but our hopes were dashed on being informed that they were only to be let by the week or month. Nothing now remained for us, save to wend our way back once more through the assembled public of Corfu, all eager to criticize our proceedings. This formidable step was at length taken; and on returning, we found, in the first place, that the rooms of the hotel were much better than we had fancied them;—but in the second place, that the landlord, from malice,—as we were not inclined, like the English people, to pass the night there, but intended to sleep on board,—would not give us any food.

A couple of gold pieces, paid in advance, soon made him relent, and he promised that, in the course of two hours, he would have a good dinner prepared for us. This time of waiting was, by dint of bargaining, beat down to one hour, for longer our hungry stomachs could not hold out. *En attendant;* we sought a palliative in a mixture of coffee-grounds and water, in the Cafè del Club, under a splendid colonnade, which nearly surrounds the handsome "piazza," in the centre of the town. Sly-looking black-eyed boys were playing around us; some of them martyrizing, in a most inhuman manner, a bird which they had caught, while others were snatching away the crutches of a poor cripple. The grand piazza, planted all round with *Ailanthus* trees, lay before us; to the left of it rose the palazzo of the governor, with its spacious portico, and its two beautiful gates;—in front of it a fountain, the basin of which surrounds the statue of Sir Frederick Adam. To the right stretches an extensive grove of acacias, in the middle of which stands the statue of General Schulenburg, who, under the Venetians in 1716, six times repulsed the Turks from the fortress; and lastly, high above the "piazza" frowns the castle, surmounted by its lighthouse. As we could still afford sufficient time, we sought out the most beautiful points of view within our reach. Art (*i. e.* the English) has done much to beautify this charmingly situated town: more especially fine is the view of it, from the foot of the fort to which we climbed.

An invitation to dine with Prince George of Cambridge, the commandant of the place, saved us from the necessity of returning to our hotel. The dinner was succeeded by a ride, in which unluckily, so many claims were made on my skill in horsemanship,—of which this was the first trial,—that I could manage to see but little of the delightful olive-forest, or of the magnificent sunset glow; and, had not our speed been somewhat abated in returning, I should have preserved but a slight recollection of that lovely evening. I do however at least retain in my mind a faint, yet pleasing picture of the beautiful, oak-like growth of the olive-tree,—of the half-clothed herdsmen, and the many-coloured flocks of goats, under the deep shade of the forest,—and of the glorious vistas of the azure sea, in which the setting sun was about to sink into its tomb. It was late when, rowed by Prince George's twelve gondoliers, we sped our way to the steamer by moonlight, over the glassy sea.

At five in the morning, on the 19th of September, we were to make another flying excursion, which was to extend across the mountainous part of the island of Corcyra, and its interesting ruins: but alas! no information was to be obtained among the learned of the town of Corfu, concerning the well-preserved remains of an ancient city named Calliope, of which all the English Hand-books are full. No one knew the name;—it was only subsequently that I learned that the disappointment had arisen out of a typographical error, Calliope being put instead of Cassiope, the ancient name of the city of Corcyra. It lies farther eastward, and still, in its numerous ruins, gives evidence of its former greatness.

At half-past five A.M., we were already on shore and in our saddles. We began by rambling through the picturesque environs of the town, in which several palm-trees already appeared. We saw two very pretty villages, one of which, Potamo by name, was full of life; but the houses every where consist merely of four walls without windows, with a flat roof. The filth in their interiors is frightful; yet the inhabitants are tolerably cleanly in their persons, especially the women, who have a mode of dress quite peculiar to themselves, and do not, like other Greek females, cover their heads with the fez.

We now proceeded on our ride without path or gate, climbing steep hills, over hedges and ditches, always aiming at the highest points. On arriving at the high ground, and finding ourselves beside a cottage, the inhabitants of which betrayed great alarm, having probably never before seen horses on their steep rocks, we got a woman to give us some grapes, which we devoured with excellent appetite, while the whole population gazed in utter amazement at the grape-eating cavaliers. Signs served instead of language, as we had no interpreter. Again we advanced, at a gallop, over what had been the bed of a river, full of stones and pebbles, till we found another rocky height to climb. Our horses clambered up like goats. We halted among the ruins of a villa, very picturesquely situated among olive-trees, where we met two tall, handsome, splendidly attired, young Greeks, who held our horses for us. I took the opportunity of sketching these fine-looking fellows with their proud and noble countenances. One was clad in a perfectly white costume, the covering of his legs alone was of scarlet cloth, with silver clasps, and his belt of red velvet, loaded with embroidery of gold: the latter contained a pair of pistols, inlaid with silver, with long narrow stocks, and two poniards, a long and a short one. The drawing caused them great pleasure, for they appeared extremely vain both of their beauty and of their finery.

Beautiful as is the thick and gigantic olive-forest in these parts, vegetation generally is dry and withered; a couple of cyclamens, and the squilla maritima, with its long leafless stalk, were the only blossoming plants; —the insects also were but few;—I saw only some beetles, *(Ateuchus,)* in the dung, some hornets and a couple of white butterflies. The people lead, in general, an idle life; for this olive-forest produces, without much exertion on their part, enough for their support; no one thinks of making new plantations; and the fields that surround the villages are neither manured nor ploughed. Each tree brings its regular income now, as was the case a hundred years since; and the vine is indigenous. It was only in the neighbourhood of the town, where the soil is extremely fertile, that we saw fields of maize, and ground laid out for the cultivation of vegetables; and there is indeed far more of all this here, than in the other parts of Greece.

I never should have imagined that the olive-tree could have so picturesque an appearance as it has here, where it equals the oak in height; the stems, usually full of holes and cavities, are of considerable size, and crowned with beautiful foliage, the shade of which is often most refreshing, when riding, in the heat of the day, on the ridge of a mountain.

Thus, by following paths over which I could not have ventured to pass on foot, we at length reached the vicinity of the town,—not a little fatigued, but still animated by the remembrance of the exquisite landscapes we had beheld among these sea-girt mountains. As I wished to make a few purchases, I gladly availed myself of the permission to absent myself from our party during the visit to the fortifications of the adjacent island of Vido. A few minutes more, and I found myself once again on board the steam-boat, and soon the Prince's gondola rowed across from the island of Vido, and gave the signal for sailing, which was immediately obeyed. Our English fellow-travellers we found all re-assembled, and our adventures were mutually recounted. About four o'clock we all dined together. On this occasion the heat of the cabin became most oppressive; moreover, just after our repast, a very uncomfortable hot wind sprung up, which caused the ship to roll violently, so that, towards evening, several of the passengers were attacked by sea-sickness. To spend the night in our cabin would have been intolerable: the heat rose to 28° Réaumur (98° Fahrenheit). I took, therefore, my sea-cloak for my companion, and slept on deck, until the drenching morning-dew drove me back into the cabin.

Meantime we had run into the bay of Patras, and were passing, now close under the coast of Lepanto; now again, still closer under that of the Morea. Upon those rocks (which were altogether bare, or had only here and there a few *maritime pines* and *tamarisks* growing on them,) many villages were pointed out as occupying the sites of celebrated cities; but I shall not weary you with an enumeration of them. None of them seemed to possess much beauty. At nine o'clock we landed at Patras, our first Greek town. This is genuine classic ground. If one had not been aware of the fact, the mighty ruins, which extend far into the sea around the harbour, as well as the earnest, solemn countenances of the soldiers who lay stretched on the beach, must have convinced one of it. We passed through a broad piazza, surrounded by small stone buildings, before reaching the town itself. Here every place swarmed with busy, active men. Some were rolling barrels; others nailing down chests; here, an industrious shoemaker was working in front of his door; there, a tailor, with at least a dozen assistants. In one spot they have already begun to dig a canal through the middle of the street; in another, a number of paviors are working at the new market-place: in short, a degree of bustle and activity reigns here, not to be met with in other large towns in Greece.

The city is quite new; of the ancient town which lay farther westward, and, according to the custom of ancient Greek sea-ports, more inland, nothing is now visible, save some heaps of ruins:—all has been laid waste by the Turks. The works of the new city, now springing up, are being carried on with great zeal; long colonnades have been built already, at the expense of Government, to mark out the future streets, although as yet neither shops nor dwelling-houses have arisen under their shadow. Farther on, towards the hills, the houses degenerate into filthy hovels; and, among the cleanly-dressed men, are to be seen on all sides, dirty, crippled beggars, and wild-looking gipsy boys: here and there we also noticed two or three old women with dishevelled hair, trailing themselves through the filth of the streets; for the beautiful springs which rise among the hills, and which ought to scatter refreshing vegetation around, no channel being dug for their water which therefore stagnates in the great heat, are transformed into a stinking marsh, reaching to the confines of the leafless, grassless, dusty plain below.

When we had ascended half-way up the hill, on which rises the old "Castello,"—still in tolerable preservation,—we again witnessed the shocking manner in which these fine springs of water are continually abused. A house was to be built: for this purpose, nothing was thought necessary but to hack up the soil, composed of crumbled ruins, turning in at the same time the water of the nearest spring, and scattering on this miry slough, a little straw and some dried grass. Lime and mortar being thus prepared, they merely built up, straightway and on the spot, the stones that lay strewn around them! Having reached the summit of the mount, we forced our way through heaps of ruins to the half-destroyed Venetian "castello." Entering at a small iron door, which was scarcely closed, we found a strong detachment of Greek soldiers, in most picturesque groups. Nothing can have a better effect than that beautiful Greek costume. Their jerkins were sky-blue with silver, the *calze* of the same blue stuff, fustanelle and ample sleeves of white, a broad sabre, several pistols, a very long musket, and the red fez, completed each man's warlike attire. Some of them were seated on a half-fallen stair, carelessly holding their fire-arms; another group was playing at cards, under the shade of a fig-tree, upon the ruins of a marble fountain; while others were employed in unloading the mules that had brought provisions. Their captain, of giant stature, with tremendous black mustachios, and with numerous medals on his jacket, was going round, reading in a growling tone the list of names, from a dirty paper he held in his hand. We ascended the tower, and soon we saw the black-looking captain defiling with his company, at a quick pace, through the field of ruins; a most picturesque sight! Lower down lay the town, in beautiful disorder; round about it the mountains of red limestone; opposite, the Albanian shores; and, in the centre of the landscape, the azure bay, thickly studded with sails. After having refreshed ourselves by admiring the beautiful prospect, we entered at another door of the fort, and here we found the spring of water encircled by fresh and lovely verdure. Peculiarly refreshing was the sight of a prodigiously large plane-tree, the only one left standing by the Turks, who spared it, because it served to hang the Greeks upon. Close beside this fountain-head, we found a small house among the trees, a little nook far too inviting for us to pass without lingering there. The inmates of the house brought chairs and tables promptly and unasked; fetched fresh water, and offered us wine grapes, and all this merely that they might enjoy the pleasure of looking at us. The fort, with its plane-tree, was soon selected as the subject of a sketch. Now the people flocked from all sides, full of curiosity; for the most part they had uncommonly handsome faces, sunburnt, but clean-looking, with an honest expression.

Two remarkably handsome lads, of ten or eleven years of age, especially attracted my attention. I drew the portrait of one of them: he stood perfectly still, with decorum and respect, not knowing what I was going to do with him. Some men, who had pressed forward to peep over my shoulder, began to notice the thing, and when at last, they discovered the likeness, they cried aloud again and again, "Καλόν! καλόν!" And now each man would have his picture taken,—each one pressed forward to the spot where the boy had stood, smote on his breast, and gesticulated with extraordinary vivacity, placing himself in the best attitude, and adjusting his dress in the most becoming manner. It was a wonderfully pretty scene. One of the most refined-looking, and best dressed among them, had the honour of being sketched; and when at last, he actually stood there upon the paper, the fellow himself and his neighbours could not contain themselves for joy; he hopped and jumped, first on one leg, then on the other, snapped his fingers, and talked on without ceasing; at length he took Count Gr——— and me aside, and drew us almost by force into his hut at no great distance, brought out his arms, displayed to us his medals won in the Turkish war, and laid before us his best belts and jackets; then he went into the little garden, tore down with both his hands some bunches of grapes, which he constrained us to accept, and gathered besides for each of us, a large nosegay of odoriferous herbs.

On returning to the spring, we there found the aged consul, bowed down with grief and hardships, who had previously announced his intended visit. He spoke little, as he only understood Italian and Greek, and looked peevish and morose amidst all our mirth, while we were amusing ourselves by making the swarthy little youngsters, with their beautiful, merry, black eyes, trundle their hoops, and leap to catch gold coins. In the mean time, Count Gr—— had collected a multitude of the older people around him, to whom he was displaying experiments with a chemical apparatus for instantaneous light. How they did stare and shake their heads, when, with a cracking explosion, the tinder was ignited! One man was bold enough to wish to try the thing himself; when he at last succeeded, he was gazed at with astonishment by the rest, and was unable to conceal his own joy, and thereupon they all in chorus shouted out their cry of καλόν! καλόν! While such entertainment was going on, time was gliding away unperceived, and we were obliged to think of retracing our steps to the town. We afterwards found however, that we had a little interval remaining before our departure, of which we availed ourselves to obtain, in a house which was quite hidden under bowers of Corinthian vines, a sight of the stores of these Corinth grapes (commonly called currants). Unluckily this pretty fruit was already spread out for drying, and the process of preparing was explained to us, without its being possible to offer us any of the high-flavoured and much-prized little grapes. We next witnessed the teaching of a troop of little children, who were all seated in a dirty hut, on a piece of coarse carpeting spread upon the ground, and receiving instruction in the art of reading from an old man. The alphabet-books, instead of being bound, had their backs fastened into a cane. The older children had a sort of catechism. Lastly, we rested ourselves for a few moments in a much-frequented cafè on the market-place. Here there was a swarm of people of every rank and condition; dirty, swarthy creatures with white mustachios, and impoverished attire; and elegant dandies with dazzling white fustanelle in ample folds, a heavy load of gold embroidery on their red jerkins, magnificent belts, tassels of a yard long on their lofty fezzes, red morocco shoes and scarlet *calze*. One among them was distinguished by his beauty, his long hair and tight-laced figure;—he was a Palikaro.

Most of the people were sitting, according to the fashion in Greece, out of doors, playing with their rosaries, and sipping a glass of water, their only refreshment. Before the principal entrance sat two musicians, making most execrable music;—one, an old man, was scraping a fiddle, which the other accompanied by scratching with a toothpick, on an eight-stringed guitar; the highest string alone was *fingered;*—the others were merely scratched on. In the interior of the cafè, leeches were also sold; they were to be seen hanging in large bottles in the windows. While I was looking at them, a fearful noise was heard in front of the house: the old man had been pushed off his stool, and robbed of his fiddle by a younger fellow, who, on his part, was now beginning to exhibit his skill. He had seen the old man richly paid, and he thought that he, as a better performer, might claim some reward. Amidst a kind of flourish of this harmonious choir, accompanied by a grunting song, we took our departure from the beautiful cafè, and soon afterwards from Patras.

The moonlight night at sea was clear and lovely; so warm that I again preferred sleeping on deck in my "*capote.*" We rose at four; for at six we were to be *en route* for Corinth, accompanied by our English friends. In the morning-dawn we already saw spread before us the harbour of ancient Corinth, the end of the Gulf, which resembles here an inland-lake, and on which is now situated the wretched nest called Lutraki. The bare rocks rise on either side to the height of a thousand feet, and shine with a reddish glare. The shores are treeless, but clothed with green tamarisks and lentisk shrubs. Besides the horses that had been ordered, we found a great number of others, which the consul, who had been sent from Athens to meet us, had provided. Thus we had great choice of them; notwithstanding which, by some mistake, I had, instead of a horse, a humble mule, an exchange which, in spite of the chain that served as a bridle, and the high horse-saddle, I had no cause to regret. Our cavalcade, amounting to at least twenty persons, moved on at a quick trot, over the sandy beach, among the green underwood. The bare mountains stretched high, and higher still, in front, and in half an hour the Acro-Corinthus, or Citadel of Corinth, lay before us. The country became more and more barren, as we drew nearer and nearer to the seat of ancient splendour, till at last we found ourselves traversing fields of stones, and heaps of ruins, without one single plant. The plain, which hitherto had been verdant, became more and more bleak; at length several melancholy-looking pieces of wall,—relics of ancient times,—obtruded themselves on us, against which were built up some windowless barracks. Six lofty and massive pillars are the only monuments which remain of departed beauty. This broad ruin-strewn plain was formerly covered with magnificent streets and palaces, from the hill of Acro-Corinthus down to the sea; now are seen only a score or so of miserable dwellings, crowded together on a little spot of ground; and about the same number of others, scattered here and there. Not a trace of agriculture is discoverable; yet large wine-casks, seen at intervals among the broken walls, betray the proximity of vineyards. We passed the Amphitheatre; Professor Ross, the celebrated antiquarian, —sent to meet us by the King,—directed our attention to the fact; otherwise I should rather have imagined the hollow area, the sides of which are somewhat excavated, to be a dried-up pond; so few are the remaining traces of masonry; not even the seats or the steps can be recognised. We did not linger in the town, but immediately proceeded on a decayed Venetian road, (only occasionally marked as such by some remains of old pavement, and which was rather a hindrance than a relief to our climbing steeds,) up the mountain to Acro-Corinthus. The road goes through chasms and over rocks, and is often dangerous, for the mountain is very high and steep. After an hour's ride we arrived at the first gate. Here the fortifications are still tolerably well kept up; there is also a garrison of about 30 men.

From this gate we proceeded on foot, halting, now at the ruins of a Turkish mosque built out of the remains of marble pillars,—now at a Grecian tombstone,—now again at a Venetian cistern, or the crumbling walls of a Christian chapel: for there is no age that has not erected its memorials here; now indeed, they are lying low in rubbishy fragments, and those of the most beautiful period are buried the deepest. On the extreme summit, we seated ourselves on two pillars of the Temple of Aphrodite, —mere broken pieces, requiring the skill of an archæologist such as Professor Ross, to trace their story,—and surveyed the Isthmus of Corinth,—the calm blue waters on either side—death-like,—without one vessel,—the two large and magnificent harbours of ancient Corinth. How narrow did the neck of land appear, when viewed from above,—how trifling the distance separating us from Helicon and Mount Parnassus on the opposite shore! These also are now but naked rocks;—these heights that once were crowned with groves of pines and oaks,—so lovely—so much sung. Pity it is indeed, that the death of all vegetation should produce in the mind so melancholy an impression; wherever one turns one's eye, trees are wanting—men are wanting;—one sees only inquisitive Englishmen, telescope in hand, searching out the traces of former grandeur. Notwithstanding the burning heat of the sun, the precious spring-water, collected in the ancient Greek subterranean water-courses—which even the many centuries of barbarism have not succeeded in destroying—never fails to rise on the surface of this rocky summit.

Under heat the most oppressive, our poor beasts scrambled like cats down these frightful roads, and soon we were all assembled to partake of a frugal dinner in a dirty inn.

Among many other bad things the wine was altogether undrinkable. The careless treatment of it during fermentation would soon cause total corruption; therefore, to preserve it, the natives add a great abundance of resin and of the needle-like leaves of the pine, so that it acquires a nauseous, resinous, rhubarby sort of taste. Having satisfied the cravings of hunger, we again mounted our steeds, to take, under the guidance of Professor Ross, a survey of the "*Stadion,*"—the great Theatre of the Isthmus of Corinth,—and of the fir-grove of Poseidon. In one hour—during which we travelled on a tolerably even road, a marvellous occurrence in Greece,—we reached the place. The theatre and the ruins of a temple lie pretty close to each other. These are gigantic monuments of ancient architecture. The stones which yet mark the circumference of the theatre, where of yore the Erinnyæ walked with slow and measured step, are blocks of from twelve to fourteen feet in length, by eight in height. That even such a work could be destroyed, and how that was accomplished, is clearly proved by the immediately adjoining ruins of a Turkish lime-kiln; a similar tale is told on the Acropolis by the halves of bombs mixed up with fragments of the capitals of pillars. Poseidon's fir-grove now consists only of a few trees, at most fifty years of age; the trees which formed the grove in old times have probably been repeatedly burned down, and the young ones are intentionally mutilated, for the sake of obtaining from them resin for the manufacture of wine. On the arena, which measures 600 feet in length, we found some pieces of mosaic and a copper coin. Excavations are more rarely made than one might imagine. Many tombs are still found in the vicinity: we witnessed the opening of one of them. We now quitted the ruins of the ancient city, and reached, in an hour from the theatre, the point of the Gulf of Corinth, where another steamer was to take us up to convey us to Athens. The place of departure, Kenkres, the ancient Cenchrea, consists of a row of mean cottages. We found there however, an almost inconceivable throng: all Greece appeared to have flowed together, as of old, to the "combat of the chariot and the song." On board the steamer people all crowded together, many still enveloped in large sheepskins, to ward off the heat; soon not a place was left free for one to move or stand, for all were lying down together *en famille* on the deck. Here were to be seen many an elegant dress, many a ponderous silver sabre or pistol, many a tight-laced figure; but few handsome faces. The Prussian minister had come to convoy us to the shore, and gave us an excellent dinner on board the steam-boat. At length the cool of the evening came, a great refreshment after so sultry a day, among such a multitude of men, closely crowded together. At half-past eight o'clock we entered the Piræus. Unfortunately, the charge of remaining beside the luggage, until the dispersing of the mass of human beings permitted it to be carried on shore, where the royal carriages were immediately to receive it, fell to my lot. The luggage was landed at last, but the promised carriages were not to be found; we therefore waited till ten o'clock: the insecurity of the roads did not allow of our lingering any longer. Luckily we succeeded, by paying a large sum, in obtaining a conveyance; and now we proceeded along an uneven country road, on our somewhat nervous journey, through a dark olive wood. I was, meantime, so much fatigued, that,—notwithstanding my having forgotten my cutlass, which I had been wearing at my side through the day,—I soon fell into a sound sleep, from which I was only wakened with difficulty on our reaching the vicinity of the city, by my companion's loud cries of "The Acropolis! the Acropolis!" It was impossible at that hour to distinguish many objects: what I could discern, a few solitary palm trees and many ruins, had a melancholy and desolate appearance. The streets were narrow; the houses like wretched barracks, full of filth and rubbish. It was eleven P.M., when I alighted at the Hotel de l'Orient. Feeling somewhat indisposed in consequence of the heat and of my exertions, I remained next day tolerably quiet at home, making only one or two very short excursions,—in company with an English gentleman,—as, for instance, to the temple of Jupiter, of which eighteen magnificent pillars, sixty feet high, yet remain standing. It is situated immediately behind the hotel, in the plain, separate from the town; for the space now left vacant, is merely to indicate the circumference of a piazza hereafter to exist. The houses are all wanting excepting the hotel and the King's palace; the latter is a costly edifice, built of marble from Mount Pentelicus; it extends over a large surface, and agreeably enlivens the desolate avenue of ruins. A flight of marble steps leads to a more elevated piazza in front of it. Imagine yourself standing on these steps; to the right is the Hotel de l'Orient, to the left the building occupied by the Bavarian embassy, which most unfortunately stands on a level lower than that of the piazza before the palace. The hill beside it is Lycabettus; then follow the palace and the columned remains of the temple of Jupiter. How melancholy the effect produced by the mixture of the relics of by-gone splendour, with the architecture of the present day!

On the following Monday, the 21st of September, I climbed, with our English fellow-travellers who had obtained a permission to visit it, to the Acropolis, which is now being cleared out and excavated. Large heaps of tombs are there scattered on every side, from which may be seen,—and their size furnishes the solution of the difficulty,—how it was that so many a block of marble, six feet in length, was forced to quit the pediment on which it had stood, and how the ground became white as snow, with crumbled marble. Many lofty columns, now prostrate and broken, which had remained erect for centuries, also show how the Turkish fire and all-devouring lime-kilns have raged here.

The impression made on first viewing the Parthenon is sublime beyond all conception; it is the most beautiful monument of antiquity that I have seen. The colossal bas-reliefs which filled up the pediment, are now in the British Museum, to which they were sent by Lord Elgin. I have seen them there, standing upon the floor, where they have a mournful aspect, as every thing must have that has been torn down from its proper position under the free canopy of heaven. The digging up and the carrying away of old Turkish mosques, and other buildings, have afforded a rich treasure of marble fragments; one shed is here filled with broken statues and friezes; another with vases and coins.

. The temples of Erechtheus, of Apollo, and of Bacchus, are now but groups of ruined pillars scattered here and there;—none of them indeed so large as the glorious Parthenon, but each, in its own way, beautiful and astonishing. Had the rays of the sun been less intensely scorching, how gladly would I have sat, for hours longer, on the high marble steps, where I beheld around me the magnificent remains of the past, while the dirt and rubbish of the present age lay far beneath.

I was struck, during my descent, by the heaps of human bones that I saw lying in every hollow place. In the city itself they have already vanished. The modern town consists, as yet, only of one street, which, with much pains, has been rendered passable;—it leads directly to the palace; in its centre stands an ancient Christian church, built in the Moorish style, dingy-looking and miserably low when compared with the shafts of those noble pillars of the temple of Jupiter. It is surrounded on all sides by booths, in which fruit and other eatables are exposed for sale;—behind it the continuation of the principal street extends to some distance, leading to the most considerable cafè of the town, which is not far from the church, the "Κουφεῖον τῆς Ελλαδος" (pronounced "*Coffion tis Ellados.*") This cafè has two entrances with glass doors; it contains a large room, with a billiard-table covered with filth, and some dirty white tables that had once been painted; we found in it a host of loungers, who were smoking abominable paper-cigars, and drinking cold water. It is, however, also possible to procure coffee, chocolate, and, by waiting patiently for the right moment, even a little ice. Untidy, barefooted lads bring what is asked for, if one has the good fortune to make oneself intelligible to them.

At some distance from the town, in a street which, as yet, is only marked out, and has no houses, stands the theatre. The university and the hospital, on the other hand, are situated in a tolerably pretty part of the neighbourhood, which is already covered with pleasant houses, and has the honour of possessing the only green trees any where to be seen. The quarter of the town nearest to the Acropolis is, on the contrary, most horrible; abounding in dingy, rubbishy ruins; yet one sees there scarcely a wall that has not variegated fragments of marble columns, or the heads or trunks of statues built up in it. The figures that usually meet the eye, running or crawling among the débris, are those of sordid, dusky-coloured boys, or ugly, tattered old hags. In many parts the rubbish is lying twenty-four feet deep; and, on attempting to excavate, one meets with the capitals of pillars that yet stand erect.

On Tuesday (the 22d of September) I had the honour of being presented to the King and Queen; and since then, I have been at court nearly every day, and have taken a lively share in the enjoyment of all the pleasure parties. The king is a young man, of prepossessing appearance, and his countenance is always marked by a friendly expression. He is habitually attired in the Greek costume, and never lays aside his broad silver sabre. He graciously did me the honour to enter at once into a long conversation with me; and, on subsequent occasions likewise, he seemed to have a predilection for talking with me on zoological subjects, especially when I had the honour of being seated opposite to him at the dinner-table. The Queen is an elegant, sprightly, active lady, of an even, bright, and happy temper,—fond of making, in person, the arrangements for all the parties of pleasure; and decidedly preferring a swift-galloping horse to a tea-party,—and social games in the open air to musical entertainments. Although the ladies of her court were clad in the graceful costume of Greece, she always appeared in a simple attire of French or German fashion.

On the appointed day the proposed excursion took place,—to the ruined mountain fortress of Phylæ, situated on Mount Hymettus. It was a most frightful ride. I could never have scrambled up these paths on foot; but, with Greek steeds, these four hours of clambering up and down again were a mere trifle, which the queen and her ladies accomplished at a gallop; while to me, the deep chasms and the loose, tumbling masses of stone afforded matter of no small uneasiness. Professor Ross always led the van, ready to solve any doubts that might arise, and to throw light on the various antiquities. Unfortunately, time is too short; otherwise I should have had pleasure in dealing out to you much learned information, which I picked up by the way.

The view from the colossal rocky masses, of which the ancient fort was composed, was indeed transporting. It included Athens,—the royal palace, shining in all its whiteness in the blue distance,—the fir-clad mountains, illumined with a rosy brightness,—and, rendering the effect more vivid,—grey, sombre-looking cliffs predominating on every side. At nine o'clock we returned to the village where we had left the carriages. It is a large and prosperous place. Here we found the royal tent ready pitched, and a liberal repast was served, in which nothing was lacking that could satisfy the most dainty palate. While we were eating, the population gathered around us, the men clothed in white woollen stuff, their heads shorn quite bare, except the long tuft of hair behind,—the women with handkerchiefs round their heads, and long white petticoats, with very pretty embroidery in black stripes. The children of rich parents were distinguished by their red caps, which were completely covered with ancient gold and silver coins, so that at a distance it appeared as if they wore helmets. Cheerful fires were lighted, and were soon burning all round the tent. Suddenly there arose a strain of mournful singing, to which the village youths, drawn up in line, under the guidance of a skilful leader, began to dance in graceful measures. In this dance, they hold each other by their hands, which are continually flourished together in the air, imitating, only with diminished vivacity, each movement of their leader, advancing three quick steps, and retreating one slow step; and the simultaneous movements of all the figures gives to the dance a certain measured and solemn air. At intervals the time is quickened; the leader, snapping his fingers, springs lightly up into the air, and then throws himself upon the ground,—still without withdrawing his hand from the line. The whole row, consequently, unites in an animated vibrating movement; and not one is guilty of breaking the time or figure.

Similar to this is the women's dance, except that they join hands alternately, across an intervening person, so that the first, third, and fifth, and again the second, fourth, and sixth, are linked together; but there is the same measured step, the same sad, monotonous, wailing melody, and yet the same passion for, and perseverance in, the dance. Men and women never dance promiscuously. To put a stop to their dancing was by no means such an easy matter, as to set it a-going. After it had ceased, we, in our turn, diverted ourselves with amusing games in the open air, in which the King and Queen again distinguished themselves by their agility. At last, at the request of her majesty, a race was run by the young maidens of the village, which caused prodigious laughter. Confectionery and money, placed on the top of a chest, marked the goal: the enthusiasm and passion of the little creatures, and the crowding about this chest, which most of them reached rather on their heads than their feet, really made it altogether a very pretty scene.

There was besides, an ease and a universal gaiety in the whole party, such as I had really not imagined could exist in Greece, in these times of great excitement, of which at least, our newspapers are always so full. When, at eleven at night, we at length got into the carriages, we heard still for a long while, the huzzas of these honest village folk; and their "Ζήτω ὁ βασιλεύς," (Zito o vasilefs,) resounded far and wide. Had I not, after this pleasure-party, enjoyed three others of similar kind with the Greek court, I should have marked that evening as pre-eminent among the most interesting and agreeable recollections of my journey. The amiability of their majesties strikes me more and more upon further acquaintance, and my taste for such festive enjoyments has also increased. Unfortunately however, I must throw on them the blame of causing this letter to be far from carefully or properly composed or written. Not one moment of my time was at my own disposal; I made numerous acquaintances, which cost me the sacrifice of some leisure; so that nothing was left but my night hours, when I was wearied with long rides, dinner-parties, and dances;—a time which one would fain bestow on any occupation, rather than on writing letters and journals. On board the steam-boat, which sails from this on the 30th of September, for Syra and Alexandria, I shall find time to fill up the arrears of the remaining five days.

If our travels continue as they have begun, my position will be a most agreeable and delightful one, and no such thing is dreamt of as over-exertion. The Greeks have been universally represented to us as thieves and brigands;—I have found only a cheerful, good-humoured, engaging people. Thus we may expect to find it also in Africa and in India, and the anticipated struggles with wild and murderous banditti will, doubtless, never be realized!

SUPPLEMENT TO THE FIRST LETTER.

ATHENS, *Sept.* 28.

My project of ascending Lycabettus, failed again this morning,—and that for the second time,—owing to my not having awaked early enough; for these pretty gauze curtains are a capital invention for warding off mosquitoes, but they are also, alas! the very best means to ensure one's morning hours being wasted.

My first visit was to Professor Buros. He had promised to take me to see the fish-market, and we set out for it accordingly, without delay. This crowded mass of booths, over the roofs of which is spread old linen cloth,—to exclude, as far as possible, the heat of the sun,—is a most odious abode, owing to the quantity of bad meat, and the myriads of flies, which literally cover the slaughtered calves like a black drapery. The fruit offered in greatest abundance is that of the *Solanum melongena* ("*Malanzars*"), or egg-plant, as well as that of another species of *Solanum*, long and thin, and of a green colour, which is very much eaten. Potatoes are a rarity there; grapes are the chief article. The fishmonger's division occupies only a small portion of the market, and is not fully frequented till after three o'clock. We were too early; however, there was already a very fine choice of fish. I particularly noticed the *Sparus erythrinus*, (Rose Sparus) and another larger *Sparus*, as also the *Exocœtus evolans*, (flying fish) *Mullus barbatus*, (red Surmullet) *Scorpœna*, (Sea-Scorpion) *Squatina*, (Angel-Shark) and *Raja (Trygon) pastinaca*, (Sting Ray).

From thence we went to the museum. A small, neat house is hired for it, by the Natural History Society, which is favoured with the King's support. On the ground-floor is the mineralogical collection, esteemed the most considerable part of the whole museum. I can only judge of its value by the mass of fossil remains from Pentelicus, and from another hill which stands very near Lycabettus. They furnish a multitude of highly interesting remains, for the most part of ruminating animals. One under-jaw appeared to me, to be undoubtedly that of a walrus; I also recognised the bones of a hippopotamus. What a pity it is that no one should feel sufficient interest in these fragments to arrange and classify them! But that is quite out of the question; —it is even fortunate that they are now at least carefully preserved.

The zoological portion of the museum is, certainly, most scantily supplied; it includes the species peculiar to Greece, and a few specimens from Brazil, obtained, either by exchange, or as gifts. They are, one and all, very ill stuffed. The only object in the whole collection worthy of notice as being really rare, is a well-preserved specimen of the *Capra Ægagrus*, from the desert isle of *Antimilo (Phyle)*. Possibly it may be altogether a new and distinct species; for who would venture to take it for granted, that the *Ægagrus* of Persia had been cast upon an isolated rock on this side of the Ægean Sea. The one in the museum has the three-ridged horns of the goat, but considerably inclined outwards. The upper parts of the animal are of a dark, its sides of a yellowish, brown.

On arriving at home, I found, to my surprise, another invitation to a fête champêtre. We started at eleven o'clock. I was in the same carriage with Mademoiselle Colocotroni, and with Dr Treiber, the King's physician; conversation, however, would not flow on as might have been desired, as I was not able to touch on any topic of lasting interest. After a drive of two hours we reached the village of Kalaki, which is surrounded by thinly-planted olive woods. There we found the red and white linen marquee, belonging to the royal family, pitched on an eminence considerably exposed to the wind. We set out immediately on horseback, and the cavalcade flew on with great resolution over a very stony piece of ground. My dapple-grey steed, notwithstanding the irregularity of its pace at a gallop, is a most distinguished brute. Dashing over thorns and hedges, and passing many a dilapidated farm, we at length reached a steep mountain-path, behind Hymettus. Our horses did their utmost, but the smooth, slippery crags of argillaceous schist mocked all their efforts, and their riders were, for the most part, forced to dismount, and to find their way on foot as best they could, through the underwood of *Pistacia Terebinthus (turpentine tree)* and pine. At last we beheld at our feet, the fig-tree, which marks the entrance to the grotto of the nymphs. We had no small difficulty however in penetrating into the interior; the ladies especially, who had however the Queen at their head to lead them on by her good example, were in a state of considerable embarrassment. By the help of ropes and ladders, which we had taken with us, we succeeded, after some time, in effecting an entrance; but,—notwithstanding all Professor Ross's learned remarks on the original use of the cave,—on its having been sacred, rather to the nymphs than to Apollo,—and in spite of the beautiful stalactites we found in it,—it failed to rivet the attention of the company beyond a very short time. The fair adventurers, already grown bolder, began to scramble up the steep sides of the cavern, upon the ladders, aided by ropes; the love of displaying their powers easily overcoming the taste for listening to the discourse of a savant. Our ride back,—for which it was at first no easy matter to recover our wandering horses,—was performed at the same pace as before; no repose was granted to our palfreys, till we found ourselves once more at Kalaki; and indeed, even then, the passion for equestrian exercise had not been sufficiently gratified, and so we visited the windmill hill, on which stands a mill with twelve armed wings. However, as the view was not particularly fine, and the wind very troublesome, we soon returned to the tent, where we gathered round a tasteful and well-replenished board. I had the honour of sitting opposite to the King, and of being interrógated by his majesty on various points, in the course of which conversation, I felt that it was not merely the polite wish to talk with every one on subjects connected with his own profession, but a real interest in science which prompted his queries. Dinner ended, the whole village population flocked together; one man beat the great drum, another played on a tin flute, which seemed to require a great effort. The sound of the music speedily invited the lovers of the dance to assemble, and the long line waved, in spiral motion, now slowly, now in more lively cadence, in graceful and measured step. This was the romaica. Another dance, performed by single dancers, or by a pair standing vis-à-vis, begins with a slow cadence, and degenerates into a bacchanalian stamping, the dancer throwing himself on his knees and then quickly jumping up, and all this with an accompaniment of snapping and piping, growing louder and more shrill with the increased wildness of the movements. Afterwards, the women also began to dance; at first among themselves, but by degrees, mingling with the lines of the men, and when we, infected with a desire to imitate them, pressed into the dance, others also joined themselves to us.

Presently we were wheeling round in the midst of them; now in a waltz,—now in a Scotch reel,—to the no small amusement of those who were performing the antique dance.* They sought to copy our modern airs and graces, but their attempts all failed, and rather afforded scope for ridicule than added to the classical effect. Our drive back to Athens by moonlight, during which I was so fortunate as to be the companion of the fair and charming *Mavromicali*,† and of Count G——, was most enchanting. Singing, and classical translations of German songs into French, contributed not a little to our entertainment.

In the afternoon of the following day, when everything was finally arranged for our departure on the morrow, I visited, in company with Professor Buros, the botanical garden. The road to it leads along a watercourse, the humidity of which produces the most glorious vegetation and rapid growth of trees. The "*Melia*

* Probably the ancient and celebrated "*Pyrrhic dance*," so beautifully alluded to in one of the stanzas of Byron's impassioned lay.

"You have the Pyrrhic dance as yet;
Where is the Pyrrhic phalanx gone?
Of two such lessons, why forget
The nobler and the manlier one?
You have the letters Cadmus gave,
Think ye he meant them for a slave?"—Tr.

† The name of Mavromicali is associated with all the most remarkable events in the history of modern Greece. The share which the now veteran patriot of that family took in the Revolution, his own sufferings, and the tragic fate of his young and noble son, by whose hand Capo d'Istria fell, are now matter of history; but we cannot better illustrate the feelings of delight and interest with which our Author found himself in company with the fair and youthful daughter of the chieftains of Maina, than by quoting the concluding paragraph of an interesting and touching account of their history, contained in a work recently published, "Wayfaring Sketches among the Greeks and Turks." "The Mavromicalis were, and indeed are, the most powerful family of their province, and are greatly respected and beloved in Maina—they themselves, from the old Bey down to his beautiful grand-daughter, the Queen's maid of honour, are each in their distinctive position the most perfect types of the true Greek aristocracy, and to great simplicity of manner they unite refinement of mind and delicacy of feeling."—Tr.

Azedarach" (common beard tree) in particular, succeeds delightfully, and grows to the size of a tree in the course of three years; it bears clusters of yellow fruit. All the trees of this "*Melia*" are transplanted hither from the botanic garden, the neighbourhood of which they mark. At the entrance we found the lady of the curator, who led us in and most obligingly presented us with bouquets. In the garden itself there is in fact not much that is remarkable. *Broussonetia*, (paper mulberry) *Melia*, (beard tree) *Cercis*, (Judas tree) and *Syringa* (lilac) flowering for the second time, *Roses* and *Costuses*, besides many fruit-trees and other nursery plants. The curator resides in a Turkish building, the external flight of steps leading to which, with a draw-bridge, yet reminds one of the Pasha who once dwelt there.

The kind lady could not resist exhibiting to us the curator's manufactory; for the garden is not his chief occupation, as one may easily perceive by the endless confusion that reigns within its bounds. He has discovered the very valuable art of manufacturing—from the refuse of the *Spuma Marina**—an elegant material, which becomes waterproof by the action of fire, and which is equal to alabaster in beauty of colour, and to porcelain in hardness, while it far surpasses the latter in lightness.

The most exquisite sunset-glow was illuminating the Acropolis as we wended our way homewards; every mountain shone resplendent in the roseate light. What a magnificent prospect! As darkness cast its shroud over the landscape, we perceived the fires of the gipsy groups on the level plain below.

Monday passed away in preparations for our departure; after dinner I rejoined the Prince at the palace,

* Sea Froth, or Keffekill, a mineral found in the Crimea, in Spain, and especially in Natolia. It is commonly used among the Turks in the manufacture of the heads of tobacco pipes.—Tr.

and about five o'clock, we drove to the Piræus. The Parthenon was shining brightly in the serene light of evening; the white pillared ruins were looking down upon us, as though they would bid us farewell,—awakening in our minds thoughts of home. At the fort we met our English acquaintances; some of whom took leave of, while others accompanied, our party. To many others besides, we bid a hearty adieu, the little bark rowed off, and at the same moment, the men-of-war lying in the harbour, thundered their farewell-salute!

SECOND LETTER.

MAHMOODEEH CANAL—THE GREEK COURT—DEPARTURE FROM ATHENS—ARRIVAL AT SYRA—THE FOUNTAIN AT SYRA—PASSENGERS ON BOARD THE STEAMER—GENERAL EL MESARI BEN ISMAEL—COAST OF AFRICA—ALEXANDRIA—MOSQUE—CAFE—CLEOPATRA'S NEEDLE—ORIENTAL GARDENS—EGYPTIAN FORT—POMPEY'S PILLAR—PALACE OF THE PASHA—MUSICANTES—DEPARTURE FOR CAIRO BY THE MAHMOODEEH—STEAMBOAT ON THE NILE—ORCHESTRA ON BOARD—THE NILE AND ITS BANKS—WATER-WHEELS—ARAB SINGING—ARRIVAL BY NIGHT AT CAIRO—HOTEL ORIENTAL—PLACE UZBEKEEH—CITADEL—BARRACKS—NEW MOSQUE—EGYPTIAN SOLDIERS—DEEP WELL—MENAGERIE—BAZAAR—FELLAH WOMEN—TURKS—TOMBS OF THE CALIPHS—MOSQUES—POPULAR AMUSEMENTS.

CAIRO, *12th October* 1844.

So I am now actually proceeding on my travels by the canal of the Nile, between Alexandria and Cairo; and, although it is not the very Nile itself, it is certainly a place from which a letter has never before been despatched to B——. The ship in which I now am, is exactly a Dutch "*Treckschuite,*" (track-boat) such as one travels in from Utrecht to Leyden,—and it is drawn, as in Holland, only with somewhat more noise, by three active horses, which the half-clothed fellows, who act as drivers, cheer on by the sound of a most abominable kind of singing, to which another man responds from on board with a speaking trumpet. The surrounding country too is quite as flat as that along the canals of Holland; but there is this difference, that there, one glides through gardens of tulips and hyacinths, and here, through the most barren and dismal-looking plains of sand.

My last letter contained a very hastily-patched-up account of Athens; but, if I recollect rightly, the last days were wanting, and you must grant me final remission as far as these are concerned, for I am not now in a condition to be making further excerpts from my Journal. I can only assure you in a few words that the King and Queen of Greece are really charming people, well worthy of being far happier than they are; for their ungrateful subjects, for whose sake the King is expending enormous sums yearly, will never be brought to acknowledge or comprehend their obligations to him. What pleasure and satisfaction were diffused throughout the court, when our Prince honoured, with his presence, its festivities, not one of which did I miss. I suspect these parties do usually savour not a little of ennui; for there is among the Greeks a great want of nobility fit to grace a court, and all Germans are banished. The society is consequently monotonous,—consisting of four or five ladies of the Queen's bed-chamber, one only of whom can speak German: several Greek cavaliers, one of whom, M. Mavromicali, the king's master of the ordnance, left a most pleasing impression on my mind; and Professor Ross, a very learned antiquarian, formerly connected with the Greek university; that university from which many a man of distinguished merit, many a main prop and bright ornament, was driven away on the 15th of September.* That great joy should be caused by the event of so amiable a prince coming, with his suite, to introduce some little variety into their monotonous life, was therefore most natural;

* The 15th of September 1843,—when the populace, with the military, assembled in the great square in front of the palace, and remaining there for ten hours, resolute in their demands, yet abstaining from all violence, compelled King Otho, who had been totally unprepared for such a rising, and who, on directing the artillery to be pointed against the insurgents, found every piece turned against himself, to grant them a constitution, to form a new ministry, convene a national assembly, and exclude all foreigners from the Court, and from every office.—Tr.

and the result was, that one fête rapidly succeeded another, and there was no end of the devices invented for giving pleasure to all. One must, to be sure, have a considerable stock of strength, and bones not easily shaken, to be able, after riding at a gallop during six hours over every obstacle, to scramble down on foot over high cliffs and huge masses of rock, leading one's horse by the bridle during two hours more; and that in places where even the Greek horses slip down beside their dismounted riders; and then, at the end of the fête champêtre, to dance without intermission during half the night, in a climate where the cool of the evening is like our warm forenoons. In all this however I took my part; and, what is perhaps yet more surprising, her majesty the Queen was ever foremost in it all, led the march at a gallop over fields of stones, where many,—as, for instance, your humble servant,—would never have dreamed of such a thing as galloping,—after the repast was ended, gave the signal for active and exciting games,—and altogether allowed but little repose to the young ladies of her court, who doubtless would often have preferred their sofas to the games of blind man's buff or of "la grace." In short the pleasure-parties to Pentelicus, where the beautiful and precious marble is quarried, and where the grove of poplar-trees,—a great rarity in Greece,—would alone make it worth one's while to lead the moonlight dance with beautiful ladies arrayed in splendid Greek costumes,—and the excursions to Hymettus and to the Grotto of the Nymphs, have left a bright picture in my mind which can never be effaced, whatever other impressions may follow hereafter.

But I am forgetting that I am on the Nile; and that it was my intention to write more particularly about Africa. I shall therefore merely touch slightly on the subject of our voyage. We sailed from Athens on the evening of the 30th of September, under the thunders of three large French and two English ships of war, all whose yards were manned. On the 1st of October, in the morning, we reached SYRA, one of the Greek isles, whose capital of the same name is very picturesquely situated on a conical hill, while two higher mountains form the back-ground. This is the Roman Catholic town. All its houses are white, and have flat roofs, upon which the inhabitants pass the night. The wide-spreading Greek town, (*Hermopolis*) situated on the harbour, is far larger, and is the centre of all the trade of the place. The consul came to meet us, and displayed his hospitality in the Oriental fashion, by setting before us sherbet and sweetmeats. We traversed the cleanly and well-paved streets of the town, which are filled on both sides with shops full of manufactured goods, chiefly the product of native industry, such as capotes, pipes, shoes, cloths, &c.; and then ascended to the summit of one of the twin hills, on which stands a convent. The road is very steep, and the streets in the upper town are narrow and dirty; a multitude of pigs blocked up the road, so that our asses had some difficulty in forcing their way through; moreover the heat was intense, and the white houses and treeless hills dazzled the eye: but when we did at last reach the top, the enchanting panorama well repaid our toil, notwithstanding the absence of all verdure save that of a few pretty vineyards. On one side is an extensive sea-view with Paros, Naxos, Delos, and a variety of smaller islands in the distance; and on the other rises the lofty hill of Pyrgos, a bare and frowning height, separated by a deep precipitous cleft from the hill of the convent on which we were standing; it was only at the foot of this mountain that we could descry a few green vineyards enclosed with walls. The path to this ravine passes over the roughest and most frightful cliffs; yet we saw on it numberless women with large amphoras on their heads, climbing up and down. They fetch the pure and beautiful water from the spring that bubbles up on that height, the only fountain in the island, and sell it in the town. On our way back we scrambled down the rugged side of the ravine. What a delicious shade did we enjoy under the large fig-trees beside the spring! Close to us was a splendid vineyard, or rather an extensive trellised bower formed of vines, on which hung bunches of grapes, such as we could only compare for size to those of Eshcol, sweet and juicy, and most refreshing, especially after we had cooled them in the fresh water of the fountain. We could willingly have luxuriated among these delights for a much longer time; but suddenly there appeared a messenger despatched from the steamer to call us back in all haste; we therefore mounted our asses, and urged on the brisk little beasts to a rough gallop. We soon reached the consul's house, and in a few minutes more found ourselves on board a large gloomy-looking French steamer, which was to take us on our further voyage. Here for the first time, the fact that we were approaching the Eastern world was, visibly and in every imaginable form, presented before us. Pilgrims from Northern and Western Africa all bound for Mecca, swarmed around us. On a many-coloured carpet lay a venerable and pleasant-looking old man, whose copper-brown complexion contrasted singularly with his hoary beard. He was clothed all in white; the end of his long scarf of thin silk, twisted round his head, and fastened into his white turban, and his broad-brimmed, red and yellow straw hat, characterised the Bedouin. But who could have imagined that this small lean man, with his delicately formed hands and feet, was the object of dread in so many battles, that same El Mesari Ben Ismael, at present French General of the Bedouin Light Cavalry? He was now going, viâ Alexandria, to Mecca, accompanied by two most captivating boys of dark-brown hue, who had not an article of raiment upon them save a soiled shirt and the red fez-cap. They seemed to cling to the aged man with extreme tenderness; and he also appeared to take in good part, and to be pleased with, all that they did; sometimes even a smile played upon those rigid features as they carried on their wild fun around him, pulling his long moustachios, seating themselves on his lap, and practising many a droll prank. There he lies upon his splendid carpet immoveable through the whole long day; his mode of killing time is to divert himself continually with a gold watch of great value, which points to half-past five when it is twelve o'clock at noon; he keeps his eye ever upon it that he may not miss his time for prayer. This recurs five times daily; he has a particular bass-mat for the purpose, which he spreads out upon the floor; then with his face turned towards Mecca, he first looks at his hands, next bends in deep reverence, hastily raising himself and standing erect, and lastly throws himself on his knees, and even prostrate with his face to the ground. This whole ceremony is performed twice on each occasion, and after it is ended he rolls up his mat and lays it aside.

A no less Oriental scene was presented before us in the other direction by three Turks, seated in a group, surrounded by their slaves. They smoked their "*Nargiles*" with the utmost gravity, gazing fixedly at the fumes rising from the water in the crystal vessels attached to their pipes. There too, were Persians, with green turbans, long flowing robes striped red and white, and splendid silk sashes; their faces characterized by long noses and large prominent eyes. I drew portraits of several of the figures that struck me most. Moreover I relieved an aged Turk who was suffering from toothache, by extracting a large double-tooth! In consequence of this, I was pressed on all sides, to partake, with these curious people, of their water-melons; and it is not my custom to scorn such well-meant invitations.

Most exceedingly did we rejoice when, at length, a loud shout announced that the African coast was in sight;—for, however novel and varied were the scenes presented on board, there is nothing of which one more quickly becomes impatient than the atmosphere of a cabin, the smell of oil and grease, the gloomy darkness, and the noise of the engine. On the flat promontory, to sweep round which we were obliged to make a great circuit, in order to enter the ancient harbour on its opposite side, we perceived several towers, or objects having that appearance. Cleopatra's Needle and Pompey's Pillar were also pointed out to us: unfortunately however the coast is so low, that all these features, seen on the level horizon, have but a miserably poor effect. Having thus nearly described a circle, we found ourselves once more beholding the prospect that we had left behind us, of the Egyptian fleet here stationed. It is said to be a most wonderful fleet;—but I must be pardoned for saying that, to my eyes, it was a most unlovely sight. Every vessel seemed to be old, ill-kept and shabby-looking; the paint of most of them was worn off, and in very few of them were there any signs of life. In these few, youngsters of dusky complexion, with red caps and white trowsers, were climbing and springing about most cleverly in the rigging.

Among the numerous little boats which made for the steamer, we soon recognised that which belongs to our consul. It was lined with crimson cloth, and rowed by twelve handsome brown sailors; at their head sat a tall, well-made, shining negro, who attracted our especial attention: he wore a white turban; his upper garment and trowsers were also white; his inner-garment of bright scarlet. We were informed that the consul was lying sick at Cairo, and had therefore sent two deputies to receive us;—one, a young clerk, whose embarrassment kept him in a constant tremble; and the other, a man of very common-place appearance. Our luggage was carried off helter-skelter, and we took our departure, pushing through the crowd of little skiffs belonging to the numerous boatmen who were eagerly flocking to the steamer. Such a shouting—such a noisy bustle amid the multitude of sable and dusky faces, with flat noses and thick lips! The turban and the single garment wound round the loins, were, generally speaking, the only raiment worn by this motley crowd. Troops of camels and of asses were stationed on the beach, waiting for the arrival of the passengers; and here a fresh dispute awaited us, which however was soon settled by the exertions of our guides. Instead of the asses, which in point of size and strength are almost equal to mules, we were fortunate enough to secure a very elegant calêche, lined with white silk. In it we proceeded to the town. The first truly foreign sight that greeted our European eyes, was a troop of dromedaries; then the strange and varied population,—the dusky Bedouins, the jet-black Nubians and Ethiopians, and the slaves from the west coast of Africa, with their frightful, broad, flat noses, called forth exclamations of surprise. The women of the "*Fellahs,*" veiled, and wrapped in blue chemises and trowsers, with their three-cornered veils of black silk, and the black circles painted round their dark eyes, riveted our attention, no less than the elaborate carved work of the projecting latticed windows. Passing through many streets, some broad, some narrow, and amidst a most animated throng of people of all sorts, we at length reached an open square, surrounded by a number of thoroughly European-looking houses. They were built, as a speculation, by Mehemet Ali, who asks a high rent for them. We halted before one of these,—the Hotel Oriental; a large stone house, with lofty saloons, all the blinds of which were closed. Behind each apartment is an alcove, with two beds; a handsome sofa, a piano-forte, and a number of Parisian engravings, adorn the rooms: the cuisine is excellent;—in a word, it unites all the advantages of a good French or German hotel; the only drawback being the nightly plague of the musquitoes, which unfortunately in this country never fail to disturb our slumbers. We spent some time, on our first arrival, in lounging on the window-seats, amusing ourselves with watching the sorrowful-looking and noiseless trains of dromedaries, laden with stones, constantly passing by, with slow and monotonous pace;—the Mahometan population, clad in the gay and motley costumes of the East; and the multitude of English and French travellers, even ladies mounted on horseback and on asses;—all seen at a glance, on casting one's eye round this spacious "*place.*" Venders of pastry and sweetmeats, of lemons and sherbet,—gracefully carrying their goods on the top of their heads,—and water-carriers, with their bags of goats'-hide,—made by skinning a goat in a very clever manner, and afterwards sewing up the neck and the legs,—some on foot, and others mounted on camels, all jostling each other among the crowd.

Two days were devoted to seeing the sights of the city, and that time proved amply sufficient for the purpose. On the very day of our arrival, we mounted our asses, and made our first giro through the town, in the course of which we certainly saw but little worthy of notice. What we most admired was the view from the palace,—which is situated at the sea-side,—and from the harem of the Pasha. We entered, and began to carry on some negociations with the military on duty as guard, and with some Turkish magistrates, who, by reason of the Ramadan, had but just assembled after sunset, to do their work by night. Thus we gradually paved the way for obtaining the favour of permission to inspect the palace. The shades of night had fallen when we remounted our asses and rode back to the town, now enveloped in darkness, relieved only here and there by the sad and murky light of a date-shop, with its small tallow lamps. These dates as they are devoured by the people here in an unripe state are remarkably pretty, of an orange or lemon yellow, and seem to invite the passer-by to partake also; but, for a European, on account of the tannin that abounds in them, they are scarcely eatable.

We drew up and dismounted in front of a mosque, from which proceeded a sound of loud singing. It contains a spacious hall, with numerous white-washed pillars; between these were bars, from which were suspended oil lamps. The congregation of the faithful stood in straight rows, one behind another. Exactly opposite to the entrance, was the sanctuary, or holiest place, the "Mahrab," a little niche, before which stood the Imaum. As often as he began to intone his plaintive chant, "*Allah el Akbar*," the whole congregation prostrated themselves, with their faces touching the ground, all striking it simultaneously. This alternate prostration and rising again of the gaily-turbaned multitude had so strange and picturesque an effect, that we could not have resisted the temptation of diverting ourselves for a much longer time, by peeping in through the grated windows and the open door, at the novel spectacle, but suddenly, a well-aimed paving-stone was precipitated into the very midst of our party. Fortunately, it merely struck me a somewhat violent blow on my side as it fell. Thus taken by surprise, we were too glad to jump hastily into our saddles, and to ride swiftly forward to the place for which we were then bound, which happened to be a café. There we were presented with small *nargilehs*, and were expected to smoke, which cost me no small effort. More to my taste was the café-noir, which, though served with the grounds in it, was not ill-flavoured. We sat on a high balustrade, with our legs dangling in the air; for our repeated endeavours to sit after the fashion of the Turks uniformly failed, so that at last we gave up the attempt in despair. In this café we saw a rude specimen of the transparencies, with figures "*à l'ombre Chinoise,*" accompanied by metrical singing with tambourine *ad libitum,* which forms the favourite substitute for theatrical entertainments among the better classes of the oriental inhabitants of Alexandria.

On the morning of the next day, (the 3d of October) I was awakened by the inflammatory stings of the musquitoes, which had penetrated within my gauze curtains. These little insects,—a species of "*Culex,*" (gnat) by no means a *Simulia,*—glide unperceived within the hangings, if there be an opening however small in any of the seams, or a hole that has been unobserved in the close examination which every curtain must needs undergo daily; and when once confined in a narrow place, they sting all the more malignantly.

Our first proceeding was to set out for one of the handsomest quarters of the city, accompanied by our Russian interpreter,—a man possessed of the minimum of good manners, and the maximum of stupidity. On the preceding day we had visited Cleopatra's Needle,—a monument which has a most dismal appearance, being half-buried in the sand, and surrounded by fallen walls of great size. The soil of this whole district of country consists, to a considerable depth, of limestone remains, the relics of ancient Alexandria. The ruins are looked upon as a quarry, and the materials for building are fetched as they are required, from this often ransacked but still inexhaustible subterranean magazine. I found in my visit to Cleopatra's Needle, little of peculiar interest, except a lizard eighteen inches in length, which, on my attempting to catch it, began to climb up the obelisk. *Salamanders* (newts) were particularly abundant here. They often reminded me of the tale of the stupid Kailun, when I saw them crawling among the heaps of stones,—the ruins of ancient palaces.

I was, on the other hand, agreeably surprised with the thoroughly modern-oriental gardens, which are most unique in their appearance, full of lofty bowers and marble fountains. We visited them on the 4th of October, riding to them through the suburb, which is close to the new harbour,—our road bordered on either side with palm-trees, raising their tall forms on the top of ruined walls; each stately tree resplendent with beautiful and abundant fruit. From time to time we heard the mournful creaking of the "*sakieh*," (water-wheel) which is usually placed on the most elevated point, under the shade of thick trees, that from it the garden may be kept continually well-watered. Pure fresh water is here a most precious thing; it is brought into the city by a single water-course only;—these deep wells afford brackish water, which may serve for purposes of irrigation, but cannot be used at all for drinking.

We entered a lofty house, of neat and almost European appearance. A long entrance-hall, paved in a sort of Mosaic, with black and white sea-pebbles, leads immediately into the first inner-court, which is surrounded with a low border of *mesembryanthemum*, (fig-marygold) while its walls are richly and beautifully clothed with a profusion of jessamine, roses, and various other elegant creepers. A long alley, laid with marble slabs, and still edged with mesembryanthemum, terminates at the great "*kiosk*," or pavilion,—a large, airy building, constructed of carved wood-work, quite in the oriental style, in the midst of which are playing numerous fountains, in handsome marble basins. Every one of the plants trained over this bower was in full flower; the fragrance of the Arabian jessamine ("*jasminum sam-*

bac") in particular, was most delicious. At this place is the entrance to the garden itself. All its alleys are separated by high enclosures, chiefly of rosemary; the loftier groves are formed of *oleander*, *orange*, and *musa* trees (the latter, plantain and banana trees); the date-palms occupy a separate division; and another is devoted to the vegetable-garden, in which are cultivated several sorts of melons, gourds and cucumbers.

As our cicerone was here seized with a violent fit of ague, we were obliged to proceed on our way unattended, and we wandered on to a steep eminence, surmounted by a fort, to which we ascended. Notwithstanding the significant gestures by which the ill-equipped garrison had warned us from above not to approach, we were soon at the top, and enjoyed a charming view of the many white mosques below, scattered among gardens of date-palms,—bounded on one side by the sea-like Lake of Mareotis, and on the other by the Mediterranean. Scarcely had we however seated ourselves on the end of a half-fallen bridge, when the soldiers, enraged at our having penetrated within their stronghold, came up to us and attempted to drive us away. One man only was bold enough to stretch forth his hand, and then indeed, it was to touch, not us, but the ass-drivers: his stick was soon taken from him, and after loud screams and stubborn vociferations on the part of the garrison,—in their Arab tongue, which, at any time, sounds like the language of perpetual disputing,—they came to the resolution of leaving us where we were. On our return, we shaped our course towards the monument that bears the name of Pompey's Pillar, and passed a fountain which pours its waters into a dirty basin, where washing was being carried on. Here we saw a crowd of filthy, screaming, wrangling women and girls, all clad in blue shifts, and indescribably ugly,—nevertheless, if they happened to be without the black veil, always catching up the ends of their garments in their mouths, and drawing them half over their faces. Many of them had their naked children sitting astride on their shoulders. The chief part of the duty devolved on men, who, standing in the basin, were scrubbing the clothes lustily.

The road to Pompey's Pillar leads over an arid, burning plain, covered with stones and sand, here and there passing over extensive burial-grounds, in which the graves are marked only by a few stones, rudely put together with mortar, and often unhewn. The pillar itself stands out pretty freely, and appears as though it must have belonged to some immense temple; but neither its capital nor its proportions have any beauty;—they bear evidence, on the contrary, of a corrupt, modern-antique taste.

From thence we turned our steps towards the Palace of the Pasha. One cannot picture to oneself a finer site for a palace. It stands close to the sea, at the old harbour, and commands a view of the whole fleet. The stairs and the audience-chamber are built of beautiful white marble: large circular halls with splendid inlaid floors, in which the most precious woods are not spared; state-apartments, the walls of which are hung with rich tapestry; handsome vases,—one of which is a present from the Pope,—and numerous paintings; the most elegant Parisian ameublements, cabinets filled with stuffed birds from Brazil,—all kept up with great care and neatness,—are to be seen within the walls of Mehemet Ali's magnificent abode. French taste has here regulated the luxury of the East. Much pleased, we quitted the palace, which, according to the fashion of all our oriental buildings, is but two stories in height.

After dinner, we sallied forth once more, and traversed on foot, in the twilight of evening, the city now enlivened by the joyous sunset liberty of the Ramadan;

passing,—sometimes through dark streets, and sometimes through market-places or bazaars brightly illuminated with paper-lanterns and filled with eatables of all sorts,—we wandered on till we reached an elegant café, where we gave ourselves up to the enjoyment of oriental scenes and characteristics. Here, in the most profound repose, the Mussulman was smoking his pipe;—brown faces mingling with black ones,—and black with copper-coloured;—tattered costumes beside those the most recherchés;—turbans and "*tarbóoshes,*" (red caps)—all in a motley crowd: in the centre of the hall a fountain was playing. The coffee and the "*chiboócks*" (pipes) were excellent,—and the jolly waiter, with his jacket and his white trowsers, presented us with mastich* for chewing, which he took out of a pocket in the top of his shirt-sleeve! To add to the entertainment, some musicantes took their places within the café; a blind boy, as singer,—and an old man, who played with a plectrum on wire-strings stretched across a board, a kind of hautboy, and the tambourin, completed the orchestra! A second singer soon relieved the first; for their performances required great effort, from the custom of constantly shaking the head, turning the eyes, and making the most inconceivable grimaces. The melody,—for the most part in a minor key,—was always either

* A custom, very prevalent throughout the Levant, and almost universal at Constantinople and Smyrna, ascribed by the inhabitants to the healthful effects of this resinous substance on the mouth: the name of *mastich* is itself derived from the use of it—*masticare.* So highly is it valued in the Island of Scio, where it is the chief export, that very strict rules are observed regarding the incisions made in the lentisk trees, and the gathering of the juice. Even in the days of Turkish tyranny, the fortunate inhabitants of the villages that furnished it, enjoyed an exemption from compulsory and unpaid labour, and freedom from every chief, save the "*Aga,*" or lord, who travelled in state from place to place, to collect the treasure; the supplying of it being limited by government to certain localities. The *Pistacia lentiscus,* from which mastich exudes, requires scarcely any cultivation; it is a beautiful evergreen, though scarcely exceeding the size of a tall shrub: the incisions are made only in July and September.—Tr.

asked for or named before-hand by the landlord, who then expressed his satisfaction by clapping his hands. The tout-ensemble made our ears ache, especially as it was so very close to us. We soon repaired to our hotel, to finish the preparations for departure on the following day.

On the 5th of October, in the morning, we went on board the vessel by which we were to proceed, on the Mahmoodéëh Canal, taking with us a good supply of provisions. Our interpreter,—a black man with fine eyes,—followed us in a small, neat track-boat, made of painted wood. The country around, destitute equally of life and of verdure, makes a melancholy impression on the traveller. Mud-huts, a "*Sakieh,*" many Egyptian vultures,* and a few miserably poor and half-savage men, were the only objects that attracted our attention. The whole course of the canal lies through a stratum of sand and clay, and in most parts the rude mound which confines it is not even clothed with grass.

It was late in the evening ere we reached the place where the canal enters the Nile, beside a wretched village, ("Atfeh") whose inhabitants dwell in common with their poultry, in a kind of swallow's nests. The junction of the canal with the waters of the sacred stream is effected, at this point, by means of a lock with sluice-gates. A stately steamer, beautifully lighted up, was lying at anchor in front of a house two stories high, in which coffee was served; and as we

* The Egyptian or aquiline vulture, (*Vultur Percnopterus*) though in its appearance and habits one of the most horrid birds that can be seen in any country, with its naked wrinkled face, black, hooked beak, long neck, and tremendous talons, is most useful, both in waging war against the innumerable mice, and still more, in clearing away the many carcases before they putrefy, and thus preventing those noxious exhalations which, in such a climate, would otherwise be so fatal. The male is nearly white; the female of a brown colour, both having black quills: this vulture sometimes measures twelve feet from tip to tip of its wings. It has no shyness, and never soars to lofty flights.—Tr.

went on board, we were greeted with loud music. We ound every thing in the boat arranged in the best possible style;—the after-deck was surrounded with purple velvet sofas; and the cabin set apart for our use was cool and airy. Certainly, whether from the effects of imagination, or really from the beneficial influence of the mild and tepid air of the Nile, with its silky, balmy softness,—we did, as we lay there stretched beside each other upon the floor, enjoy a slumber so refreshing that no other could be compared to it. Meantime, every three or four hours, all the numerous domestics belonging to the vessel renewed, *in pleno*, their vigorous exertions in the way of performing, with the accompaniment of drums, kettle-drums and serpents, airs of Bellini or of Donizetti; it never occurred to any one among them to think of our poor ears being torn to pieces by their discords; on the contrary, all this was done for our entertainment, till at length we gave them clearly to understand that we were no amateurs. In the morning, (on the 6th of October) we partook of a most scanty breakfast, as our provisions were rapidly disappearing. We were therefore most agreeably surprised, when, at dinner, the cook of the steamer set before us a great number of dishes, all choice Arabian dainties, for the most part consisting of very greasy preparations of rice or of flour,—several of them really excellent,—but many, according to our taste, too fat and doughy.

But truly, neither the good fare, nor the noisy Egyptian music and drumming, could indemnify us for the ennui of watching the view along the banks of the Nile. The broad expanse of water, turbid and of a dark yellow colour, winds through a low and barren plain, which displays none of the fresh verdure that one might expect to see so soon after the inundations. On the exterior margin of the river only, is there a little half-dried-up grass, to consume every particle of which with all possible expedition, affords matter of rivalry to the young camels, and to the numerous herds of buffaloes, which stand up to their muzzles in the muddy water. Here and there, appears a palm-grove, of from fifty to a hundred date-palms; as far as I could judge, the height of some of these trees might be eighty or ninety feet. They all make a fine show at present, adorned with a rich crop of remarkably pretty clusters of red or golden fruit. When passing under those that grew close to the water-side, we could descry, in the dark object appearing from under the crest of rich foliage at a great height, the figure of a man, busily employed in gathering the fruit into a straw mat, which he had contrived to wind up with him to that elevated position, while the assembled population below were eagerly watching his proceedings. The usual rule is for each of these palm-groves to have a hamlet situated at no great distance from it; but it may be often sought for in vain, for it requires an eye accustomed to such a country to discover its position. The material of which their huts are built is the black soil beneath their feet, pieces of which they bake in the sun, into a sort of rude bricks, or indeed, often mere clods; with these they construct, at pleasure, round, square, or conical buildings, usually not exceeding four feet in height; a single aperture answering the double purpose of door and window. The whole hamlet, when viewed from any point in the vicinity, resembles nothing so much as a collection of swallows' nests, built close together. How horrible the interiors of these molehills are, is evident from the apparently indelible filth which cleaves to these miserable, degraded, swarthy-brown creatures, although they seem to facilitate the promotion of cleanliness by diminishing their wardrobe to the last degree! How pitiable and shocking is it to behold the unfortunate men with rough, hard ropes fastened obliquely across their breasts, dragging the boats up the river against the current, their bodies dreadfully excoriated, and covered with sores, like our worst cart-horses! The women wrap themselves in long dark blue garments, one end of which is used to cover the head; the black half-veil is never wanting, even in cases of most extreme ugliness; it is a long three-cornered piece of silk, fastened with brass buttons to the top of the cap or hood, so as to hang from below the eyes. The effect of the whole costume is abominably bad.

Here and there was to be seen a large lake, the remains of the late inundation; beside it, almost invariably, a group of acacia or sycamore trees; beneath their shade a few buffaloes, working a powerful "*Sakieh*" for the irrigation of some fields of wheat or of Indian corn, ("*Doóra Shámee*") while the overflowings of the plentiful stream, thus raised, serve to nourish the grove itself. This "*Sakieh*" is a very simple machine, consisting of a large wheel, on the outer circumference of which, all round, are fastened earthen pitchers; these draw the water out of a small trench close beside the wheel, raise it up, and pour it into a wooden trough or channel. The mournful creaking of these wheels resounds throughout every part of Egypt, as an accompaniment to the yet more mournful singing of the drivers of the oxen; for the Arab never engages in any occupation without accompanying it by singing. This art does indeed at present occupy a very low place in the scale of cultivation; they sing every thing through the nose, or at best, squeeze out their tones in a most extraordinary manner. Their melodies are, for the most part, in minor keys, and have but few notes; the chief art in executing their airs, is to drawl out a succession of wild cadences, which, doubtless, many European artistes might vainly endeavour to imitate. They have a strange, and often even an unpleasant sound, but they produce an impression of surprise which is certainly somewhat striking.

From time to time, though rarely, I observed, on the banks of the river, a flat field covered with tall, rush-like grass, but no general verdure was spread over the level surface. Here and there a branch of the Nile was glittering in the distance, or its course was marked by a small, white sail, usually of a quadrangular form, and fastened to a pole, which lies obliquely across the mast-head.

The captain had given us a promise that we should be in Cairo before three o'clock; but the current was too strong, owing to the subsiding of the inundation, to allow of our advancing rapidly, and so hour after hour passed away. Towards sunset the Pyramids at length appeared. Like grisly phantoms, they stood there on the red horizon, and riveted our every look, until they vanished in the dim twilight. Sable night now met us in deepest gloom, and still not a light was visible, not a vessel, nothing to announce to us that we were drawing near to a capital city, containing a population of nearly two hundred thousand inhabitants. Our impatience was excited, and not so easily quieted, although the swarthy orchestra, with their white jackets and trousers, used their utmost exertions to break the drums of our ears, and thus to arrest our attention. Their performance being at length concluded, we took refuge in our usual evening entertainment, singing, and the banks of the sacred stream soon re-echoed the sounds of our German national airs. A deep stillness was spread over all around us on board, and the brown-looking Fellahs crept out on every side, attracted by the charm of a strain of singing so new to them.

At length Cairo lay before us,—at least, many lights were glimmering on the shore. Our steamer made a most awkward and unskilful turn, by which a small bark laden with stones was run down, and several men were thrown into the river; sounds of fearful altercation and loud cries of murder were raised, and not words only but blows were exchanged. On the shore, there now appeared people bearing large iron vessels like barrels, fastened to poles, and filled with burning wood, straw or shavings, to serve as flaring lanterns. Nothing was to be seen of the promised carriages; asses however were standing in readiness; brown, wild, banditti-like men were brandishing their sticks, with frightful cries, each goading on his beast. We mounted, after having made the necessary arrangements regarding our baggage, leaving one of our servants with the interpreter, to remain beside it,—a precaution which, owing to the disorderly state of the country, the narrow streets, and the midnight robberies which frequently occur, was assuredly very necessary,—and urged on our asses, laden only with the most indispensable parts of our luggage, to a swift gallop. Thus our cavalcade dashed on towards the city,—the two guides, torch in hand, leading the van,—like hounds upon the scent, as we passed through the thick gloom of close and narrow lanes, and over roads often blocked up by rubbish and by vehicles of divers sorts and sizes. A little disaster, viz., one of our cavaliers, who had the encumbrance of the heavy money-box, being thrown from his ass, though fortunately he escaped unhurt, was the only adventure that befel any of our party; and the mirth occasioned by the novel scene of our nocturnal entry, lasted till, after half-an-hour's ride, we found ourselves at a stand before a large gateway. It was the Hôtel Oriental,—a house very prettily situated, and with something very English in its appearance. The gate was opened, but we sought in vain throughout the spacious building for waiters or domestics of any kind, while the impudence of the ass-drivers could scarcely be held within bounds, even by the aid of our sticks. After sundry fruitless endeavours, we succeeded in rousing a most somniferous negro, who spoke a little Italian; he speedily put an end to our difficulties, by means of a long whip of hippopotamus' hide, (called "*koor-bag*") with which he dealt fearful blows to the right and left among the sleeping men who were stretched, without any covering, on the ground on all sides. As to our rooms however, we had, in the first place, great difficulty in convincing the people of our identity, and thus obtaining possession of the apartments ordered for the Prince and his suite,—and, at one time, it really seemed as if we had here bid farewell to the civilized world. Nevertheless, the beds in which, thoroughly wearied, we shortly sank to rest, were very good; the curtains were thick and without any holes, so that musquitoes ("*Mücken*") from without, and grumblings ("*Mucken*") from within, were equally excluded. It was not till the following morning that we were made aware of the advantages which our suite of apartments possessed. The landlord,—a Frenchman, proprietor also of the above-mentioned hotel in Alexandria,—full of apologies, introduced us to a handsome "*salon*," and a dining-room furnished with Turkish divans. The walls, throughout, were adorned with very pretty English and French engravings, and in the salon was a piano-forte, and one by no means devoid of merit.

It is now once more day. The Venetian blinds are opened. What an enchanting prospect! To our left, a long row of oriental houses, with richly carved "*mushrebóohs*," (latticed projections instead of windows) interspersed with mimosas and palm-trees, rising picturesquely above the garden walls: the long line of houses and palaces is terminated by a tall and splendid minaret: several similar buildings, gaily painted red and white, appear in the foreground: the centre of the back-ground is a grove of palms gracefully pencilled against the blue horizon: adjoining it, to our right, tower the two gigantic Pyramids of Geezeh. They supply in some measure the place of hills, which are wanting to perfect the beauty of the landscape. To our right on the horizon lies the desert, easily recognisable by its atmosphere; over it floats a thick vapour of yellowish greyish hue. The foreground here however is all the prettier for this; it consists of a thick forest of acacias, clothed in the freshest vernal green, and broken at intervals by flourishing fields of maize; in the centre of the picture a small piece of water, bordered by *Labbek acacias.* Near this basin passes one of the greatest thoroughfares leading to the city: it extends across the wide square called "*the Uzbekéëh,*" upon which the windows of our hotel look out. A multitude of asses laden with fruit, followed by swarthy young drivers, is approaching the town; then draws near a long train of slowly-pacing dromedaries, each fastened by a rope to the one before it: women in blue shifts and trousers, a large urn on the head, a smaller one on the uplifted palm of one hand, and often a naked infant astride on the shoulder of the other side; white Copts with their black turbans; black Nubians with their long white togas; lean, wizened, filthy-looking Arabs; and fat, well-fed, cleanly Turks and Armenians; all are moving on, *en masse*, towards the city. Close in front of our windows the eye is refreshed by the rich foliage of acacias and sycamores. It is impossible to describe the delight we feel in once more beholding really green trees, which we have mourned the want of ever since we quitted Vienna. Here is shade; here is water; here are clean beds and a most comfortable breakfast. Having done honour to the latter, our curiosity could be restrained no longer. We jumped upon the backs of the asses that stood in readiness under our windows, and off we set, without loss of time, bound for the interior of the city of the Caliphs.

A totally new world here opens upon the traveller's astonished gaze; he knows not where first to cast his eyes; whether upon the gay and motley dwelling-houses adorned with carved work, upon the magnificent ruined mosques, or upon the shops of the wealthy merchants, and the crowded and various mass of human beings gathered together from all the nations of the East, which swarms around. It was scarcely possible to penetrate the throng that pressed closely on us, for the usual width of the streets is only from four to six paces. Our interpreter, armed with his formidable hippopotamus' hide whip, compelled, without further ceremony, by a few powerful lashes, all loiterers to make way; and quickly cleared every obstruction from our path. Even the heavy-laden camels were forced to yield to such treatment, and so we advanced with tolerable speed. We are generally accompanied in our more extended rides by one or two janissaries, (commonly called "*Cawàsses*") whose constant attendance often becomes quite an oppression; as, though they make a very fine show, they are not of the slightest use; for no one dreams of such a thing as being attacked by robbers, and the accounts given by travellers on this point are greatly exaggerated.

From the moment when a European first enters the streets of Cairo, his mind cannot fail to be impressed with the thought that he is within the precincts of a city degraded, impoverished, and weakened by famine and by plague, whose only attraction now is what remains of its ancient splendour. But this splendour of bygone ages was so great, and so closely interwoven with the whole structure, and with the very being, of the city, that a long period of sanguinary barbarism has failed altogether to oblitorate it. Wherever he may turn, the elaborate wood-carving of the airy "*mushrebéehs*,"—the beautiful bronze gates of the fallen palaces,—the half-immured sculptured ornaments, scattered amid the remains of ancient mosques,—all testify to the refined taste, and the skill in art, of the era of the Caliphs. Fortunately, scarce a drop of rain ever falls among these ruins: if this were not the case, it were hardly possible that so many relics of the fine arts, of the eleventh, and even of the tenth, century, should have been preserved; for, since that glorious era, nothing in the way of repairs has been attempted, but on the contrary, every thing has contributed to reduce the beautiful monuments of antiquity to mere heaps of broken fragments, which have supplied building materials for many edifices of more recent date.

As far as I can recollect, it was on our first day (the 8th of October) that we repaired to the citadel, thence to enjoy a general survey of the whole city. There lay,—stretching over the broad plain beneath, clothed in a tint of sombre grey,—the immense extent of the capital. The suburbs, whose houses are only built of mud, have a most woeful appearance; beyond them again, are spread immense heaps of rubbish and débris, through which it was necessary to cut in forming the roads. Within these outskirts of the city,—in melancholy and deathlike prominence,—are scattered some few very ancient mosques and minarets, more durable than all else around them,—now, alas! only inhabited below by dogs,—above by turtle-doves and ravens. Casting our eyes round the circumference of this mighty wreck, we were enabled to form some idea of the vast size of the city of old. Formerly it had a population of eight hundred thousand souls; the present inhabitants scarcely amount to two hundred thousand! Immediately below the citadel,—which rests upon a solid foundation of limestone-rock,—are a number of long, mean, grey buildings, which, with their flat roofs covered with camels' dung instead of asphalte, and with their windowless walls, look like paste-board boxes. They never exceed eight or ten feet in height, while each occupies a surface of twenty feet square. These are temporary barracks, in which the soldiers are living, with their wives and children,—a fearful crowd!

Grey is the colour that predominates throughout the entire city; here and there only, a minaret of graceful architecture, painted red and white, gladdens the weary eye; or the dome of a mosque of ancient date, shining through the net-work or tracery of chiselled stone. Most willingly did we bestow a long and lingering look on the Pyramids, which stand out,—bright and glorious in the clear sunshine,—amid the golden haze that overhangs the desert. Between them and the town, there is a welcome stripe of verdure,—trees in fresh and rich foliage, scattered over fields of wheat or of maize. Again, and yet again,—in many a distant spot,—we descried the source of all these blessings—the Nile,—glittering like some great lake, among the trees. To our left, we observed a small wood of palm-trees; the edge of it forms the boundary of the desert. To our right,—like a long, straight, whitish wall,—extend the limestone mountains of the "*Mokattam.*" The circumference of modern Cairo is still very great, in proportion to the number of its inhabitants; being twice—perhaps nearly thrice—as large as that of Berlin. The immense heaps of ruins, and the almost uninhabited streets of some quarters, often consisting, in great part, of fallen houses, are however necessarily included in this measurement.

On our descent from the highest point of the citadel, we visited, in the first place, the half-finished mosque, begun by order of the Pasha;—an edifice on a very grand scale, but executed in a corrupt, half-Moorish, half-modern style. Its chief beauty consists in the exquisitely-marbled oriental alabaster of its pillars,—some fifty or so of which are already standing,—the yellow marble of its niches and friezes,—and its various Mosaic pavements, formed of the most valuable stones found in Egypt. It is strange that the Pasha, who undertakes so many great architectural works, should never have thought of repairing any one of the ancient mosques, which are of such uncommon beauty.

We next made an attempt to obtain a sight of part at least, of the interior of the Pasha's palace. A veteran officer procured for us permission to enter, although we had at first been refused.

But what was our surprise and disappointment, when, on being ushered into the suite of apartments surrounding the parterre, we found ourselves in a large antechamber, with straw mats, and white-washed walls coarsely painted in grey and red stripes. Even the reception rooms were not much better, and they contained, in the shape of furniture, only soiled and torn red divans, placed against walls that had once been white. In the front court lay a detachment of Egyptian militia, whose arms and equipments were most minutely examined by our party of inquisitive strangers. An Egyptian soldier is by no means an ill-looking personage, and one might fancy him well-treated, if one did not know that parents here often put out an eye of one of their children, or cut off the fore-finger of his left hand, that they may save at least one of their sons from becoming the victim of the Pasha's cruel tyranny in his military service. The infantry wear loose blue jackets, white waistcoats, red belts, white loose trowsers fastened by means of garters at the knee, white gaiters, reaching to the ankle, and red slippers on their stockingless feet. Their head-gear consists of a red cap, similar to the Greek fez, but here called "*tarbóosh.*"

Below the citadel there is an extremely curious

well,* the only one in all Egypt, for the people universally drink the water of the Nile. It is said to be of great antiquity, and is known by the name of "*Beer Yoosef*," or Joseph's well. Its depth is supposed to be not far from three hundred feet. It is hewn in the limestone rock. Round the well itself is an ingeniously constructed winding staircase, with windows in its inner wall, which, from their great depth, afford but a small portion of light.

Near the foot of the citadel, and adjoining it, is a small side building, which contains Mehemet Ali's ménagerie. A few lions and hyenas are there attached by huge ponderous chains to the walls of their close and dirty cells. The animal most worthy of note is a serval ("*Felis Serval*").

On our way home we visited a bazaar. The streets of the bazaars, like all others, are only four or five paces in width. They are unpaved, but usually covered by an awning, stretched across from the higher stories of the houses on either side, which casts a mysterious gloom over the whole scene. The merchants deal in silk goods, a few of which are of home manufacture, but the greater part imported from Constantinople. There also are to be seen tailors selling ready-made clothes; numerous appraisers, ("*dellalin*") carrying about silver and gilt arms and weapons, shawls and pipes, both nargilehs and chibouques; and squatted down in the midst of the crowd, dirty little imps, sucking sweet citrons and pomegranates. The ordinary attire of these young boys is a shirt of blue cotton with loose sleeves fastened up by means of a red woollen cord thrown over the neck and

* *Minutoli* affirms that the well has been called "*Beer Yoosef*," to mark it as containing the tomb of the patriarch of that name.—*Editor*. The name really derives its origin from the renowned *Saladin*, ("*Yoosef Salah-e'-deen*,") the founder of the Eiyobite dynasty in Egypt, who, in the twelfth century, while occupied in enlarging, improving, and fortifying his capital, discovered and cleared out this very ancient well.—Tr.

crossed behind. Boys rarely wear the turban; they usually content themselves with the *tarbóosh.* The merchants who carry on their trade in silks and mouthpieces, are for the most part Turks, and are clean, and finely dressed after the fashion of their nation. A wealthy Arab always wears a white shirt and white trowsers, and binds round his waist two broad silken sashes. A jacket of silk or of cotton tissue, with the sleeves slit up, or a loose bed-gown reaching to the ankles, yellow slippers next the skin, with red ones over them,—the former having no soles,—complete his costume. The women of the common fellahs may be seen here in numbers, with their naked infants, covered with filth and vermin. These women sell a sort of flat cake, or tough, half-baked, white bread, and also cucumbers and sweet citrons. Their dress is a kind of long, blue garment, ending in a hood that covers the head. The black veil, which is drawn tightly up to the bridge of the nose, is fastened by a brass clasp, formed of three little buttons strung upon a wire, to the end of this long garment, which hangs down on the forehead. Many of them however, even young women, are discontinuing the use of this most irksome veil; they compensate for the want of it by holding a tip of their long drapery between their teeth, and cast a blinking, one-eyed glance at the stranger. The custom of painting the eyes dark-blue with "*kohl,*" ("*antimonium crudum*") and the nails red with *henna*, has become common even among the lowest ranks. The constant habit of carrying a burden upon the head has given to these women a stately, swimming mode of walking; and from the same cause, not merely to prevent their long loose sleeves from falling over their hands, they are wont to raise their hands as high as their heads, holding back their flattened palms, which altogether gives a strange, balancing air to all their movements. Belts or sashes they never wear;

consequently, even the most slender figure has a plump and full appearance. Although so careful in concealing their faces, they do not scruple to be considerably à la découverte otherwise, owing to the very broad opening at the neck of the garment. Blue drawers, of the same stuff as the chemise, are an indispensable part of their costume, but shoes they have none. These are considered an appendage peculiar to ladies of distinction, who generally appear in the streets mounted on asses, and numerously attended. Their garments are usually white instead of blue, and a small black cloak of stiff silk, which is thrown over the head and shoulders and hangs down the back, forms a striking contrast with the rest of the costume. They sit astride in men's saddles, with very high stirrups, into which they are raised with extreme difficulty.

Great luxury is displayed in the way of fine horses and beautiful trappings. The saddle-cloths are of purple velvet richly embroidered in gold, and with thin plates of gold fastened on them. Suspended round them, are as many tassels as can possibly be crowded on them.

Almost all persons of any consideration are Turks, and for the most part belong to the army. They are attired in the Turkish fashion, with the exception of the turban,—which is but rarely to be seen in its original rich and ample form,—wearing loose drawers falling over the knee, a sort of "*calza,*" (or covering for the leg) an embroidered jacket, usually of blue or brown, a broad silken girdle, in which are placed several pistols, and a short sabre in a silver scabbard. The red fez universally prevails.

Strikingly characteristic, among the mixed crowd of gaily and variously apparelled folk, is the dark figure of the Copt,—with his yellow complexion, and his vacant sycophantish countenance,—generally all in black,—dress and turban. A much larger turban, also of black, is worn by the lawyers and by the expositors of the Koran. Those persons who can boast of a particularly holy descent, are marked by the green turban;—but indeed I saw this only in the mosques.

On the second day of our visit to Cairo, (the 9th of October) we made an excursion to the so-called *Tombs of the Caliphs.** We rode out by the gate nearest to the *Mokattam* hills, to visit, in the first place, the *Mosque of "El Káëdbai,"* a building of the 15th century. A large, half-ruined, temple-like edifice was opened to us: it is surmounted by a dome and an elegant pointed minaret. The stucco of the ceiling has fallen off, the beautiful painting has become effaced, and the designs of the arabesques that covered the side walls and surrounded the quadrangular windows, are only occasionally to be recognised. The strong latticed gratings of cast bronze are yet in good preservation, and no less so the doors of entrance, with their hinges and mountings of bronze. This is indeed no matter of surprise, considering the dryness of the atmosphere. The inlaid floors, on the other hand, have suffered greatly; they retain but few traces of the splendid Mosaic pavements, composed of yellow and black marbles and of alabaster. The actual place of interment of "*El Káëdbai*" is beneath the vault of the dome. Here, in an ancient block of granite, are exhibited the footprints of Mahomet himself. The Sultan's tomb is enclosed by a grating of carved wood, formerly gilt, the openings of which are so narrow that it is no easy matter to see through it the large Koran lying on the grave. The magnificence of the sculptures of the dome can now be distinguished only by isolated fragments here and there; the masonry is however,

* These are, properly speaking, not the Tombs of the Caliphs, though among European travellers they are always known by that name, but those of the Memlook kings of the Circassian dynasty, founded, in the 14th century, by Sultan Berkook. The Tombs of the Caliphs were of much older date, and occupied the site of one of the Bazaars, in the city of Cairo itself.—Tr.

generally speaking, in excellent condition, and what injuries it has met with are such as could very easily be repaired.

We now rode forward over the wide and desolate field of ruins:—hillocks of from thirty to fifty feet in height, formed entirely of potsherds and broken water-jars and various wrecks of buildings of every age, lay scattered all along our path, marking the extent of the city of the Caliphs. Soon we reached the burial-place, which is only in some few places enclosed by walls. Ancient mosques and domes, pointing out the tombs of the Caliphs, here rise on every side. Several of them are covered with designs of great beauty, elegantly traced with the chisel in the limestone walls, which look as though a web of delicate embroidery had been thrown over them. We entered one of the most remarkable of these monumental mosques,—that of "*El Bérkook*,"—which dates from the 14th century. Owing to its distance from the city, a wonderful degree of stillness reigns within; the only sounds of animation throughout the precincts of its deserted walls proceeded from some little children, belonging to poor families that have taken up their abode in the lateral recesses of the mosque. The large, open court, in the centre of which is a fountain overshadowed by trees,—is surrounded by arcades: the slender pillars that support these have capitals adorned with a variety of Arabic designs: the grating of wooden fret-work, now grown grey with age, but still bearing marks of having once been gilt, struck us as peculiarly handsome. This mosque is without a dome.

Our third day (the 10th of October) was occupied in sight-seeing among the mosques of Cairo itself. We visited so many that my memory can scarcely present a full and distinct picture of each; there are still eighty of them in a habitable state, within the capital: if those that are now in ruins be included, the number mounts up to at least two hundred. The entrance-porch, surmounted by a lofty cupola, is usually the most magnificent part, and often contains the tomb of the founder. The actual mosque consists of large, open spaces or courts, surrounded by splendid colonnades. In the centre is a large quadrangular space, with marble pavement, and lofty, highly ornamented walls or colonnades; its only arch above,—the free canopy of heaven. In this inner court, and under the colonnades, prayer is offered up. What a beautiful spot for worshipping God! How much more majestic and sublime in reality than many a Gothic cathedral, where adoration is poured forth amid darkling gloom! Here the glorious vault of heaven itself, with its unchanging and unsullied blue,—seems to rest, like a vast dome, on those lofty walls of sculptured stone. In the middle of the above-mentioned open quadrangle rises a beautiful fountain, generally built of, and covered in with, marble; a few palms surround the basin in which every individual of the congregation of the Faithful may quench his thirst and perform his prescribed ablutions. Palm-mats are spread beneath the colonnades, which are often formed of six or seven rows of magnificent marble pillars. On that side of the building which is toward Mecca there is a niche in the wall, of superb workmanship,—a sort of Holy of Holies. Every Mohammedan slips off his shoes on entering the colonnade:—our not being able to do the same with our boots,—whatever might have been our willingness to comply with the custom,—often gave rise to curious scenes; more especially in the much frequented mosques, where we were, on more than one occasion, saved from acts of violence only by the energy of the "*Cawâss.*"

The great mosque of "*El Moâiüd*" lay the nearest to our hotel,—on the opposite side of the covered street. It has a magnificent entrance, somewhat resembling a gigantic grotto of shell-work, with hundreds of small niches in the noble porch, which is sixty feet in height. An immense bronze lustre, shaped like an ark, is suspended from the huge dome by two long chains, the third being broken: turtledoves were nestling in it. The dome was originally covered with skilful wood-carving, some fragments of which yet remain, and even here and there betray the fact that they once were gilt. The open court, with its fountain in the centre, is of surpassing beauty; its marble pavement, untrod by the rough step of boot-clad feet,—retains its brilliant polish, so that we were actually forced to draw straw "*babooshes*" (slippers) over our European chaussure.

The Mosque of "*Teyloon*," ("*Tooloon*") now in ruins, is a giant structure, and left a peculiarly grand impression on my mind. The colonnades that surround the immense open space in the centre, are forty feet high, and are supported, not by the pillars only, but by lofty pointed arches of most graceful proportions and beautiful workmanship.* Here and there, where the more recent parts have given way, the exquisite workmanship of the original edifice is clearly visible. Some portion of the gilded wainscotting is here still preserved, although the mosque is of the ninth century. A few ancient tablets of black porphyry are inserted in the walls near the principal entrance, and contain *Cufic* inscriptions.

We found our way into yet a third mosque, that known by the name of "*El Az'har*," (or "*the splendid*") which boasts a peculiar sanctity.† It contains, within

* These are among the earliest specimens now in existence of the pointed or modern Gothic style of architecture, which appears to have been introduced into Europe by the Crusaders in the 12th century, after they had become familiar with it among the Saracens.—TR.

† *Mr Lane*, in his work on the *Modern Egyptians*, mentions that, until the French invasion, neither Jew, Frank, nor any other Christian, was suffered to pass *before* this mosque.—TR.

its enclosure, a very large space of ground, covered with outbuildings; a poor's-house; a sleeping apartment for pilgrims; a library; a celebrated college in which instruction is still given and professors deliver lectures; and bath-rooms, in which the barber carries on his shaving operations,—all are connected with this large and many-pillared edifice! There was, within, a crowd of the faithful: some were cowering down to the ground, reading the Koran, and bending the upper part of the body up and down as they read;—others were pursuing us with hissing and snapping noises, continually pointing to our feet, and making gestures significant of putting off our obnoxious shoes. Meantime our *Cawáss* defended us from the obtrusive, by lashes which, with his ever-ready whip, he dealt largely round on every side, while the servants of the mosque,—with their long black gowns, and yellow under-garments,—struck in valiantly, contributing, with their long canes, not a few blows to our protection.

On the fourth day, (the 11th of October) we visited one of the greatest mosques,—that of "*Sultan Hassan.*" It stands in a large "*place,*" in which, at the time of our visit, a conjuror was performing his wonderful feats, for the edification of a numerous circle of spectators, of all ages and of every class, which had gathered round him. The chief exhibition of leger-de-main that we witnessed consisted in one of the audience cracking a very dreadful-looking whip violently round the bare head of the merry-andrew,—a tall, lean, swarthy-brown fellow,—a performance apparently attended with some danger; while the bald-headed victim so skilfully adapted himself to each twist, each movement, of the lash, that he was never touched. The people were likewise amusing themselves by swinging in balancing-wheels, horizontal and vertical, —and by carrying on, in booths and tents, a variety of games,—in the invention of which, all Arabs are most fertile. They were also lounging about their cafés,—or at least places where coffee is retailed,—which consist of a row of little boxes like hen-coops, made of plaited palm-twigs, on which the guests seat themselves to drink their coffee out of extremely diminutive cups, and to smoke their pipes. "*Sherbet*" may also be had at any of these stands; *i. e.* syrup of any kind, as mulberry, apricot, or plum, mixed with water. None is a more general favourite for this drink than that of violets: to me the verdigris colour of the beverage always appears somewhat suspicious.

The magnificent mosque occupies one whole side of the piazza, and is, like most of the others, painted in stripes of red and white. This colouring of the walls, which does not at all harmonize with the elegant decorations of the windows, must surely have sprung up in these latter days of degeneracy in the fine arts, and thus have been unconnected with the original architecture. The turrets are of cast bronze, scattered over with innumerable little projections and ornaments of irregular and convolute form, the design of which is not easily traced. The interior of the porch too, with its lofty arches, and the portals at the entrance, are adorned with a multitude of small niches, of workmanship so delicate, so much resembling exquisite stalactites, that one can never weary of examining it. The height of the walls is seventy feet to the roof, which is likewise full of these stalactite-hung niches, while a row of them forms a cornice immediately below it. The principal entrance leads to the tomb of Sultan Hassan; it is a large vaulted dome of immense height, adorned above, all over, with that curious sculptured niche-work, which I can designate by no name save that of stalactite-covered niches. There are upon it abundant traces of former gilding. The half-broken windows are extremely beautiful specimens of arabesques;—they are filled with glass of the most brilliant and varied colouring; but they are placed at so great a height, that the rays which they admit shed but a dim twilight on the scene below. The pavement is of the finest mosaic, formed of porphyry, jasper and marble; in its centre, placed against the east side-wall of the building, is the massive but simple tomb-stone, concealed behind a lofty grating of most elaborate design, partly of iron and partly of wood, on which marks of ancient gilding are also observable. On the splendid pavement within, lies a huge Koran, in characters of red and gold, said to have been written by a son of Hassan. All here is on the very spot on which it lay when the mosque was first built, well-nigh five hundred years ago. Since then, one generation after another has marvelled at the vast expenditure of magnificence and of skill,—and although none has ever possessed the art and the means requisite to repair the injuries that the edifice has gradually received,—yet a religious awe has withheld the hand of mischief or of revenge from approaching these monumental shrines,—and the mildness of the climate has tended to preserve sculptures of wood and of stone, which in our less genial climes, would have been reduced, by the vicissitudes of the weather, to a mass of rubbish and of desolation. How often, as I crossed the threshold of these lofty and mysterious halls, so sublime in their simplicity, so tranquil and hushed in their magnificence, have my thoughts wandered to the "*thousand and one nights,*" and to their enchanted palaces, which, for many a long century, no foot had trod. Often too am I involuntarily reminded of "*Aboo Hassan the rope-maker,*" and of "*the blind Ali Baba,*" when, in walking through the streets, I see the industrious artisans sitting in their little shops,—mere stalls hollowed out in the walls,—whose only opening towards the street, serves the double purpose of door and window. The front part of each shop is laid with carpeting, on which the passer-by may seat himself to transact business or to indulge his love of gossip. Here, generally, may be seen the proprietor reposing cross-legged, with his clean jacket of silken stuff, and his white turban, now busily plying his needle,—now making the air resound with the blows of his hammer, or now again smoking his nargileh, after the fashion of every merchant in the bazaar.

On the same day on which we took our general coup-d'œil of nearly all that was most remarkable among the mosques, we were also honoured with an audience of the Pasha. At seven o'clock in the evening, an equipage all glittering with gold, came to convey us to the palace. Two Moors with burning pitch-rings ran before us; and horsemen in bright uniforms surrounded the carriage, which proceeded rapidly on its winding way through the narrow streets of the city. In front of the palace, we alighted with all possible speed, and escorted our royal master up the flight of steps, and into a large but not very elegant saloon, containing only red divans, and at one end of the room two candelabra, six feet high, between which stood a wax taper, which was lighted as the Prince entered. The Pasha's interpreter, *Chosreu Bey*, a short, thick-set man, with piercing, rolling eyes, came forward to receive us, led us up to his highness, and presented us. We jumped up, not without difficulty, upon the high seats, in which operation our spurs were a sad hindrance. In the first place, a long pipe richly set with diamonds, was brought to the prince by the commander of the forces; next, a similar one to each of us,—silver trays served to support the pipe-bowls. I smoked with the utmost gravity, at the same time straining every nerve to follow the interpreting of the conversation, which was no easy matter, as I had the most distant seat. Coffee was next handed round, in tiny cups, by the great dignitaries. It was perfectly black, and boiling hot; nevertheless etiquette required that the whole should be swallowed at a draught. This I really could not accomplish; I delivered over my cup to the officer in waiting, after having merely taken a sip. He hastily covered it with his two hands, according to prescribed custom, as if he were endeavouring to catch an insect in it.

This letter must be despatched in an unfinished state, as I had been misinformed as to the hour for sending it off. I shall write again from Suez, where I expect to find time to describe the pyramids, and to say something concerning the remaining days of our stay in Cairo.

SUPPLEMENT TO THE SECOND LETTER.

FROM THE DIARY.

On the 13th of October, we ascended the pyramids of *Gizeh*, to which, by the bye, I think such a miserable little place, situated too at such a distance from them, has no right to give its name. The Pasha had supplied us with horses,—stout, gentle beasts; so we galloped on as far as the Nile, and then proceeded to Gizeh, where we visited, in the first place, the ovens for hatching eggs. These are low chambers, built of earth, and raised against the walls of the dwelling-houses. The openings are one foot above the ground, and about two feet in diameter. There were six of them at each side of the house, filled with dust and ashes to the height of about half a foot. Beneath them are the ovens for heating the eggs: in each chamber five or six hundred eggs are packed: a man creeps in daily, and turns them with great care. The usual temperature of the chamber is 31-5° Réaumur, (103° Fahrenheit.) In twenty-one days the chickens are hatched;—a third part of the eggs, or rather less, comes to nothing; the hatching is carried on only during three, or at most four months of the year, from

January to April; this is probably owing to the difficulty of procuring food for the young chickens.*

Our road from Gizeh lay through several delightful woods of palm-trees, whose crops of dates had just been gathered in. The ordinary dwellings of the Fellahs are under the palm-trees; for they betake themselves to their mud-built hovels only in cases of necessity and distress. Their children are prowling about the morasses and the remains of the inundation all day long. Under these palms, tillage is carried on; with a very simple plough to be sure;—yet the fields are, as far as we could see, well cultivated. The greater part of the plain was still covered with water; and, on this account, we could approach the pyramids only by making a great circuit, riding along a narrow dyke. At length we reached the desert, over the flat surface of which, mounted on the swift coursers of the Pasha, we flew on at a most rapid pace towards the pyramids. The population of the surrounding villages,—for the most part Bedouins, rushed out to meet us, with loud shouts. Among them I descried one thick-lipped, flat-nosed native of western Africa. Each of us selected his men to act as guides, or rather was selected by them;—and so we proceeded to the Pyramids.

First, however, we saw the noble and pleasing Sphinx. How much is it to be regretted that the calcareous sand of the desert is constantly, more and more, threatening to bury it! and that the soft calcareous rock out of which it is hewn is so light and crumbling, that the

* This singular and ingenious art of hatching eggs in ovens is peculiar, not only to Egypt, but to one place in that country,—the village of *Berme*, in the Delta, the inhabitants of which disperse themselves throughout the land every autumn, the trade passing as an heir-loom from generation to generation. Besides their board, and a fixed payment for their superintendence of the eggs, they are entitled, if more than the guaranteed two-thirds come to maturity, to retain the overplus. Their peculiar skill consists, not so much in the construction or arrangement of the "*mamals*," or hatching-houses, as in the nice regulation of the fires.—Tr.

nose has vanished altogether, and the bosom too is decayed and full of holes.*

The pyramid which we first visited was that of *Cheops*, the *Great Pyramid*. On its interior wall, close above the entrance to the king's chamber, are the hieroglyphics, engraved by Professor Lepsius.

We descended the first, or outer passage, the entrance of which is about a tenth of the height of the pyramid. Here the regularity of the steps,—or outer tiers of stone,—ceases. The stones above the opening are immense, wedge-shaped blocks, resting against each other. We descended with twenty candles, each of us taking two men to assist him;—it cost us some trouble to drive back the remainder of the crowd, and we could not accomplish it without causing much uproar;—indeed, notwithstanding all our exertions, a black supernumerary contrived to smuggle himself in with our party. The descent of the steep passage was accomplished rather by sliding than walking, and in the course of it we were often obliged to bend ourselves quite double; however, the guides assisted us to the utmost of their power, and never suffered us to fall. At length, having ascended the second passage, and proceeded to a lofty gallery, we

* *Sir Gardner Wilkinson*, in his "*Modern Egypt and Thebes*," informs us that from the accumulation of sand the entrance into the Sphinx is now concealed, and even its position unknown. In a Greek inscription cut on its paw, bearing the signature of Arrian, which Sir G. W. quotes, with Dr Young's English translation of it,—allusion is made to the motive which led the Egyptians of old to place their great monuments so close to the edge of the desert. They were, the poet supposes, unwilling to sacrifice, even to purposes so noble, any portion of land which could be cultivated. It appears from the accounts given by Sir G. W. and other writers, that the Sphinx was originally an object of adoration,—that the space between its legs was a sacred area,—that an altar stood between its paws,—and that the entrance to this sanctuary was flanked by sculptured lions. Many traces of red paint remain on the Sphinx, and on the fragments near it. It was formerly protected from the sand by brick walls. Hieroglyphic inscriptions may still be seen on the granite tablet upon its breast.—TR.

reached the King's Chamber, a large, dark hall, into which no ray of light has ever penetrated. It is formed of blocks of granite, and the only thing it contains is a rude sarcophagus, of the same material. Another chamber, called the Queen's, which we had the same difficulty in approaching, contains nothing except bats. One of our attendants crept into one of the air-channels, (which are not much more than one foot square,) for the purpose of catching some of them, and he was lucky enough to seize a few. The species is the "*Vespertilio Barbastellus:*" it has a long tail, and ears meeting above the nose.

The ascent on our return, climbing up the narrow outer passage, was yet more difficult than the descent: we were most heartily rejoiced when it was all over, and we saw the light of day once more. After a short interval of repose, we ascended quickly, on a broken part of the pyramid, to its summit, on which is a flat space, upwards of thirty feet square. We had wished to breakfast on that elevated platform; but we found the heat too great, and contented ourselves while on the top with emptying a bottle of champagne to the health of our king. One of our guides now volunteered to perform within five minutes the exploit, not only of scrambling down the Great Pyramid, in the ascent of which we had occupied more than a quarter of an hour, but moreover, of climbing up that of *Cephren*,—or of *Belzoni*, whichever you may be pleased to designate it,—which, near its top, is still covered with its casing, and almost inaccessible to a European;—and actually the five minutes had not yet perfectly elapsed, when the fellow was heard shouting to us from the apex of the second pyramid. A few minutes more,—and he was with us again on that of Cheops,—and all this without being in the least out of breath. Both of these pyramids are about 450 feet, more or less, in height:*—the third, that of Mycerinus, which stands at a little distance, is considerably smaller.

After remaining for some time on the top, we again descended to the plain,—passing over the face of this mighty work,—this monument of the now mysterious ages of the past. Our horses were standing in readiness below; we resolved to strike off by another road:—no sooner said than done. But soon we came to a halt before a trench, formed for irrigation from the Nile, which crosses the path; we leaped in, and fortunately reached the other side in safety, although the water was up to our pommels, and our horses were shying at the dogs of the Bedouins who were swimming close beside us. Thoroughly soaked, we proceeded on our journey. A numerous flight of birds, game of various kinds, besides mews, herons, and kites,—tempted us to indulge in the pleasures of sporting; however nothing was shot except one owl. It was the *Strix noctua*, or *snowy owl*. We passed the ruins of a handsome bridge, dating from the time of the ancient Arab kings,—and towards evening, having traversed flourishing fields of maize in most luxuriant verdure, we found ourselves at Gizeh, and soon afterwards reached Cairo.

* According to the calculations made by *Sir Gardner Wilkinson*, the present perpendicular height of the Great Pyramid is 460·9 feet: its present base is 732·0 feet, according to his measurement: its perpendicular height, when entire, he calculates to have been 480·9 feet. This differs but slightly from the measurements of *Coutelle*, as quoted in the second volume on "*Egyptian Antiquities*," published by the Society for the Diffusion of Useful Knowledge. *Colonel Howard Vyse's* measurements would considerably reduce the present perpendicular height. Sir Gardner Wilkinson reckons the present perpendicular height of the pyramid of Cephren to be 446·9 feet, and the present length of its base 690 feet;—its former perpendicular height 453 feet. These measurements very nearly coincide with those of *Colonel Howard Vyse*,—and do not differ materially from those of *Jomard* and of *Belzoni*, as quoted in the above-named work. *Sir G. Wilkinson* gives the present perpendicular height of the pyramid of Mycerinus as 203·7 feet,—its present length of base as 330·0 feet,—and its former perpendicular height as 218·0 feet.—Tr.

On the 15th of October, in the most oppressive heat, we made an expedition to *Sakkâra.** We crossed the Nile at Old Cairo; and thence followed the left bank of the river for the distance of five leagues. One beautiful palm-grove succeeded another;—everywhere we saw a cheerful and well-fed, though very dirty population, some of whom were engaged in preparing the "*néeleh,*" (indigo). It is, while boiling in earthen vessels, crushed, to the sound of noisy singing.† At length we reached

* Supposed by some writers to derive its name from *Pthah-Sokari*, the god worshipped at Memphis.—Tr.

† We find, in an interesting article on Indigo, contained in the 3d Volume on "*Vegetable Substances,*" published by the Society for the Diffusion of Useful Knowledge, that the method of preparing indigo in Egypt differs essentially from that pursued in British India, in the West Indies, or in North America. In all these countries, though the mode of proceeding varies in different places, it may be said to consist generally of three parts, carried on successively in three large vats,—viz. fermentation, agitation, and precipitation: whereas in Egypt the plants are dried, previously to being put into earthen jars filled with hot water. They are then worked in these, with a palm branch, in the manner of churning, until the whole of the colour is pressed out. The liquid is next strained through the bark of a tree into another jar: it is left there for eight days, during which time part of the water escapes by trickling through a small aperture half-way down the side of the vessel, leaving the sediment at bottom. This residuum is afterwards poured into a broad but very shallow hole formed in the sand, which absorbs the remaining liquid and leaves the indigo in solid cakes. The Egyptians and the Hindoos are the only people who scald or boil the indigo instead of fermenting it: their method is said to produce less colouring matter, and a less permanent dye. The fermentation of it is attended, however, with so much difficulty and uncertainty, as to have caused more numerous failures, in proportion to the number of persons engaged in the factories, than almost any other branch of speculation. Many workmen die from the noxious vapours of the indigo, and the refuse water would poison the brooks, if suffered to flow into them. The *Indigofera anil* requires great heat; it is sown in narrow furrows, two or three inches deep, about a foot apart from each other. The Egyptian peasants sow it once in seven years, and obtain two crops annually. The plant is stunted and shrubby; its stem hard and ligneous; its growth straight and delicate; its smooth pinnated leaves, and bunches of small, purple, papilionaceous flowers emit a faint but pleasant smell: the seeds are contained in brown pods. A few centuries since, even after Marco Polo had described the indigo plant of Asia, Europeans persisted in believing it to be a mineral substance. So strong too was the jealousy of it in Germany, that it was known as "the devil's dye," and in consequence of the prejudice against

Mitrahenny, the neighbourhood of the ancient *Memphis*, now only distinguished from the rest of the plain by immense heaps of ruins, which resemble rather a mountain formation than fragments of ancient works of architecture. Not a pillar is to be seen,—not a block of marble; —all is overgrown with palms.* Some wandering Bedouins had pitched their tent not far from this sacred spot, and they gave us a friendly invitation to enter and to share their coffee. After remaining a short time among them, we proceeded along the dykes as before, and reached the termination of our ride in two hours. A plunge in the last basin of the inundation, refreshed us greatly, and whetted our appetite for breakfast, of which we partook at the base of one of the largest pyramids. This pyramid is of easy ascent; it is built in the same manner as that of *Cheops*, but inferior in height,

any rival of the German woad, an oath was even recently (if indeed it be not still) imposed on the Nuremberg dyers, who thus annually perjured themselves by a pledge not to use indigo!—TR.

* How strikingly does this vivid picture of the present desolation of the ancient capital of Lower Egypt, the renowned *Memphis*, *Menoph*, or *Noph*, —which superseded Thebes as the metropolis of Egypt,—illustrate the fulfilment of that short but comprehensive prophecy uttered by the mouth of Jeremiah, ch. xlvi. ver. 19, "Noph shall be waste and desolate, without an inhabitant." Many are the denunciations, contained in other passages of Scripture, against this city. Had Dr Hoffmeister visited Memphis at a more favourable season, he would doubtless have mentioned the celebrated *Colossus of Rameses II.* It is however, when the Nile is high, nearly covered with water, and from the same cause some parts of Memphis are then unapproachable. The colossus is, though much broken, still more than 42 feet in height. It is supposed by some to mark the site of the great *Temple of Pthah*. Two statues of red granite, and some other figures, likewise remain. Yet even during more favourable months, comparatively little is to be seen to mark the sites of the famous Temples of Serapis, of Pthah, and of Apis. In the latter, the god Apis, the black bull, was kept and worshipped. To the north and west of the city, in ancient times, was an artificial lake, believed, as were many other wonders, to be the work of Menes,—the mythic king;—its position can now scarcely be traced. Sir G. Wilkinson believes it to have been near the dyke below Sakkara,—probably the spot where we shall find our author enjoying the refreshment of bathing. The Colossus of Rameses II. is the property of the British Museum, but is left in Egypt on account of the expense of transporting it to this country.—TR.

(though upwards of three hundred feet high) and far more decayed. Having crossed the high mounds of rubbish accumulated from a great number of pyramids, part of which are still surrounded by walls that may be easily traced, so that they appear quite like church-yards,* we descended into the subterranean chambers of the ancient tombs. The entrance of the one we visited is between masses of rock, half closed up by the sand that obstructs it. After a descent of twenty feet, we entered a dark cavern; in the back-ground appears a handsome and spacious hall supported by pillars: all its walls are adorned with splendid hieroglyphic tablets, executed in the hard lime-stone: the ceiling bears traces of painting, which has indeed here and there preserved its brilliancy wonderfully; but the lovers of art have made fearful havoc all round. In one very deep recess is a descending shaft; Count O——— caused himself to be let down by a rope, but after arriving at a depth of 40 feet, and at the end of the rope, he could scarcely see the bottom.†

The graves of animal-mummies, (ibises, oxen, sheep, snakes, &c.) situated in the neighbourhood, near the vil-

* The pyramids of Sakkara and of Dashoor, all standing near each other; those of Abousir are but a few miles distant.—Tr.

† The tomb here described may very probably be that alluded to in the work above quoted, on "*Egyptian Antiquities*," where we find that "Captain Caviglia cleared one out to the depth of sixty feet, and found at a little distance, to the south of the well's bottom, a chamber containing a highly polished sarcophagus without hieroglyphics." Among the innumerable tombs, extending for miles round Abousir and Gizeh, are many rude paintings and sculptures, valuable as illustrative of the customs and civilization of ancient Egypt. Sir G. Wilkinson particularly describes one vaulted tomb of hewn stone, of the time of Psammeticus II.,—which he considers to be probably the oldest existing specimen of a stone arch, having been built 600 years before the Christian era: arches, formed of crude brick, are indeed found at Thebes, in tombs of the 16th century, B.C. Sir G. W. also suggests the idea that the chamber, of which he traced the base, in one of the crude brick pyramids at Dashoor, must have had a vaulted roof,—and he quotes the supposition of Dr Richardson, who thought that Asychis,—a king of very ancient, but uncertain date,—in boasting, as recorded by Herodotus, of the superiority of his brick pyramid over those of stone, must have referred to the invention of the arch, and to its being the first specimen of it.—Tr.

lage of Abousir, we only found after a difficult search; and a very long rope was necessary, to let us down the half-filled-up shaft.* While being drawn up again, having seen little or nothing, my hands slipped, I lost my hold of the rope, by which I was endeavouring to pull myself up, and fell, when I had nearly gained the top, down again to the bottom,—a great depth. With hands excoriated and shockingly wounded, I at length contrived to get out, and, mounted on an ass, not without pain and difficulty, I reached the Nile, by which, fortunately, we were to return home: for I should have been utterly unable to hold the bridle. At midnight we found ourselves standing before the gates of Cairo, and it was only owing to a lucky accident that we were suffered to enter, though ignorant of the watchword.

A subsequent excursion to *Heliopolis*,—the ancient "*On*,"—the city of philosophers, close to the modern *Mataréeh*,—afforded us but little satisfaction. We found only an elevated part of the surface, marked out by its solitary obelisk, and by a profusion of ruins.† The return home, under the shade of *gum-acacias*, beside the water-trenches supplied from the Nile, was most agreeable. The fields were full of "*Hibiscus esculentus*," (*Baniah*,) and of "*Indigofera*," (*Néeleh*). At the outskirts of a little village,‡ surrounded by well-cultivated

* Mr Lucas, who, in 1714, wandered, by the aid of Ariadne's thread, through nearly all of these catacombs, imagined, from the embalmed ox-heads found there, that the god Apis had been buried in them.—Tr.

† These ruins, among which are those of the great Temple of the Sun, and the Avenue of Sphinxes, are however, to the antiquarian, of great interest, and the obelisk is extremely curious, independent of the associations connected with the city where Plato and Herodotus studied: which, in Strabo's time, was already deserted. The place abounds no less in Scriptural than in classical associations;—we read of Joseph marrying the daughter of its priest, (Gen. xli. 45). Its usual Hebrew name was *Bethshemesh*,—"House of the Sun;"—but it is mentioned under the name of *Bethaven*, or *Aven*, "House of Vanity,"—with Noph and other cities, in the denunciations against Egypt, uttered by the voice of inspiration. (Ezek. xxx. and Hosea x.) A similar prophecy is contained in Jeremiah xliii. 13.—Tr.

‡ Probably the village of Matareeh, which is full of ancient fragments.—Tr.

fields of "*Ricinus*," (castor-oil tree) we were conducted intó a garden, where, in the centre of a flower-bed, the point of a gigantic obelisk projects above the ground. Its hieroglyphics are almost entirely filled up by the nests of mason-wasps. Apricot and peach trees encircled the granite block. Who can tell what may be its appearance or its language, at the depth of fifty or sixty feet below the present surface of the soil!

I had, during our stay in Cairo, the pleasure of forming several interesting acquaintances. Among the foremost of these was that of the Pasha's physician in ordinary,—*Klot Bey,*—which dates its commencement from a visit which we paid him. His house has nothing distinguished about it; but ostriches and gazelles are running about in its court, in which we also saw the young lion sent by Professor Lepsius, and destined for Berlin. Klot Bey's collection of Egyptian antiquities contains much that is of interest. He is liberal-minded, and full of independent thought as a physician. He expresses himself remarkably well, and would do honour to a professor's chair, if indeed he is as deep and well-grounded in his scientific knowledge as he is agréeable in conversation;—and of this I could form no opinion in so short an acquaintance. He has gained great honour by the operations he has performed in cases of the leprous tumour so common in Upper Egypt, which is not very rare even in Cairo. He has described the mode of performing it in a treatise which he published on the subject. I was also introduced to *Dr Pruner,* another physician in ordinary, a medical man of great experience. Among his orthopædic patients, whom he has consigned to the care of *Dr Schledehaus,* I saw several most successful cases of cure in club-foot of the second and third degree. I happened to be at this Orthopædic Institution on the day on which we were to dine with the Pasha. At about half-past two o'clock, I hurried back to the hotel, and saw, to my horror, the Pasha's equipage just driving off from its entrance. What a disappointment! How much should I have enjoyed seeing His Highness at dinner;—and it was vain to hope for another opportunity, as our departure was at hand.

On the 17th of October, Count G——— set out for Suez, with a view to making arrangements with the captain of the "*Hindostan*," as to our further route. We accompanied him, as he rode through the gate of Cairo late in the evening, and parted at the spot where the bivouacking detachment of cavalry had pitched their tents, at the edge of the desert. A few flying excursions in the environs of the capital, which we made specially for the sake of sketching,—and a visit to the Pasha's garden at Shoobra, occupied us during our remaining days at Cairo. On the evening of our last day, (the 19th of October,) soon after we had returned from our day's sight-seeing, and while we were enjoying our tea on the balcony of the hotel, cries of most agonizing distress, mingled with imprecations uttered in the French tongue, suddenly burst forth below our windows. We saw a man, in white under-clothing and without shoes, running to and fro before the sackiyeh, making violent gesticulations, and apparently in a state of fearful despair. It was our landlord, M. Coulomb. The inquisitive soon formed a circle round him, while some more sensible and active neighbours brought lanterns to illuminate the depths of these horrible pits, and their half-rotten water-wheels. The surface of the water is ten feet below the level of the ground, and below that again is muddy, slimy water, fifteen feet deep. Any one who, in the dark, may approach too near the edge of the pit, and thus fall in, is gone; nothing can save him. The descent of this pit is extremely difficult, and some time elapsed before any one could be found willing to venture down. At the end of half an hour, after many fruitless attempts, they succeeded, by means of letting down several men, in recovering the body of a young man,—the younger brother of M. Coulomb. He was instantly put into bed, and we cut every article of clothing off his body. A slight degree of warmth was still perceptible. Dr Schledehaus was fortunately with us, and he assisted me in my endeavours to restore animation; Klot Bey also came, after I had sent for him twice. We laboured on till night had passed away:—we sat beside the dead till two o'clock in the morning; never intermitting our exertions in rubbing and warming the lifeless frame. At length the conviction forced itself upon us that all human help was vain; it had come too late. Death had but too surely grasped his victim. What an awful night was that! On the very day that followed it, a simple funeral procession was seen to wind its mournful way from before the gate of the "*Brothers Coulomb.*"

Our baggage had been sent before us to Suez on the 18th of October, as we had succeeded, through the obliging civility of the officials connected with the Bombay steamer, in obtaining berths for our voyage to that place, although at first the captain had refused to augment the ordinary number of passengers. We had had some hopes of being still able to secure berths on board the steamer "Hindostan," bound for Calcutta; however we were informed, even at Alexandria, that, almost invariably, every berth was taken before the departure of the overland mail from London, and we therefore contemplated, with quiet resignation, the unpleasant prospect of being obliged to wait at Bombay a whole month, for an opportunity of proceeding to Ceylon. As the shades of evening were closing around the spacious Uzbekeeh, on the 20th of October, the Pasha's dromedaries were seen standing in front of our hotel;—one among them,—elegantly caparisoned, and distinguished also by its light and slender form,—was destined for the Prince's own use: The others were all large, indeed gigantic creatures. We speedily mounted, and rode off towards the desert. The slow jolting motion of the dromedaries when walking, was soon pronounced by every one to be quite intolerable; their trot we found somewhat less irksome: even at the end of the first quarter of an hour we were so weary of the constant swinging, and of being thrown backwards and forwards in saddles fastened with bands or thongs, and with very high stirrups which uncomfortably forced back our feet, that every one of us heartily wished the ride at an end: in fact the fatigue was so great, that not having yet recovered from the sleeplessness and the exertions of that last dreadful night, I sunk repeatedly, notwithstanding the violent motion, —which I can only compare to the game of tossing a fox in a blanket,—into a weary slumber: I was however, much to my regret, wakened each time by the cries of the anxious dragoman, who feared that I might fall from my unpleasant elevation.

Thus we rode on uninterruptedly, during twelve long hours. At length we perceived, by the first light of morning dawn, a well-built house in the midst of the desert:—it was No. 4, one of the stations or hotels, which the Transit Company* has built, for the accommodation of the numerous travellers who cross the Isthmus of Suez in their public carriages or vans. Every stranger is free to enter; only he must pay one pound sterling for the mere permission to do so, and every other charge is proportionably high. Wearied as we were, we hastened forward towards this most welcome resting-place, where we enjoyed an excellent breakfast, and some hours' repose in capital beds,—and moreover, towards

* The Peninsular and Oriental Company, which has now been relieved, by the *Pasha's* Transit Administration, of the charge of the Egyptian part of the overland route.—Tr.

evening we all voted ourselves greatly the better for a remarkably good *English* dinner.

Such are the English! Every where, even in the most desolate solitudes, they introduce their "*Comfort!*"

As soon as the heat of the day was over, we were once more on our road, mounted on our heavy beasts. In a little while, night overtook us; and, whenever the moon was obscured by a passing cloud, or when one or another of our little caravan yielded to Morpheus,—the party were in danger of being scattered. The desert is parched and barren; behind No. 4, is a ridge, which runs from west to east.* There is said to be much underwood upon it, well stocked with game:—the only plants that I observed were a strongly scented *Artemisia* (Wormwood), and various kinds of *Salsola* (Salt-Wort). A multitude of fantastic forms floated before me as I sat dozing in my saddle; but no Jackals, no Hyænas, no Jerboas appeared, although we could see distinctly, even to some distance, in the clear moonlight. We arrived, quite exhausted, at about three A.M., on the 22d of October, at the station No. 6. Here the charge made for our coffee and eggs was a guinea and a half. After a few more painful hours on the backs of our dromedaries, morning dawned upon us; there appeared to the north, towering in the crimson light of sunrise, the outline of a mountain ridge;† and the Red Sea itself burst upon our sight. Birds well known in Germany were here greeted by us as welcome messengers from home:

* The sandhills of *Undtham*. The defile of *El Muktala*, near No. 4, is generally supposed to be that through which the Israelites passed from *Migdol*.—Tr.

† The *Kolzoom* mountains, which give their name to the adjacent part of the Red Sea. *Kolzoom*, signifying destruction, is supposed by some to have reference to the destruction of Pharaoh's host; while most authors derive the name from the ancient Greek town and fort of Clysma.—Tr.

—we saw the *Charadrius Morinellus* (*Dotterel*), and the *Motacilla Alba* (Wagtail), frequently, throughout the desert, and before that, we had had the joy of meeting our good old friend *the Stork* in vast flocks among the palm-groves of Sakkarah.*

We were now obliged to muster all our remaining strength;—but indeed our faint embers of energy were soon extinguished under the intense glow of the ascending sun, which rendered the shaking pace of our dromedaries more than ever irksome:—our legs were stiff and aching, and every joint seemed to have grown rigid. At about half-past seven A.M., we were at length in sight of Suez,—a small and dirty town: ruins upon ruins meet the eye on every side, and, among them all, the traveller seeks in vain for any abode fit to dwell in. The

* Those readers who may be familiar with the domestic life, and we may add with the popular songs of Germany, will at once understand with what warm and tender feelings a German must welcome, in a foreign land, this home-bird, which, from year to year, he has been accustomed to regard as a member of his family. In Germany, in Holland, and in parts of France, boxes or wheels are placed on the housetops to entice them to settle there, and a house which is never visited by one is deemed unlucky: each stork returns to its own nest, and various experiments have been tried to prove this fact. One gentleman in Poland is even said to have fastened an iron collar, with the words "*Hæc ciconia ex Polonia*," to a stork in autumn; and to have welcomed it back in spring, adorned with a golden collar, bearing the inscription, "*India cum donis remittit ciconiam Polonis.*" The storks arrive in Germany and Holland about April; and in August the whole flock re-assembles with confused noise, and, on the signal being given, they depart for Egypt, Barbary and the East. They seem to migrate from a real love of travelling; for even at Bagdad, and other places where winter is never severe, they regularly depart in autumn. In Egypt they feed on frogs, and thus are of great use. If they are loved in Germany, they are venerated in Oriental countries, where they destroy serpents and other vermin: among the ancients they were held sacred. Adrian commemorated by medals the fact that a stork built its nest on the Temple of Concord, regardless of the noise and bustle of the capitol. The quality specially venerated in this bird among the Greeks was its filial piety. Its peculiar instinct regarding its migrations is strikingly alluded to in the Divine warning by the mouth of Jeremiah, (Jer. viii. 7,) "Yea, the stork in the heaven knoweth her appointed times, and the turtle, and the crane, and the swallow, observe the time of their coming; but my people know not the judgment of the Lord."—Tr.

hotels are falsely so-called, for any hen-house might be as worthy of the name. Yet how delightful to us was the long-wished-for moment, when our dromedaries, with a deep groan, knelt down in front of one of these wretched abodes! We had scarcely assembled round the breakfast-table, when the Captain of the Hindostan was ushered in. He came to offer us cabins, and most comfortable accommodation in every way, on board the Calcutta steamer. This was joyful tidings, for we had all been quite in low spirits, in consequence of our previous unsuccessful efforts to obtain a passage for Ceylon direct. The arrangements were concluded at once, and our luggage was sent for to the Bombay steamer, and immediately put on board the "*Hindostan.*"

The day fixed for sailing was the 25th of October.—*En attendant,* we made several excursions among the adjacent mountains, the *Gebel Attáka.** This range rises,—to the west of Suez, at a distance from it, as the crow flies, of about three leagues,—from a plain but slightly elevated above the level of the sea, and covered with travelled fragments of hard limestone rounded by friction, and of a dark brown colour. In the wide plain between these mountains and the Red Sea, everything bears the traces of some violent action,—apparently that of a stream of water:—all the fragments of stone lying on its surface have evidently been detached from the mountain above. Several distinct channels of considerable depth, marked by white calcareous sand, unite themselves with the bed of one larger stream. The explorer who may trace the latter up that part of its course, which is visible from Suez, will find himself advancing towards the hills in a direction from north-east to south-west, the highest turn only leading him

* Tradition attributes the name of these mountains "*Attaka*" (deliverance), to their having looked down on that great deliverance recorded in Exodus xiv.—Tr.

due south. We rode into the bed of this river, and followed it towards its source, till we found ourselves at the foot of a precipice, where, apparently, a waterfall of from forty to fifty feet in height, had worn the rocks into hollow grottoes and deep creeks and basins. Before we reached the turn in the bed of the stream, we had, on either side of us, a rampart,—eighteen or twenty feet high,—consisting entirely of debris:—probably once the bed of the river, which may here have deepened its channel as it flowed on. The mass *in situ* here consists of a brownish-grey limestone, the fragments of it greatly resembling pebbles. It is so hard as to emit sparks when struck with the hammer: the formation at the foot of the mountain is the hardest: higher up we came to regular, horizontal strata, which, at a height of about 500 feet above the channel of the water, are quite white. I should reckon the highest point, to which we had no small difficulty in ascending, to be from 1500 to 2000 feet above the level of the sea: it is a sort of terrace, strewn with broken fragments of travelled stone; the abrupt declivities on which we had clambered up are, in some parts, covered with these, while elsewhere there are deep cavities, formed by the undermining and wearing away of the summits of these rocky masses. The question which presents itself on examining these appearances, is,—what was the undermining agent?—for water there is none. This roughness and inequality of the surface rendered the scramble a difficult and tedious affair. About 100 feet below the highest point of the Gebel Attaka, I saw a perfectly white, sharply marked line drawn horizontally along the summit. I contrived, by dint of scrambling, to reach the spot;—even on my way to it I found fragments of *selenite* and of disintegrated *gypsum* in great abundance. The white streak is an *anhydrite* of remarkably pale, clear colour, in contact with a stratum of brownish limestone of moderate hardness. In this stratum I missed the distinct fossils, a profusion of which I had observed throughout the lower limestone stratum, and saw merely organic remains extending across the stone like a delicate tracery; —very small shells and the remains of *ecthrinites*. The ridges of nearly all the highest mountains are on one and the same level.—There are no plants on these bare declivities, whose every stratum may therefore be distinctly traced. The bed of the stream however,—which appears like a large, deep groove, sharply drawn, from the height downwards, in the smooth limestone,—forms an exception in this respect.—We saw, among its white rounded gravelly stones, large bushes of the blue-leaved *Capparis* (caper-tree), fragrant *Artemisia* (wormwood), Lavender, and a few *compositæ*. The only living creatures that we caught a sight of, were a few large vultures *(Vultur cinereus)*, and some smaller birds of prey belonging to the falcon tribe: unfortunately we did not bring down a single bird.

We embarked on the 25th of October, but did not actually sail until half-past ten on the 26th. Our voyage on the Red Sea presented very little to interest us. On the 28th of October, the weather became unfavourable;—thunder-clouds darkened the clear sky, and lightning flashed across the firmament. A great number of flying fish *(Exocœtus volitans)*, afforded us some amusement for a short time, rising suddenly from the water, shooting up like rockets, and fluttering about in the air for eight or ten seconds. We also observed a screech-owl, whose persevering efforts,—notwithstanding the comparative nearness of land,—to remain close to the ship were regarded as an evil prognostic. The storm however did not burst upon us till the following day, and it was not a very formidable one. Another owl, which established itself on the mast, was shot, but unluckily it dropped into the water, so that I could not obtain possession of it. Two harmless wagtails,—driven out to sea by the wind,—were added to our ship's company; they made a hearty meal of the insects that were flying in swarms about the sheep on board. A flight of rose-coloured locusts was also seen; a considerable number fell down upon our vessel:—they were about six inches in length, and their wings were spotted with brown.

On Thursday the 29th of October we reached the island of *Harrisch*, and passed beneath its crater-walls; it consists almost entirely of extinct volcanoes. One crater, the side of which is partly washed away by the action of the sea, so that its interior lay open before us,—seemed to me the most interesting point: its sides are covered, almost down to the edge of the water, with black slags and other volcanic remains: the upper margin is of red earth. Even with the aid of the spy-glass we could not discover the slightest trace of vegetation. A bed of white sand, visible on one solitary spot, was at first declared by one of the passengers to be *guano;* the captain however contradicted that idea: the white streak contrasts strikingly with the reddish-grey of the soil.

On the 1st of November, at ten o'clock in the morning, we landed at Aden, the southernmost point of Arabia, glad to find ourselves safe on *terra firma* once more, having escaped the dangers of the Red Sea. At four o'clock we set out on our sight-seeing expedition. The sun was hot, and the atmosphere glowing; notwithstanding which we proceeded rapidly, in order to have a general view of this mean place, this town of huts,—and to be on board again in the evening. Aden is the crater of an extinct volcano, which the English have transformed into a fort: it possesses little interest of any kind. Nevertheless we wandered on till it had become too late to return on foot. We therefore despatched an old Arab who had invited us into his rush-built hut, to procure asses for riding. The asses however did not make their appearance; there came instead a couple of camels, which, protesting against such treatment, we refused to take, proceeding forthwith to make the best of our way on foot;—at the gate however we were met by a party of wild-looking Arabs, who were bringing the wished-for asses, but they demanded a most exorbitant hire, and insisted on its being paid beforehand. After long and noisy bargaining, we mounted the beasts, the fellows being to all appearance quite contented. We had scarcely ridden on a few yards, when, with most impertinent threats, they demanded full and instant payment of the sum originally demanded, and even attempted to make a violent assault upon us. Fortunately they were unarmed, and although they constantly followed us at a distance of from fifty to eighty paces, they did not venture to molest us on our return, which, indignant at their knavery, we accomplished on foot, leaving the asses behind us. After a forced march of about half an hour, over cliffs and across narrow defiles, we reached the shore, quite exhausted, and delighted to find the little boat in readiness to convey us out of the reach of our pursuers, on board our steamer.

The monotony of our further voyage to Ceylon was only relieved by the view of the large island of *Socotra*, and a day before we arrived at our destination, by the verdant and palmy isles of the Archipelago of the Laccadives.

THIRD LETTER.

CEYLON—POINT DE GALLE—THE CINGALESE—QUEEN'S HOUSE—THE GARDEN—WALK ALONG THE COAST—BOTANIZING EXPEDITION—CAPTAIN CHAMPION—DEPARTURE FROM POINT DE GALLE—STORM—RECEPTION AT COLOMBO—SIR COLIN CAMPBELL—MR ANSTRUTHER—CULTIVATION OF CINNAMON—ROAD TO KANDY—PALACE OF THE KINGS OF KANDY—BOTANIC GARDEN—SUGAR PLANTATION—THE TEMPLE AND THE DALADA—JOURNEY TO THE MOUNTAINS—RAIN-WORMS—COFFEE PLANTATIONS—RAMBODDA—THE NUWERA ELLIA CONVALESCENT STATION—THE CHASE—WILSON BUNGALOW—ETTEM PITYA—BADULLA—INHABITANTS—ENVIRONS—DAGOBAH—JOURNEY FROM BADULLA—TALDENIA—ELEPHANT HUNT—BOBOLA—JUNGLE—GALBOCKA—ELEPHANT HUNT—SAVAGE NATIVES—PALEVALLAH—THE ELEPHANTS—ARRIVAL AT RATNAPOORA.

MADRAS, *Dec.* 24, 1844.

UNFORTUNATELY, during my stay in the island of Ceylon, a pressure of accumulated business, and the hurry of travelling, prevented me from giving you some earlier token to prove how often my thoughts have been with you all; and, during our voyage to India, we had such weather that, tossed by the rough billows, and surrounded by a crowd of sea-sick passengers, I found letter-writing quite impossible.

After a somewhat monotonous, but, in point of weather, most favourable voyage from Suez, on board the large steamer "Hindostan," we were once more rejoiced by the sight of green land. The company on board was very agreeable, and there were between thirty and forty ladies; but the number of passengers was too great: it amounted to about a hundred and fifty. We had therefore no lack of entertainment and conversation; yet we were all right glad when our voyage of nearly four weeks was at an end. As we approached the Island of Ceylon, the rich and verdant foliage of its shores,—among which we soon recognized woods of cocoa-nut trees,—stood out in more and more marked relief from the deep blue of the mountain forests in the back-ground.

Two hours yet elapsed, and we slowly entered the rock-bound harbour of *Point de Galle*, at the southern extremity of the island. How bright and glorious were the thick groves of palms; how striking the contrast of the white foaming spray dashing over the black cliffs, as seen against their dark verdure! Soon our vessel was surrounded with small boats, formed of the stems of trees bound together. Larger canoes,* each consisting of the hollowed trunk of one tree of a very pretty colour, also came alongside: fastened to their sides by cross sticks, were pieces of wood, of half the length of the canoe, which floated on the water to prevent any danger of capsizing. With such craft as these, known by the name of "*Orowah*,"—the Cingalese venture far out on the open sea. Lean, copper-coloured men, with lively black eyes, finely chiselled features, and raven hair twisted in a knot behind, a scarf girt about them as their sole attire,—were sitting in these frail barks. Among them were young boys of most lovely countenance, whose rich, flowing black hair fell over their backs. This motley throng surrounded the "*Hindostan*" in strange groups, while the prince and his suite bid a hearty farewell to their amiable fellow-passengers, who were to sail on their further route in that good ship. The governor's boat was now seen approaching from *Galle*;—we jumped on board

* Dr Davy, in his account of a journey in Ceylon, thus mentions the crossing of the "*Kotmale Ganga*." "We were conveyed over in a canoe of the rudest construction, which, it might be inferred from its appearance, would hardly carry a single man, and yet it conveyed three or four with perfect safety. It consisted merely of the rough trunk of a jaggery palm, hollowed out, and supported on each side by a plantain-stalk as out-riggers."—Tr.

her, and, with ten red-hosed rowers to speed our flight, and entertain us with their abominable singing, we bounded over the surf and gained the shore.

The sun was shining with glowing heat, and the aromatic fragrance of the island of spices was wafted softly to us on the breeze. Suddenly transferred from the clear and elastic atmosphere of the ocean to this hothouse air loaded with the scent of rich flowers, I felt almost like one recovering from an illness, who, on a mild spring day, steps for the first time into the soft luxuriance of the flower-garden. It is very remarkable how far out at sea one begins to perceive this balmy perfume; although it is not indeed the scent of *cinnamon*, as travellers fabulously assert, themselves deceived by a common trick of the ship-surgeons, who, as the vessel sails past Ceylon, secretly sprinkle a few drops of oil of cinnamon upon the deck!

A great crowd of natives, in every imaginable variety of costume, received us as we set foot on land;—foremost among them were the "*headmen*," distinguished by a blue Dutch coat, and a large East Indian handkerchief thrown round the loins, so as to appear like a sort of under-petticoat. A large comb of the finest tortoiseshell confines the hair, which is neatly turned back over the top of the head, and hangs in plaits such as young girls wear in Germany. Small in stature, and of delicate and slender form, they have a somewhat effeminate appearance; however, the eye soon learns to perceive real beauty in the shining, coffee-brown skin, the refined features, and the large black eyes of the true Cingalese. The natives of Malabar are essentially different from them;—they are marked by a greyish-brown complexion, a stronger system of bones, a flat nose, and short, often shaggy hair, which is cut and never plaited;—and are, for the most part, a very ugly race. There were also, among the varied multitude several "*gentlemen*" of ancient Portuguese and Dutch extraction. The antique costume which they sport is truly singular. It consists of a head-dress somewhat resembling a college cap, a jacket richly embroidered in gold, with enormous buttons, the sleeves slit up to the elbows, and simple East Indian handkerchiefs hanging over their short drawers; large ear-rings and a multitude of rings on their fingers mark their affluence. The largest part of the population,—scanty as is the clothing of most of them, especially of the younger men whose only garment is a coil twisted round their loins,—carry parasols of Chinese manufacture, of bamboos and varnished paper. We pressed forward through the crowd,—which we had difficulty in penetrating, as we were crushed and stared at on all sides,—to the ancient, moss-grown Dutch gate. Opposite to it was the place of our destination, an open building, of somewhat venerable appearance, one story high, surrounded by an airy verandah,—with the figure of a cock* and the date 1687 over the entrance. It was the "*Queen's house,*" or governor's residence. Of its large rooms, paved with stone, three were prepared for our reception. They have doors, which, indeed, serve the purpose of windows also, both towards the verandah and the inner gallery, and contain, in the shape of furniture, only large beds, measuring eight feet square, with muslin hangings round them.

* The town of Galle is indebted for its emblem,—a cock,—to an etymological error of the Portuguese rulers of Ceylon, who associated the name *Galla* with *Gallus*,—a cock,—whereas *Galla*, in Cingalese, means a rock; thus the name is really derived from the situation of the town and harbour. In like manner, "*Pedura-tal:a-galla*," "*a mat-wove rock*," has been transformed by the English into "*Pedro talla-galla*," as though some great Don had immortalised his name by bestowing it upon that peak; whereas, in fact, the Portuguese never reached that part of the island, and the name was given in consequence of a rush used in mat-making being found in abundance on that mountain. One of the most absurd of these misnomers is that by which the hill of "*Mattan-Pattena*," near Kandy, has been designated by the British, "*Mutton-button!*"—Tr.

But a peep into the garden soon enticed us away from our spacious apartments into the luxurious freedom of the open air.—What a splendid profusion of red and yellow *Hibiscus*,—what beautiful, rich, velvety turf, such as I have never seen since I was in England! Here the gorgeous *Plumeria*, with its sweet fragrance, there gigantic banana-trees, *(Musa Sapientum)* Papaws, *(Carica Papaya)* and bread-fruit trees, *(Artocarpus incisa)*, towering above the walls. We descended a flight of steps,—green from the continued warm moisture,—into the tree-garden, or shrubbery, which is on a level twenty feet lower. It is a perfect wilderness, peopled by innumerable animals. Among the tall grass,—which was full of long-tailed green lizards,—were shining forth blue creepers of wondrous beauty, (the *Clitoria)* and a number of red-blossomed balsams, *(Impatiens coccinea)*; above them rose bread-fruit trees, with dark, shining, sinuated leaves, at least a foot in breadth and two or three in length, white stem, and rough, heavy, round fruit, of a greenish yellow colour,—the elegant *Papaw tree*, with regularly tapering, hollow stem, from the top of which bursts a tuft of rich foliage, each leaf broad-spreading like an umbrella, thick clusters of fruit somewhat resembling small melons hanging below the crest of leaves. Here too we found the plantain-tree, *(Musa Paradisiaca)* universally known in India as the *Banana tree:* its reed-like, thick, sappy stem bears the leaves, which are eight feet in length and two or three in breadth, springing in an upright position out of its top; but their thin and tender texture, while it exposes them to be torn by the wind, causes them to droop gracefully as they expand. Who could imagine that this tree, with a stem of one foot in circumference, and twenty feet in height, and with foliage so luxuriant, is the growth but of one year? The fruit grows in thick, regular clusters, on a spike hanging from the top of the stem, at the axil of the tuft of leaves;—this spike or fruit-stalk, which is about four feet long, has usually some eight or ten clusters of fruit nearly a foot in length, each of which, again, contains some twenty or thirty plantains. This beautiful greenish-yellow fruit has a charming effect, amid the freshness of the gigantic spreading foliage; its flavour is far more delicious here than at Cairo, where we had it at dinner daily. Each plantain is about four inches long; its skin is soft and leathery; beneath that is a pulpy fleshy substance, very sweet, and without either seeds or kernel.

The *bread-fruit tree* bears a coarse, hard fruit, which is often dressed and eaten by the people here in an unripe state, but which, when fully matured, contains among the seeds a milk-like fluid said to be sharp and acrid.* We have not tasted this fruit, but it is clear that the eulogies of many travellers, who speak as if nothing could bear comparison with it, are not merited.

The fruit of the Papaw tree resembles a melon; having like it, flesh of a yellowish colour, which however

* The natives of Ceylon (as we are informed by Dr Greville in the Botanical section of the "Account of British India,") also eat the fruit of the *Artocarpus integrifolia*, or Jaca tree, which, elsewhere, is not held in great esteem. The *Jaca* is a larger tree than the bread-fruit tree, and of extraordinary aspect, bearing its ponderous fruit on the trunk and arms. Each fruit contains several hundred seeds three or four times as large as almonds. Of the bread-fruit, the variety most esteemed in the South Sea Islands contains no seeds; the tree propagates itself by suckers from its creeping roots. It fruits during eight months of the year, and the Tahitians use a sour paste made of its fruit, called "*mahie*," during the remaining four. The bread-fruit of Ceylon is much used for curry, and as a vegetable sliced and fried. The praises of this wonderful tree, of every part of which the South Sea Islanders make some use, have been sung by Lord Byron in the following lines:—

> "The bread tree, which, without the ploughshare, yields
> The unreap'd harvest of unfurrow'd fields,
> And bakes its unadulterated loaves
> Without a furnace in unpurchas'd groves,
> And flings off famine from its fertile breast;—
> A priceless market for the gathering guest."—Tr.

becomes pinkish as it ripens. It is inferior to the multitude of curious and delicious fruits of Ceylon, only from having a peculiar,—to most palates unpleasant,—taste of the seeds of Indian cress.

I searched for some time in vain, among the superabundant vegetation, and the many perfumes that loaded the air, for the cause of one peculiar and most overpowering fragrance. At length I discovered its origin in a tree, twelve feet in height, with thick and clumsy branches, long, narrow leaves, and large, white oleander-like flowers.—It was the *Plumeria*,—a sacred tree, which generally, when in an open place, is deemed worthy of a stone enclosure. Close beside it I found another tree, which makes but little show; it bears bunches of brown flowers, and a green fruit resembling cucumbers, close to its stem. The *Appoo* (butler or head man-servant) made signs to eat; I bit the fruit, and found it to be a very quintessence of sourness.—It was the *Bilimbing*, (*Averrhoa Bilimbi*).*

The humid, vapoury atmosphere which pervades these shades, under the massive bowers of foliage so gigantic, is most favourable to scorpions and serpents. A long, slender, brown lizard, with triangular head, was also sliding about among the branches; and a species of large carpenter-bee (*Xylocopa*,) was filling the air with its loud humming. Crows,—whose screams are far more discordant than that of any crows at home,—were perched on all the trees, and casting an inquisitive and impudent glance at the foreign intruders.

After breakfast,—at which meal, by the bye, I made acquaintance with a profusion of tropical fruits new to me, Pompoléons, or Shaddocks, *(Citrus Decumana,)* Jamboos, *(Eugenia Jambos,)* and mangoes, *(Mangifera)*—we could restrain our curiosity no longer, and sallied forth once more into the open air, to become

* This is a favourite fruit in the cuisine of Ceylon.

more at home among the magnificence of tropical nature. Our abode was within the walls of the old citadel; we therefore passed out by the same gate by which we had entered on our arrival. Here, for the first time in my life, I saw large piles of green cocoa-nuts. The effeminate Cingalese were lying in groups upon the ground, playing with stones of many colours. We met venders of *Betel leaves* and *Areca nuts,** distinguished Cingalese borne in their palanquins, herds of buffaloes and Zebu oxen, yoked to vehicles made of a sort of basket-work plaited of the leaves of the cocoa-nut tree.

An avenue of *Hibiscus* trees with large yellow flowers afforded us refreshing shade; the sea, dashing high on our right, shed a coolness through the sultry air. We now entered the town itself, which is separated from the citadel by a wide "place." It consists of only two long streets, formed of small one-storied houses. On a foundation wall, two feet in height, built of stone, rest wooden pillars, which, with a wall of hurdles, support a broad overhanging cocoa-nut tree roof: tiles are seldom used. At the back of the deep verandah is the entrance to the one solitary apartment. The proprietor sits or lies on the raised floor above the foundation wall, beside his wares or the implements of his trade. In the street through which we walked, there were only petty merchants or shop-keepers, dealing, for the most part, in spices and aromatics, pepper, turmeric, ginger, cardamomum, salt and saltpetre: all their goods were reposing beside each other in perfect harmony, spread in little heaps on fresh banana-leaves. We also saw among their stores, rice, and various sorts of grain, among the rest, several kinds new to me, such as "*amou,*" "*core*

* The nut of the *Betel tree (Areca Catechu,)* so constantly used by the natives of India and the adjacent countries, who chew it as tobacco, is cut in slices, sprinkled with lime, and mixed with the leaf of a kind of pepper, which is consequently known as *Betel-leaf.*—Tr.

can," and "*habby,*" all somewhat resembling our millet, (*Setaria Germanica.*) Suspended to the roof we saw pretty basket-work cages, in which were speaking mina-birds* and parrots. We provided ourselves in this bazaar with parasols of Chinese manufacture, a most necessary weapon of defence in heat so overwhelming, the thermometer being at least up to 35° Réaumur, (111° Fahrenheit.) Most of these shop-keepers have learned a little English, so that we could make ourselves intelligible to them. Our appearance among them in our travelling attire, brought a crowd of people,—themselves without any,—to walk round us; a number of children in particular, with lovely, soft, black eyes, and many of them with thick silver bangles on their ankles, were running merrily about. Every thing here indicates prosperity and contentment; not a careworn or sorrowful face is to be seen. Not a creature thinks of such a thing as hard work; for why should they make life a burden, when they may, without much trouble, subsist for the whole year on cocoa-nuts and rice?

We now entered a thick grove of bananas, and of cocoa-nut and betel trees, which begins at the edge of this bazaar town, and continues along the coast. Nothing can be more graceful than these latter loftily-waving, slender, palmy trees, with their bushy crowns, bending downwards in delicate feathery curves. How heavy and clumsy does

* Mr Wilson, the distinguished ornithologist, in the history of British India of the Edinburgh Cabinet Library, gives the following account of this not very commonly known bird. "It is somewhat larger than a blackbird; its plumage is of a rich silky black, with a white spot about the central edge of the wing; the bill and feet are yellow, and a peculiar fleshy appendage or caruncle stretches from the side of the face, and behind each eye, to the back of the head. This bird is easily tamed, and perhaps the most accomplished linguist of all the feathered tribes; it imitates man's voice much more accurately than a parrot, and may be taught to pronounce long sentences in the most clear and articulate manner. It is consequently held in the highest esteem by the natives, and is sometimes brought alive to European countries; the moral purity of the English tongue is not however always exhibited as the result of its maritime education."—Tr.

the African date-palm, to say nothing of every European tree, appear in comparison of them. The deep azure of the sky, and the white surf breaking high over the dark rocks of the coast, fill up the picture, and the effect of contrast in the whole is most strikingly beautiful.

It is impossible to describe the wondrous impression made upon the traveller by the luxuriance of tropical nature; the warm, humid, heavy air, laden with the perfumes of spices and of cocoa-nut oil, and the fairy-like glancing of the light,—clear, though partial,—through the thick palmy crests above. A rich under-growth of yellow, red, and blue campanulas, surrounds the neat dwellings,—built in the old-fashioned Dutch style, with small verandahs at their sides, which, without being dignified with any particular name, are scattered along the road towards Colombo. Old Dutch inscriptions are to be met with frequently in every direction, on brick walls half decayed and green with moss,—as though one had wandered into some desolate region, long deserted by mankind. Every thing produces an impression of dreaminess and of repose.

Wherever the palm-trees are not enclosed within garden walls, the ground is covered with thick underwood, diminishing in height as it approaches the sea. Little green serpents abound in the copse; beautifully painted crabs run about the stones, taking a hasty side-leap when pursued, and concealing themselves beneath the luxuriant tendrils of the beautiful, red-flowering *Ipomœa*. The *Bromelia Ananas* (common pine-apple,) and the *Pandanus* (screw-pine,) succeed well here, growing wild on bare parched cliffs, only nourished, apparently, by the constant moisture of the atmosphere. How I longed to seat myself, and to sketch those magnificent groups of bread-fruit, mango and palm trees; but again, might I not replenish my botanical box with some of those splendid creepers or lilies; or waylay those lizards three feet long,—on their black and yet mossy rocks;—or drag out that little dark fiendish scorpion from its retreat beneath yon stone; or, last not least, possess myself of those span-wide, black-winged, gaily-spotted butterflies. Here are Priam and Helenus; there, Aristippus and Agamemnon.*

It was high time for luncheon before we returned home; yet you will not be surprised when I tell you that, the moment our repast was ended, I begged to be excused from accompanying the Prince, in order to make a botanical excursion. Ascending a hill which, in the forenoon, we had passed to our left, I wandered up towards the source of a little brook. The soil consists of a yellowish red clay, probably caused by the decomposition of clay iron-stone, and mingled with red fragments of harder consistency.† I was joined by many inquisitive

* Not heroes or philosophers, but the "*trivial names*" of various butterflies! We may quote, by way of explanation, a paragraph from the article "*Entomology*," in the Encyclopædia. "In the vast multitude of butterflies, the greatest part of which are foreign and extra-European, and to whose food and manner of life we are utter strangers, it was impossible to give significant trivial names. Linnæus, therefore, by way of simile, has taken the names of the *Equites* from the Trojan history. They consist of two troops or bodies; of which one contains the sable, and, as it were, mourning nobles, having red or bloody spots at the basis of their wings. These receive names from the Trojan nobles; and the most splendid among them bear the name of Priam. The other body ornamented with a variety of gay colours, are distinguished by the names of the Grecian heroes; and as in both armies, there were kings, as well as officers of an inferior rank, those elegant butterflies, whose hinder wings resemble tails, are distinguished by some royal name. Thus, when Paris is mentioned (knowing that he was a Trojan, and of royal blood) we look for him among those of the first section; *i.e.*, those of a sable colour, spotted in the breast with red, and having their hinder wings resembling tails. When Agamemnon is named, we at once find him among those nobles which have variegated and swallow-tailed wings. But when Nereus is spoken of, we readily know him to belong to the last section, having wings but no tails." The *Equites* are the first of the six classes into which naturalists divide the *genus Papilio;* the others being, 2d, *Heliconii;* 3d, *Parnassii;* 4th, *Danai;* 5th, *Nymphales;* 6th, *Plebeii.*—Tr.

† Dr Davy, who, in his "*Account of the interior of Ceylon,*" gives a full description of the soils of the island, says, "The best and most productive soils of Ceylon are, a brown loam resulting from the decomposition of gneiss or granitic rock, abounding in feltspar; or a reddish loam, resulting from

natives, who, on observing the objects of my pursuit, assisted me in gathering flowers, and showed great delight when I caught butterflies. One of them, indeed, seeing my perplexity, as I was despairing of being able to maintain my equilibrium on the two thin bamboos which served as a bridge, offered to carry me across the little stream. Although our conversation was generally confined to dumb-show, I noticed that they cried "*hondey*" when pointing out any thing good, or that had a pleasant taste or perfume,—while, if the fruit was poisonous, or if the flower had a disagreeable odour, their exclamation, accompanied by a gesture significant of throwing it away, was, "*nodderkey, nodderkey!*" They seemed to look with compassion at my endeavours to catch insects, or to kill lizards,—while at other times they shook their heads at me in an expressive manner; for the mass of the native population,—excepting, of course, the intruders from Malabar, and the Persian Mahometans, commonly called "*Moörmen*," are all Buddhists.*

the decomposition of clay iron-stone, called in Ceylon, Kabookstone." Dr Davy observes that there is, in the soil of the island, a great scarcity of vegetable, and also of calcareous matter, which he attributes to the rapid decomposition caused by the great heat, and to the heavy rains.—Tr.

* Reference is here made to the first great commandment of Gautama Buddha, viz. "From the meanest insect up to man, thou shalt not kill." The religious scruples of the Cingalese are not, however, generally as strict as our Author appears to have imagined from these gestures; they are frequently guilty of killing animals of every sort, with the exception of the cobra de capello, which is deemed sacred, from a tradition of its having miraculously sheltered Gautama under its uplifted hood from the scorching rays of the sun, when he had sat down to rest. All those individuals however who consecrate themselves to the service of Buddha rigidly adhere to this grand precept; thus Major Forbes, in his "Eleven Years in Ceylon," mentions the "*Pirankada*," or water-strainer—used by devotees to prevent the destruction of the animalculæ which they would swallow imperceptibly in drinking unstrained water." He also mentions the strict obedience rendered by all natives to this law when they visit Buddha's sacred mountain, commonly called Adam's Peak; he says, "At Diabetme," (four miles from the Peak) "the fowls were killed that we might require during our stay at the holy footstep, as no follower of Buddha would break his first commandment within the hallowed precincts which, with to-morrow's dawn, we are about to enter."—Tr.

Having obtained a rich booty, I returned home towards sunset: the lightning was flashing tremendously, and I had scarcely reached our airy dwelling, when a sudden and fearfully violent shower burst upon it, while the rolling thunder pealed, and the brilliant lightning cast an almost uninterrupted glare. The flood that immediately, after a few minutes' rain, surrounded the house, enlightened me as to the necessity for its being raised above the ground by a foundation-wall of five feet in height. As soon as this tropical water-spout was over, and the darkness of night was spread over the scene in deep and sudden gloom, every tree was illuminated by countless fire-flies, various species of Coleopterous insects—*Elater noctilucus*, (night-shining skipper,) *Lampyris noctiluca* (glow-worm,) and *Cantharis*, so that the garden appeared like an assemblage of brilliant "Christmas trees;"* and the evening concert of the

* The author refers to a favourite amusement in the domestic circle in Germany, at the festivities of the parting year,—doubtless one of the bright visions associated in his mind with the recollection of that "cloudless childhood" which, we are told, he enjoyed under his parents' roof. It has now become familiar to many in this country; but to some it may require explanation. The Christmas-tree is a young fir, straight and shapely, usually from three to six feet in height, which occupies the centre of a large table, to which the guests or the juvenile circle are not admitted till all is ready. Those who are initiated into the mysteries of the tree are busily engaged on Christmas eve in decking its rigid branches and sombre foliage with everything that is bright and gay. Lighted tapers, of every hue, are ingeniously fixed to the extremities of the branches,—bonbons of many colours, grapes, oranges and cherries are suspended from them in most inviting confusion, and last not least, hanging in the midst of them, and scattered on the table below, are gifts, each bearing the name of the friend for whom it is destined. The pot in which this tree stands is usually strewn with such flowers or verdure as the season may afford, and the ensemble is extremely pretty. Another kindred and very popular custom, is that of placing a Christmas-tree, adorned by the maternal Pomona, with a rich crop of such fruit, to which every member of the family circle contributes some gift,—beside the couch of the sleeping child, before that merry morning dawns upon it. Such then was the "*Noctiluca,*" accompanied too by simple and characteristic melodies, a curious contrast to the "evening concert of the tropics" described above, which glittered before the mind's eye of the youthful traveller whose thoughts so often wandered to his father-land.—TR.

tropics began with redoubled zeal. The musicians are *Grylli*, (crickets and locusts) *Cicadæ*, (frog-hoppers) ten or twelve distinct species of *Rana arborea*, (tree-frogs) *Geckos*,* and several small owls. This sylvan population kept up a noise which baffles all description:—humming and chirping, croaking and squeaking, whistling and whizzing, clicking and clapping,—as in the tale of the "enchanted castle." There are some species of Cicadæ, of great size and of wonderfully beautiful colours; these are the chief culprits in this nocturnal breach of the peace; for the ear is soon accustomed to the mill-like sound of the long-legged tree-frogs, which usually greet their pursuer with a pert and fearless croak from within the large calyx of some gorgeous flower.

We had, ever since our arrival at Cairo, acknowledged the utility of the ample bed-hangings;—here too they are indispensable, for there is a great abundance of musquitoes, which, however, I thought somewhat less cruel in their attacks than those of Egypt.

Next day, (the 14th of November) we set out very early on another excursion. The Prince had gone before us:—we found him seated in the middle of a little palm-garden, busily engaged with his pencil, and surrounded by inquisitive Cingalese. They had placed a chair for him, and had regaled him with fruit, which luxury they now offered to us: we also, before joining the Prince, had received from another party of hospitable Cingalese the same kindness.

Inscribed on a solitary house among the palm-trees, we read the words "Comfort-place." As we were very thirsty, and the outside of the house looked most inviting, we entered, with the intention of purchasing refreshments of some sort. At our request, the inmates

* A species of pale brown lizard, so named from the peculiar sound of its shrill voice.—Tr.

forthwith brought cocoa nuts, the first fresh ones that I had tasted. The fruit is taken in an unripe state, when it contains clear water* in its centre, as is the case with unripe hazle nuts. This cool beverage, which has a mingled sweetness and sourness to the taste, we all thought most delicious. By breaking the nut quite open, one may take out with a spoon, from within the shell, the flesh which is just beginning to form: in colour and consistency it resembles the white of a light-boiled egg; its taste is like that of sweet jelly, with somewhat of a nutty flavour. It was only now that we discovered that we were being entertained out of pure hospitality; even the domestics declined receiving payment. Here, for the first time, we became acquainted with palm-sugar, called "*Jaggery*": its colour is brownish, like that of the coarsest bonbons, but the flavour remarkably pleasant. It is made of the juice of several species of palms, which is obtained by cutting off the end of the flower-sheath, and binding it up above the wound, and it is never allowed to ferment.† Great quantities espe-

* Commonly called "*Cocoa Nut-Milk.*"—Tr.

† The juice thus obtained—averaging nearly two hundred pints from each tree—is called Toddy: it is sometimes drunk fresh,—sometimes fermented into vinegar or wine,—sometimes distilled into Arrack: when intended for Jaggery, the vinous fermentation is checked by putting a little lime into the earthen pots in which it is gathered, and the sugar is made by boiling. The use of Arrack is lamentably prevalent among the degenerate Cingalese of the lowlands, while in the interior, Gautama Buddha's prohibition against all kinds of fermented liquor is more strictly obeyed. The gathering of the juice is not unattended with danger; to save themselves the fatigue of frequently ascending and descending the tall and branchless stem of the palm, the indolent Cingalese fasten coir cordage from tree-top to tree-top, and traversing these aerial passages with little care, they often meet with accidents, which, from the height of the trees, generally prove fatal. It has been said by Humboldt that wine, oil, wax, flour, sugar, salt, thread, utensils, weapons and habitations, are all afforded by the palms. Innumerable indeed are the uses made of every part of the tree, and of its fruit, so that it may well be called the staff of life in the countries of which it is a native. "The hundred and fifty uses of the Cocoa-nut tree" are familiarly spoken of in Ceylon, while in the figurative language of the East, the eight hundred and one of the Palmyra palm have been celebrated in a Tamul poem called Tala Vilasam.—Tr.

cially are made from the juice of the "burning, or thorny-leaved palm," *(Caryota urens,—" Ketool Gaha,")* a palm-tree distinguished by the long feathery leaflets of its bending leaves, which give it less of a curly appearance than other species of palm. It is not quite so tall as the cocoa-nut tree, but of somewhat thicker stem than the slender Areca.

Just as we were about to depart from our "*comfort-place,*" Count G——— returned thoroughly drenched; he had been shooting birds in a neighbouring rice-field, and had brought down a brace of young Minas, with imperfectly formed caruncles.

In the afternoon I visited the only botanist* of this island,—Captain Champion,—a very well informed person, to whom I was indebted for many curious facts. Notwithstanding Thunberg's residence of half-a-year in Ceylon, and the researches of Wallich and of many others, a little trouble is sure to be rewarded by the discovery of many new plants. A botanical expedition was forthwith agreed upon, and we proceeded in Captain Champion's gig to an unfrequented part of the country, about four miles from the town, where we alighted, and scrambled over rocks and hills. I was greatly exhausted by the burning sun,—and did not therefore gain as much information as I might have desired in that ramble, which was my only initiation into the Flora of the tropics. I felt almost overwhelmed by the crowd of objects of interest: no one that my eye was wont to behold;—all was new and strange. A violent shower overtook us on our return; however we arrived just in time for me to see the whole of the Captain's beautiful collection of insects. The result of this first exposure

* The only one then resident in the island; Dr Gardner, the distinguished Superintendent of the Botanical Gardens at Kandy,—one of the first botanists of the age,—being, as Dr Hoffmeister subsequently mentions, absent on a visit to Madras for his health.—Tr.

to a tropical sun was a violent swelling in my face, which ended in an abscess above the eye. A melancholy surprise moreover awaited me on my return to my quarters at Queen's House: I found myself robbed of a large portion of my wardrobe. Part of my linen, —some silk handkerchiefs,—all my knives,—and my case of surgical instruments,—were gone. I gave the alarm; no one could have committed the theft save the roguish servants, half-a-dozen of whom were always crowding around me, and whose noiseless step, as they enter the room, may easily pass unobserved. There is no power of locking one's door; and the sentinel stationed at the gate had put us off our guard. A strong representation made to the principal officer of the household succeeded so far as to recover my surgical instruments. This was our first misadventure;—how many others were yet to come!

We now took leave of the civil and military officers of the place, Mr Cripps and Captain Thurlow, and, at four o'clock in the morning, on the 15th of November, we set out on our journey in what is here called a "*diligence*," or "*mail-coach*," which in fact consists merely of a box made of boards, with a linen roof spread over it, and with seats too narrow for one man, but which, on the present occasion, must needs suffice to contain two! Notwithstanding our being deprived of the power of moving freely, great contentment reigned among our party, as we proceeded on our palm-o'ershadowed way, keeping close to the coast, and watching the reflection of the still young and harmless rays of the rising sun in the ocean's clear and placid face. We crossed handsome bridges over more than one broad stream. There was ever something that was interesting to look at, now the *Pandanus* (Screw-pine) growing to an uncommon height beside the sea,—now stately palms rearing their crowned heads towards the sky,—or again fishermen's boats, drawing in their heavy nets. We were ferried across two small streams, whose banks were indeed enchanting. Along the whole road we saw the people adorned in their gayest style, in motley and picturesque costumes; the head men with their Dutch coats and their insignia, and the wealthier part of the Malabar population distinguished by a number of rings in their ears and on their fingers. They all saluted the long-expected Prince* with the deepest respect, folding their hands before their faces, and slightly bending forwards;—nevertheless it was not difficult to discover in them symptoms of disappointment, when they beheld,—instead of the Oriental Potentate, loaded with gold and jewels, mounted on an elephant, and wearing a crown,—only Prince Waldemar in his simple travelling dress: it was evident that their imagination had conjured up some extraordinary coup-d' œil. They have, in the East, no conception of the simplicity of a German Prince.

When breakfast-time arrived, a man, clad in white costume,—of considerable embonpoint, and singular stiffness,—drew near to our vehicle, and saluted the Prince. In broken English, but with great cordiality, he requested that the coach might draw up, and caused coffee and plantains to be handed round. He was a Dutchman,—a relic of his nation in Ceylon: joy and brandy were equally beaming in his eyes. Before we drove on, he brought out a long-treasured-up, and really very pretty pair of old-fashioned wine-glasses, and entreated the

* Instructions had been sent by the Secretary of State for the Colonies,—Lord Stanley,—to the Ceylon Government, to receive Prince Waldemar in a manner becoming his rank, and suitable to the intimate and friendly relations existing between Great Britain and Prussia,—and to afford him every aid and facility on his travels. In pursuance of these directions, arrangements were every where made for the Prince's reception by the native chiefs in the provinces, and for his being treated with the honours due to the Governor himself.—Tr.

Prince's acceptance of them so earnestly, that his Royal Highness could not do otherwise than graciously receive the gift. Brittle goods in our narrow coach! Before we came to the next station, the precious glasses were no more. Near it we breakfasted,—in company with a very interesting and agreeable English gentleman, Mr Anstruther, and his lady, who escorted us from Galle to Colombo,—at the house of the local magistrate, Mr Gibson. The country now became hilly: broad and well-made roads conducted us up the ascents; they were bordered, on either side, by a row of old, Dutch buildings, charmingly situated among thick, and extremely rare, flowering shrubs; tall *Arecas* and *Cocoa-nut trees* formed a continued and delightful shade;—vehicles, drawn by fine brown and white oxen, with long, moon-shaped horns, bearing their yoke, of simple construction, on their humps,—met us repeatedly. At one spot we alighted, for the sake of watching the fishermen as they drew in their nets. Several kinds of mackerel and many gaily spotted kinds of *Scarus* and of *Chœtodon* were lying there in heaps upon the beach. The fishermen were toiling on, regardless of the scorching sun, accompanying their every movement with a strain of mournful singing, which strongly reminded us of the Egyptian boatmen.

Four o'clock arrived, and with it the storm which, during this monsoon, pays its daily visit with almost unvarying punctuality. According to established custom, it commences with a few heavy drops, which are the immediate precursors of a sudden and most violent shower.* On this occasion it was a perfect water-spout, so that we seemed to be driving through a lake, and it was vain to think that we could escape being completely soaked. The shower-bath had exhausted itself

* Amusingly described by Major Forbes as "a combination of Scotch mist, English thunder-shower, and tropical water-spout, more resembling a general water-fall than anything called by the name of rain."—Tr.

in about an hour; and, in a very short time, all the water had run off, and our road was once more dry: indeed in spite of the heavy rains, I have never seen either high-roads or paths better than those of this island. How brightly did every leaf now shine after the refreshing rain, how sweetly did the flowers give forth their fragrance, and the little birds their song! This is one of the phases of nature, which I had frequent occasion to admire in Ceylon.

Thoroughly drenched, we found ourselves at a halt beneath a triumphal arch, formed of cocoa-nut leaves, and erected at the margin of a broad and noble river, nearly equal, in its body of water, to the Rhine; it was the KALLOO GANGA. On its opposite bank lay the town of CALTURA, whose streets we could distinguish from afar. We saw, in the boat which conveyed us across the ferry, several men afflicted with leprous eruptions, and with elephantiasis. This disease disfigures its unhappy victims frightfully: they have however fortunately almost always one sound leg, compared to which the swollen one appears like a huge shapeless lump. Cases of this malady abound in this part of Ceylon.* Another triumphal arch had been erected on the north side of the Kalloo Ganga; it was constructed, according to the fashion of the country, of bamboos, hung with white or pale yellow festoons of young and tender palm leaves, and very tastefully decorated, in the centre and on each

* The disease is limited to the south-western coast; Dr Davy alludes at some length to the prevalence of it in the district between Colombo and Matura, which he attributes to the temperature there being throughout the year high, and the air the greater part of the year loaded with moisture. Elephantiasis is also common in some parts of the continent of Asia, particularly at Cochin; hence it is frequently called "*Cochin leg.*" Cases of actual leprosy are of rare occurrence in Ceylon, and are transmitted to the Government Leper Hospital, near Colombo, where however the number of patients is never considerable. Dr Davy mentions that there is scarcely any species of cutaneous disease, of which he has not seen an instance among the natives. —TR.

side, with the panicles of banana flowers, reminding us of the Thyrsus of Bacchus with its vine leaves and ivy. We were received, at this place, by a deputy sent by the Governor of Ceylon, who conducted us to His Excellency's equipage. Thence we advanced at a rapid pace towards Colombo, changing horses every half hour. We were preceded by two finely equipped outrunners, (horse-keepers) who wore red and white turbans, short breeches, and sleeves trimmed with red ribbons. The country now became more and more beautiful at every step: nature and art seemed to conspire to render the landscape a charming one;—picturesque country-seats,—a rich vegetation,—several rivers flowing softly between banks of exquisite loveliness,—distant vistas of mountain scenery,—and the mellow radiance of evening light over the whole;—the scene was like one vast and blooming garden. For a considerable distance we passed on between the most celebrated cinnamon gardens of Ceylon:* the cinnamon trees however though brilliant from their shining foliage, are mean-looking, as contrasted with the luxuriance of the varied vegetation around, and are kept, by pruning, to a height of only about twelve or fifteen feet. The sun was beginning to dip

* These gardens, though the boast of the island,—the south-west part of Ceylon being the only country of which the cinnamon tree is known to be a native—are comparatively of recent formation. A strange idea had obtained among the Dutch rulers of Ceylon, that the spice was only valuable when growing wild in the jungle, and it was never cultivated till after the year 1766. The Dutch were strict to the extreme in their monopoly of cinnamon. The injuring of the trees, peeling any portion of the bark, exporting or selling cinnamon,—were all crimes punishable with death.—To keep up the price, bonfires of cinnamon occasionally perfumed the streets of Amsterdam, as recorded by M. Beaumare, who witnessed it in 1760. Besides constantly supplying the European market, Ceylon exports large quantities of cinnamon to South America, where it is in daily use among the workmen, as a preservative against the noxious effects of the fumes of quicksilver used in the mines. Of the bales of cinnamon imported into Great Britain, far the greater proportion is not for home consumption, but for the foreign market,—being exported to Spain, Portugal, and other Roman Catholic countries, where it is largely used, with frankincense, &c., in the services of the Church.—Tr.

behind the glorious horizon as we approached the capital: a courier was despatched before us, to announce that the Prince was at hand. The whole population were on the *qui vive:*—dandies in European attire, mounted on wretched nags, saluted us as we drove through the handsome open square in front of the town; —and we could distinguish, among the varied crowd, many well-dressed English gentlemen, and even gay ladies not a few. It was a most cheerful scene, and our satisfaction would have been complete, had our own appearance been in character with this grand and triumphant entry; but wetness and filth had, at the last stations, conspired to the no small injury of our never very splendid habiliments!

On reaching the gate of the Fort, we were greeted with military music, and with the firing of cannon, which noisy salutations were reiterated on our finally halting in front of the magnificent "Queen's House." The Governor and Commander-in-Chief, Sir Colin Campbell, a venerable old man, with hoary head, gave us a most kind reception; and Captain Maclean* conducted us to our respective apartments, in a wing of the Palace, opening into the garden. Unfortunately, my swelled face prevented me from appearing at table, so I passed a quiet evening on the sofa. Here again, we were followed, at every step, by a host of copper-coloured domestics,—men and boys,—some wearing jackets, others wearing no clothes at all; many and vain were my attempts to get rid of their attendance; before I was aware of it, the sneaking fellows were at my heels again.

Next morning brought me a multitude of butterflies, and some of our party shot many birds of various kinds, *Oriolus, Crax, Gracula, Erodias,* &c. I carefully skinned them, and had left them for a few minutes to dry in the sun, when the native servant came running in, and

* Sir Colin's son-in-law and Aide-de-camp.—Tr.

said, "Master, crow come, take yellow bird." I turned round to look, and it was even so; half of my birds had disappeared! Without delay, I took what remained with me into my room; however, at the end of half an hour, I discovered that millions of microscopic ants had, in spite of the arsenic with which they were prepared, nibbled every morsel of skin from off the feathers! But a glance at my cases of insects completely overwhelmed me;—the whole treasure was reduced to powder—Oh that I could have wreaked my vengeance on the small but silent foe! But the ants were marching in endless procession,—a long sable line,—up to my glass of eau-sucrée, which was thus gradually becoming a mass of dead bodies; while there sat the crow, in undisturbed tranquillity, at the open door, as if, in contempt, mocking my distress.*

I saw but little of the city, as my swelled face excluded me from all pleasure-parties; however, in spite of it, I made various purchases in preparation for our journey into the interior of the island, such as tin-boxes, spirits and glasses. On the next day, (the 17th of November) I was able for the first time, to appear at breakfast, "tiffin" (or luncheon) and dinner, of course always dressed, as etiquette requires, in white trousers, black satin waistcoat, dress-coat and white neckcloth,—

* The crows are here so tame and impudent, especially within the Fort at Colombo, that it is scarcely possible to leave a breakfast table unprotected, lest they should carry off everything eatable. Their appearance is remarkable; they always sit with their mouths open, as if suffering from the heat, and their peculiarly loud and hoarse cry grates upon the traveller's ear, and seems to haunt him wherever he goes. Major Forbes thus notices them;—"On arriving at a rest-house you are immediately attended by several crows; as soon as you are seated, one or more of these harpies, having settled beyond your reach, in defiance of all threatening gestures, commences forthwith to screech at you with expanded beak and drooping wings; halt where you will,—unpack when you may,—only look up into the trees above, and you will see one crow at least, with his head on one side, peering into your provision baskets, as if he were sent to take an inventory!"—Tr.

most oppressively hot! The Prince had been invited, and took me as his companion, to lunch, at twelve o'clock, with Mr Anstruther,* whose courteous attentions we had already enjoyed on our journey from Galle. I never met with a more amiable and pleasing man. While we were partaking of his splendid déjêuner, some of his people were brought in to exhibit before us the mode of preparing cinnamon.† The shoots of one year, which are about the thickness of one's thumb, are cut off, and stripped of their leaves. The cinnamon-peeler (or *chaliah*) seats himself on the ground, and with his long knife,—convex on one side and concave on the other,—makes an incision the whole length of the shoot; he then very skilfully, with the curved point of his knife, separates the bark from the wood: the next operation is to scrape off, with the utmost caution, both the green inner rind or epidermis, and the greyish outer covering, or thin skin: the bark, which is not thicker than parchment, and is at first white, when laid to dry in the sun soon assumes a yellowish, and after some time a brown

* Then Colonial Secretary in Ceylon.—Tr.

† The Cinnamon tree usually yields a double harvest yearly; the first, or great one, from April to August;—the second, or lesser one, from November to January. The several processes in the preparation of Cinnamon are commonly entrusted to separate classes of "*chaliahs.*" The fragrance diffused around during the operation is very strong, although it is an error to imagine that any odour is perceptible in passing through a plantation of cinnamon trees. The leaves of the cinnamon have a flavour of cloves, and from them clove-oil is distilled in large quantities. Camphor is also sometimes made from the root of the cinnamon tree, though that substance is more commonly obtained from the Camphor tree of Japan and China, the *Laurus Camphora.* The shining dark green leaf of the Cinnamon tree is remarkable for its beauty when first opening; it presents a picturesque mixture of tender yellow and flaming red. The coarser kinds of the spice are known by their darker colour, thicker consistency, more extreme pungency and bitter after-taste. The refuse is distilled for the sake of its water and its golden-coloured essential oil. The fragrant, yellowish white flower, resembles that of the *Saxifraga umbrosa,*—London Pride. The fruit, in form like an acorn, but smaller than a pea, if boiled, yields an oil which, when cold, becomes a solid substance like wax, and is formed into candles, which emit an agreeable odour.—Tr.

hue, curls up together, and the cinnamon is then ready. When fresh, it is extremely burning to the tongue; the footstalks of the leaves, on the other hand, have a very pleasant taste, and it is much the custom here to chew them. The cinnamon-tree (*Laurus Cinnamomum*) is planted in a poor and sterile soil,—a silicious sand, formed by the disintegration of quartz. Great heat and frequent rains are the only requisites to ensure its successful growth.

In Mr Anstruther's garden we saw the Nutmeg tree, (*Myristica moschata*) loaded with fruit: the nutmegs, in appearance, somewhat resemble dark yellow apples: when pickled in an unripe state, their flavour is excellent. We saw also the betel-pepper shrub (*Piper Betel*, or "*Kapooroowell*"),—the Jamboo tree (*Eugenia Jambosa*),—the Malay Apple tree (*Eugenia Malaccensis*, or *Rose Apple*),—the Clove tree (*Caryophyllis aromaticus*), the so-called Almond tree,* (a species of *Terminalia*),—the Mango tree (*Mangifera Indica*),—the Sugar-cane (*Saccharum officinarum*),—and Bamboo-cane (*Bambusa arundinacea*). A profusion of fruits, not to be surpassed in excellence, were spread before us at the déjeûner: we had, besides pine apples and bananas,—the yellow Mango, which is about the thickness of one's fist, of an irregular round shape, and its kernel enclosed in a very juicy pulp or flesh; it has a peculiar fragrance, not unlike that of common Jessamine. The Jamboo has a sourish taste, like an unripe Gravenstein Apple; its colour is perfectly white. The Guava (*Psidium pyriferum*) is a small pear, with soft, melting flesh, and somewhat of a musk perfume. The custard Apple (*Annona*

* Probably the species mentioned by Royle, who, in his Illustrations of the Botany of the Himalayan Mountains, thus writes, "The kernels of T. Catappa have the same name, *Badams*, applied to them, as to those of the common almond; they are eaten as such, and are very palatable. I have seen the trees as far north as Allahabad, in gardens. Those of T. Bellerica and T. Moluccana are also eaten."

squamosa,)—a thick-skinned, scaly, green fruit, not unlike the cone of a pine tree, and with a rich creamy pulp. The Cashew Nut tree *(Anacardium Occidentale,)*—has a fruit nearly similar, in size and shape, to a pear: the only part that is eaten is the nut, of a kidney-bean form, attached to the outside of the fruit at the lower end, the hard shell of which encloses a kernel of most agreeable flavour. In addition to all these fruits, the "*Pompelmoes,*" a species of very large and highly-perfumed Shaddock, with bright pink pulp,—and many other varieties of the Orange tribe, were placed before us. But the fruit among the whole multitude, which met with most commendation, was the "*Rambutan*" (or Nephelium) a large, fleshy berry, exactly resembling the *Solanum Lycopersicum* (Love Apple or Tomata,) only perhaps somewhat smaller: it has a delicious sourish sweetness, and contains a thick, white kernel: it grows upon a large myrtle-like tree, *Nephelium lappaceum*, or *Euphoria Nephelium.*

In the evening a splendid dinner was given by the Governor in one of the handsome state apartments of the Palace. The table was groaning under the rich display of silver plate; there was a servant standing behind the chair of each guest, while two or there dozen more were running hither and thither;—for the same man who pours out the wine, will not touch a plate; and he who trims the cocoa-nut oil lamps, and arranges the wax candles, could not think of such a thing as fetching a chair. Every one has his own appointed office to perform, and it requires no small degree of study to define the limits of each man's duty. It is often necessary, when one requires some slight service, to address one self to four or five different attendants, and each one may perhaps refer one to some other person.*

* Dr Hoffmeister seems to have attributed to the rules of caste what in fact results rather from the local etiquette of society. The former is much

A most important office devolves on the man who during dinner time keeps in motion the large, heavy, beautifully painted board,—equal in size to the table over which it is suspended; which is done by means of strings which pass through the wall. This ever-swinging board is the *Punkah*, the cooling effect of which is much needed during the hot operation of dinner, while at the same time, on those unaccustomed to it, it has a somewhat soporific effect. All the rooms are quite open towards the verandah, which, for the sake of coolness, surrounds each story; windows there are none. Great luxury reigns here in the article of light: each apartment is lighted by lustres, be it ever so far removed from that in which the company are assembled. Our own rooms had each of them, two lamps, two candles, and a lustre, which last I found much "*à charge*," as it was only with great difficulty that I could extinguish its brilliant light. Cocoa-nut oil is burned in all the lamps here. We see it solid in our perfumer's shops at home;—here, under the influence of a temperature averaging about 24° Réaumur (86° Fahrenheit) it is a liquid, clear as water, or sometimes, of a pale yellow colour.

On the 18th of November we set out from Colombo, for the far-famed city of KANDY,—the capital of the ancient Cingalese rulers, those proud and mighty Kings.

less strict in Ceylon than in Hindostan; so that except in the household of the Governor, a very moderate number of domestics, not exceeding that of a European establishment, suffices for all the work.

Etiquette however requires that at a dinner party each guest should bring his own servant to attend upon him at table. The peculiarity of moral character among the Cingalese,—familiar to all residents in Ceylon, viz., their habitual dishonesty concerning any matters not committed to their care, and about which they do not therefore consider themselves responsible, and their scrupulous honesty concerning whatever has been entrusted to them, has led to a custom regarding these "guest's servants," which is repugnant to European feelings; when the operation of cleaning the plate begins, they are one and all, put into a separate apartment; and instances have been known of newly arrived British residents, scorning such vile suspicions, and paying dear for their mis-placed confidence.—TR.

Historical notices would fill more space than I can afford to bestow: I may just mention that it was only in the year 1815, after repeated insults offered to the English, that the last Tyrant-King, who with his Prime Minister or Adikar, Pilimé Talawé, had, in 1803, barbarously massacred a body of English troops, was captured and dethroned. His name was Sree Wikrimé Rajah Singha: he died in 1832.*

A vehicle similar to the mail-coach from Galle, and by no means more roomy, conveyed us on our journey to the interior. The officer selected to accompany us was the Governor's Aide-de-Camp, Captain Maclean, an amiable, kind-hearted man, not at all military in his appearance.

As we drove out of Colombo, I had for the first time an opportunity of seeing something of the town, which is built chiefly of brick, but contains many very neat houses, or I should rather say cottages, of one story. We also passed several of the wonderful monuments of antiquity;—temples, covered with rudely sculptured ornaments, lions, dragons and volutes. The city is of immense extent, and a large proportion of its inhabitants are Moormen, distinguished by the turban, the short drawers, and the showy belt,—and Malabars. These last are rendered conspicuous, not only by their iron-grey complexion, but by painted stripes of white, red, and yellow, variously combined, with which they adorn their

* In Dr Davy's "*Account of the Interior of Ceylon*," the reader will find a narrative of the events preceding and connected with the convention of 1815, by which the British Government obtained possession of the whole island. The interval between 1805, when an armistice concluded the war of 1803, (which led to the massacre of the British troops under Major Davie,) and 1815, when war was again declared under Lieutenant-General Sir Robert Brownrigg,—may be justly characterized as "The Reign of Terror." Among the many victims of the cruel jealousy of this last despot, was the guilty First Adikar himself, Pilime Talawe. The English guaranteed to the Kingdom of Kandy, its old government, religious liberty, and protection in the laws and customs of the land.—Tr.

foreheads:—they are Brahmins. Persians, too, are to be seen there: their national costume, their long black beards, yellow skin, and aquiline noses, strike the eye of the traveller.

Among the Cingalese, as among the Hindoos, there is the distinction of castes, which is marked chiefly by the greater or lesser abundance and luxury of the wardrobe; all are not allowed to wear jackets.* There are also some "*outcastes*," or people not belonging to any caste, who are looked on as outlawed, and, notwithstanding the efforts of the English to protect them, meet with contumely and ill-treatment.†

* The population of Ceylon is, according to Dr Davy, divided into four principal castes: the 1st is the Royal caste; the 2d, that of the Brahmins; the 3d is composed of three subdivisions,—viz. merchants, cultivators of the earth, and shepherds; the 4th includes sixty inferior grades of society, or low castes,—among the rest, fishermen, smiths, tailors, and other of the most useful trades, with executioners and tom-tom beaters! The small proportion of the two highest principal castes has, in a great measure, saved Ceylon from the degrading mental and political despotism which has been the bane of Hindostan. According to ancient Cingalese law, the use of gold ornaments was limited to royal personages, and the favoured few who had received them from the hands of royalty. The jacket,—which, as well as the flat cap, and the privilege of wearing several similar garments one on the top of the other, is a badge of high caste,—is, as we are informed by the same author, always thrown off on entering a temple: any one who does not uncover his shoulders is supposed to entail on himself boils and cutaneous diseases in another state of existence. The Cingalese Christians and the Malabars, though not of any caste, are not outcastes, being attached to the cultivators (of the 3d caste), and to the fishermen (of the 4th) respectively. These native Christians are believed to be descended from the converts,—often compulsory,—made by the Portuguese: their religion is very degenerate, and while preserving many tenets and practices of Popery, appears not untainted with Buddhist superstition; its only minister, the Sachristian, is mentioned by Davy as "an ignorant man, who cannot read, and knows only a few prayers by heart;" till about thirty years since, none of these people had ever seen a Cingalese New Testament. A purer form of Christianity had, however, been introduced into the north-western part of Ceylon, at a very early period, by the Nestorians; and within the last 50 years of British rule, the number of native Protestant Christians, which was very considerable under the Dutch, has greatly increased: various European and American Protestant Missionaries having laboured in the joint cause of education and Christianity.—Tr.

† The *Rhodias*, or out-castes, are mentioned by Dr Davy as "the descendants of those who were punished by being made out-castes, for continuing to

An admirably engineered road leads from the low, flat country that borders the coast, to the mountains of the interior;—from the fresh and verdant fields of rice and the groves of cocoa-nut trees, to the black and frowning masses of gneiss rock. What a glorious magnificence of colouring among the rich bowers of these forests! Not one withered leaf is there; every tree shines brilliant,—each in another and yet another tint of verdure, and each more vivid than the last!

In the early part of our route, one village quickly succeeded another; but, as we ascended higher, the country became more tranquil and lonely. We had begun to feel the heat very oppressive before we gained the high and wooded region above.

The view from these heights,—looking back over the plains below,—baffles every attempt at description: it dazzles the delighted eye. Amid the lavish abundance of objects new and wonderful to us, I may mention at least the Talipot tree, or Great Fan Palm, (*Corypha umbraculifera*). We saw, here and there, towering high above the tops of all other trees, large and bright green crests;—in one spot we observed, shooting up from the centre of this splendid crown, a solitary flower of resplendent whiteness, and of immense size. This was the

eat beef after its use was prohibited,—and of those who have since been degraded for high treason." The former crime was perpetuated by the peculiar tax imposed on them; for "they were required to furnish hides, and hide-ropes for taking elephants." During the native sway, they were subjected to many indignities and sufferings,—forced to live in open sheds, prohibited from approaching a temple, &c. Dr Davy mentions a singular circumstance as resulting from the dread of their contaminating touch; certain Rhodias being suspected of a murder, the Cingalese, commanded by our government to make them prisoners, refused, saying that "they could not pollute themselves by seizing them, but would willingly shoot them at a distance." The Rhodias still preserve the Buddhist religion, and its sacred language, the *Pali:* yet they are abandoned by the teachers, and excluded from the rites and sanctuaries of Buddhism. Dr Davy records one instance of a priest who, when rebuked by the king for preaching to the Rhodias, nobly replied, "Religion should be common to all."—Tr.

celebrated Talipot, the umbrella-leaved palm, which flowers but once, immediately on reaching the acmé of its lofty stature, and then dies! Each leaf is a circle of five feet in diameter, folded together in a marvellous manner. These leaves are, throughout the highland districts of Ceylon, used, after the leaf-stalk has been cut off, as umbrellas;—they are also highly esteemed as furnishing writing materials, for which purpose they are cut up into strips, and written upon length-ways, with an iron style.*

We alighted at one of the steepest parts of the road, to enjoy more freely a full survey of the landscape. No chasm or precipice was visible in all this rugged mountain pass; every thing was overgrown and concealed by green bushes and giant trees. How many beautiful plants,—*Orchideæ* and *Liliaceæ*,—did I gather during that day's journey! and on every side I met with trees new to me, many of them clad in wondrous and gigantic foliage,—scarcely one of which I had ever seen before!

Here, for the first time, we observed a herd of mon-

* The leaves of the talipot tree, each of which, when fully spread out, can shelter seven or eight persons beneath its wondrous circumference, were,—as we are assured in histories of the native governments of Ceylon,—formerly the badges of rank in the various castes, the grade of each man being marked by the number of them which he was permitted to have borne before him as fans. But their most singular quality perhaps is their durability, a proof of which is the well-known fact that, while, among the Cingalese, some sacred records are inscribed on plates of bronze bordered with silver, those of most importance in the worship of Buddha are committed to laminæ of these leaves. Dr Davy, in describing a journey in the interior of the island towards the east, thus speaks of this tree, which he, in a note, designates the "*Licuala spinosa*," though our Author, in common with most writers, describes it as the "*Corypha umbraculifera.*" "This noble palm," he says, "has been the subject of a good deal of fabulous story. It has been called the giant of the forest; but, like the cocoa-nut tree, it is never found wild. Its blossom is said to burst forth suddenly, with a loud explosion; but it expands gradually and quietly. When its flower appears, its leaves are said to droop, hang down and die; but they remain fresh, erect and vigorous, till the fruit is nearly ripe, and their drooping precedes only the death of the tree, which speedily takes place after the ripening of the fruit. Even the disagreeableness of the smell of the flower has been exaggerated greatly."—Tr.

keys springing about among the branches; although they were at a depth beneath us of nearly four hundred feet, the noise of their chattering was distinctly audible. We could trace, to a great distance, by the shaking and breaking of the boughs, the direction of their gambols. A multitude of green parrots, with large, red bills, (*Psittacus Alexandrinus*, or Alexandrine Parrakeet,) were flying among the underwood; but so jealous were they of being approached, that we could not catch one.

The rocks, in the neighbourhood of the last station on this road, are clothed with three or four different species of beautiful red and white *Impatiens* (Balsam) and the roadside below is enlivened by a species of *Coreopsis*, (Tick-seed sunflower) with a great profusion of yellow flowers. Beyond these nearer and smaller features of loveliness, we had the magnificent prospect of a forest of lofty trees, clad in sombre green. There were *Myrtus*, (Myrtle) *Rhus*, (Sumach) *Laurus*, (Bay-tree) and many others;—and, pre-eminent among them all, the wonderful *Ficus Indica* (Banian-tree.)*

* This tree, which seems to stand alone even among all the remarkable productions of the vegetable world in the East, is considered sacred among the Hindoos, who believe their god Vishnu to have been born under it, and consider its long duration, its outstretched arms, and overshadowing beneficence, as emblems of the deity; hence probably its Linnæan name of Ficus Religiosa, which however is more commonly applied to the poplar-leaved Banian, or "*Bo-tree*" of Ceylon, which is there held sacred to Buddha.

The Banian is propagated not by seed, but by fibres thrown out by all the branches, which grow thicker and stronger as they descend to the ground, where they finally take root, each parent tree thus forming a grove, in appearance so singular as to baffle all description. Its vast and many-pillared tent of rich foliage,—supported by a multitude of trunks, adorned in its season with a very small, fig-like, scarlet fruit, and its dark recesses nightly illuminated with myriads of fire-flies,—seems to the European traveller like a magic scene of romance. The Brahmin loves to dwell beneath its shade, and a temple may generally be seen at no great distance from its circle. The most remarkable of these trees that has been described, is said to grow on an island in the Nerbudda, ten miles from the city of Baroche, in the province of Guzerat;—the name "*Cubbeer Burr*," was given it in honour of a saint. Though many of its roots and stems have been carried away by high floods, it is said still to measure two thousand feet in circumference by the stems,

At this last station the people had erected some of the elegant triumphal arches already described. From thence to Kandy the road was lined with cottages on both sides. I cannot imagine on what grounds Ceylon is affirmed by some to be a thinly peopled country; in this district, the huts continue for miles together, with-

and the over-hanging branches cover a much larger space,—its larger stems amount to three hundred and fifty; the smaller to more than three thousand, and new roots are descending in profusion. Hindoo festivals are at stated seasons held there, and it is said that seven thousand persons find shade under its branches, which are filled with green wood-pigeons, doves, peacocks, singing birds, large families of monkeys, and multitudes of enormous bats.

The Banian is beautifully described in the two following passages, so characteristic of the two poets.—Tr.

"Branching, so broad along, that in the ground
The bending twigs take root; and daughters grow
About the mother tree; a pillared shade,
High over-arched, with echoing walks between.
There oft the Indian herdsman, shunning heat,
Shelters in cool; and tends his pasturing herds
At loopholes cut through thickest shade." Milton.

"'Twas a fair scene wherein they stood,
A green and sunny glade amid the wood,
And in the midst an aged Banian grew.
It was a goodly sight to see
That venerable tree,
For o'er the lawn, irregularly spread,
Fifty straight columns propt its lofty head;
And many a long depending shoot
Seeking to strike its root,
Straight, like a plummet, grew towards the ground.
Some on the lower boughs, which crost their way,
Fixing their bearded fibres, round and round,
With many a ring and wild contortion wound;
Some to the passing wind, at times, with sway
Of gentle motion swung;
Others of younger growth, unmov'd, were hung
Like stone-drops from the cavern's fretted height.
Beneath was smooth and fair to sight,
Nor weeds nor briers deform'd the natural floor;
And through the leafy cope which bower'd it o'er
Came gleams of chequer'd light.
So like a temple did it seem, that there
A pious heart's first impulse would be prayer."

Southey.—*Curse of Kehama.*

out intermission; and they appear to be inhabited by a people blessed with plenty and with contentment.*

Soon we left the forest behind us, and descended once more into a broad plain covered with fields of rice,—or, as they are here called, *Paddy-fields,*—whose verdure is so fresh and sappy that the finest crops of wheat in summer would look dingy and faded beside them. These, together with the Areca and Palmyra palms that surround the enclosures, the short, crisp tufts of the Sago palms, and of the wild date trees, and the dark forests of the mountain-tops at no great distance, form a picture no less charming than it is varied in its features and colouring. The ditches beside the road are almost everywhere overgrown with a beautiful species of Cassia, which grows to the height of five or six feet, and has a long Thyrsus-like flower, of such a flaming golden hue, that I would give worlds to be able to transplant it into any of our gardens in Europe. I am assured here that no description of it has been given to the world.

But now we were again climbing a steep hill, and threading our way through populous streets. We were followed by a crowd of several hundreds, in procession; —all must needs see the Prince,—for a European prince had never before set foot in Ceylon! We drove on, through narrower and yet narrower streets;—passed beneath one elegant arch after another, all formed of bamboos and tender palm-leaves; and at length were met by a deputation consisting of officers connected with the local government. After receiving the Prince at the gate, they rode on into the city, with their scarlet uniforms and gold épaulettes,—a brilliant escort, to usher in our queer old tub of a coach! Close to the gate, again, stood, waiting to meet his Royal Highness

* Nevertheless, though this part of Ceylon is populous, it is by no means erroneous to state that the island generally is very thinly peopled. Its ex tent is twenty-four thousand square miles,—the number of its inhabitant amounts only to fifteen hundred thousand.—Tr.

long rows of "headmen" and priests, the former arrayed in robes of white muslin, and decked with gold ornaments. These headmen,—for the most part aged men, with hoary beards,—wear a most singular costume; their head-dress,—the large flat round cap, made of white muslin, or occasionally a square one, of scarlet and gold;*—their raiment, a small tight jacket, with large buttons, often formed of precious stones, and short, full, plaited sleeves;—over it they twist several ample pieces of muslin, all the ends of which are bound together in front beneath the broad golden girdle, so that their figure gains a wonderful degree of rotundity. The girdle is of the richest gold embroidery. They also wear long chains round the neck, bangles on the wrist, and heavy rings, all of gold. They are the only individuals, among the whole nation, who claim a right to wear trowsers: these are fastened with a frill above the ankle, and, being made of the whitest muslin, produce a picturesque effect, contrasting with the dark bronze or coffee-colour of their arms and feet. To heighten the singularity of their figures, they wear round the neck a large crisped ruff, such as preachers did with us in days of yore.

Now commenced a strain of loud music, which I can only compare to that which we are wont to hear as the accompaniment of dancing bears and capering monkeys. Amid the sounding of fifes, the rattling of tambourines, and the rolling of drums,—the various musicians, clad in

* The court head-dress of the Adikars only: it has an elevated peak in the middle, surmounted by some bright gem: inferior headmen wear the round, white, flat cap. The distinguishing insignia of the Adikars however,—though probably not seen nor heard amid the din of tom-toms and the waving of banners on this occasion,—are their silver sticks and immense whips, the latter described by Major Forbes as eight or ten feet in length, two inches in breadth, and as producing a report almost equal to firing a pistol. Each Adikar is attended by a confidential servant carrying a silver betel-box, and followed by persons holding long-handled fans, ornamented sticks, spears, bows or guns.—Tr.

gay jackets, and, according to the national fashion, wearing Indian handkerchiefs instead of trowsers, danced and jumped with most animated gesticulation, to the no small detriment of their rude harmony. Suddenly there appeared three elephants, constrained to adapt their heavy pace to the marked cadence of the music. A grand display of silk banners,—shot through and through,—and of gold brocade, grown black with age, were next paraded before us. Then followed a strain of singing, which might have charmed the tiles from off the roofs, had there been any; and, in short, these festive and characteristic demonstrations were so deafening and so exciting as to border on the disagreeable; at least we were by no means sufficiently prepared to act our part with perfect self-possession during a reception so overwhelming.

At length, however, we drove up to the quarters which were destined for us, a palace, in comparison of which that at Colombo is a mere nothing. In the centre of a lawn, carpeted with the smoothest and richest turf, adorned, here and there, with scattered groups of Magnolias, or "*Rocu-trees*," in full flower, stands a handsome edifice of marble whiteness, surrounded by regular colonnades, and remarkable for the airy and elegant style and the beautiful proportions of its architecture. An extensive park, in which flowers, butterflies, and leeches might be seen in equal abundance, stretches along the sides of the hills, encircling the whole valley, and, at every point, an exquisite mountain landscape opens upon the view. We were obliged to make our toilet in all haste, for the Prince had accepted an invitation to tiffin at Colonel Macdonald's.

The residence of this officer is the ancient Palace of the Kings of Kandy, towards which accordingly we soon turned our steps. A building of but one story, with a front several hundred feet in width, but of no great depth, flanked at each end by an ancient temple, was seen before us at the extremity of a little valley. A short flight of steps leads to the principal entrance, in front of which its present occupant has erected a verandah. The door is of clumsy device, supported by posts in the shape of dragons. The walls are five feet in thickness, as are those of the ruined dwelling of remoter date. The one long hall of the interior has been divided into several apartments, and side-rooms also branch off from it. The walls, although in most parts covered with a thick coat of whitewashing, retain, here and there, traces, reaching up to the low ceiling, of battle-scenes, in which several leopards, a female figure and that of a man, are still discernible. On the spot where, for five hundred years, the great and half-deified Kings of Kandy sat on their throne of gold, unapproachable by any of their subjects save the Adikars alone, now stands the elegant tea-table of an English lady. This article of furniture is, by the bye, a fine specimen of the Point-de-Galle inlaid work, on which are expended the varied beauties of Ceylon's ninety-nine species of costly wood. The skilful artificers of Galle tempt the traveller with exquisite productions of their art, splendid boxes and cabinets in particular, all which are, of course, quite beyond my purse.

Towards evening I was tempted, by the infinite multitude of fire-flies which were fluttering over the lawn, to step out upon its velvety grass, and succeeded in collecting several dozen of those splendid insects. When dinner-time arrived, I observed, to my horror, in the brilliantly lighted apartment, that my white trowsers were streaked with blood! I was not long left in suspense as to the cause of the disaster: this was our first acquaintance with those leeches with which we afterwards became but too familiar. I actually found several hundred of them clinging to my legs; they had penetrated through my trowsers; however I freed myself by means of the established recipe of lemon-juice of these unwelcome guests.*

We went on the following day, the 19th of November, to visit the Botanic Garden, which is at the distance of about half a German mile from the present outskirts of the decayed and fallen capital, and on the bank of the Mahawelle-Ganga, which we crossed by a very handsome bridge of satin-wood, called the *Peradenia* Bridge.† The Botanic Garden is full of curious and valuable plants; every kind of spice and aromatic plant, and a multitude of very rare trees from the mountainous districts of Ceylon, loaded with blossoms and with fruits, are there collected. Among the Chinese fruits, none could bear comparison with the delicious *Litchi*, which indeed surpasses every fruit that we had hitherto tasted. It is somewhat larger than the finest strawberry, and contains, beneath a thin leathery rind of dark red colour, a white semi-transparent pulp or jelly of most exquisite flavour. Another variety of this fruit, of larger size, and prickly, is, if possible, yet more agreeable to the taste. These are the produce of different

* The Ceylon leech is of a brown colour, marked with three longitudinal light-yellow lines; its largest size is about three-fourths of an inch in length, and one-tenth of an inch in diameter: but it can stretch itself to two inches in length, and then becomes sufficiently small to be able to pass between the stitches of a stocking. It is nearly semi-transparent in substance; in form, tapering towards the fore-part,—above, roundish,—below, flat; it apparently possesses an acute sense of smell, for no sooner does a person stop in a place infested by leeches, than they crowd eagerly to their victim from all quarters, unrestrained by the caprice sometimes so annoying in their medicinal brethren. Loss of blood, itching, and sometimes slight inflammation form the extent of their injuries in the case of a person in good health, but animals suffer more severely from their attacks.—Tr.

† A very remarkable work of architecture, constructed by Lieutenant-Colonel Fraser, Deputy Quarter-Master General. It is mentioned by Major Forbes, as "a light and elegant arch of satin-wood, two hundred and five feet in length."—Tr.

species of *Dimocarpus;* or *Euphoria.** I also saw, for the first time, a most singular species of Banana, a tree from Madagascar, which, from its leaves springing from the two opposite sides of the stem only, has the appearance of having been crushed or flattened. The sheath that encloses the leaf emits, when punctured, a considerable quantity of very sweet juice; from which circumstance the tree is known, among the English, by the name of "*Traveller's Friend.*" Mr Gardner, the superintendent, was at Madras on account of ill-health; we were however received by a native, whom we found well qualified to act as a most efficient cicerone, and even acquainted with the botanical names of the plants, and their classification.†

We hurried on from thence, to see a great sugar-plantation. It was harvest time, and all hands were busy at work. The sugar cane which has been cultivated in Ceylon for the last twenty years, is not any of the species indigenous to the island, having been brought from the Mauritius. The native kind, known by the name of "*blue cane,*" produces only half the quantity of sugar obtained from the *Saccharum officinarum.* The cane is planted in October, and is cut for the first time

* Many varieties of this fruit are known in China. The common *Litchi* is covered with prickly scales, and larger than the first fruit here described, being about two inches in diameter; the Longan is also prickly, but smaller, and brown instead of red. But Mr Davis, in the second volume of his work on China, mentions the "*Loong-yen,*" or "*dragon's eye,*" as much smaller and of smoother skin than the common Litchi, known in Bengal. It is probably the first fruit described above by Dr Hoffmeister. These fruits have been ripened in hot-houses in England, and are well worthy of being more frequently cultivated. The Dimocarpus is a tree of moderate size; its bark of a rich brown; its leaves resembling those of the laurel; its fruit growing in bunches, on stalks several inches in length, at the extremities of the twigs, each individual fruit hanging on a short separate stalk, the appearance of the whole tree being extremely graceful.—TR.

† This native is well known to British residents in Ceylon as an excellent botanical draughtsman: it is understood that an almost unrivalled collection of botanical drawings, accurately representing the flora of Ceylon, may be found buried in some musty cabinet, belonging to the government of Kandy. —TR.

at the end of fourteen months, after which the usual interval allowed is from ten to twelve months. New plants are required in five years. The soil most adapted for its cultivation, is a red clay, which results from the decomposition of a species of black porphyry, and is here called "*Kabook.*"

When fully ripe, the sugar cane* is cut above the stole, and the upper part is used as fodder for cattle, while the remainder of the cane is divided into three long pieces: these are pressed between two fluted iron cylinders, placed one above the other, but in an oblique position, from which process they are brought out flattened and tolerably dry, so that, after being exposed for a short time to the sun, they are used as fuel for heating the caldrons. The juice pressed out in this cylindrical mill runs into a cistern, capable of containing about three hundred gallons, and four ounces of quicklime are added to the mass, to facilitate the separation of all feculent matter, by causing it to rise to the surface of the juice, which now assumes a yellow colour. From this large cistern it runs into the first of a succession of boilers, in each of which the heat is kept up to a temperature higher than the preceding one; that of the fifth and last averaging 240° Fahrenheit, and mounting finally to 260°. At this point the sugar is ready to granulate, and it is then drawn off, through a grooved channel, into large four-cornered trays, or shallow vessels, to cool. The scummings of the third and fourth coppers are constantly returned into the two

* Few writers, in describing a sugar-plantation, dilate much on the appearance of the cane,—the laborious operations of planting, hoeing and cutting, and the interesting proceedings of the mill and the caldron, being the all-engrossing topics. Yet the sugar-cane is distinguished by the elegance of its golden stem streaked with red, and its dark verdure, and, above all, by the beauty of its silvery, arrowy blossom, which by some travellers has been compared to a light and graceful plume of white feathers, tipped with lilac, rising in the centre of the tuft of leaves.—Tr.

first, in which at last nothing but scum remains, and this, with the molasses, (which, when the sugar is newly casked, drain through plantain stalks fixed in holes left in the bottoms of the hogsheads), and an admixture of water, is fermented upon the spot, and distilled to produce Rum. One gallon of cane-juice yields about a pound of sugar. The manufactories are almost all in the hands of English managers; at Point-de-Galle only did we meet with a native manufacturer. The cultivation of the sugar cane is of recent date in the island, and admits of being much extended and improved.*

Again we sat down to a sumptuous repast, at which there was no lack of Champagne. But far more interesting and enjoyable, in my opinion, than the succession of splendid banquets, was our visit to the principal temple of Kandy, which contains the far-famed "*Dalada*," a boasted relic of Buddha himself, (in reality, a tooth formed of ivory) on the possession of which that of the kingdom of Kandy itself was believed to depend. The flame of rebellion was kept alive among the people by their Adikars, until this shrine was taken by the English.† The temple is a mere wooden edifice, but mark-

* The hope here expressed, then cherished by many, has not been realized, and while coffee plantations, spice gardens, and cocoa-nut grounds are more or less flourishing in Ceylon, the attempts at introducing the cultivation of the sugar-cane have altogether failed, and those best acquainted with the island have come to the conclusion that the climate is unsuitable.—TR.

† This far-famed relic has shared the numberless vicissitudes common to all similar objects of superstitious veneration, whether Pagan or Popish, Oriental or European. After working, as tradition affirms, extraordinary miracles on the Indian Continent,—which left permanent results in the altered faith of ancient kingdoms and the unrelenting wars waged by Brahminism against Buddism,—the sacred tooth of *Gautama Buddha* was taken, —according to Cingalese legends,—by a Prince and Princess true to his religion of peace, from the besieged sanctuary at "*Dantapoora*" to the island where the Buddha had lived and died. Major Forbes gives several arguments, at great length, for believing "*Dantapoora*" to be identical with the sacred Juggernaut. Since its home has been in Ceylon, the tooth has been far from leading a life of peace;—but whether it was, or was not, taken by the Portuguese in the 16th century, seems to be a question beyond the

ed by its height, as it has two stories. The unpretending entrance, with its flight of steps on each side, recalled to my mind that of a village church in Germany. Priests, in rich attire, and decked with many ornaments, met the eye in every direction, and the walls were covered with emblems and decorations of brass. We first ascended, by one of the flights of steps, to the sanctuary, which is closed with folding doors of gilded bronze, and into which not a ray of daylight ever penetrates. Within its sacred walls, on a large table, hung with white shawls and gold brocades, stands the shrine of the Dalada. It is a casket in the form of a bell or

power of any writer finally to settle. Not only do its worshippers deny this to have been the fact, but they maintain that on the conquest of the kingdom of Kandy by the English in 1815, the relic never fell into their hands, not having been surrendered by the natives, who still considered it their own and clandestinely removed it from the *Dalada Malegawa* at Kandy. It was recovered from them by the English towards the conclusion of the rebellion of 1817, and Dr Davy, who was then in the country, and who afterwards, in company with the Governor, Sir Robert Brownrigg, had an opportunity rarely enjoyed by any European, of very closely inspecting the tooth and all its karanduas, thus speaks of the impression produced by the capture.—"When the relic was taken, the effect of its capture was astonishing, and almost beyond the comprehension of the enlightened:—'Now (the people said) the English are indeed masters of the country; for they who possess the relic have a right to govern four kingdoms:—this, for two thousand years, is the first time the relic was ever taken from us.' And the first Adikar observed, 'That whatever the English might think of the consequence of having taken Kappitipola, Pilime Talawe, and other rebel leaders, in his opinion, and in that of the people in general, the taking of the relic was of infinitely more moment.'" In 1828, Sir Edward Barnes, then Governor, caused the Dalada to be publicly exhibited at Kandy, with great pomp: it had not been displayed to the crowd of worshippers since 1773. An interesting account of the magnificent and characteristic scene presented on this occasion, on which the Buddhist relic became the political tool of a Christian government, and many forced worshippers were drawn to its shrine by worldly interest rather than by superstition, is contained in the first volume of Major Forbes's work. The Dalada was, from the year 1817 till 1847, kept under the custody of the British government, and to its disgrace as a Christian power, British soldiers mounted guard over it day and night. Within the last few months, however, it has been made over to the votaries of Buddha, to dispose of as they please, greatly to the discomfiture of the priesthood, who foresee that the relic and its worshippers must fall into contempt when no longer upheld by the British government.—TR.

dome, of purest gold, richly studded with gems. Behind it are large plates of gold, inscribed with a variety of characters or emblems. The casket opens by a small door below, of which the governor and the chief priest have each a key.* Beside the great casket, or "*karandua*," as it is called,—that contains the "*Dalada*," stands a smaller one, which is commonly used in processions,—and, on the same table or platform, are numerous small golden figures, of rude workmanship. On two side-tables, loaded with gold and silver brocades, are placed lamps of silver gilt, fragrant from the sweet cocoa-nut oil that feeds their flames. The walls are hung with costly Indian shawls of most beautiful design. An adjoining apartment, from which also the light of heaven is excluded, was resounding with loud and stunning music,—the beating of the "*tom-tom*," or drum, accompanied by a strain of singing calculated to break the tympanum of any unaccustomed ear. The half-howling, half nasal melody executed by three youngsters, rung its changes in a high and squeaking key,—all the variety of its tones being comprised within the interval of a third! Its sound seems now always to echo on my ear, whenever I smell the exquisite perfume of the *Plumeria*-flower, with which the floor and the tables were strewn in this sanctuary. The singers moved their heads backwards and forwards, and made most piteous grimaces as they sang.

We next ascended the other stair, which, by a similar folding door, leads into a secret closet, very like the former one. In this closet or small room stands, or

* This outer shrine, or Karandua, is, according to Dr Davy, five feet four and a half inches high, and nine feet ten inches in circumference at its base. He found it on close inspection to be only of silver gilt, and the gems of very little value; some even of coloured crystal. But within this Karandua are four others, all of pure gold, richly wrought and decorated with diamonds, rubies and emeralds, and each wrapped either in muslin or in tinsel. —Tr.

rather lies,—Buddha himself, as large as life, with staring eyes, a delicate nose, and a very yellow complexion, his hand supporting his head, and his face and hands the only parts that are not gilded.* Other figures are placed beside him, of which one represents his wife, but the others are borrowed from the worship of the god Brahma, and stand there, as our interpreter informed us, rather as ornaments than as objects of adoration. Here again, is an abundant display of sheet-gold, of costly banners, rich brocades, and other objects of value, studded with precious and rare gems, such as sapphires and rubies of extraordinary size.

On returning to our quarters, I found that my pockets had once more been thoroughly rifled. In the hurry of changing my clothes, I had left my purse in the pocket, where it had not long been suffered to remain; fortunately however it contained only a few shillings, some Egyptian money, and a little collection of ancient copper coins of Ceylon.

A stud of horses was purchased in preparation for our further journey into the mountainous region of the island;—very pretty,—but mischievous and snapping little creatures.

At break of day on the 20th of November, thus

* Major Forbes informs us, that the images of Buddha are only represented in three positions,—viz., sitting cross-legged, standing as if preparing to advance, and reclining on his side, with his head resting on a pillow; he is generally represented clad in the yellow robe, but one of pomegranate colour is also canonical. His statues are not placed in the temples as objects of worship, but to recall more forcibly the founder of their religion to the minds of its votaries. Corresponding to the mild tenets of Gautama's religion, are the offerings made in his temples: ornaments are presented to the Wihare; but flowers, remarkable for fragrance and beauty, are alone offered before the figure of the Buddha." The Buddha here mentioned, is of course *Gautama Buddha*, the divinity of Ceylon. The records of no less than twenty-five Buddhas are preserved among the Cingalese, but Gautama was, according to Cingalese history, the founder of the national religion, which is now however greatly altered and corrupted. It is distinct from the Buddhism of Thibet, Japan, or China.—Tr.

mounted, we took our departure from the filthy streets of this poverty-stricken city, and, crossing the Paradenia bridge, we proceeded on our smooth and easy road, without meeting anything worthy of notice, till at about eleven o'clock we halted for breakfast. Soon after we had resumed our march, such a storm burst upon us, as I had never before witnessed. In an instant we were soaked to the skin; even my journal and sketch-books I was unable to protect. But we rode on bold and undaunted, during two long hours of this pelting rain, gradually ascending higher and higher among the hills. At the end of that time, we had reached a considerable elevation, probably about two thousand feet above the sea, and were pleasantly reminded of the fact by the unusual coolness of the atmosphere. I, for one, certainly benefited by this shower; it had lured forth from their retreat several *rain-worms* of five or six feet in length,—the very reptile that I had beheld with so much interest and astonishment in the museum in Paris several years ago. I sprang from my horse with lightning speed, to catch some of them, but it was not without much difficulty that I succeeded in getting hold of those strong and active creatures. *Scolopendræ* too, (Centipedes) of enormous size, and rolling *Onisci*, as large as walnuts, were creeping out. To my great regret I did not obtain possession of a single bird among the many that we that day shot, as they all fell irrecoverably into the depths of the tall grass. Towards evening we reached a miserable "*rest-house*," which did not offer any conveniences or comforts, not even that of a fire to warm ourselves and to dry our clothes. Most opportune therefore, and most thankfully accepted, was an invitation to partake of the hospitality of a German planter, who, with his brother, is cultivating coffee-plantations of considerable extent, in a tract of land cleared by fire of its primitive forests and jungle. Under the friendly roof of the Messrs.

Worms, of Frankfurt, we ate a hearty dinner, during which conversation flowed on most pleasantly in the German tongue. The house was indeed a small one, and could scarcely include the whole of our number beneath the shelter of its thatched roof; nevertheless we were, one and all, as cheerful as heart could desire. A rich collection of serpents and of insects, caught in the immediate neighbourhood, contributed not a little to my share of the amusement. Somewhat less agreeable, however, than this social evening, was the night,—a cold and misty night it was too,—which we passed on the damp ground, where rats were swarming, with little or nothing spread below us. Next morning, (the 21st of November) we inspected the coffee plantation, still black with the embers and scattered ashes of that proud and ancient forest, of which a few tall Mango trees are still left,—spared as monuments of their fallen race!

After bidding a hearty farewell to these kind "countrymen," we proceeded to visit another plantation, on a larger scale, which was on our way. From thence we rode on, without further halt, through shady forests,—whose underwood was enlivened by magnificent butterflies,—and found ourselves still continually ascending, our road winding along the edge of lofty beetling cliffs of granite rock, as we drew nearer and nearer to the table land of the ridge above. Here and there we saw, amid the thick and gloomy forests, a spot which, by means of fire at the dry season, had been cleared out and opened to the light of day, that it might be used forthwith for a coffee plantation. In the ravines or little glens among the higher mountain-tops, we observed several large waterfalls, and as the rushing torrents dashed their silvery foam over the edge of a cliff into some deep chasm, the distant roar was wafted over to us on the mountain breeze. At the foot of one such cascade we passed close to the spot where its fallen waters precipitate themselves into their black and turbulent pool, and it cost us no small trouble to guide our steeds across the ford below. As for mine it violently broke loose from me, and on my attempting to regain my hold, it kicked and struggled so that its hind-feet struck me on the breast; I fell to the ground, and during a few minutes, gasped for breath: however, I soon discovered that none of my ribs were broken, and that I was in a condition to resume my journey, though not without some difficulty.

We soon reached our breakfast-station, RAMBODDA, a little spot at an elevation of two thousand feet, encircled by magnificent cascades, whose tops we could frequently distinguish amid the lofty peaks above. I was busily occupied among the productions of the vegetable world around, and the geological wonders of the masses of rock, which abound with cinnamon stone; while the Prince was taking possession, with his pencil, of some of the beautiful waterfalls.

Beyond this station, our road became more steep, and the flora underwent a marked change: we were now at no great distance from one of the highest passes of this mountain chain. The forest rose to a gigantic height, and appeared nearly black from its vast bowers of dark foliage: soon, moreover, a heavy mist sunk down upon us, so that we were enveloped in midnight gloom;—the bright spots were indeed few and far between. The darkness was almost total when we gained the head of the pass; we could just discern a few dirty hovels, surrounded by barricades, before the entrance of which we saw our hitherto naked "*coolies*,"* wrapped in some scanty covering, and shivering round a fire. Our kind friend Captain Maclean, who, on account of the weakness of his little horse, and the strength of his own constitution, always

* The native term used to designate those hired bearers, who carry the traveller's baggage suspended on long poles across their shoulders.—EDITOR.

started half an hour before the rest of our party, had obtained information regarding the dangerous character of this place. We were assured that the multitude of wild elephants in this neighbourhood, which are wont to march in single file, perfectly at their ease, along the beaten paths, rendered it impossible for us to proceed without torches or flaming firebrands. Travellers had often before found the road blocked up, and had been forced to retreat in danger of their lives. In spite of all these representations, the absolute necessity of carrying firebrands was not, in our opinion, very clearly proved: the Prince gave the decisive word, and we proceeded along the dangerous defile without a single torch. We had not advanced far, when some fresh heaps of dung were observed, confirming the truth of the statements made to us. We rode on nevertheless, and not one of these objects of dread was heard,—much less seen,—by any of us.

The wild elephant is a bold and formidable animal, which, without pausing long, takes a sure aim at its victim. Those most to be feared are the solitary males, which, being thrust out of the herds, often lie in wait for any one who may pass that way, and put him to death slowly, and with the utmost deliberation.*

After another hour and a half of utter darkness, we descried the lights of the Convalescent Station of

* The "*hora-alias*," or "*rogue elephant*," is not only dreaded by travellers, but regarded with almost superstitious horror by the Cingalese, who believe it to be a rebel and criminal member of society, exiled from the herd by common consent, and held in abhorrence, mingled with fear, no less by its former companions than by man. He usually ranges within a forest circle of from ten to fifteen miles, and takes far greater delight in a human victim than his more social brethren do. Major Forbes even says, "having once overcome their dread of man, and made a successful essay, homicide seems to them a favourite amusement." He mentions an instance of a rogue elephant, without any irritation or apparent inducement, coming at mid-day into an open field, trampling a woman to death, and straightway returning, calmly and slowly, to its forest.—Tr.

the English troops, NUWERA ELLIA, which is situated as high as six thousand four hundred feet above the level of the sea. We were ushered into a pleasant, although lowly dwelling; on the spacious hearth of its principal apartment were blazing huge logs of wood, a luxury we had not enjoyed for many a long day, but which was by no means superfluous here. The mist was now falling, and with it the thermometer. The temperature, which in the morning had been 24° Réaumur (86° Fahrenheit) now sank to 10° (55° Fahrenheit). Alas! even here, tired to death as we were after our long ride, we were not to enjoy repose;—we were constrained, in consequence of receiving an invitation to dine with Captain Kelson, to make our toilet without delay. While at dinner, I had well nigh fallen asleep, and was only occasionally roused from my half-slumbering state by one or other of the gentlemen asking me to drink wine with him. Never was I more thoroughly frozen than on our return from the dinner-party; the way was long, and there was hoar-frost. I found the thermometer in our room standing at 8° (50° Fahrenheit), in the open air at 6° (46° Fahrenheit), and it even fell as low as 5° (44° Fahrenheit).

A party had been arranged for a hunt on the morning of the following day, the 22d of November. The surrounding woods were said to be full of elks. *Elk* is the name given, in Ceylon, to a very large species of greyish brown deer, with long hair: it is the *Cervus hippelaphus* or *unicolor*, or moose-deer.* A numerous pack

* This animal must not be confounded with the *Cervus Alces*,—elk, or moose-deer,—the name *elk* being erroneously applied by British residents both in Ceylon and on the continent of India to more than one species of stag, while the real elk or moose-deer is not found in Asia except in its northern regions. Mr Wilson, in his notices on the zoology of British India, mentions that "the *rusa* group of stags is entirely Asiatic;" it is distinguished by the roundness and peculiar formation of the horns. That naturalist describes the Gona Rusa (*Cervus unicolor*) as "the largest species of Ceylon," surpassing

of bloodhounds, and a no less numerous body of quick-scented natives assembled round the "*rest-house,*" for the purpose of raising the game in the thick and often impenetrable underwood, here known as "*the Jungle.*"

This sweet, inviting spot, Nuwera Ellia, lies in an open plain among moor lands, encircled on every side by craggy mountains, which, in our climate, would be clad in eternal snows; bold and lofty peaks tower to the very skies; among them the highest summit in the island, is Pedro-tallagalla, which rises to the height of eight thousand four hundred feet above the sea.

The level ground, on which, scattered here and there among the thick bushes, stand the few detached buildings of which Nuwera Ellia (or New-House) consists, is but two thousand feet beneath this high level; no wonder therefore that the whole vegetation of the neighbourhood should assume altogether a new appearance, and more of a European character. Few trees are to be seen; among these I may mention *Rhododendron arboreùm* (tree rhododendron) with its flowers of burning crimson, *Viburnum opulus* (the "snow-ball tree," or guelder rose,) *Euonymus* (the Spindle-tree,) and several species of Acacia. The peach, the apple, and the pear tree thrive extremely well here; and above all, the potatoe, and every possible variety of European vegetable, turnips, cabbages, &c., &c.—One object the eye seeks in vain in all this highland district; I mean the fir-tree; —for throughout the whole of Ceylon no trees of the order of *Coniferæ* are to be seen. The moors are

in size the stag of Europe. The throat is loaded with long bristly hair, the tail is short, and the general colour is a uniform dark brown. This animal is very bold and fierce, and dwells in the jungle and the deepest recesses of the forests." The Great Rusa, (*Cervus hippelaphus*) is numbered by Mr Wilson as a species found in continental India, (chiefly Bengal) and in several of the Asiatic islands; its size exceeds that of the *unicolor*, being nearly equal to that of a horse. It has trifurcated horns, very coarse hair, of a fulvous brown in summer, changing in winter to a greyer hue; the tail is rather long." It is sometimes known as the great *Axis*.—Tr.

overgrown with a kind of hard grass, two or three feet high,* among which luxuriate many beautiful alpine varieties of *Campanula* and a most fragrant species of *Physalis*, (Winter-cherry) I think, probably, the *Physalis pubescens*,—all in as great abundance as the stinging nettle in our meadows! The winter cherries are here called *Cape gooseberries*, and no fruit makes a better tart.

This beautiful retreat is said to have been discovered by a rich English gentleman, (I think his name was Horton) while engaged in a wild boar hunt, and I am assured that he laid out the ground as a park some fifty years since. Be that as it may, the posts of a spacious gate-way, rising above the moor, still meet the eye; and the place all round them, wherever it is not too boggy, is covered with thick bushes of *Pelargonium*, *Tagetes*, and various other plants, all of which we are wont to see in pots; and which are here probably the relics of former cultivation.†

* This is the *Lemon-grass, Andropogon Schœnanthus*,—one of the most characteristic productions of Ceylon, and of some parts of the adjacent continent. It is the general covering of such parts of the hills, near Kandy, as are not overgrown with jungle; and in its young and tender state affords good pasture to buffaloes; it emits when bruised a strong lemon-scent, which, although pleasant at first, becomes if one is long exposed to it, particularly oppressive. Its taste is a refreshing acid.—TR.

† A slight confusion, not surprising in a stranger and a foreigner, seems here to have arisen on the subject of names. Nuwera Ellia, though visited and described by Dr Davy in 1819, when its solitude was but rarely broken by the natives who resorted thither in quest of iron or of gems, was little known to Europeans till, in 1829, Sir Edward Barnes, then Governor of Ceylon, having accidentally wandered thither in the chase, fixed upon it as a military convalescent station, and built the residence above alluded to. Its wonderfully temperate climate, 65° being reckoned its mean temperature by day, and 55° by night for the entire year, freedom from piercing winds, and proximity to the mountain peaks, and the extraordinary purity of its water, render it equally salubrious and congenial; there are also chalybeate springs in the neighbourhood. The "*fifty* years since" spoken of by our author is thus probably an error for *fifteen* years since. But the allusion to the "gentleman of the name of Horton," doubtless refers, not to Nuwera Ellia, but, to an interesting wild, and solitary table-land, at no great distance from it,

The chase had already commenced, when I set out on my rambles with the intention of climbing several mountain-summits; unfortunately, I was unable to advance beyond a very short distance, for the bushes are thorny and impenetrably thick. I therefore turned my steps in another direction, towards the pass which we had ascended the evening before. Here my toil was amply rewarded by scenery of surpassing loveliness,—deep and narrow glens, half filled up in some places by fallen trees stretched across them,—mountain streams winding their rugged way beneath,—and on all sides a smiling lawn, carpeted with exquisite flowers. I soon heard in the thicket, at a great depth below me, the clamorous cry of the hounds; the crashing and breaking of the branches approached nearer and nearer, till at length an animal of large size sprang out of the jungle, and crossed the road with one mighty bound, only to vanish instantly amid the thick wood on the other side. It was probably an elk. Shortly afterwards I fell in with the whole hunt in the valley below. Their toils had been unrewarded, for the object of their pursuit was too swift both for huntsmen and for hounds.

known as the Horton Plains, thus named in honour of Sir Robert Wilmot Horton, Governor of Ceylon from 1831 to 1837. A picturesque description of the primæval desolation of these plains,—the most elevated in the island, —of their sombre forests,—and mountain ramparts,—and of the adjacent sources of the Bilhool-Oya or Walawe River, and the Mahawelle-Ganga, is given by Major Forbes: One of his characteristic touches is as follows:—"In these vast jungle solitudes, on the ascent from Nuwera Ellia, on every twig, round every tree, the stilly damp of ages has twined a mossy vesture: their mouldering rocks, moss-clad forests, and silent plains offer so few signs of animated nature, that the notes of a small bird are a relief from universal stillness; and the occasional rise of snipe is absolutely startling. In following up the green banks of a rill on one of these mountains, I called to my companion and proposed a change of direction; he answered, 'Very well.' Instantly, as if these words had burst the magic spell which bound the demon spirits of the waste, the joyous sounds, 'very well! very well! very well!' came hurrying forth from every copse and winding glade in these, the farthest bounds of the forest labyrinth."—Tr.

After breakfast, the party undertook a second hunt, and returned triumphant with a large and handsome elk. In the evening a dinner was given to the hunt in the rest-house; the company however broke up early, as we were to start at day-break.

Day-break did arrive indeed; but the whole country around, with the sole exception of the spot where we were, was enveloped in mist so dense, that we were obliged to wait till it should disperse. As soon as this was the case, we proceeded at a swift gallop, down another pass in the mountains,—a steep and long descent. Our road was here for the first time circling round bare hills, on which herds of buffaloes were grazing; the highest ridges alone were crowned with wood. Here suddenly the formation changes from the primitive masses to secondary lime-stone, dolomite, and lumps of ironstone in a state of disintegration:—the yellow soil abounds in mica. We reached an open and elevated platform, from whence we had an opportunity, which we had never before enjoyed, of seeing in perspective the singular and manifold crossings of the valleys below.

We found ourselves, at one o'clock, at our station, "*Wilson Bungalow,*"—a lonely hut, surrounded with a verandah, as are all the other rest-houses. After breakfast, a snipe-shooting expedition was agreed upon, in which Captain Maclean and I took no share, as he was withheld by the fear of wet paddy-grounds, and I by the desire of botanizing. The shades of evening had fallen ere our gentlemen returned,—drenched up to the shoulders,—from their toilsome day's sport. Twelve brace of snipes and a number of other birds were however spoils that consoled them for all their fatigues.

Near this station the paddy-fields begin to assume the form of terraces,—the mode of cultivation prevalent throughout the interior of Ceylon. Along the gently sloping valleys, these enclosures,—each levelled to a depth of about a foot or a foot and a half lower than the one immediately above it,—are surrounded with low walls of earth.* There is never any lack of water, for the rains are regular and abundant.

We made ourselves as comfortable as circumstances permitted in our "rest-house," and after a few hours' sleep on the hard ground, started at three o'clock in the morning on the 24th of November. The moon was still shining brightly, and the sun did not rise till three hours and a half of our journey had passed away. When the clear light of day dawned on us, we found ourselves on the brink of a deep and precipitous chasm,—the rugged bed of a mountain torrent. The road, newly made and covered with soft, loose earth, was only a few feet wide, and was continually yielding beneath our horses' tread. We were ever and anon climbing,—and again descending, —now a steep part, now an easy one,—but constantly skirting the channel of the stream. On a bare rock in the middle of the river, we saw a large troop of monkeys, leaping in merry gambols: immediately on perceiving

* For the purpose of securing copious irrigation and inundation, which are not allowed to depend on the rains, however regular and abundant; water being, as we learn from Dr Davy, "sometimes conducted two or three miles along the side of a hill, or occasionally even carried from one side of a mountain to another by means of wooden pipes." Of these picturesque terraces, which, in some places not exceeding three feet in width, resemble the tiers of seats in a vast amphitheatre, Dr Davy thus speaks:—"Among the mountains, paddy-fields are a succession of terraces or flights of steps; and in each field the crop may be in a different stage of growth, in some just vegetating, in others full-grown, ripening, or ripe;—there, at the same time, you may see the labourers at all their different operations,—banking, ploughing, sowing, weeding, reaping, and treading out the grain." The diligent cultivators of these verdant terraces may recall, to the minds of some travellers, the industrious vine-dressers of our Author's native land, who, on the sunny banks of "*Father Rhine*," may be seen toiling to carry, not water, but manure, to the objects of their care. In these two species of husbandry, so opposite in many respects, there is this point moreover in common,—that no portion of ground, however short and narrow, is left uncultivated. The paddy-ground, being ploughed while under water, and again irrigated after seed-time, is not drained till the crop is nearly ripe, when the water runs off to the terrace below, and so flows on from one to another.—Tr.

our approach, they sprang with the greatest agility, by means of an overhanging tree, to the opposite bank. They were *Silens, (Inuus Silenus)* a species of short-tailed monkey.

Towards eleven o'clock we reached the station at which we were to breakfast,—Ettem Pittya, a rest-house like the preceding ones, built on an isolated rock. Here again, the population of the surrounding district, with their headmen, had assembled to salute the Prince, and to see him pass beneath the triumphal arches of bamboos and palms which they had erected in honour of his visit. From this place we had a distance of fourteen English miles to traverse before arriving at our place of rest. The valley continued without any new feature, and we perceived scarcely any difference between the scenery here and that of our morning's ride: it was not till we descended a very steep declivity, and once more beheld the region of palms and bananas, that we found more variety among the objects around us. I was however so much fatigued, that my only recollection is of having passed under two more of those beautiful decorated arches, and of having seen and pursued a porcupine, before descending into the lovely valley of Badulla.

Badulla, situated in a very charming open valley, and surrounded by tall and majestic cocoa-nut trees, was a most welcome retreat for travellers wearied with the severe exertions of a twenty-five miles' ride over difficult mountain paths. The town itself is small and neat, consisting of two broad streets, which cross each other and seem to stand in the midst of a pleasant garden. The houses are of one story, built of bamboos, and covered with the leaves of the cocoa-nut tree; each house has but three walls, the fourth side being open, and serving at once for door, window and shop. Here are seated, distinguished by the turban, the sun-burnt Moormen, grave and serious-looking: they form the great majority of the merchants and dealers, selling chiefly English stone-ware and ironmongery;—there, the Cingalese venders of fruit and grain,—the "*topetty*," or coil of white muslin girt about the loins, their only garment; and the broad tortoise-shell comb fastening the plait of their long black hair;—again the eye is struck, among the varied groups that pass before it, with the picturesque figures of native females, wives of wealthy Cingalese,—their ample dark-red garment (the "*hala*") thrown over the left shoulder, and confined by a silver girdle, their hands and feet adorned with rings and bangles,—dragging behind them naked children, whose arms and legs are loaded with cumbrous ornaments of silver, like those of their parents:—or again, shaven priests, with the toga of flaming yellow wrapped proudly round them,—silent and solemn, like Plato or some other philosopher of ancient times. The men of poorer and more degraded castes are not privileged to wear anything save the simple "*topetty*,"—but indeed even those of higher degree usually content themselves with a long piece of cotton cloth, covered with Indian patterns, which is wound about the loins and hangs down to the ancles. This garment, together with the long plaited hair and the large comb, gives to their naturally slender and delicate figures a most feminine appearance. But to my eye there is something pretty and engaging about these cheerful, friendly people, with their black eyes and their shining, olive-brown skin; and more especially about their lovely little ones, who unfortunately however have the greatest dread of Europeans. Would that it were but possible to win these people from the use of their betel-nut, which dyes their lips a vile yellowish red, and their teeth brown, and distorts their mouths with a perpetual grin! It is really impossible to imagine anything more disgusting than this unnatural custom. The Areca nut, the unslaked lime, and the betel-pepper leaf, are all individually, and much more when united, things fit only for poisoning rats.

The ugliness of the women is, notwithstanding their picturesque ensemble, quite equal to the beauty of the men. One sees only withered old hags with skins like parchment, and even a Cingalese belle has, at twenty, all the air of being a grandmother with the weight of sixty years on her head,—which is probably the consequence of their being married when mere children, from ten to twelve years of age.

At the extremity of one of the streets of the town, a most enchanting landscape opens upon one: lofty mountains in the back-ground,—a glorious forest of tall cocoa-nut trees, of Areca and of Palmyra palms, close to the outskirts of the town; the underwood, beneath the deep shade of their thick bowering foliage, consisting of various blossoming shrubs,—their lovely flowers, for the most part white and of an Oleander-like form, breathing celestial perfumes, and large Convolvuluses, white, or of a deep blue, twining high into the air round all the branches, —and, not to be forgotten, the elegant *Carica Papaya*, (Papaw-tree) with its crown of spreading, sinuated leaves, —rising among orange-trees of every sort, with their shining foliage and their tempting fruit.

Between the trees on the roadside appears here and there a small cottage, in which some old woman may be seen, offering for sale the beautiful, fragrant, yellow fruit of the Banana-tree:—goats, not unlike fawns in appearance and colour,—are seen running about on every side, amidst groupes of young children, whose only pretence of clothing is a simple coil twisted round them.

In the evening I walked with the Prince along this magnificent avenue. Few only of the people followed us, in spite of their curiosity; for it was late, and these superstitious folk have an extreme dread of the Evil-Spirit, although I fear they have not any distinct or lively impression concerning God.* As sunset draws near, the fragrance of the numberless flowers becomes more delightful; the air is soft and balmy as on a fine summer evening at Home; and throughout all nature, life seems to begin with renewed freshness. Myriads of frogs cause the air to resound with their voices, croaking in every variety of tone;—the palm-trees are filled with minas,—black, thrush-like birds, with long yellow legs and reddish yellow flaps or caruncles hanging below their eyes. These birds, in concert with the crows, keep up a most intolerable screaming; and a host of insects, members of the numerous families of frog-hoppers, grass-hoppers, crickets and locusts, chime in with their soprano to complete the harmony of the concert. Several of these minas, whose peace, as they are held sacred, had never before been broken by the shot of a gun, fell by the Prince's aim.

To our right hand, at the end of the grove of palms, stood a house of very singular appearance, raised on a high foundation-wall of stone, but constructed in a neat and tasteful style, of fine wood, with a carved roof, altogether much resembling a Swiss cottage. It was the priestly dwelling-place:—opposite to it was the entrance to the "*Dagoba,*" or Buddhist sanctuary. We ascended a ruined flight of stone steps, which leads into the interior of a spacious walled enclosure. Tall palm-trees here

* The Cingalese have engrafted on their original Buddhism many strange and incongruous superstitions, demon-worship, planet-worship, and, like the refined idolaters of the days of St Paul, (Acts xvii. 23,) the worship of "*The Unknown God,*"—their "*Abudha Deiyo.*" The red-eyed demon, pestilence, the demons of the forest and of poisonous plants, and other objects of this worship of fear, they seek to propitiate by offering a red cock; but the peculiar offering made to the "*Spirit of the flood,*" "*Ganga Bandera,*" a personification of the malaria sometimes prevalent on the banks of all Ceylon streams, differs from all the rest. A miniature double canoe, canopied with cocoa-nut leaves, is filled with betel, grain and flowers, and launched upon the stream; in a sickly season, a whole navy of these tiny barks is resorted to as a sure defence against the "*river-fiend.*"—Tr.

cast their shade over an edifice, the most extraordinary I had ever seen. A large, round, bell-shaped building of stone, from forty to fifty feet in height, rises from within a double enclosure, skilfully constructed of brick, but now fallen into a state of dilapidation. Nothing reposes on the foundation below, except this great circular dome, which is smooth as the globe of some huge lamp. Every thing is grey with age, yet in the coating of plaster that covered the whole, traces of figures and of volutes or arabesque devices were here and there discernible. The summit appears to have been of old completely gilded; and the base must have been very elegant, and finely fluted;—but not a window, not a door, not an opening of any kind could we discover in all this mysterious edifice, which in fact contains nothing except a relic of Buddha,—a tooth or a bone,—to which the priests gain access by a subterranean passage. Close beside this colossus stands a modest and unpretending "*Wiharé*," or idol-temple, a whitewashed building, surrounded by a verandah, the roof of which is supported by elegant wooden pillars. Within these holy walls stand, ranged in front of a most frightful image of a sleeping Buddha, a table covered with odoriferous flowers, and a variety of bronze vessels amidst a profusion of cocoa-nut-oil lamps. We met two very filthy-looking priests, who without hesitation permitted us to enter, and to examine both the architectural masks on the walls, and the wooden Buddha. A multitude of copper drums and tambourines were hung up in the verandah before the sanctuary;—it was lucky for us that they were not put into requisition, as at Kandy, for an accompaniment to a shrill and screaming song. A number of small mud-huts, like stables or pig-sties, stand round the temple; I was unable to discover the use for which they are intended, or to obtain any information on the subject. But the most beautiful object by far in the scene around these sacred precincts was a very ancient *Bo-tree, (Ficus Religiosa)* with its mighty boughs and knotty roots. The Bo-tree is a species of fig, with small poplar leaves, which terminate in long pointed ends; it is numbered among the sacred trees, and grows to an immense height and strength: trees of a hundred feet high are by no means rare in the primitive forests of the island. High above their broad and spreading masses of foliage rise the slender, tapering palms, shooting up their bright crests into the air like rockets, to a height of a hundred and fifty, or two hundred feet.

Suddenly plunged in "darkness visible," and guided only by the uncertain brightness of the fire-flies, which were dancing in myriads around the crowned summit of each lofty tree,—like gay and variegated fire-works,—or by the glimmering of solitary cocoa-nut oil lamps shining in lowly cottages,—we found our way back to our "*Bungalow*,"* at the farthest extremity of the town. Meanwhile, during our absence, a plan had been agreed upon with the officer in command at this station, the renowned elephant-hunter, *Major Rogers*,† by which we were to start the following morning for an elephant-

* Such is the name given in the East to houses erected for the accommodation of travellers.—W. Hoffmeister.

† Major Rogers, no less excellent as a civil administrator than unrivalled as an elephant shot, is since dead. How striking the analogy between the touching fate of this fearless man, who had lived to recount so many hair-breadth escapes, and whose life had been replete with such romantic dangers, and that of the youthful traveller, who, at the very moment when his every vision of happiness seemed to have become a reality, and when even the most adventurous parts of his wild and remote travels had been safely passed through, was cut down by a death no less unexpected in its form than sudden in its stroke! It was not by the oft experienced fury of the elephant,—nor in the din of the battle-field, that Major Rogers fell; but by the dread artillery of heaven, as he stood alone in unshared, unthought-of danger. He had taken shelter with some other travellers in a hut during a thunder-storm; after a time he went to the door to see if it had cleared off; the next moment there was a vivid flash of lightning and violent clap of thunder,—he returned not,—his companions went to the threshold,—and found only his lifeless remains.—Tr.

hunt in the heart of the forests and jungle, a three days' journey from Badulla. I was obliged to pack immediately in all haste, that I might be in readiness early enough in the morning.

At five o'clock A.M., on the 25th of November, our horses were waiting for us to mount and go: the "*coolies*" or bearers, had gone on in advance with the cook, and had taken all the luggage. Major Rogers, and his amiable and pleasing companion, the local Judge, a young gentleman of the name of *Layard*, made their appearance in most extraordinary costumes,—large, loose, linen jackets, hats of basket-work plait, "*leech-stockings*," reaching above the knee, and over these a sort of mountain shoes. Such is the habiliment necessary in self-defence, on account of the plague of this country, the Ceylon leech, which abounds in these parts. Without delay we mounted our steeds, which bore us swiftly, over well-made roads, to the first mountains of the range, the out-posts as it were of an enchanting Highland country. Our road, engineered by our friend Major Rogers himself, in long zigzags up the steep acclivity of a very high hill, commanded a prospect ever varying, and ever more and more expansive over the valley of the river below, which, when we began our ascent, had been enveloped in mist. In many parts, little brooks, still swollen from the heavy thunder-showers of the preceding day, crossed our road. For some hours we enjoyed most lovely views,—rice-fields, banana-gardens, and palm-groves, clothing the sides of the rich valley at a great depth below us;—at the end of that time we found ourselves plunging into the deep forest: the road, though newly cut through it, had in many places been washed away by the rushing torrents of rain: towering masses of rich and varied foliage rose in every direction above and beyond the magnificent evergreens, which shone brightly on either side; already had the trees, through which this opening had been so recently cut, met over head and formed a bower; already had conical hills arisen on the middle of our path, —the newly constructed abodes of the *Termites fatali* or *bellicosi*, (white ants):* such is, in these climes, the profuse luxuriance of nature! With us long years are spent in planting and careful and anxious training, to obtain a tolerably flourishing shrubbery; here on the contrary, vegetation often threatens to dispossess mankind of their domain, and to bury villages and paddy fields in one mass of coppice. This bushy underwood or "jungle" as it is called, grows so thick, so thoroughly interwoven with gigantic creepers and thorny parasites, that, in many parts, it were vain to attempt to force a passage through it. The elephant alone,—the monarch of this wilderness,—stalks through it all, and treads down the crashing woods with his giant pillars as he goes.†

In some places immense roots of mighty trees present

* Such are the amazing dimensions of these wondrous structures, formed by insects not exceeding a quarter of an inch in height, that Bishop Heber describes some which he saw in Bengal as looking, at a distance, like the stumps of decayed trees: they were five or six feet high; probably seven or eight in circumference at the base, and partially overgrown with grass and ivy. Mr Smeathman assures us that "when these hills are little more than half their height, it is the practice of the wild bulls to stand as sentinels on them, while the rest of the herd are ruminating below:" he adds, that he has himself stood, with four other men, on the top of one of these hillocks at its greater height, to watch for a vessel in sight. The pinnacles which give to these conical edifices so remarkable an appearance, are the columns prepared to support and divide future arched apartments, and are mentioned by naturalists as affording evidence that these insects project their arches, and do not make them by excavation. Tr.

† Probably a scene such as Dr Greville alludes to when he says, "A species of *Trichozanthes* ascends to the tops of the highest branches, and produces a beautiful white flower, with a fringed border, but which, expanding only in the night, is rarely seen; while the abundant fruit, nearly as large as a small orange, and of a vivid scarlet colour, is very ornamental. So numerous are climbers of this description, that trees and shrubs are lashed as it were together, and the forests and jungles often thereby rendered impenetrable except to wild animals."—Tr.

themselves as obstacles to the traveller: in others, we heard, to our amazement, that the overgrown thicket of from twelve to fifteen feet in height, through which we had to force our way,—was the growth of but one year and a half, before which time that part of the forest had been burnt down for the sake of cultivation. Did not pieces of charred wood and black streaks of coal on the newly laid road confirm the truth of this statement, it would be difficult for the stranger to credit it.

On the margin of a clear and rippling stream, and encircled by trees of enormous size, lies TALDENIA,—a solitary bungalow. There Major Rogers' cook had prepared a capital breakfast for us,—eggs, roast fowls, and curry with abundance of rice. Curry is a national dish in all these lands, and is never wanting at any dinner or breakfast, either in Ceylon or India. It is left to the cook's discretion and skill to furnish a new variety of curry each day; for the "de quoi" is a matter of indifference. Every kind of meat, poultry or game, fish or shell-fish, may,—by a plentiful addition of Cayenne-pepper, cardamums, turmerick (which gives the sauce a sulphur yellow hue) and the juice of young cocoa nuts as the main ingredient of the sauce,—be transformed into a curry: rice is an indispensable auxiliary, softening the pungent heat of the dish in so far as to enable one,—after having persevered in the experiment for a few weeks,—to eat it with some relish. The exquisite fruits of the country never fail to make their appearance at table: they are very highly prized at first by Europeans, but when the charm of novelty has passed away, they cease to be so irresistibly inviting.

The well-made road soon came to an end on the other side of Taldenia, and the continual leaping and clambering, under the scorching rays of the sun, threw our horses into a great heat. The deep and almost unbroken shade of the trees, in many parts of the way, was however most refreshing. We forded three or four swollen and impetuous streams, whose banks were steep and rugged. We were soaked up to our chests; but had always the sure prospect of being soon dry, from the violent exercise. On reaching the high ground, towards noon, we observed the fresh dung of elephants,—a most agreeable surprise for all the sportsmen. Their footsteps were immediately tracked, and a numerous train of runners and of coolies was soon dispersed through the jungle to start the herd. The horses were to be led forward to be out of the way: I remained at the halting-place, my surgical instruments in my hand, prepared in case of any accident rendering my services useful. Not long after the thick bushes had closed behind my companions, and I had been thus left standing in perfect solitude, I heard at a great distance, the heavy crashing tread of an elephant. My first thought was to satisfy myself as to the height and strength of the surrounding trees, that I might, in case of necessity, take refuge in them, should an elephant chance to pay me a visit.

At the end of three hours, the sportsmen issued out of the jungle, with clothes much torn, without having been able to fire a shot; but,—His Royal Highness and the Major were missing! Suddenly we heard two shots quickly succeed each other, followed by a trumpet-note, the elephant's cry of distress. We waited in intense anxiety, and had soon the joy of welcoming among us those whom we had missed. An elephant had been shot, first by the Prince and then by the Major; but as to killing it, that is a very different affair. The rules of the chase are these;—the hunter pursues his victim,—whose track the natives never fail to find,—through thick and thin; which, amid jungles, dense even to darkness, is not accomplished without violent exertions. On approaching it, he advances to within four or five paces, and fires precisely at the moment when the animal is preparing to charge his assailant. There are however but two spots at which a shot, fired from this distance, is instantaneously fatal, namely, above the eye close to the front of the ear,—or, if the elephant is rushing upon the hunter face to face, just above the root of the trunk; all other wounds, even when the gun is loaded with heavy balls, only serve to make him furious. It is therefore really not saying too much when I affirm that elephant hunting is an excessively dangerous amusement. How easily may the gun, put out of order by the wet, or by the rushing and pressing forward through the thick bushes, miss fire at the critical moment! Besides, what a sure aim and what cold blood are requisite in firing, to hit exactly the mortal spot!

In the evening, at the little village of PALEVALLA, we partook of an excellent, though simple repast, consisting of snipes, which we had ourselves shot; after which, wrapped in our cloaks and lying on straw mats, we enjoyed very sound slumbers, notwithstanding the rain which was constantly trickling through the roof of palm leaves. The whole population was a-foot as we entered the place, pretty-looking little men of dark-brown complexion, who, in the heart of this wilderness, cultivate rice to a considerable extent, and manage their terraces and the enclosures by which they parcel out their small pieces of land, with great skill.

On the 26th of November we started at five o'clock in the morning, while it was still dark, crossed a deep river flowing between steep banks, and reached, about nine o'clock, another small village, BODOLA, where we took breakfast. Even here everything was adorned in festive style, to receive the Prince;—the "headmen" appearing, as usual, covered with jewels, with their white muslin, and their broad, flat, round caps. We sat under a palm-roof, upon large benches, low, but very wide. These are in universal use, both for sitting and for sleeping:—they are plaited of the young leaves of the cocoa-nut tree; instead of Chinese varnish, they have always a covering of cow-dung, which is assuredly filthy enough, but is said to be the only means of guarding against the destructive *Termites* (white ants) and *Eumenes* (carpenter wasps). Houses formed of bamboos, and all plaited walls of matting, are plastered in the same manner: nothing can be more frightful.* Our cottage was shaded by a beautiful and gigantic tamarind-tree *(Tamarindus Indicus)*, the pods of which contain a semi-fluid pulp of a most agreeable acid, which is a favourite refreshment in this country: the tree resembles an Acacia.

This village marked the utmost bound of cultivation: beyond it we entered into the thick masses of a primeval forest. Its deep and awful gloom almost made me shudder; I was overpowered by the feeling of the mighty difference existing between it and anything I had ever before seen. The huge stems of its trees stand close beside each other; creepers, of almost tree-like growth,

* In speaking of the hosts of insects and reptiles so peculiarly characteristic of this island, Major Forbes says—"After a heavy shower, the houses in Ceylon are invaded by snakes and venomous insects: centipedes and scorpions are the most numerous of these intruders; the bite of the former and the sting of the latter being equally severe, but neither of them dangerous to adults in good health. Myriads of white ants soon begin to fill up the glass shades that surround every lamp for the purpose of preserving the flame from being extinguished. Flying-bugs, beetles, car-wigs, and eye-flies add to the masses that hover round your person, overspread the tables, or scramble over each other on the floor: these insects are far more disgusting and troublesome than their larger brethren, usually classed as venomous, or considered as dangerous." The proceedings of the white ants are perhaps the most insidious; sometimes undermining the floors and posts, sometimes reaching the roof by one of their covered ways, and intersecting it with pipes and galleries, they take possession of the dwelling, filling up the cavities which they have gnawed within the posts with tempered clay, which soon hardens, so that the wooden posts seem to be transformed into stone pillars; but almost all these foes have the good taste to object to the peculiar species of plaster, which, as the minor evil, is so commonly adopted in Ceylon.—Tr.

often bind together three or four of the sturdiest among them, already partly dead, or, as it were, caught in this strong embrace while in the very act of expiring. More than once I saw only one stem, of moderate thickness, and winding round in a spiral form. I was at first not a little surprised and puzzled at the sight of these gigantic cork-screw trees, until I discovered their origin. It was the stem of the creeper; the trunk round which it had twined, oppressed by its weight, had rotted and worn away, and it was left alone and unsupported. I did not see many flowers; light and air are lacking for them in this place; but the whole vigour of the plant was thus expended on the foliage which was proportionably rich and beautiful.

In some places, foaming mountain torrents, which have washed away the soil from the roots to the depth of four or five feet, made it by no means easy for our horses to proceed; frequently also they were obliged to shape their course round thick imperishable stumps, or huge stems of fallen trees. Occasionally we came to an open space, covered with luxuriant grass, where the sweetest flowers were unfolding their beauties, and swarms of butterflies fluttering around; but soon we plunged once more into the deep and solemn shades, where our swift steeds were impeded in their onward course by many a mass of those bare and knotted roots, or by dark waters, whose depth we could not ascertain. The path was so narrow that we were forced to ride in single file, keeping close behind each other, that our party might not be scattered. For six long wearisome hours we rode on, straining every nerve for speed; at length we reached our goal, the centre of the forest, where a few huts had been erected for our accommodation.

This place is called Galbocka. Three huts contained our whole party. Their walls were formed of dried leaves and twigs, their roofs of palm-leaves and grass, and their gutters of the bark of trees. Four posts stuck into the earth, with six or seven sticks fastened diagonally across them, formed the table; chairs there were none; but, on the other hand, the walls were hung with white cotton, and a curtain of the same material covered the doorway. The floor was somewhat sunk in the ground, and during continued rain it soon filled with water. Such were the "*comforts*" of our eight days' residence at *Galbocka.*

Every morning, before night had fully yielded to the dawn of day, we started from our lurking-place, in pursuit of elephants, which are met with in large herds; and usually, even before sunrise, we were wet to the skin. When the natives perceived, by their quick scent or otherwise, that the elephants were at hand, which they announced by a particular sign, we all instantly dismounted, and the huntsmen rushed, head-foremost, through the thicket, while I remained with the attendants at the halting-place. The crash of an elephant, running at full speed, may be heard at the distance of half a mile; a whole herd makes a noise such as one might imagine from an avalanche falling over a vast forest. The terrific and portentous cry, not unlike a fearfully loud note sounded from a broken trumpet, is uttered by the mighty beast at the identical moment in which it turns around, either to crush its enemy, or itself to receive the fatal ball. I therefore always knew, even at a distance, when the crisis of danger had arrived.

On one occasion I had remained nearer than usual to the hunt, because the danger of being isolated in a broken and rocky ground, all alive with elephants, is really greater than that of following close to the chase. Suddenly a crash was heard to the right and to the left, —behind us sounded a trumpet-tone, and before us appeared the head of a huge and powerful animal, stirring among the thick bushes;—we were standing on a smooth rock, only slightly elevated above the surrounding ground. How fortunate that just then, Major Rogers, the most expert marksman of the hunt, was close to us. He sprang in among the elephants, and, advancing towards the one nearest him on the right, to within the length of its trunk, he fired a shot into its ear; then turning with lightning speed to the one on the left, he discharged the contents of his other barrel into its temple. Both fell with a hollow groan, as if blown down by a sudden whirlwind; the others, on hearing their giant comrades sink crashing into the bushes, hastily fled; for their fall produced a resounding noise like the report of two distant canons.

After that day, I had seen enough of elephant hunting, and always sought some pretext for remaining at home. On the following day, Major Rogers killed a female elephant, and by that one shot he brought down two victims, for she crushed, in her fall, a young one that was running beside her. Besides these, a young elephant had been already numbered among the slain, and many were wounded. The Prince himself was at one time in instant danger of being overtaken by an elephant rendered furious by three wounds in the head. Fortunately the creature was laid low by another shot.

On the day immediately preceding our departure from Galbocka, a large elephant was shot by Count Von O———, and, as it was doubtful which ball was to be considered fatal, and to whom the tail,—the usual trophy of elephant hunters,—was justly due, I set out with the Count, to examine the dead body.

Silent and noiseless, we rode along the narrow paths, when the rising sun had scarce begun his course. Our copper-brown guide often stood still to listen, and branched off from the straight road, to avoid bringing us into contact with a numerous herd. We were obliged to make great détours, to reach the spot, where the colossus had fallen. There he lay beside a little brook,—the ground on every side crimson with his blood: on his mouth and on his proboscis,—the only parts vulnerable to them,—we saw marks of the claws and teeth of the blood-thirsty *Chittas** *(Leopards)*. Unluckily for me, they had already departed before our arrival. The elephant, although reckoned one of very considerable size, measured but eight feet from the crown of his head to the sole of his foot; so much are we often deceived in our ideas of their height. It had only very short straight tusks, one of which we extracted, after inconceivably hard work, which lasted an hour and a half, in the course of which we were so covered with blood and perspiration, that we looked rather like savages than civilized Europeans. With toil and difficulty, and after many wanderings, we regained our station: for indeed it is no easy matter to ride through these wild and ancient forests, on untrodden paths;—and the horses must have strong bones, and be well shod, not to lose their footing and fall on the wet and slippery roots of the trees.

Thus our forest residence was brought to a close. We had, during that week, several opportunities of becoming acquainted with the half savage natives of that district, who flocked even from distant parts to see the

* Not the "*Chittah*," or hunting tiger of Hindostan, *(the Felis jubata)* but the "*Kotia*" *(Felis Leopardus)* of Ceylon, which is remarkable for its fear of man, and seldom attacks a human being except in self defence; yet it has been known to brave even the presence of the lord of creation in its eagerness to seize its favourite prey, the dog. Instances are common of the most extraordinary panic being produced among cattle by the mere smell of a Leopard. The Cingalese of the mountainous interior wage inveterate and successful war against this enemy in many ways. Some naturalists assert that the "*Kotia*" though generally agreeing with the description of the leopard more than with that of the panther, has some peculiarities not found in either of these quadrupeds; among others that it cannot entirely retract its claws into their sheath: it sometimes grows to eight feet in length, and its skin is valued for its great beauty.—Tr.

Prince. This too was the only place where we saw real barbarians, that is to say, beings destitute of all religion and morality, and without even a glimmering idea of the habit of social life. They dwell among the lofty forests, in mud-built hovels, under the shelter of palm leaves; wearing no manner of clothing save a scanty apron fastened by a string round the waist; and carrying the javelin and the bow and arrow. The Cingalese of the lowlands know them by the name of Veddahs,* and look upon them with great contempt, notwithstanding their claims to descent from a higher caste.

The first time that I beheld these beings they made a truly horrible impression on my mind. In the midst of a heavy rain, we were informed that they had arrived, and were ready to perform their dance in our presence:

* The Veddahs,—a remnant of the aboriginal inhabitants, driven into the forests of Bintenne and Veddaratta, many centuries since, by an invasion from Hindostan,—are divided into two classes, the village and the forest Veddahs. The former though savage in their appearance and dress, and almost without civilization, have fixed habitations formed of the bark of trees, and some communication with the other natives, with whom, however, they do not mix. Ignorant of every social rite, not distinguished among themselves by names, superstitious in their fear of evil spirits though destitute of all idea of a supreme or beneficent God, or of a state of future existence, and rewards and punishments, and consequently without knowledge of right and wrong, unable to count above five, having no idea of medicine, making no attempt to bury their dead, themselves living almost solely by the chase, cultivating a very little Indian corn in the most primitive manner, and occasionally allaying the pangs of hunger by eating cakes of decayed wood mixed with honey, or meat preserved with honey in the hollow of a tree stopped up with clay, never seeking to possess any manufactured articles except arrow-heads, attached to this savage freedom and satisfied in every respect with their own condition, they seem degraded almost to the level of brutes that perish. Yet the forest Veddahs are more barbarous still. Living in the forests without dwellings, or any means of subsistence except the chase, they are subject to Cingalese of the adjoining districts, whose cruel policy it has ever been to increase that degradation which enables themselves to obtain ivory and venison in barter for the most valueless articles.

But within these few years much has been done for the civilization of this unhappy race. The late lamented Governor, the Right Hon. J. A. Stewart Mackenzie, set apart an annual sum to be applied towards furnishing them with huts, seed-corn, and agricultural implements; and a school was successfully established among them at his own expense.—Tr.

forthwith appeared six small, lean, bronze-coloured men, with raven-black hair, long and dishevelled, hanging down their backs. One fellow only was somewhat taller than the rest, yet his stature did not appear much to exceed five feet. Their eyes were rolling and unsteady; —their language was a hoarse, yet loud sounding cry; and their dialect intelligible only with great difficulty to the Cingalese of the plain. They were all shivering from wet and cold; nevertheless they seemed to be in a highly excited state, and most impatient to begin the dance. It consisted in a sort of hopping to and fro, on alternate feet, at first moving slowly, but gradually quickening their step, which they accompanied with frightful contortions of their eyeballs, while they held down their heads, bending low. An aged man, whom at first we had not observed, rehearsed a few words, apparently questions, to which one of their number always replied with great vehemence. Presently their movements became very quick and impetuous;—and now they jumped backwards and forwards on the heels of both feet, tossing their arms about with such fearful violence, that we were in fear of their dislocating all their joints. Suddenly one man fell headlong into the mire, which had been routed up by this tremendous exercise, and writhed, arms and legs, in violent convulsions.

We had had more than enough of this horrible spectacle. Money was distributed; but they did not know it, and it required much talking to make them comprehend that copper coins were of less value than silver. A pocket-handkerchief, which Major Rogers bestowed on the occasion, had a much better effect; the fortunate individual, to whose lot it fell to receive it, immediately fastened it round his loins, and danced as if beside himself; but soon he also was prostrate in the mud. And now the others must needs have pocket-handkerchiefs also; a piece of cotton cloth was torn up and distributed among them, which they joyfully twisted about their heads; further demonstrations of gratitude they seemed ignorant of, and instead of any such, they recommenced their shocking and convulsive dance, which could not easily have been brought to a conclusion, had not the idea occurred to the Prince of offering them brandy. We were aware that they were reported to have a violent aversion to this liquor: at first not one of them would venture to taste it; at length the old man alone took a few drops, after which he assured them all that the drink was excellent. Thereupon a second fellow tried it too; he opened his mouth very wide, and poured about half a tumbler down his throat at once. What screams, what horror! In accents of most bitter lamentation he assured his companions that he had swallowed fire, pointing at the same time to his stomach, and bending double and writhing in a most piteous manner. They immediately chimed in with his howling, cast an anxious look around, and then all simultaneously fled, suddenly and with lightning speed.

Only once, since that day, have I met with any of these wild and shaggy men; it was at a station near to Badulla. They were carrying bows and arrows,—the former, handsome ones of red wood,—and were shooting in capital style. Mr Layard promised sixpence to any one of them that could shoot his hat; it was forthwith suspended upon a pole at a distance of sixty paces; yet, notwithstanding the evening twilight, it fell, pierced through, at the first shot.

On leaving Galbocka on the 30th of November, we had great difficulty in passing the mountain streams, (the Ootiyawa Oya) which were in high flood;—our strong steeds however carried us through, steep as were its banks and impetuous its waters. In the evening, we came to WELLAWA.

Next morning, (the 1st of December) we started very early, and reached our breakfast station BOBOLA by ten o'clock. We slept that night at PALEVALLA, from which place another adventurous elephant hunt was undertaken on the 2d, in which however not one elephant was brought down. I had remained with the servants, in a large paddy-field, and was catching insects, while the other gentlemen were following the chase. All of a sudden, I saw the whole of our natives rush precipitately to the trees. I deemed it advisable to do the same myself with all possible speed; for a loud crash and crack announced that an elephant was at hand, and with furious and rushing speed approaching nearer and nearer to the spot on which we stood. Scarcely had I left the marshy flat behind me, and taken refuge in a tree, when a powerful elephant issued, at a quick pace, from the thicket. A loud shout, which resounded from the troop of natives,—the cry of the elephant drivers,—caused him to turn aside, and soon his ponderous steps were no more heard. The thick underwood does not retard his heavy trot, more than the tall grass of a meadow the galloping of a horse.

With regard to the size of elephants, I have had convincing proof that the reports current among us are much exaggerated. I have not in this country seen one that exceeded eight feet in height. The tame ones in India are said to be larger. Then another popular error is to suppose that every male is furnished with tusks. This is quite untrue. Among a hundred elephants four or five only have perfectly formed tusks. I was assured of this by Major Rogers, who has killed at least fourteen hundred elephants with his own hand. When, six years ago, he had reached his thirteenth hundred, he ceased reckoning any longer. His whole house is filled with ivory; for among the hosts of the slain, more than sixty were tusked elephants. At each door of his verandah stand huge tusks, while, in his dining-room, every corner is adorned with high piles of similar trophies. Most fearful adventures indeed has he gone through. On one occasion an infuriated elephant so trampled and crushed him with its feet and trunk, that it was only the depth of the hole into which the latter had cast him, that was the means of saving his life. Several of his ribs on the right side were broken by this stamping, which is the usual mode in which an elephant despatches his enemy; his right arm was also broken in three places, and the shoulder dislocated besides. He has seen two of his fellow-sportsmen, by similar treatment, perish before his eyes; he himself, of iron constitution, has escaped with his life, and a fearful revenge indeed has he taken for his defeat in that memorable adventure.*

The elephants commit great ravages in the rice-fields and the plantations in these parts. It is calculated that, notwithstanding the frequent hunts, they annually increase by six or eight hundred. The northern parts of the mountain district, which we have not visited, are quite depopulated by them; on the roads which lead across them, the thickest trees are provided with ladders that they may serve as places of refuge for wanderers. The extermination of these wild beasts is therefore, for the present, not to be thought of; a slight consolation or the zoologists of future days.

The hunt of the 2d of December was the last that we witnessed. We now returned to Taldenia, a distance of

* The account given by Major Rogers himself of this fearful adventure was a very remarkable illustration of that wonderful presence of mind by which he was characterized. The infuriated elephant seized him and carried him off in its trunk; his friends followed, and found him lying on the ground with several severe injuries. He related that he had frequently before reflected what he should do under such circumstances, and had resolved to make no struggle or resistance, a resolution which he had kept, and to that he attributed his escape.—TR.

six miles, on untrodden paths. The ascent was so steep on the smooth face of the cliffs, that our horses were forced to scramble like goats, while their riders, leading them by the bridle, were in constant danger of being dragged down and falling with them. Already twilight was drawing on, and we were to arrive at Badulla that evening. Just at the most difficult spot, the misfortune befell me of my horse slipping down into a hollow and breaking the saddle-girth; however, with efficient assistance at hand, the injury was speedily repaired. We passed the BADULLA-OYA, whose waters reached to our waists, and soon found ourselves once more at TALDENIA. Thence we proceeded at a hand gallop; lame as our poor horses were, they were urged on to great speed by vehement laying on of the whip. Nevertheless, night and total darkness overtook us, and a rough and weary journey of ten long miles yet lay before us. Our party was much scattered, and kept together even in groups of two or three with difficulty, and only by dint of calling and screaming. How, in those dark hours, we crossed the slender bamboo bridges, and threaded the steep and narrow paths, without meeting with any misadventure, is to me quite inconceivable.

At BADULLA a rest of three days was agreed upon, and the baggage, grown quite mouldy, was, for the first time for eight days, dried in the sun and thoroughly overhauled. Not a single boot was whole, not an article of raiment remained entire, the linen was beyond the power of any washing to make it white, and the trunks had so completely burst open that we were obliged to fasten them up with ropes. I turn from my stockings and my leather trowsers, which now feel exactly like boards, to conclude, in all haste, the narrative of my journey. We spent the third and fourth of December at Badulla. From thence we set off on the fifth, and on the eighth, after a three days' ride through the mountains, by way of HABOO TALLA and BALLANGODDE, we at length reached RATNAPOORA.*

* "The city of rubies," so called from the gems found among the hills, and along the beds of the small rivulets in the neighbourhood.—TR.

FOURTH LETTER.

RATNAPOORA—THE GEM FISHERY—JOURNEY TO ADAM'S PEAK—MOUNTAIN FORESTS—CEYLON LEECHES—PALABADOOLIA—PILGRIMS' ROAD—LADY BROWNRIGG'S RESTHOUSE—SUMMIT OF ADAM'S PEAK—TEMPLE—RETURN TO COLOMBO.

Patna, 27th January 1845.

I must now carry you back some few miles, to Ceylon, and to the most interesting spot in all the "island of spices," viz. Adam's Peak. We arrived at RATNAPOORA on the 8th of December, and rested in a most inviting bungalow, a country house open on every side,—where we recovered from the fatigues of our journey and the adventurous hardships of elephant-hunting. Two days must needs suffice for that purpose, during which we were entertained,—"*on ne peut pas mieux,*"—by the very youthful, and, in spite of his name, very delicate, President of the district, Mr Power.

The town is charming from the beauty of its situation, although of its ancient monuments nothing now remains; for vegetation and humidity soon destroy what no one ever repairs. Notwithstanding this, an air of antiquity is cast over the whole scene. Scattered over a hill-side, on the banks of the noble KALU-GANGA,—not very close, for the river is a dangerous neighbour,—are the detached buildings, with broad roofs and deep verandahs, which constitute the town. The larger dwellings among them are painted white and yellow, and have a foreground of lovely green turf, with thick flowering shrubs, and large yellow bell-flowers and passion-flowers. Gorgeous bread-fruit-trees, and the species of *Terminalia*, here known, by reason of its fruit, as the Almond-tree, are the chief ornaments of this town;—both are distinguished by their smooth white bark. As the natives here content themselves with merely a slight piece of cotton cloth in the shape of raiment,—so, in like manner, I have not seen a single stem in Ceylon which wears a covering as thick or as rough as that of the sturdy trunks of our oaks at home; nearly every tree here has a polished, shining bark.

One street only, in the town of Ratnapoora, consists of contiguous rows of houses; it is the Bazaar, in which here, as in other towns in Ceylon, the spice-warehouses predominate; for curry is almost the only dish among many thousands of the inhabitants. Here may be seen, however, besides, many interesting productions of Cingalese art and industry. Very frequently, we observed the stone-polishers moving their leaden wheels by means of a sort of violin-bow: their turban and their somewhat lemon-coloured complexion mark them as Moormen.

The celebrated precious stones of Ceylon are brought chiefly from Ratnapoora, and form a principal article of trade. We fortunately happened, on the first day of our stay at that place, to meet with a certain stout little gentleman in a white jacket and trowsers,—a most kind and friendly person,—who accosted us in Dutch with much politeness, introducing himself as the Superintendent of the Gem-fishery. He requested to be allowed the pleasure of doing the honours of the place to His Royal Highness, by causing his men to carry on their fishing operations before him,—for gems are here fished up in a most singular manne , after the fashion of a pearl-fishery.

On the following morning accordingly we wended our way down towards the bank of the river,—the Kalu-

Ganga. There are but few spots at which it shows itself from between the gay border of gigantic bamboos, with their elegant golden stems, and their fresh, verdant, sappy foliage, which grows so thickly on its margin.* At one of these openings, which we reached after a toilsome march through half-submerged fields of rice,—all swarming with land-leeches,—lies the gem-fishery. A small tributary stream, which at this place flows into the Kalu-Ganga, forms the treasure-bed. Here we saw six reddish-brown natives, standing in the water, which reached up to their breasts, and working about in it

* The real Bamboo, (*Bambusa Arundinacea*) as distinguished from the many species of tall and luxuriant reeds or canes which travellers often dignify with that name. Its manifold uses among the Chinese are well known. Travellers indeed assure us that, in the Celestial Empire, scarcely any thing is to be found by sea or by land into the composition of which bamboo does not in some way enter: bridges of bamboo we have already found alluded to by our Author;—ropes and sails are formed by twisting or plaiting split bamboos: houses are constructed of them,—walls, roofs and gutters; to say nothing of all the furniture they contain,—mats, screens, chairs, tables, bedsteads, bedding, &c. &c. The young shoots, boiled or pickled, are a favourite article of food in some Eastern countries; and in China, in addition to all these uses, which are more or less common also in Ceylon, we must not omit to mention its value as a material for manufacturing paper. This is made of the second bark and ligneous substance of the first year's shoots, which,—after being steeped in muddy water for about fifteen days, then covered with lime, and then again washed and bleached,—are boiled in large coppers. Next follows the operation of crushing with a pestle, by which the whole mass is reduced to a thin paste. The paper is finally made by mixing gum-water, and the juice of a particular kind of plant, with this paste, in the large reservoirs out of which it is taken in bamboo-moulds. Naturalists describe several varieties of *Bambusa Arundinacea,* known in India and in the adjacent islands, all of which grow to the height of a tree. The *Bamboo Ily* of Malabar, which, like the Talipot tree, flowers but once, grows to the height of sixty-six feet. The *Bamboo Zelin,* of Java and Malacca, reaches that of fifty feet. But the variety most common in India has been described by many travellers as growing even as high as eighty feet. In the Moluccas, flutes and fishing-rods, pikes and arrows, tobacco-pipes and writing-pens, are numbered among the endless uses of some peculiar species of bamboo. While some kinds are mere hollow reeds, others have hard and solid ligneous stems. In Ceylon, as in other Oriental lands, most dangerous effects arise, in case of fire, from the use of hollow bamboos in building houses, the confined and rarified air within them bursting forth with a tremendous explosion. —TR.

with long mattocks. They were standing in an oblique line across the stream, and shovelling up from its bed, against the current, the mud, in which the precious stones are contained. The depth of the hollow, which they had thus dug in the channel, was apparently not less than twelve or fourteen feet. They collected all the slime or mud into heaps at their feet; there the water as it flowed on, washed away the finer particles of silt, so that the coarse sand and clayey gravel only remained. Every half-hour they dipped down, holding flat baskets in their hands, which they brought up full; they then swung them backwards and forwards in the water, with much caution and neatness, to separate all the lighter parts of their contents, after which they carried the baskets filled with coarse sand and gravel to the shore, there to undergo examination. Besides granulous lime and lumps of blue clay and flakes of mica, there was contained in the mass thus fished up, a gaily variegated sand formed of fragments of quartz, feltspar, rubies and topazes. Rubies of large size are extremely rare, and fine sapphires yet more so; topazes on the contrary, or yellow and yellowish-green sapphires falsely called topazes, are more frequently met with.

Unfortunately for us, not one fine gem was fished up that day, save perhaps some few dark blue sapphires, which were not of very particular beauty. Meantime I amused myself by watching the magnanimous composure of the worthy Dutchman, who, clad in his white jacket, and never for a moment partod from his clay-pipe, gazed with unruffled serenity the whole day long, at the unproductive labours of his gem-fishers.

The following day (the 9th of December), by the time we had concluded a very hearty breakfast, cavalry horses were standing in readiness at our door to carry us to the foot of Adam's Peak. The weather was mild and lovely: the early part of our road, passing over the richest turf, traversed plantations of slender and delicate Areca palms, whose graceful crests, by the bye, my eye misses sadly in India. We proceeded among cocoa-nut and spreading umbrageous bread-fruit trees, which conceal low and homely cottages built of loam; under the shadow of their broad roofs may be seen groups of black-haired, naked children playing in the shade, while their mothers, —wrapped in light webs of white cloth, and wearing massive rings of silver on their ancles,—are diligently turning the spindle replenished with wool. The husband sits there beside his industrious spouse, and imagines,—like our tobacco-smokers lounging on their sofas,—that he is abundantly occupying his every moment, while he chews his betel, and calculates, perchance, how long the clusters of bananas hanging over his head may yet last. On all sides one sees either groups of cottages or scattered dwellings, and nowhere is it possible to point out the spot at which a village begins or ends.

The surrounding accompaniments of the more distant villages are rural and attractive in no ordinary degree. The aspect of their well-cultivated fields is far more varied than that presented by the crops of wheat, barley and oats, which chequer our home landscapes. I never beheld a more exquisite verdure than the fresh velvety green of the young rice, before it is in blossom; beside it are fields of "*coracan*," *(Eleusine coracana)* clad in sober brown,—others in which the rich ears of yellow maize already begin to swell, and yet others in which may be seen the different grasses here cultivated as grain. Everywhere, even when only a single row of houses bordered our road, we found the accustomed triumphal gateway,—a simple arch, over which the golden-tinged verdure of the young cocoa-nut leaf was gracefully twined, while the centre never failed to be adorned by the beautiful blue flower-sheath of the banana, and a gay profusion of fruits and flowers.*

For nearly two miles our road was lined on either side with garlands of exquisite creepers,—whose luxuriant tendrils furnish thread to fasten the wreath,—mingled with bamboo canes and palm or cocoa-nut foliage. The arranging of these elegant playthings, connected as they are with all the pomp and circumstance of many a ceremony, forms a favourite amusement among the indolent Cingalese, and whole villages volunteer their services in erecting arches or in weaving festoons.

At each triumphal arch, a troop of peasants in festive attire, their hoary-bearded chiefs at their head, was usually assembled to see and to salute the Prince.

We soon passed the limits of the lowland country; wild brooks and rivers, flowing between steep and rugged banks, began to offer no slight difficulties to the unskilful rider: the way became narrower and the ascent more abrupt, and soon we found ourselves skirting the edge of bold precipices, commanding glorious mountain views. How splendid is the picture formed by a rich palm-grove, with blue mountains towering into the clear sky behind, and soft wooded hills in the nearer distance; and how fresh and fragrant are the thick bushes which clothe the fore-ground! Rare plants here displayed their beauties around us; among them the wondrous Pitcher-plant, (*Nepenthes distillatoria*) with its curious little vessel suspended at the point of each leaf, was growing luxuriantly in the coppice, twining its tendrils round every bush, and waving its long pitchers, often nearly a foot in length, from every branch. From time to time, at a turn or opening of the path,

* Dr Davy, when travelling with the Governor, Sir Robert Brownrigg, in 1817, saw many of these decorated archways, which the Cingalese take such delight in erecting, formed by transplanting whole trees of the Banana or plantain bodily.—Tr.

we were agreeably surprised by a view of Adam's Peak itself,—with its slender, pointed summit,—suddenly bursting upon us. Meantime we had yet—before reaching the mountain—to pass through three deep valleys, fording a multitude of rushing streams, and toiling down their steep banks and up again.

Now, however, the forest assumes an aspect of lofty grandeur. The well known Bo-tree *(Ficus religiosa)*, and two other species of Indian Fig-tree, all of them without fruit, and quite unlike any other tree in appearance, with some twenty or more sturdy stems, all meeting in a single crown above, produce a wonderful and strange effect. Here the tall Ebony-tree seems to pierce the azure vault with its sombre, almost black, foliage, which hangs around the white stem only after it has risen in solitary and leafless magnificence to the height of forty feet above the ground; beside it the Calamander, and the *Pterocarpus Sandalinus* (Red-Sandal-wood tree); they are both however much more rare. Pepper vines and a profusion of very beautiful Ferns so cover nearly every stem, that it is often difficult to distinguish the actual foliage of the tree itself; each twig moreover nourishes a multitude of superbly-flowering parasites, generally of the honey-suckle and epidendrum tribes.

Here, in this region of noble forests and redundant vegetation, at a height of at least sixteen hundred feet above the sea, the difficulty of the ascent increases considerably. The moisture which is continually trickling down, has transformed the narrow path into a tangled mass of slippery roots twisted across the steep sides of the rocks. We were obliged to have our horses led on before us, which was not particularly agreeable where the blood streaming down their legs made us conscious of the more than ordinary abundance of those land-leeches which are the true plague of Ceylon. Rain having fallen on the previous day, millions of them had been lured out; they soon covered our clothes, and doubtless sought to spy every opening, however small in order to torment us horribly. The most careful and ingenious precautions in the way of covering our feet and legs were all in vain; for these little creatures, which are often no thicker than a needle, work their way through the stuff, or else crawl up to the neck, where they are still more disagreeable. Our Cingalese attendants suffered less than we did, in spite of their bare feet, for they have an art by which they very cleverly strip off these cunning foes.

Now again, the forest is interrupted by a flat space, overgrown with jungle so deep and dense, that the traveller, if he stray from the right path, may sink in its dark mazes and be absolutely lost. At the extremity of this plain lies PALABADOOLLA, a small place consisting of a few mean huts, chiefly inhabited by priests, with shaven heads and yellow robes. One of the huts had been arranged and decked out for our reception; that is to say, the walls—consisting of mats woven together and plastered with cow-dung—were hung with a gay drapery of red and white cotton; four posts had been stuck into the mud-floor, and cross sticks placed on the top of them to form a table, and a low, broad bench made of plaited twigs had been placed beside it to represent at once beds and chairs. The sportsmen set out on a shooting excursion before dinner, from which they returned, bringing few birds indeed, but a plentiful supply of leeches.

After a few hours' rest, we started with early dawn, on the 10th of December,—leaving all our luggage behind us,—for the ascent of Adam's Peak. Here the tropical vegetation ceases; long ere now we had bid farewell to the palmy groves;—yet for some distance further, the thick and gloomy forest, with its masses of dark verdure, cast on us a welcome shade as we proceeded on our toilsome climb. We had nothing now before us but to clamber up the steep ascent, over the wet, smooth rocks, or the slippery roots, without a halt or a resting-place.

As the path up to Adam's Peak is annually trod by many thousands of pilgrims,—Mahometans as well as Brahmins and Buddhists,—one might expect to find there an easy way; but on the contrary, nothing has been done but what was absolutely indispensable; here, against a cliff so steep as to be quite impassable, a ladder of feeble twigs has been placed;—there, in some peculiarly polished and slippery part, a few steps have been hewn out of the living rock. With these exceptions, the gnarled roots of the *Sideroxylon*, (Iron-wood tree) and the *Laurus*, (Bay-tree) are the only evidences to mark that human feet have traversed these solitudes. But these are indeed sufficient to prove that this must have been a beaten track for centuries; for how many a step must have been imprinted, ere naked feet could have left their traces on these hard and imperishable sorts of wood; and yet in many spots the roots actually appear like worn-out flights of steps! After a fatiguing march of an hour and a half, we came to the ruins of a small house, in which we rested for a few moments; the chill and most unpleasant misty wind warning us not to linger long. Shortly afterwards, we passed the last broad bed of a river, a place not unlike the Bodekessel at the Rosztrappe in the Harz Mountains; but what a lavish profusion of flowers! Out of the bare slabs of rock spring three varieties of Balsams, each of which might be the ornament of our green-houses, while in other places, a luxuriant carpet of exquisite ferns and mosses is spread over the black cliffs; the former, so elegant in the forms of their leaves, that it seemed as though the fantastic imaginings of some gifted artist had been pencilled before our eyes. The splendid flowers of the tropics here give place to a fresh, vigorous Alpine vegetation; many things reminded me of our own mountain glens;—the *Germander*, ("Forget-me-not,") and *Crucianella* ("Cross-wort,") look quite like Europe; but their colours are more vivid, they have somewhat of tropical brilliancy, and seem to be fashioned on a larger scale.

Climbing several steep rocks,—on whose surface are chiselled figures of Buddha and very ancient inscriptions,—we scrambled on with the aid of hen-roost ladders and roughly hewn steps. Now the path led us, to our great annoyance, after having ascended the abrupt elevation, down a no less abrupt declivity; now we were forced to wade, for a quarter of an hour, through running water; or again, to scale cliffs so smooth, and as it were polished, that to fall was inevitable, and to escape with unbroken bones, almost more than we could hope for. How delicious and refreshing here were the fruits of the burning zones that now lay far beneath us,—the cocoa-nuts and the oranges, which our natives had carried up with us! Those Cingalese were running and springing in advance of the party, like goats, though they were bearing heavy burdens on their heads; they climb the smooth rock so nimbly and easily with their barefeet, that I began to esteem our pilgrimage as far more meritorious than that of the unshod Buddhists.

Much fatigued, we arrived towards the end of our fourth hour, at one of the elevated platforms, a level, open space; the sharp peak,—a single conical mass of rock,—rises majestically beyond it. It was the first time that we had beheld its full outline; but, how were we ever to gain its summit? The feet of a fly or of a lizard seemed to be indispensable requisites for accomplishing that exploit. A small rest-house stands in the centre of the little valley. Its interior presents nothing but bare, grey walls; the light finding its way in through the door: a most uninviting abode we should have pronounced it, had not the blazing fire kindled by our excellent cook, and the savoury fumes of his most distinguished curry, promised us some comfort. Soon however we were driven by a sharp current of air,—to which, spoiled by the climate and the dwellings of Ceylon,* we had become extremely sensitive,—from within the inhospitable walls of "*Lady Brownrigg's Rest-house.*" This lady had indeed actually been there, and the building had been erected at her expense. I regard her, in her pedestrian activity, with far higher esteem than Countess X———, who was dragged up the Pyramids by her arms: the ascent here is in many parts no less steep, and far more slippery.

You will easily believe that, having been accustomed in the lowland valleys, to a heat of from 22° to 24° (about 81° to 86° Fahrenheit) we felt the air now, at a level of nearly six thousand feet, cool and thin. But indeed the thermometer had fallen even here only to 14° (59° Fahrenheit) which at home, is not reckoned cold enough for lighting our fires.

We were still separated from the Peak by a valley, or more properly speaking, by one deep glen and two narrow ravines; it really provoked me thus to be obliged to descend again, and to relinquish the advantage I had but just gained with so much toil and trouble. On arriving at the actual base of the cone or peak, we observed

* A curious contrast in this respect to the dwellings of European residents on the continent of India, as subsequently described by our author, where artificial refrigeration is promoted by a constant thorough draught. Major Forbes thus alludes to the precautions against malaria so necessary in Ceylon: "The malaria generated in flats or jungle districts might in a great degree be prevented by having the houses, particularly the sleeping apartments, elevated at least six feet above the ground. Permanent Cingalese houses are always raised considerably above the surrounding country, and constructed so as to prevent a current of air passing either through the inner court or any of the surrounding chambers."—Tr.

a remarkable change in the vegetation. But lately we had once more found ourselves amidst shady wood; here it suddenly ceased, and we should according to one's usual experience in ascending lofty mountains, have expected to meet with pines and firs, but of such trees there is not the slightest trace; any more than of the beautiful *Gentians* of the Alps, or of the lovely *Ericas*. But what a glorious compensation! The naked rock cannot indeed here produce trees of lofty stem and spreading shade, like those we had left behind us; but their place is immediately supplied by a forest of magnificent Tree-Rhododendrons, from fifteen to twenty feet high, which predominates more and more towards the summit. The dwarf underwood between them consists of myrtle-like plants, many of which have a delicious fragrance.

From time to time we had splendid panoramic views of the mountain glens and the lower ranges of hills; and in a deep vista below, but at no great distance, a narrow stripe of the sea,—of whose immediate proximity we could scarcely persuade ourselves,—was glancing brightly in the sunshine. The mountain is not higher than those which travellers commonly climb in Switzerland; but no where in that land can the eye measure the height, by comparison with a plain so nearly on the level of the sea. On that side of the peak on which the path leads up, all vegetation ceases at some six hundred feet below the highest point; not indeed by reason of the great height, but because the summit is one single huge mass of rock, —gneiss with hornblende,—without the least covering of soil on its steep sides. Here the traveller, if at all inclined to giddiness, can scarcely escape suffering from it. A most singular expedient has been resorted to for diminishing the dangers and difficulties of pilgrims in the way. To hew steps in these mighty rocks, would have been too great an undertaking; instead of attempting it, numberless chains, of every variety of link, are riveted into the living stone. They hang in dozens to the right and to the left; some antique and rusty, some of newest stamp; for it is esteemed a meritorious work to lay one of these chains along the path, that so, if any pilgrim should chance to fall, he may be caught in this iron net-work. After dragging myself up for some fifty paces or so, as if by a windlass, I reached a sort of flat landing place, upon which one may set foot to ground firmly, and enjoy a breathing-time; but immediately I beheld, to my horror, an overhanging precipice, which I could scale only after a most aerial fashion, by the help of strong iron chains. The end of the ascent is extremely disagreeable; an iron stair is here suspended in the air, and has been so completely forced out of its original position, that the steps are now nearly perpendicular. When this last difficulty has been overcome, the cry of "Land, Land!" may at last be raised, and the pilgrimage is completed!

The Prince was the first to gain the summit, followed by Count O——. I had too many plants packed all about my person, besides being encumbered with the weight of sundry apparatus, to allow of my sharing the honour. A stair leads up to the entrance of the walled enclosure which surrounds the apex of the peak. The flat space within the wall, in the centre of which this highest cone rises, measures about seventy feet by thirty. The height of the conical apex is about eight or nine feet. The whole of the eastern side is resplendent with the gorgeous scarlet blossoms of the *Rhododendron arboreum*, and an exuberant abundance of other flowers of unrivalled beauty luxuriates among the thick grass. Everything that here meets the eye is strange and wonderful. The most singular object is a small temple of iron-wood, adorned with much carved work, under a low roof of tiles: I should think it is about eight feet in height, and covers a space of ten feet square. Within is to be seen the holy relic which attracts such multitudes of pilgrims, the celebrated "*Sree Pada,*" or sacred footstep, believed by the Cingalese Christians and Mahometans to be that of Adam; by the Buddhists, of Gautama Buddha; and by the Brahmins, of Siva. The rocky mass, on which this footstep is engraven, forms the floor of the little wooden edifice, dignified with the name of temple. There is certainly here to be seen something resembling a foot-print, an impression between five and six feet in length, and upwards of two feet in width, in which the partitions of the toes are very clumsily restored or formed with gypsum; but what cripples should we all have been, if our great progenitor Adam had stood on feet like this! The mark of the sacred footstep is enclosed within a golden frame, studded with gems of considerable size, a few only of which are genuine.

Here, upon this desolate spot, thousands annually perform their superstitious devotions. The rule prescribed for pilgrims is, to scale the mountain in a single march, and then, having offered up their prayers, and presented their sacrifices of money or of fruits, at the shrine, to descend without casting one look around,—a most arduous exploit indeed! Under the roof of this sanctuary, a filthy-looking priest was idly lounging beside a dish containing some pieces of money: a significant wink intimated to us his expectations. On a few shillings being cast in, the servant of the god hastily gathered them up, and set down the tempting money-plate in its proper place.*

* As our author was precluded, by the season at which he ascended the Peak, from witnessing the proceedings of pilgrims on its summit, some notice of them here may not be unwelcome to the reader; we therefore quote Dr Davy's account of the pictuesque scene:—"The next morning, immediately before sun-rise, we were wakened by the shouts of a party of pilgrims just arrived; . . . . . . it consisted of several men and women, native Cingalese

For a very short time only, after arriving on the summit, did we enjoy the extensive prospect, which, though magnificent and striking, is certainly rather too monotonous to be called beautiful. All around nothing meets the eye but mountain-tops, clothed with thick and verdant forests; this ceaseless wood covers almost everything that could add the charm of variety to the scene. The mountain features of the landscape immediately surrounding the Peak, are so lofty that scarce any part of the low country beyond is to be seen, and merely an occasional glimpse of the ocean. We had gazed but a few minutes at the view, when a fresh north-west wind enveloped, first the more distant summits,—then those near at hand,—and, lastly, the peak itself, in a rolling drapery of dense mist. Thus isolated, we bid adieu to the world without, and wrapping ourselves in our Greek "*capotes*," we sought shelter in our huts, the walls of which consisted, as usual, of bamboos interwoven with palm-leaves, while the only comforts they contained

of the interior, all neatly dressed in clean clothes. They immediately proceeded to their devotions: a priest, in his yellow robes, stood on the rock close to the impression of the foot, with his face to the people, who had ranged themselves in a row below; some on their knees, with their hands uplifted and joined palm to palm, and others bending forward, with their hands in the same attitude of devotion. The priest, in a loud, clear voice, sentence by sentence, recited the articles of their religious faith and duties; and, in response, they repeated the same after him. When he had finished, they raised a loud shout; and, he retiring, they went through the same ceremony by themselves, with one of their party for their leader. An interesting scene followed this: wives affectionately and respectfully saluted their husbands, children their parents, and friends one another. An old grey-headed woman first made her salams to a really venerable old man; she was moved to tears, and nearly kissed his feet; he affectionately raised her up. Several middle-aged men then salamed the patriarchal pair; these men were salamed in return by still younger men, who had first paid their respects to the old people; and lastly, those nearly of the same standing slightly salamed each other, and exchanged betel-leaves. The intention of these salutations, I was informed, was of a moral kind,—to confirm the ties of kindred,—to strengthen family love and friendship, and to remove animosities. . . . . . . Before the pilgrims descend, they are blessed by the priest, and exhorted to return to their homes, and lead in future virtuous lives."—Tr.

were three benches formed of sticks, and a table to correspond. A sharp wind from the north-west was whistling so keenly through our by no means air-tight walls, and the atmosphere felt so frosty, when, drawing our cloaks closely round us, we lay down to sleep after our repast was ended, that we rose in turns through the night, to rekindle, by means of exercise, some life and warmth in our benumbed limbs.

At six o'clock in the morning of the 11th of December, the thermometer had fallen to 6 above the freezing point (46° Fahrenheit); we therefore all gladly welcomed the proposal of being speedily on the move for our return. On reaching the lower end of the chains,—after descending a part which now seemed even more nervous than it had done on the ascent, notwithstanding our being preserved by a sea of white mist, from the giddiness of a bird's eye survey over the panorama that lay deep below,—we observed the undoubted traces of an elephant, a neighbour whose nearness we had little suspected during the past night. If an animal so colossal can indeed find means, with the aid of bushes, to drag its ponderous limbs up these precipitous masses of rock, the question next occurs, how can he successfully accomplish the descent; for to scramble down is far more difficult than to climb up?* This we knew for certain by our own experience; for we could only proceed down

* Major Forbes adduces, in proof of the hardihood of the elephant, the fact that in Ceylon "it ranges over every part of the island, voluntarily clambering to the summits of the highest mountains, and undergoing a change of temperature which, from the plains of Bintenne to the top of the Pedrotalla-galla, is sometimes not less than 50°, with a difference of elevation of full eight thousand feet." Among other illustrations of his theory that "the instinct of the elephant is not of that superior order usually assigned to it," the same writer mentions its adventurous temerity, in a manner quite tallying with the remarks of our author: he says,—"it is fond of clambering up steep hills, and does not shun slippery rocks, on which so clumsy an animal is necessarily insecure. I have known three instances in the Matale district alone, of elephants being killed by falling down precipices."—Tr.

these steep paths by springing and rushing forward without a halt, which caused no small concussion of our vertebral and bony system, while more serious and really deplorable results followed from the injuries inflicted on the system of boots and shoes!

It had been settled that the whole distance, which in the ascent had occupied six hours and a half, was to be traversed now at one pull;—we were to be at the foot of the Peak in four hours;—but, alas! in one hour and a half our whole party was scattered, and each was scrambling on his solitary way as best he could. As I lingered to gather seeds and plants, or to hammer stones, I was now far in the rear, and now again leading the van, so that I had an opportunity of witnessing the sufferings of each individual of our long train. Here, one was limping on with a sole-less shoe; there, another was running almost barefoot; while our afore-named friend, Mr Power, exhausted by exertions to which he was unaccustomed, was supported by two natives. The Prince was soon an hour in advance of all the rest. When I at length arrived at Palabadoolla, with my pockets heavily laden, I found his Royal Highness fast asleep!

At this place we made only a short halt, necessary in order to exchange our tattered habiliments for others; after which we moved on with weary limbs, through the odious part of the country infested with leeches, towards the spot where our horses were to be in readiness. No horses were there; we were therefore obliged to proceed on foot, wading through a deep brook, with the dismal prospect before us of running on, footsore as we all were, for nine or ten miles. We had begun to resign ourselves to our hard fate, when the tardy steeds made their appearance. We now rode on swiftly to Ratnapoora, where a little repose was granted to our worn-out limbs, whose every joint ached for a long time afterwards. On the 13th of December, we sailed, in a large boat, most tastefully decked with garlands of fruit and flowers, down the beautiful Kalu Ganga to CALTURA. It was a charming voyage, and, as we glided along, many monkeys and beautiful birds fell by our sportsmen's guns.

Arriving at Caltura on the evening of the second day, the (14th of December) we found one of the Governor's carriages in waiting, which conveyed us in an hour and an half to Colombo. There we were hospitably entertained for five days more, at the end of which time we embarked on board the English war-steamer, "Spiteful," Captain Maitland, for TRINCOMALEE.

FIFTH LETTER.

DEPARTURE FROM COLOMBO—TRINCOMALEE—MADRAS—THE ROCK-TEMPLES OF MAHAMALAIPUR—CALCUTTA—LORD HARDINGE'S PALACE—BARRACKPORE—THE PALANQUIN—FLATS OF BENGAL—GAYA—ENVIRONS OF THE TOWN—TEMPLE OF VISHNUPADDA—THE PRIESTS—PATNA—OPIUM CULTIVATION.

PATNA, *28th of January*, 1845.

ON the afternoon of the 18th of December, we took our departure, in the splendid war-steamer Spiteful,—placed at the Prince's disposal by Queen Victoria,—from the beautiful town of Colombo, from the kind old Governor, from our dear friend and companion Captain Maclean, and from many other kind friends and acquaintances. Rounding the southern extremity of the island, we landed, after two days, on its north-eastern coast, in one of the most beautiful harbours of the world, that of TRINCOMALEE. Two days were passed in the chase, and in catching insects, amidst the magnificent forests that clothe the shores, and the little islands by which the harbour is closed in. The Admiral gave us a costly and brilliant entertainment in his fairy palace on shore; and we enjoyed rides along the coast, under the ever-smiling sky which seemed to gaze upon the responsive smiles of the placid ocean.

When these two days had flown, we bid farewell to the lovely island, not without deep regret. The feeling was universal among us, that we were in all probability leaving behind us the most beautiful part of our travels. We had scarcely cleared the harbour (on the 22d of December) when the sea became very rough: we had a very bad passage, and suffered much from sea-sickness. On the 24th, we reached MADRAS, a beautiful and imposing city;—mountains alone are wanting to make the scene incomparably fine. The Governor, the Marquis of Tweeddale, vacated his whole palace for our reception, and went into the country, without troubling himself much about us. The pride and pomp of the English "*haute noblesse*" are, here in India, yet more intolerable than in London; for here persons assume the air of Princes, who, in their native land, would only play a subordinate part. I was, at any rate, spared much ceremony by this treatment; and the only oppression was the many dozens of servants, in red and white attire, with "*chowries*" and peacock-tails, who with noiseless tread followed our every movement.

After a succession of grand dinner-parties, and a wonderful Christmas fête, on a terrace paved with marble,* illuminated with countless bright chandeliers, and fragrant with the perfumes of a thousand flowers, wafted by the fresh sea-breeze,—altogether resembling a scene in fairy-land,—we quitted Madras on the 28th of December, and sailed upon a rough and tempestuous sea, some distance southward, to visit the rock sanctuaries of the famous temple-city of MAHAMALAIPUR. We were kindly accompanied by Mr Elliot, a gentleman well versed in natural science, who was to explain to us the wonders of these architectural monuments. The place is about thirty-five miles to the south of Madras. We were borne over the surf and landed on the shore with

* The pavements, walls and pillars, so frequently supposed by strangers to be of marble, are in reality plastered with "*chunam*," a kind of fine lime, in common use throughout India, but for which Madras is particularly famous: it is there made of calcined shells, and, being susceptible of a fine polish, is employed in the decoration of those villas scattered among gardens and avenues to the south of Fort George, which constitute the European town of Madras.—TR.

great difficulty, in a fragile bark, whose planks were fastened with cocoa-nut fibres ("*coir*") instead of nails, and stopped with tow; it was kept in motion by twelve wild-looking rowers, stripped to the skin, and plying their oars to the measured sound of horrid cries and screams, under the name of singing. The coast is very flat, yet I have never seen a higher surf. Our Hindoos availed themselves most skilfully of the rushing flow of the last huge wave, to deposit us, without too complete a soaking, on dry land.

On the shore I found large fragments of extremely fine-grained gray syenite scattered through the coppice. Further on, I found the same stone in immense blocks, forming large platforms, with deep hollows like small lakes, which, notwithstanding the immediate neighbourhood of the ocean, are filled with fresh water. A piece of rocky ground,—not unlike the "*Devil's Wall*," in the Harz Mountains,—contains the wonderful remains of the primeval sanctuaries: each rocky mass is transformed into a splendid temple, with beautiful figures and sculptured ornaments, all hewn in the living rock.

The first monuments which presented themselves to our view were at a distance of about four hundred paces from the edge of the waves;—two masses of solid rock, some eighty feet or so in length, and, I should think, from forty to fifty in height, separated from each other by a narrow cleft, and covered from top to bottom with finely executed figures, most of them as large as life. Upon the wall to the left side of the cleft, the principal figure that strikes the eye is that of a penitent, Arjuna, who is represented standing on his left foot, with his arms crossed above his head. On his left stands the god Iswara, pointing to him with one hand. Close beside these and above them, are several rows of figures, with a very singular head-dress, half-kneeling, half-walking, doing homage to the penitent. The two lower rows again consist of animal figures only,—monkeys, lions, tigers, antelopes and birds. It is remarkable that several of the figures,—chiefly those on the right-hand side,—are looking towards the cleft, into which is stuck a female figure with a lofty head-dress; though this statue, also of hewn stone, is evidently of more recent date. On the solid block, to the right-hand side, are the principal objects of the whole scene,—a very beautifully executed elephant with its young one, almost as large as life, and in excellent preservation, except that the tusk is broken off. It stands next to the ground; above it again, are seen two rows of male and female figures, in attitudes of devotion. These are of peculiarly beautiful workmanship, and sculptured in bold alto-relievo.

Proceeding in a south-westerly direction, we soon found ourselves in front of the first of the seven temples hewn in the rock. It contains a cave, the roof of which is supported by eight pillars, while empty niches appear at the farther extremity. In another is found the recumbent image of the god Vishnu, with his left knee raised up, and a female figure sitting upon it. The largest of these cavern temples contains, in the background, a very fine basso-relievo. Vishnu is supporting with one hand a falling vault: there is much power and expression in this figure: the two females also, shrinking back in terror, are by no means bad; but unfortunately the moisture which continually trickles down has done considerable damage. Several architectural remains in the neighbourhood are easily distinguished as of more modern date, by their being formed of hewn stones joined together, instead of being excavated and sculptured in the living rock; many of them are however also in very good taste.*

* Probably the same mentioned by Mr Hamilton in his "*Account of Hindostan*," as "a pagoda of stone, and dedicated to *Siva*," whereas "all

Our return to the ship was more dangerous than our landing, as the breakers drove us back towards the shore. The billowy walls, towering to the height of ten feet, at first appeared impregnable, and twice was our rude Indian bark dashed back upon the coast with a crashing sound; at length however the dauntless sailors succeeded in bringing us safely across the swell. The native boats are wooden vessels, like large shapeless cauldrons, ten or twelve feet in depth. Their thin planks are fastened together with cocoa-nut ligatures, which gives them such elasticity, that they can endure the most violent shocks without going to pieces. Their great depth keeps them well above the water. Pieces of wood are fastened across the boat, adding firmness to the whole, and serving as seats to the rowers. The latter are, by reason of the great length of their oars, not unfrequently thrown overboard, and on this account, a boat of this sort known by the name of "*Mussoolah*," is usually accompanied by a smaller craft, called "*Catamarran*," the duty of which is to pick up any person who may fall into the water. The "*Catamarran*" consists merely of three or four thick logs of wood, upon which the rower kneels and paddles with a board, sometimes

the most ancient buildings and monuments at Mahabalipuram, (Mahamalaipur) are consecrated to *Vishnu*." The place is commonly known by the name of "*the Seven Pagodas*," though in fact that number of temples does not exist there. The modern name of Mahabalipuram signifies the "*city of the great Bali*," a character very famous in Hindoo romance. The sculptures are supposed by some writers to refer chiefly to the exploits of that deified hero, as well as to those of Krishna, Arjuna, and other actors in the war celebrated in the "*Mahabarat*." Mr Hamilton mentions the appearance of the lion,—represented as much larger than the natural size,—as remarkable, from the fact of that animal being unknown in the south of India. He supposes the whole of the sculptures to have been rent by some convulsion of nature before they were finished. Brahminical tradition records the existence of a great capital near these temples, and the raging surf, believed to have encroached on the coast of Coromandel generally, is said here to break over the ruined monuments of a forgotten splendour. By some however the seat of the Great Bali's kingdom is placed on the western coast of India.—TR.

to his left and sometimes to his right side. A vessel, or rather raft, of this description is often swallowed by the waves, and as often rises again to the surface. The only article of clothing worn by its sailors is a sharp conical straw hat, shaped like a long paper cornet, in which they usually carry letters on board, from residents on shore.

On nearing the steamer, a fresh difficulty presented itself, as to jumping out on the ladder to climb her side; for we were now too low by a few yards, now again too high, to set foot upon it, so violently was our boat tossed up and down by the waves.*

We arrived, after a six days' voyage, within the domain of the GANGES, and, on the 3d of January, landed in the city of Calcutta. We were received in the palace of the Governor-General, Lord Hardinge,† a residence far handsomer than the Castle of many a German Prince.

CALCUTTA is not a place that would please me in the long run. The city is a strange medley of, on the one hand, the most splendid palaces, and on the other, the most wretched bamboo huts. The population is no less diversified. Here the eye is struck by "coolies," or porters, their burdens poised upon their heads; or palanquin-bearers, of reddish brown complexion, who run about, through the live-long day, with their heavy pole on their bare shoulders; there, by filthy Mahometans, driving before them a pair of mean and unsightly bullucks yoked to a cart, formed of bamboos roughly fas-

* A difficulty by no means unheard of to most natives of our sea-girt land, but which, to a traveller whose home was so far inland, and whose only embarkations hitherto had been amid the facilities of frequented ports, might well appear an adventure worthy of being recorded among the perils of the mighty deep!—TR.

† We copy, in this instance, without correction. Our author, from a confusion into which foreigners,—puzzled by the dignity of high official rank and the familiar English sound of "*my Lord*,"—often fall, and which led him to commit one or two other mistakes regarding proper names, designates the Governor-General by a title which he did not live to see conferred upon him.—TR.

tened together, with creaking solid wooden wheels; or again, by the most elegant equipages on the face of the earth, drawn by horses of the noblest Arab blood; seated within, are gay and fashionable ladies; mounted behind, livery servants glittering with Indian gold and stuffs of the finest tissue; thus one is surrounded at once by the utmost splendour and the greatest poverty, the proudest pomp and the most abject degradation.

In this place every one is held in servile dependance on the etiquette of distinguished society. To appear on foot is held quite inadmissible; only the brown Hindoos of the lower castes think of doing such a thing. A palanquin, or a carriage, is the proper and genteel mode of conveyance.

The innumerable domestics of the palace, who watch one's every step, but, to those who cannot make themselves intelligible to them, are not available for any real service, seem to me even more oppressive here than the similar hosts at Madras or at Colombo. I am provoked to anger or to laughter, when I am panting for a glass of water, and the servant brings me ink.

The uniform of these dark and handsome men is extremely tasteful and showy. Most of them wear scarlet coats, loaded on the breast with gold lace, and flat turbans, also of scarlet, with white centres. The upper servants are old men, with fine hoary beards,—a picturesque contrast to their long garments of bright red, adorned with a profusion of gold embroidery. The runners, grooms and coachmen, are equipped in shorter coats of dark blue, flat turbans of the same colour with red crowns, and short white breeches; those in charge of the plate, the treasurer of the household, and the upper and under servants of his department, wear white coats, blue sashes, and white turbans with blue centres. The total number of domestics required in the Government House is three hundred and seventy two!

The climate here is most agreeably temperate and spring-like; indeed there is a marked difference, if we compare it with Ceylon; for there are but few flowers here at present, and the trees have generally lost at least part of their foliage; yet, notwithstanding these appearances, the noon-day heat is overwhelming, and it is impossible to venture out of the house before four o'clock. At that hour the scene becomes gradually more animated upon the "*Course*," a broad street near the river, kept constantly moist by means of water sprinkled from leather tubes. There the "*haut ton*" of the English population are assembled, in carriages or on horseback, all in the finest toilets. Every one bows and is bowed to, and so presses on through the crowd, which often, towards five o'clock, is very considerable. As certainly as every fine gentleman takes his "*tiffin*" at one o'clock, and enjoys his "*siesta*" at three,—so certainly is he to be seen on the "Course" at five, in elegant equestrian costume, not omitting white kid gloves. There yet remains the toilsome operation of dressing for a seven o'clock dinner-party, and the exertion that must needs be made to enjoy it; and then, about nine or half-past nine o'clock, the hard day's work of a man of fashion in this metropolis is completed. He may stretch himself upon the sofa and smoke a cigar, till it is time to exchange his vigils for the charms of sleep, by throwing himself into the four-post bed which invites him to repose, with its gauze curtains, and more than a dozen of pillows.

During the whole of our stay, there was no lack of splendid dinners, concerts, &c., &c.; a ball was moreover given in honour of the Prince; but I could form no judgment as to the merits of these entertainments, for a multitude of necessary occupations gave me so much running hither and thither through the day, that all desire to join in the dance had passed away. For the same reason I could only pay flying visits to the museum and the beautiful Botanic Garden.

We spent some time at the Governor-General's very pretty country residence at Barrackpore, at no great distance from Calcutta. There is an aviary and a beautiful menagerie, in which are to be found remarkably fine specimens of the Entellus—and Hooloc monkeys and pheasants of almost every kind met with in the Himalayas.

On the 12th of January, I paid a visit to Dr Wallich,* the Superintendent of the Botanic Garden, which is a perfect Paradise, charmingly situated on the banks of the Ganges. I went down the river in one of the Governor's boats,—swift as an arrow,—rowed by sailor boys in gay jackets of various colours. It was yet early, and the January sun had risen but a little while before. A light veil of mist cast its drapery over the white colonnades of the elegant country houses; verdant shrubs and majestic trees clothed the banks of the broad stream as far as the eye could reach,—only occasionally interrupted by rich and velvety lawns. "What a magnificent fairy-like prospect!" I was silently exclaiming to myself: at that moment my eye was diverted by a flight of crows, rising into the air with loud screams. The dead body of a white man, perfectly covered with crows, immediately floated by. Nothing can equal the inconceivable impudence of the birds that hover about the Ganges. No one shoots at nor disturbs them, because they fulfil the duties neglected by the indolent police: consequently, besides crows, hundreds

* By the kindness of Dr Wallich, the translator has been favoured with the perusal of a letter addressed to him by Dr Hoffmeister from Barrackpore, in which he expresses not only his grateful recollection of his agreeable intercourse with that eminent Botanist, but his regret that untoward circumstances had prevented his enjoying, in more frequent visits to the Botanic Gardens, the opportunity of increasing his scientific knowledge, and thus more fully preparing himself for his Himalayan tour.—Tr.

of kites and vultures, adjutant-birds and minas, are to be seen in every street, and on the roofs throughout the city.* Swarms of brown kites fly beneath my window, and seat themselves so close under it, that I could strike them with ease; while a flock of those bare-necked, thick-billed, giant storks, is in the habit of taking possession of the lion and the unicorn, in the arms of Great Britain, on the highest ridge of the roof at Government House,—thus producing a most ludicrous effect.

After a residence of fourteen days at Calcutta and Barrackpore, every thing was prepared for our journey to Patna. The Prince and Count O—— had started from Barrackpore on the evening of the 19th of January, because more than two persons cannot be expedited in palanquins at once, on account of the great number of bearers that would be required to be in attendance at the stations. On the following evening, the 20th of January, we bid a hearty farewell to the Governor, the amiable Lord Hardinge, and took a more formal leave of his suite. Captain Monro accompanied us till we were shut up in those horrible boxes, palanquins, in

* The carrion birds and pariah dogs of Calcutta, with the foxes and jackals which, emerging from the jungle after sunset, make night hideous with their howls, are encouraged in their audacity by the share of dainty viands left from the well-replenished boards of European residents, which falls to their lot,—the religious prejudices of the natives preventing their tasting any food prepared by those not of their own religion or caste, and moreover limiting them almost entirely to the use of vegetable food.

But the sight of these insatiate animals is connected,—in the minds of those acquainted with the dark horrors of the sacred stream,—with scenes still more revolting than the floating by of a solitary corpse,—viz., the "*Shussan*," where the bodies of the dead are burnt, and the "*Ghauts*" where the dying are carried, living victims, and left to die. Captain Williamson, in his Oriental Memoirs, describes another melancholy feature of the latter custom: that when a person has been thus carried to the place appointed for death, he is, in the eye of Hindoo law, dead; and in the event of recovery, finds himself an outcast: not even his own children will eat with him, or afford him help: he is held in abhorrence, and has no resource but to betake himself to a village inhabited solely by persons under similar circumstances.—Tr.

which, from this place forward, we were to pursue our journey through the plains of Hindostan.

Never shall I be reconciled by use to this species of vehicle: to me it appears, to begin with, sufficiently horrible to see men toiling on like draught-cattle. Picture to yourself a wooden box with a wide opening at each side;—fastened lengthways across its top, is a strong pole, the two ends of which rest on the shoulders of the four bearers:—within this machine the traveller lies stretched at full length, panting under heat the most oppressive, or if he attempts to leave his doors open, suffocated by the dust: for the weight of the vehicle is considerable, and the weary bearers, unable to lift their feet high, continually raise all the dust of roads that have not seen a drop of rain for the last four months. These toil-worn beings cheer on their steps by a plaintive groaning song, which at first has a most dolorous sound, like a wail of agony, but to which the ear becomes accustomed, as to the irksome creaking of a wheel; while the unwilling eye gradually learns to behold their excoriated shoulders and the wounds on their bare feet, with the same measure of indifference with which one is often forced to look upon the rubs and sores of a cart-horse at home. Yet, upon the whole, if driven to a choice, I should prefer a long palanquin journey to a long sea-voyage: for nothing can equal the monotony of the desolate waste of waters, on which, frequently, not one of the many wonders that travellers describe is to be seen, or at most, but an occasional flying fish or leaping dolphin; while the dancing motion of the ship incapacitates the landsman for any employment, and throws him into a state of misanthropic indolence. In the palanquin the traveller has at any rate the power of occupying himself; and though he can see but little, there may chance, in that little, to be some scenes or objects new to him.

The balancing motion of my vehicle, together with my previous fatigues, caused me to fall ere long into a deep slumber. In the middle of the night, I suddenly felt the palanquin set down with a hard jerk, and saw, by the clear moonlight, that we had halted at the edge of a broad river. With great difficulty we made ourselves intelligible to our bearers: they were paid off, and we were ferried across the stream; but on the other side we found not a creature. After we had called in vain, loudly and long, some men at length appeared, stupified with drink. The ferry-men were not satisfied with the money given them, and, with the utmost composure, they produced their "*tarif*," a huge black board, on which the rate of fares was marked.

At length matters were adjusted, and we advanced with fresh vigour. We had left Hooghly to the east of our course. When the sun rose, its rays disclosed before our eyes an interminable plain, covered with parched grass, which, if the rustling wind chanced to agitate its withered blades, had a truly wintry effect. About one o'clock, the heat had increased to 27° (93° Fahrenheit); the air moreover was so full of dust, that my thick hair appeared as if powdered, and my nose and eyes were in a state of inflammation.

It was not until we reached Gaya (on the 22d of January) that we were once more gladdened by the sight of rocks and hills, to break the monotony of the arid desert. The change in the dress and language of the population had struck us much even on the second day. On the third, we met numbers of pilgrims. Their costumes were picturesque,—no longer the unvarying white cloth, twisted in many folds round the shoulders, breast and loins, as in Calcutta,—but here, a rich Cashmere of azure blue displayed its ample drapery,—there, a mantle of dark yellow,—or again, a ponderous silken tunic, with embroidery of gold; the headgear too was changed from the protuberant and massive turban to a flat cap of elegant form and colour. We saw here men of strong and vigorous race. Most of these people wore tight breeches, and were armed with an iron buckler on the back, and a long sword at the left side. Here and there a mighty elephant drags his massive pillars tardily along, bearing a whole family upon his back,—that of a wealthy priest, or of a Rajah, —with the sum-total of their household-goods, consisting of a few coverlets, which also serve as cloaks, a set of copper drinking vessels, and a kettle in which to boil their curry. The whole treasures of the wardrobe are usually heaped on the owner's person, for the sake of display; what need then of carrying trunks, any more than furniture or domestic utensils? A Persian merchant, with the green turban, reclining at his ease, and smoking his hookah, rolls past in a light vehicle, which resembles a small quadrangular turret, with a canopy over-head, and running upon two wheels; the pole is fastened to a knob or hump of leather on the horse's back; and the Arab steed is driven by an attendant of sable hue.

The station of Gaya was at length reached, on the 24th of January, and we were able to shake off the dust, and enjoy the refreshment of a bath.

Huge rugged masses of gneiss, and hills of débris of the same formation, encircle on every side this beautifully-situated town, and the dusty, desolate plains, and scorched wearisome roads, are soon forgotten, when the traveller finds himself suddenly transported to a smiling valley, where fields of opium are succeeded by terraces of rice, where tanks of fresh water are surrounded by verdant and flourishing gardens, and where one draw-well after another pours forth its limpid stream to refresh his languid eye. Here is the home of that vigorous and umbrageous tree, the Palmyra Palm (*Borassus flabelliformis*) with its thick and fan-like bowers of foliage: here too flourishes that most beautiful of all Indian trees, the tamarind. Its tender and fragrant verdure, as it spreads its graceful shade, here, over a white, conical, Hindoo temple,—there, over a group of simple clay-built cottages,—or again, over the colonnades of English country seats,—adds an indescribable charm to the scene.

How delightful is it, seated on the gnarled root of one of these trees, high on some rugged crag, to enjoy the coup-d'oeil of the whole city in its long extent, with its clear and glassy pools,—their broad steps enlivened by groups of maidens busily washing, and their basins, by elephants bathing at their ease,—its many and various towers and minarets, and its white-domed mosques,—in short, with all its sundry oriental characteristics, standing out in picturesque prominence amid the velvety verdure of Indian vegetation! What animation in those dusty streets below us! what a motley mixture of vehicles and of figures! palanquins, chaises, gigs, elephants with their lofty baldachins; women, with large rings of gold hanging from their nostrils, and a profusion of massy silver bracelets, bearing huge jars on their heads; native soldiers, in their gay uniforms; and other men with their long web of dirty white wrapped round them, and their large shoes with long and pointed ends. Much indeed did I regret that time failed me for taking sketches.

On the morning after our arrival, we visited one of the greatest temples in India, that of *Vishnu-padda;* it is built of a beautiful shining dark-gray stone: and is equal in circumference to many a little village. The principal edifices stand on a high granite rock, and produce a most singular effect, surrounded as they are by a number of low colonnades full of inscriptions and of images of Vishnu. A pointed tower, some forty or fifty feet in height, divided into several stories, and ornamented by numerous volutes, but without a single window, contains the holy images and the footsteps of Vishnu.* Its interior is constantly illuminated with lamps, and filled with the fragrance of choice flowers. The entrance to the sanctuary is from within a quadrangular temple-building close at hand, whose round dome is supported by two colonnades, one above the other. The pillars form two rows all round, an outer and an inner one, and in each of these every four pillars are clustered together: the outer line consists of six of these groups; the inner one of four; the height of the columns does not exceed eight feet.

Under the colonnades, and in all the courts and vestibules, we saw multitudes of pilgrims, who had flocked hither only to sacrifice their savings to the avaricious rapacity of the fat priests. It is well known that he who arrives at the shrine in opulence, returns in beggary; the priest obtains possession of his carriage and horses, or, if he has none, of the very coat he wears. Stupidity and worthlessness are painted in the countenances of these priests, beyond all description. There sits one of them, overgrown and unsightly, idly squatting on the ground, a most disgusting object; before him stands a pilgrim, pointing to three superb Japan bedsteads, hung with coverlets of costly silk, and watching

* The far-famed sanctity of Gaya, which extends to the plain of the river Fulgo, on which the modern town is built, below the temple-crowned rock, is attributed by the Hindoos to its having been the scene of Vishnu's great victory over the Asoor, or giant and infidel, Gaya, who was pressed down to the infernal regions by the foot of the god; while the Buddhists believe this spot to have been the birthplace, or the residence, of their great prophet and legislator. The annual number of pilgrims was believed by Mr Hamilton (writing in 1820) to amount, in times of peace, to 200,000, and the revenue derived by the British Government from the pilgrim-tax, increased in proportion to the magnitude of the ceremonies performed, is stated to have risen, in 1816, to 230,000 rupees. Mr Hamilton speaks of this influx of devout pilgrims, as the fruitful source of the numerous crimes, for which the province of Bahar is remarkable.—Tr.

the keen glance of those greedy eyes, as they scan and estimate the gift. It does not suffice,—money must yet be added; and then the ceremony begins. In the first place, the pilgrim's feet are washed, then rubbed with a golden ointment, and a flower of jessamine is next laid upon each foot. This operation of ablution and anointing is performed by a young boy, who represents the family of the priest, and another person who acts as an assistant. This done, the pilgrim receives a pot containing a brown salve, with which he anoints first the priest, and afterwards his two coadjutors, on the forehead, the breast, and either arm. He then draws forth from within a bag, several garlands of flowers, some formed of African marygold, others of jessamine, but all richly adorned with silver spangles; throws one over the priest's head, and another over his folded hands, and proceeds to crown the other personages of the scene with similar wreaths, during all which operations, sundry prayers and apophthegms are muttered in a solemn whisper. When the ceremony is concluded, the pilgrim departs, minus his money, his gifts, and, if he has faith sufficient, his sins also; and wends his way home from the sacred shrine with light heart, and yet lighter purse. It is truly deplorable to behold haggard and tattered mothers, with their half-famished infants in their arms, carrying their last handful of rice as an offering to the temple; cocoa-nuts too, and necklaces of flowers, are presented by many a poverty-stricken worshipper. To me it is inconceivable how the English can tolerate so mighty an evil! Venders of sacred flowers, among which Jessamine, Marygold and Everlastings predominate, are seated on all the steps, offering their fragrant goods for sale. Two thousand priestly families are said to be maintained at Gaya alone, by the offerings of the pilgrims.

The surrounding country is well cultivated; it produces great quantities of opium, and four varieties of rice. The smallest of these is distinguished by its red husk, and known by the name of "*Chaul;*" the large grained pure white sort is called "*Choola.*" I also saw a species of vetch ("*Kooltee*") with long kidney-shaped seeds, besides durra-grass ("*Chinura*") and another kind of grain, called "*Koorshee.*" Only a small quantity of sugar is made from cane grown in these parts, and it is very black and ugly; *Jaggery,* or Palm-sugar, is unknown here; palm-wine is however made from the wild date tree *(Phœnix sylvestris,)* which is quite disfigured by the numerous incisions made in its young shoots.

We left Gaya on the evening of the 25th of January, and arrived at PATNA on the following day. It was stormy weather, but without rain; the trees had a very wintry appearance, for they do not here preserve that perennial verdure and never-ending succession of blossom, which characterize those of Ceylon.

Patna,—the far-famed land of rice,—is not to be compared with Gaya in point of beauty; the surrounding country is flat and dismal. The banks of the Ganges,—that sacred stream, painted in the stanzas of our poets as flowing amid varied loveliness and roseate fragrance, are in reality sandy and arid, monotonous, and without any refreshing verdure. The town of Patna extends up the river for ten miles; from no point therefore can a general survey of the whole be obtained. It is said to contain 52,000 houses, *i. e.,* clay-built hovels; and a population of 380,000 souls. We are quartered at a considerable distance from the actual town, in the beautiful and commodious country residence of the Commissioner of Revenue and Circuit of the Province of Bahar,—of which this place is the capital,—a most kind and friendly person, Mr Ravenshaw.

We visited the town, to take a glance at the few remarkable objects which it presents; a Mahometan burial-place, a few mosques, and the opium factory. The immense quantity of opium here produced filled me with amazement. No less than 160,000 "maunds," (or 12,800,000 lbs.,)* of opium are obtained in, and exported from this place annually; Gaya exports 40,000 maunds, (3,200,000 lbs.) This must be consumed entirely among the opium-eaters of China; for none of it is sent to Europe. The manufacture is extremely simple. After the flower has passed away, the green poppy-heads are wounded with an instrument exactly fitted for the purpose; the juice which exudes is scraped carefully together; and when, in the process of drying, it has reached a certain fixed point of inspissation, it is rolled up in balls weighing five pounds, and wrapped in the dried petals of the poppy. The opium-fields are now in full flower, and bring vividly to my recollection our own poppy-fields in Germany, but with this difference, that here the Ganges performs the work of preparing and cultivating the soil, the produce of which, year after year, continues the same, and always fetches the same unvarying price. The profits derived by the English from this branch of trade are enormous.

Our residence at Patna was concluded by a ball, given by the British regiment stationed at the neighbouring cantonment of Dinapore, on the evening of the 30th of January.

From this place we are to proceed towards Nepaul, to penetrate into the interior of that country, as the Rajah of Nepaul wishes to receive the Prince's visit in his capital city of Cathmandoo. We shall make a stay of about a fortnight there, before entering into the proper region of the Himalayahs, among the high mountains of which range we are to spend the hot season, viz., the months of April, May and June.

* The maund is here calculated, according to Ward and Hamilton, at eighty lbs.—Tr.

SIXTH LETTER.

SUGOULI—THE RAJAH AT SUGOULI—FRONTIER FOREST OF NEPAUL—BECHIACO—MOUNTAINEERS—FAKEERS—DILL BICKRAM—NEPAULESE SOLDIERS—VALLEY OF THE RAPTY—BHEEMPHED—PASS OF SISWAGHURRY—THE TAMRA KHANI NUDDY—VILLAGE ARCHITECTURE IN NEPAUL—CHITLONG—PASS OF CHANDAR-GIRI—VIEW OF THE VALLEY OF CATHMANDOO—TANKOTE—RECEPTION AT CATHMANDOO—MARTABAR SINGH—ENTRY INTO CATHMANDOO—THE CITY OF CATHMANDOO—PALACE OF THE BRITISH RESIDENT—AUDIENCE OF THE RAJAH—SANCTUARY OF SAMBHUNATH—GREAT HUNT—JOURNEY TO NOYAKOT—PASS OF KAULIA—VIEW OF THE CHAIN OF HIMALAYAS—THE DHAWALIGIRI—MOUNTAINEERS—TEMPLES OF NOYAKOT—RETURN TO CATHMANDOO—PARTING FESTIVITIES.

CATHMANDOO, *26th February* 1845.

WE were at first assured that we should never be able to cross the boundary of the KINGDOM OF NEPAUL,—but patient and resolute perseverance have enabled us, not only to enter, but to penetrate into parts which, for a long period, have been unvisited by any European; and we have now been, for the last fourteen days, resident in its wonderful capital.

The Prince had started in advance, from Patna, on the 31st of January;—our palanquins followed on the next day. Passing through MUZUFFERPOOR on the 2d of February, and MUTEARY on the 3d,—we reached, on the 4th, the last British station, SUGOULI. I arrived there one day later than the Prince and the Counts, in company with Mr Fortescue, a very agreeable and accomplished English tourist, who had recently united himself to our party. We were received in a most friendly and hospitable manner by the amiable officer in command at the place,—Major Wheeler. The pleasant society we here enjoyed, soon consoled me for the loss of forty rupees, which had been most artfully stolen from me at Muzufferpoor; but there is little of interest in the flat, steppe-like country around.

At sunrise, on the 5th of February, the magnificent summits of the eastern Himalayas appeared in view; but it was only for the space of an hour or so that we feasted on the sublime prospect of those majestic, snow-capt peaks, which indeed rise like some strange and incongruous apparition, beyond the parched and arid steppes:—the vision passed away; and again the horizon was flat and monotonous as before. How dreadful to live, year after year, at such a place as this! Yet there lives, at Sugouli, an aged Rajah, who was great and powerful in former days, but who now maintains, for his amusement, only an army of elephants, and a stud of some forty or fifty horses. The latter are, for the most part, white, with their tails dyed red; they are of Arab, Turkish, Persian, and Chinese breeds. Of the herd of elephants some are of considerable size; but the largest, whose height does not much exceed nine feet, is a "*Mukua,*" *i. e.*, an elephant with short, straight tusks, which never grow. An ingenious plan has however been devised, to remove this obstacle of its appearance on state occasions; large and handsome tusks being inserted by means of holes bored in the shorter ones.

The soil of the flat plain in which Sugouli is situated, consists of a rich, yellow clay; and as there is never any want of water,—there being, in every field, at least one draw-well, if not several,—it is well adapted for the cultivation of *Sesamum** (oil plant), *Ricinus* (castor-

* The culture of the *Sesamum Orientale* (or oil-plant) is very easy, and the oil is readily obtained from the seeds by expression. Nine pounds of seed yield two quarts of oil; which, when it is first drawn, has an unplea-

oil tree), and several other oleaginous plants, as well as of *Cajan* (pigeon-pea), and some species of barley. *Opium* is likewise produced here in moderate quantities. The few straggling trees, here and there met with,—of the *Bombax*, and of the *Erythrina* genus (silk-cotton tree, and coral tree), were adorned with the embryo blossoms of Spring.

After "tiffin," i. e., about five o'clock in the afternoon, on the 5th of February, we took our departure from Sugouli, and just as the first shades of twilight were falling, we were ferried across a broad river, the *Sakorona*. At the first station on the other side we were detained for two hours by the non-arrival of our luggage; cudgelling and money were necessary to stimulate the zeal of our bearers and coolies. Towards day-break, on the 6th of February, we found ourselves in a wild, moorland region, overgrown with tall, hard grass, which, especially in those places where it had been burnt down for the sake of securing young pasturage, proved extremely irksome to the feet of our palanquin-bearers. The thermometer about seven A.M. showed only 4° of Réaumur (41° Fahrenheit,) and at sunrise the snowy summits of the Himalayas, gloriously illuminated by the radiant glow, once more appeared in the north-east, as if rising immediately from the vast plain. The frontier village, BISSOULI, lies within the limits of this steppe. Its meadows, clothed with fresh verdure, and surrounded with hedges, —and its beautiful and gigantic "*Peepul*" tree *(Ficus Religiosa,)* in the centre of the village, have a most pleasing effect.

At half-an-hour's distance beyond Bissouli is the beginning of the Nepaulese border forest; at first thin and

sant taste of mustard, but this soon passes away, leaving a very sweet and pleasantly favoured oil, admirably adapted for all the purposes of olive oil, with this great advantage, that it does not contract rancidity, though kept for many years. The seed itself is much valued as an article of food in many parts of Asia and Africa.—TR.

open, but soon becoming an impenetrable thicket, in which the beds of streams form the only paths. How refreshing to our weary sight was this forest,—the first that we had seen since quitting Ceylon,—and now doubly welcome after we had so long languished amid the heat and dust of the monotonous plains of Hindostan! The edge of the wood consists of several varieties of *Ficus (infectoria, Bengalensis, religiosa,)* of *Bauhinia,* (mountain ebony) and of *Dalbergia,* with an occasional *Erythrina,* (coral tree) but without the least admixture of underwood, as that is destroyed by the frequent conflagrations of the grass. Further in, among the depths of the forest, the *Shorea robusta,**—that magnificent Saul-tree,—chiefly predominates; but it is mingled with the *Cratæva,* (Garlic Pear) the *Feronia,* (Elephant Apple) the *Guilandina Bonduc,* (Nicker tree) the *Myrobalanus,* or *Terminalia Chebula,* and several varieties of extremely thorny *Acacia.* The spots on which the grass had been burnt last autumn were shining with a rich carpet of wonderfully beautiful sappy-green: the trees, many of them yet leafless, reminded us that we were in early spring; the *Bombax heptaphyllum* alone, (seven-leaved silk-cotton tree) was in the full glory of its gigantic, crimson blossoms.

At the end of four hours we reached the bed of a broad stream, which was covered with débris of grey sand-stone, quartz and granite, and altogether destitute

* It is described by Dr Royle, in his splendid work on the Botany and other branches of the Natural History of the Himalayan Mountains, as remarkable for its size and beauty, and as affording the best and most extensively used timber in India,—it yields in great abundance the resin called *dhoona,* which is used for the same purposes as pitch, and in Indian temples for incense. The natives in some parts of India apply the wood in several of their superstitious ceremonies,—as for instance, if witchcraft is suspected by them, branches of the Saul-tree are marked with the names of all the females in the place, married or unmarried, who have attained the age of twelve, and then, at early dawn planted in the water for four or five hours; the person whose name is written on the branch that withers first, is at once convicted and condemned.—Tr.

of vegetation. Here and there a little spring was gushing forth in the dry water-course,—the bed of the river CHERIA, which, in the rainy season, is an impetuous torrent. Its lofty and rugged banks are formed of grayish-white compact clay, intermixed with sand and mica, rising, at one bend of the stream, to a perpendicular height of about three hundred and twenty feet. Water still flows in the channels of some of the tributary rivulets, but, on reaching the empty bed of the Cheria, is soon dried up.

At one such confluence, close to the edge of the precipitous and elevated bank on the left side of the river, lies the Post-station of BECHIACO,* a wretched village, containing about a dozen huts. It is deserted during the summer, as is indeed the whole surrounding district, on account of its "malaria,"† which engenders a malignant and fatal kind of fever. Whence does this noxious miasma arise? The soil is dry and stony; far and wide not a marsh is to be seen in this part of the country. May not the rapid and copious evaporation of the many springs impregnated with oxide of iron, that flow in these deep ravines, be the possible agent in producing these baneful exhalations?

The steep ascent beyond this point rendered our palanquins useless: nimble horses of a small breed were

* The name, according to Hamilton, signifies a place abounding with scorpions.—TR.

† The Mal Aria region,—called Tarai or Tarayani,—is a tract of country from twenty to thirty miles in width, between the hills which form the southern boundary of Assam, Bootan, Nepaul Proper, &c. &c., and the flats of Hindostan. It is covered with luxuriant vegetation; the exhalations from the numerous springs which have their rise among the neighbouring mountains are confined by the dense forests; the ground during spring is covered with fallen leaves, which are rotted by the first rains of the hot season, and to these, among other causes, has been attributed an atmosphere so unhealthy that no European can encounter it for any length of time with impunity. Its effects were fatal to a large body of British troops in 1772. The natives call it "*Ayul*," and suppose that it proceeds from the breath of large serpents, which they believe to inhabit the forests of the Himalayas.

therefore in readiness to bear us on our further route, over the smooth, pebbly surface; while the care of our luggage devolved upon a troop of bearers,—thorough Mongolians in their appearance,—who carried it in light baskets on the nape of the neck, steadying the heavy burden by means of a broad strap placed across the forehead.

How striking is the contrast between the inhabitants of the plains and those of the mountain forests of this frontier! Never by any chance does one see the luggage-bearer of the plain carrying any thing upon his back; the heavy tin chests are swung in pairs,—one hanging at each end,—on a bamboo pole laid across the shoulder;—here, on account of the more convenient and easy mode of bearing heavy burdens, half of the former number of bearers suffices for the same luggage. The inhabitants of these parts are distinguished from the Hindoo race, no less by their lighter, and somewhat yellowish complexion than by their broad noses and angular faces; the hair, too, is not cut, but hangs loosely down, or is arranged in long plaits. The men wear jackets and drawers, instead of the simple web of cotton which forms the costume of the Hindoo. Their feet are shod with straw sandals, a necessary protection against the sharp pebbles. A strong knife, called the "*khukri*," curved inwards, and with a broad end, with which they hew down trees as thick as a man's arm, is stuck within the girdle, in place of the iron-tipped bamboo staff, or of the long, straight sword, which the inhabitant of the low country wears on his shoulder as he marches along. Heavy amulets, always formed of one of the precious metals, and of Agalmatolith, are here suspended round every neck. The costume of the women differs yet more from the simplo apparel of the Hindoo female; they wear jackets and petticoats, and are fond of displaying heavy rings of gold in the ears and nostrils: they too are not unfrequently armed with the "*khukri*."

We met numerous *Fakeers*, the only travellers who, attracted by the many spots of holy ground within the kingdom of Nepaul, tread these dreary solitudes. Each one of these beings seemed to be more revolting than the last. They are, for the most part, young men, and their life is one of ease and good cheer; for, in every place their impudence procures them money. Their raiment, when, indeed, they have any, is a cloak of orange colour; their face is smeared over, as is the whole body, with ashes, which gives them a horribly cadaverous hue; their hair, long and dishevelled, is either dyed a pale reddish-brown, or covered with a wig formed of tufts of camel's hair, and powdered with ashes: not unfrequently moreover they put on the top of this, by way of an additional head-dress, their iron pot or stew-pan! Many among them carry a sort of guitar with wire chords, or a hand drum. They invariably act the part of tyrants towards the poor; often have I seen them busily inspecting the baskets of the heavy-laden bearers, and appropriating to themselves their victuals.

We now wound up the narrow glen* of a tributary

* The border country of Nepaul is well described by Dr Buchanan Hamilton as follows:—"Bounding the Tarrai, to the north, is a region nearly of the same width, consisting of small hills which rise gradually towards the north, and watered by many streams that spring from the southern faces of the first lofty mountains, to which these hills gradually unite. The channels of these rivers or torrents are filled with fragments of granite and schistose mica; but the hills themselves are generally composed of clay intermixed with various proportions of sand, mica and gravel. The lower part of these hills, and some of the adjacent plains, are the grand site of the Saul forests. Higher up, the hills are covered with a vast variety of trees, and among those of the north are many pines, and an abundance of the Mimosa, (*Acacia Catechu*) from which the Catechu is made. The hills are in some places separated from the high mountains by fine valleys of some length, but considerably elevated above the level of Hindostan Proper. In the country west from the Ganges, these valleys are called by the generic name of *Doon*, analogous to the Scotch word *Strath;* but towards the east the term is un-

stream, until we reached a chain of hills extending from west to east; and crossing its steep ridge by the CHERIA-GHAUT, (Pass of the Cheria) entered another and a broader valley, which proved to be only a bend of that of the Cheria, which we had quitted soon after passing Bechiaco. The forest consists here almost exclusively of stately *Saul-trees*, (called *Sakua* by the natives) the timber of which is considered, next to that of the Dalbergia Cissu, the finest in this country, and is conveyed from this district to many distant parts; even at Patna, it is used for making the many thousand opium chests, which are exported for the Chinese market.

Before entering the vale of the RAPTY, one of the most considerable and most interesting valleys of the outposts of the Himalayan chain, we were obliged to cross the river KURROO,* and to proceed, for several hours, along a plain covered with travelled fragments such as we had continually found beneath our feet in the other river-glens. Towards evening the tents of Major Lawrence at length appeared in view; they were pitched at some distance before us, in the retirement of a deep valley, beside the village of HETHAURA, on the banks of the beautiful Rapty. Here the Prince had halted on the preceding day, and in a little while we saw him returning with his suite, all mounted on elephants, from a hunt, in which their booty had been but small; not a single deer, leopard, nor wild boar had rewarded their toils. Uncertain traces only had been met with of the rhinoceros and elephant. Besides this sudden rencontre with our friends, we were surprised by the unexpected and magnificent apparition of a detach-

known, though such valleys are of frequent occurrence. Among the spurs and ridges of the hills there are many narrow valleys or glens, which possess a rich soil, yet are totally neglected.—TR.

* Probably the "*Karrara*" of Hamilton, which flows into the Rapty below HETHAURA.—TR.

ment of Nepaulese troops, which had welcomed the Prince on the frontier. A Nepaulese of the highest rank, *Dil Bikram, (Dil Bigrum Thappa)* nephew of the Minister, was at their head; a fine looking young man, slender and elegant in his figure, with very beautiful and delicate, almost feminine features,—long, curling, black hair, a light, somewhat European complexion, and without beard. The uniform worn by the military is remarkably showy and picturesque; it consists of a red or blue jacket with slashed sleeves, short white linen breeches, a broad sash, and a low sky-blue turban, resembling indeed rather a college cap, though called by the former name, and adorned in front with a silver crescent. They are strong, well-made men, more stalwart, and less Mongolian in their appearance than the mountaineers; their open countenances and bold bearing made a most agreeable impression upon us. They are admirably drilled, and the word of command in use among them is English, though so much corrupted as scarcely to be recognized.

This escort defiled before us on the following morning, (the 7th of February) accompanied by four large elephants, and, advancing in front, guided us through the intricacies of those confused ranges of hills, and of the rocky paths of those border forests, to all which the kingdom of Nepaul is indebted for its unapproachableness. Dil Bickram was still beside us, mounted on his dapple-grey steed of Chinese blood, which was ever fresh and unwearied, notwithstanding the eccentricities of his march, as he crossed and re-crossed the road, dashed forward to the front of our long procession, or again drew up the rear of the whole train. He gave evidence of his passion for the chase by firing at every parrot that flew within reach. Most ludicrous scenes were caused by the officious zeal of his twenty or thirty vassals, all of whom watched his every movement. His greatest pleasure was, at each halting-place, to make his appearance in a new costume, each being if possible more costly than the last. His usual dress was a short, purple Chinese coat, bordered with fur, a round Chinese scull-cap of velvet, with four projecting points, tight breeches of rich brocade, and white leather stockings, over which were drawn peaked shoes of velvet, or exquisite little boots of gold.

The vale of the Rapty, along which our course lay, is one of the most beautiful I ever beheld. The river is clear and rapid, though not very broad; and its course winding and varied between rocky and broken banks. Its margin is richly clothed with beautiful bushes; the giants of the forest here recede, and make way for underwood of luxuriant growth; *Justicia, Leea, Phlomis,* and many other woody *Labiatæ,* were resplendent with their gorgeous blossoms; the *Bauhinea scandeus,* (Climbing Mountain Ebony) and several varieties of *Dolichos* twine into elegant festoons among the leafy summits of the graceful *Acacias.*

Higher up the stream, the valley, at first wide and open, becomes narrower and more rocky. Its rugged sides are formed of gneiss, alternating with granite and quartz-rock, here but slightly disintegrated, in comparison of the upper part of the Cheria Ghaut, where I saw smooth cliffs upwards of two hundred feet in height, which at first sight appeared to consist of sand, but, on close examination, proved to be masses of disintegrated gneiss: deep hollows are there excavated by the river, while these frowning battlements rise lofty and perpendicular, on either side above its rocky bed.

The first three hours of our wanderings through the vale of the Rapty were most enjoyable; afterwards, the constant crossing from one bank of the stream to the other, which brought us into rather too close contact with its waters, rendered our way somewhat fatiguing and unpleasant.* The valley does not open out until it approaches BHEEMPHED, the first Nepaulese military station; there its breadth is so great as to enable the traveller to survey the towering summits and bold features of highland scenery which bound it. The height of the nearer hills, I should estimate, by a rough guess, to be from three to four thousand feet; they are all sharp ridged; no broad mountain-tops or table-lands are to be seen. The valley of the Rapty at Beemphed runs downward from E.N.E. to W.S.W.; but the sharp-crested mountains on either side, form an acute angle with the course of the glen, and each range seems to throw out projecting spurs to meet those of the opposite chain.

From Hethaura to Bheemphed,—our next station,—is a distance of some twenty miles. At the latter place we rested for the night, and early on the next morning (the 8th of February) we set out to ascend the pass of SISWAGHURRY. The road here winds up an extremely steep conical hill, formed of sand-stone, and covered with rolled fragments. We reached the summit only after a fatiguing climb of three hours: It is covered by a Nepaulese fortress, strong and in excellent repair, which seems to render the approach from this quarter,—already made sufficiently difficult by nature, altogether impracticable to a hostile army. Here, for the first time, I saw a few firs (*pinus longifolia*) upon the hills, mingling with the acacias and saul-trees: the temperature, which, in the valley below, averaged 15° (66° Fahrenheit) had fallen on the summit, at half-past eight, A. M., to 7° 6′ (about 48° 30′ Fahrenheit) from which we may fairly infer that

* Hamilton mentions that, from the extraordinary windings of the Rapty in this narrow defile, it is crossed no less than twenty-two times between Hethaura and Bheemphed.—TR.

the height of theh ill is somewhere between five and six thousand feet above the level of the sea.*

Wé followed, for some time, the ridge of this pass, proceeding in a north-westerly direction, and thus enjoyed an opportunity of observing the marked difference between the north and the south and east sides. The two last are bare and treeless, while the former is clothed with noble forests:† our admiring attention was particularly attracted by the dark crimsoned flowers of the rhododendron, which, growing to a height of above twenty feet, spreads over the northern side of every mountain-top in the Siswaghurry range.

It bears a great resemblance to the *rhododendron arboreum* of Ceylon; and the thick clusters of its flaming crimson blossoms may be seen, even from a great distance, glowing amid the dark verdure of its shining foliage. The common name by which it is here known is "*Gurahss;*" its flowers, being esteemed holy, are an article of trade usually offered for sale at the temples, and the snuff made of the bark is excellent. Besides this gorgeous tree, I remarked here two species of oak, growing to the height of forty or fifty feet, the "*Bhansh*" (*Quercus semicarpifolia*) and the "*Bhalath,*"—both superb trees.

From the heights of Siswaghurry we first obtained a

* Hamilton mentions, that the name of the fort,—"*Cheesapany*, or *Cheesaghurry* is derived from a spring of cold water, which, according to barometrical observations, is situated 5818 feet above the plains of Bengal."—Tr.

† Dr Royle alludes to this peculiar feature of the Himalayas as one of the difficulties in accurately defining the three several belts into which he divides their slope: He says, "A further difficulty is also produced by the great difference in the vegetation of the northern and southern faces of the very same range or mountain, so that frequently a straight line running along the summit of the ridge may be seen dividing the luxuriant, arboreous and shrubby vegetation of the northern face from the brown, barren, or grassy covering of the southern slope. This difference may be ascribed in part to the greater depth of the soil on the northern face; but chiefly, I conceive, to the less direct influence of the solar rays on this than on the southern side."—Tr.

view of the beautiful vallies of NEPAUL PROPER. A plain of no great extent appears near the horizon to the north; while, in the foreground, a labyrinth of rocky glens, all originating in the steep acclivity on the north-eastern side of the Siswaghurry range,* stretches to the open country below. We soon looked down upon one of the most considerable of these glens, as it lay immediately below us, bending and winding towards the east-south-east; it was the valley of the TAMRA KHANI NUDDY, or COPPER-MINE RIVER.

A shady and pleasant path through the thick forest brought us, by a descent of some three thousand two hundred feet, to the margin of the Tamra-Khani's clear waters, near which the wood ceases. Tall ferns,—the first we had seen on the continent of Asia,—nearly conceal the numerous small brooks which gush down the rugged declivity. The masses of stone which here present themselves,—Grauwacke-schist and a loose clay-slate,—forming a narrow and indented defile, control the course of the river, which winds its way in a thousand turnings through these laminated rocks. Considerable quantities of copper and of iron are found here, and I observed slags lying in many places. It is a curious fact that cow-dung is here used as fuel for smelting the ore, although there is no lack of wood for that purpose. We passed not far from the copper mine, but were not permitted to see the mining operations, nor to examine the ore.

We had scarcely emerged from the wild and rugged ground at the head of the glen, when we began to perceive a striking contrast between the unproductive waste of the wooded ravines through which we had hitherto passed, and the careful cultivation of the valley of the Tamra Khani. Here no thicket of unfruitful bushes,

* Properly the range of the *Lama Dangra* mountains, Siswaghurry or Cheesapany being the name of the pass.

no rank exuberance of luxuriant grass is to be seen; but we beheld, spread before us, a richly dressed valley, every inch of it improved, even to the foot of the distant mountains, and terraced fields laid out on the steep acclivities; while the freshest vernal green,—the young shoots of barley, their second crop,—gladdened our weary eyes. How delightful, after the tedious and arid plains of the Indian lowlands, to enjoy the refreshing prospect of fertile and verdant fields; and, instead of the sultry atmosphere and burning dust of the banks of the Ganges, to breathe the mild and elastic air of these mountain recesses! A net-work of little trenches, which catch every drop of water that finds its way down the slopes, extends between the narrow terraces, presenting no small obstacle to the traveller as he skirts the hill-side.

After a march of an hour and a-half, we quitted the valley, and once more ascended the higher ground on the left bank of the stream, where the road zigzags, for some distance, up the southern slope of the hill,—scorched by the glowing sunshine,—and then continues along the top of its broad ridge. This elevation commands most lovely views of the deeper valleys to the westward, gay with green meadows and pleasant villages. The red tone of colouring spread over the sandstone hills in the immediate foreground, and the naked appearance produced by the absence of wood, give to this landscape a certain resemblance to many of those in Greece; but the dreams and illusions to which such reminiscences give rise are speedily dispelled by the sight of beautifully cultivated lands, and of clean and tidy cottages. Nothing strikes the traveller, coming from the flats of Hindostan, more than this last feature of the altered scene. There, the eye is wont to behold only mud-walled hovels thatched with straw or with rushes,—their single opening answering the double purpose of door and windows,—or huts constructed of a few bamboos, and villages which seem to consist of a solid accumulation of filth, while the sole occupation to which their inhabitants apply themselves is the manufacture of fuel from cow-dung: how gladly, on the other hand, does one here welcome the sight of neat houses built of wood or of brick, which display, not cleanliness only, but elegance and taste. On the front of the lower part of the building is a kind of portico, the roof of which is supported by carved pillars, and the four or five centre windows of the first floor are decorated with a profusion of beautiful wood-carving, which vividly reminds me of Cairo. The roof is formed of small tiles* with a double curvature. Every thing proves that Chinese art has found apt scholars on this side of the Himalayas. In these villages we remarked, among the neat dwellings, a multitude of small chapels,—simple edifices of stone with projecting roofs, which contain Lingams and images of the gods; occasionally also temples, of six stories in height, elegant fountains and tanks, lined with stone to a great depth, and provided with stone or metal conduits.

Towards evening, we reached the plain, which we had seen at a distance in the morning, from Siswaghurry. It is watered by a small stream, and bordered by a dense forest, extending over the foot of the Chandar-Giri range, which, like a lofty rampart, separates it on the north side from the valley of Cathmandoo. We pitched our tents in an open space beside the village of Chitlong; but they afforded imperfect shelter from the chilliness of the night, which, even on our arrival, was most unpleasant. When, about the dawn of day, we were preparing to start, the thermometer was standing at 2½° (about 37° Fahrenheit); however, the climbing of those steep schis-

* These tiles,—however insignificant the subject may appear,—have attracted the attention of other writers. Dr Buchanan Hamilton describes them as flat; of an oblong form, having two longitudinal grooves, one above and another below, which fit into the adjacent tiles, the whole being arranged and put on with peculiar neatness.—Tr.

tose rocky masses, of which the south side of the mountains consists, speedily warmed our benumbed limbs. The forest here consists of spiny-leaved oak, with various species of Bay-tree, *Berberis*, *Vitex* (Chaste Tree), and a beautiful variety of *Prunus:* the bushes most prevalent among the underwood are of the *Daphne cannabina*, which is remarkable for the fragrance of its blossoms, and from the bark of which a coarse kind of paper is manufactured. We recognised with delight, among the luxuriant creepers, our own German Ivy, twining its tendrils in the humid moss; Violets also, *(Viola serpens)* and *Potentillas*, in full flower, were shining forth from its velvety carpet.

A toilsome climb of two hours and a-half brought us to the naked and rocky summit of the mountain, where a sharp westerly wind, with a temperature of 4° (41° Fahrenheit) made us fully sensible that we had gained a point of considerable elevation.

On this narrow path, we met numbers of heavy-laden bearers, carrying spices, fruit and salt, or large sacks of cotton. This is the only access permitted to the kingdom of Nepaul from the south-west; a more easy and convenient one does indeed exist, but the Government has made it forbidden ground. Report commonly alleges that guards have been stationed to ward off intruders; we found subsequently that facts do not corroborate this statement; the natives are however deterred by fear from venturing, even when heavy laden, on that tempting path.

The roof of a half dilapidated house seemed to present an admirable point for obtaining a panoramic view of the magnificent landscape, which was spread out below. We scrambled up to it accordingly; but how bitter was our disappointment, when a dense mist, suddenly rising, cast its gloomy shroud over the whole scene! Near as the snowy mountains now were, we could only distinguish a vague and spectre-like outline of their westernmost peaks;—the three large towns, and the numerous villages of the valley of Cathmandoo, undefined and melancholy-looking, were seen dimly peering through the haze. We little knew what glories this unlovely weather was concealing from our view, until, on our return, we enjoyed the prospect in its fullest beauty.

We were much struck by observing the great depth at which the valley of Cathmandoo lies, in comparison of that of Chitlong, in which we had passed the night: the difference between their levels may be estimated at about eight hundred feet. The height of this pass is eight thousand five hundred feet above the level of the sea: the plain round Cathmandoo lies upwards of four thousand feet below this elevation; and the Chandar Giri mountain rises so abruptly, that, from the head of the pass, we cast our eyes down an almost perpendicular declivity of that entire depth. The path, in descending, was therefore extremely fatiguing, and not without danger; moreover, the crumbling yellow sandstone, of which the whole northern side of this ridge consists, and the mica-schist, so abundantly occurring in it,—which, in a state of disintegration, forms a very slippery, yellow clay,—offer no secure footing, on which the weary traveller may venture to rest. To add to these difficulties, the path is so narrow, as to be often obstructed by the trains of bearers, and the groups of women and children.

Who could have imagined that, on mountain paths such as these, on which neither horses nor draught-oxen are put into requisition, the loaded elephant could drag on his way? Yet, in the middle of this rugged steep, we met this patient slave, panting under the weight of an oppressive burden! He was sliding, with the utmost caution, down the mountain-side; at all the steepest points carefully placing his hind feet between his front ones, at the same time using his trunk as a fifth foot, and thus testing the firmness of each stone before he hazarded his bulky frame upon it. Meanwhile, he seemed to know the danger well, and to be full of anxious fear; we had ocular demonstration that this was not causeless, in the three or four huge carcases which, on nearing the base of the mountain, we saw lying beside our path; every such fall is certain death to this massive and unwieldy beast.

In half-an-hour we reached the valley, and found, in the neighbourhood of the town of TANKOT, tents prepared for us to breakfast in; near them lay another detachment of troops, sent forward to meet the Prince. Major Lawrence, British Resident in Nepaul, had prepared us for a very magnificent reception; our travelling guise was therefore laid aside; and, mounted on horseback, we pursued our course along a nearly level plain. The road leads, in a north-easterly direction, to Cathmandoo. To the north, narrow ranges of hills of moderate height,—branches of the Chandar-Giri mountains,—extend as far as to the banks of the BOGMUTHY, which, flowing towards the south, forces its way through the lofty ramparts of the Chandar-Giri, at a point farther east than the pass. This breach in the south-western barrier of the valley forms its second approach, to which I have already alluded.

Crossing one of these low ridges, a splendid view of the capital burst upon us; it stands in a valley watered by the many streams tributary to the Bogmuthy. To our right, on the summit of an eminence, stands KIRTAPOOR; before us, to the left, rises,—amid a grove of beautiful and shady trees,—the Temple of SAMBHUNATH; here and there little hills, richly wooded, break the outline of the terraced fields, which are shining in the early stage of their lovely verdure. In the horizon the glorious snow-capt peaks of DHAYABUNG and GOSSAINTHAN are towering to the skies; in the middle distance below them are the lofty terraced banks of the Bogmuthy, which form the back-ground immediately behind the resplendent roofs of the many temples of CATHMANDOO.

Proceeding along narrow but well-paved roads, between hedged terraces and smiling villages, we arrived at the first bridge of the BISHMUTTY, an elegant structure of red brick, whose top however is formed merely of cross-laid beams, the principle of the arch being unknown in this country. Much industry has been bestowed on the making of roads; in each village they are neatly paved with bricks, like those in the cities of Holland.

A numerous and motley throng had assembled on the other side of the bridge; a long file of soldiers in their red and blue jackets, and a troop of elephants, splendidly caparisoned with silken stuffs and plates of gold and silver, and surmounted by gilded "*howdahs*," had been marched hither, and were drawn up to receive the Prince. A spacious tent of blue and white cotton, with silk curtains, was pitched on the level ground beyond: there we were welcomed by Captain Ottley, Assistant-British Resident, and Dr Christie, staff-surgeon of the small body of British troops in this place, both in full uniform.

We dismounted, and were conducted within the marquee; but we had scarcely seated ourselves, when the arrival of the Nepaulese Minister,—Martabar Singh,—(Magnanimous Lion) was announced. His appearance was like the rising sun,—clothed entirely in gold tissue, resplendent with emeralds, pearls and diamonds, and so fragrant of sandal-wood oil and otto of roses, that it almost suffocated one! On the breast he wore three large plates of gold covered with insignia and inscriptions, the badges of his dignity; round his neck hung thick strings of pearls; his head-dress was the flat turban of Nepaul, made of Chinese brocade, studded with pearls, and surmounted by a bird of Paradise; his ears were adorned with large hoops of gold, and his arms and each of his fingers were encircled with brilliants. He was mounted on a tall white steed with blue cockades and golden trappings.

Such was the picture presented by Martabar Singh,—Minister and Generalissimo of the kingdom of Nepaul,—of proud and stately mien, tall, handsome, and corpulent, with a keen and lively eye, a small aquiline nose, a magnificent black beard, and long raven hair. He was immediately followed by two of his sons, arrayed in every colour of the rainbow. Next to them appeared Dill Bickram Thappa,—gorgeous and shining beyond what we had ever seen even him before,—and Djung Bahadur,—a kinsman of the Rajah, a man of very intelligent countenance, by far the most educated and agreeable of them all; he too was overloaded with superb silken stuffs, with pearls and glittering arms. Twenty or more officers, equipped in simple red and white uniforms,—some of whom were veterans with silvery beards, though still vigorous and strong,—brought up the rear of the procession.

Martabar Singh advanced to meet the Prince, first made a most graceful "*salam*," then stepping forward about two paces, bowed himself over the left, then over the right shoulder of the object of his salutations, in a way similar to what is practised in embraces on the stage; a second salam, and a retreating step, concluded the ceremony, which each of our party was in his turn obliged to undergo. His sons too, and the officers, all performed it with the same formal solemnity, the whole operation occupying, as you may imagine, a considerable time.

This done, we seated ourselves on the chairs which stood ready in the tent, and a short but most interesting conversation took place, during which Major Lawrence, Captain Ottley, and Dr Christie, had enough to do to satisfy every claim upon them as interpreters, both in putting questions and in answering them.

The interview however soon broke up, as it was now time to mount the richly caparisoned elephants, which stood in readiness to bear us in triumphal procession to the capital. The foreign guests were led to their respective elephants after a fashion resembling that in which a gentleman leads the fair ladies in a quadrille: first advanced Martabar Singh,—on his right hand the Prince, on his left, Major Lawrence; Dr Christie and I were conducted in like manner by a brother of Djung Bahadur. We mounted our howdahs; peacock's tails and Chinese parasols were put in requisition, and thus we all marched forward towards the city, to the sound of a variety of musical instruments, among which bagpipes, clarinets, kettle-drums, bells and triangles played the most prominent part.

An endless multitude of strange and motley figures covered the terraced fields on either side of the road. We here saw the most singular and varied costumes; among them that of the BHOOTEAS, the inhabitants of BOOTAN, with clumsy stuff boots, coarse felt coats, thick tufts of hair, and a completely Mongolian physiognomy: men and women among them are dressed alike. The NEWARS,* or aboriginal population, are clad, in spite of

* Few subjects seem to have been more fertile in discussions among those acquainted with the historical records or the conflicting creeds of these Eastern lands, than that of the various tribes inhabiting the mountains and plains of Nepaul. According to Dr Buchanan Hamilton's account of Nepaul, "all that have any pretensions to be considered aboriginal are by their features clearly marked as belonging to the Tartar or Chinese race, and have no sort of resemblance to the Hindoos." Of such aboriginal tribes, that author notices no less than 9 or 10, distinguished by various habits and pursuits, shades of civilization and religious tenets. The Newars, who form the majority of the inhabitants of Nepaul Proper, are described as a race addicted to agriculture and commerce, and far more advanced in the arts than any other of the mountain tribes. Their style of building, and most of their arts, appear to have been introduced from Thibet, and the greater part still adhere to the religion of the Buddhists, but on the other hand, they have adopted

the cool atmosphere, in little more than a broad web of cotton cloth; the GORKHAS, or conquering race, sport jackets and trowsers, and even shoes. Troops of fakeers and of other beggars were slowly advancing before us, and uttering most doleful cries as they passed.

We looked down from our lofty seats at this crowd and bustle far below, through which the elephants were slowly making their way. The singular and picturesque city,—with its gay temples, and elegant brick structures,* its gardens, whose orange trees were loaded with golden fruit, while plum and cherry trees were in the full glory of their blossom,—was extended before our wondering eyes. The bridges threatened to give way under the mass of human beings, which rushed together to see us pass through the last branch of the BISHMUTTY; for our elephants must needs wade through the stream, since the bridges are too feeble to support the weight of these mighty animals.

We entered the city itself through several very narrow streets, whose entire width was just sufficient to admit of an elephant passing along. The rich wood carving lavished on the rosettes of the windows, on the pillars, architraves and corners of the roofs, reminded me of many an ancient German commercial city; yet, on the other hand, the Oriental character stamped on the whole scene is very conspicuous. The gilded roofs of the

the distinctions of caste, have rejected the Lamas, and have a priesthood of their own, named Bangrus. These people partake freely of every kind of animal food, and are prone to habits of intoxication.

* This epithet, which, applied to edifices of red brick, may appear somewhat inappropriate, is explained by the account of Nepaulese architecture given by Dr Buchanan Hamilton. He says, "The Nepaulese have peculiar moulds for the bricks used in cornices and other decorations, and for the fronts and ornamental parts of their best houses they make smooth glazed bricks, that are very handsome. They have, in the alluvial matter of the plain of Nepaul, large strata of particularly fine brick-clay, and in the lower hills are found masses of a hard red clay, called "*Lungcha*," which they use for painting the walls of their houses."—TR.

temples, hung round with bells and adorned with flags of many colours, and the gigantic images of stone, betray the influence of Chinese taste. The rain, which was falling in torrents, did not prevent our gazing with surprise at many an ancient and splendid edifice, nor admiring the skill in the fine arts displayed in the horses, elephants and battle scenes, carved on the houses, the rich designs of window rosettes through which the rays of light penetrate, the colossal dimensions of the hideous monsters of stone, (toad-headed lions, dragons and rhinoceroses) and the many-armed red-painted images of the gods.

More surprising than all the rest was the coup d'œil presented by the market-place, notwithstanding its moderate size. On either side of it stands a great temple, whose eight stories, with their gilded roofs, are peopled by innumerable minas and sparrows. A flight of broad stone steps guarded by two monsters, leads up to the entrance of the temple; above, gigantic rhinoceroses, monkeys and horses adorn the edifice. The multitude of these strange figures, the stunning noise that resounded from within, the antique gloomy air of the surrounding houses, with their projecting roofs, and the solemn grandeur of the whole scene, awakened in my mind a feeling as though I had been suddenly carried back to some city of a thousand years since: I was involuntarily reminded of the description which Herodotus gives of ancient Babylon. For how long a time may all these things yet continue to appear exactly as they now do! The durable wood, the indestructible stone,* and a people who, like their kindred and instructors, the Chinese, cling to all that is primitive,

* Described by Dr Buchanan Hamilton as being found disposed in vertical strata, in large masses, as containing much lime, being very fine-grained, having a silky lustre, cutting well, and admirably resisting the action of the weather.—Tr.

unite in effectually resisting the destroying influence of Time.

We rode on, meantime, through a high, but narrow gate-way, into a court, where we saw several tame rhinoceroses, kept here on account of the custom of the country, which requires that, on the death of the Rajah, one of these creatures should be slain, and imposes on the highest personages in the state the duty of devouring it!*

Passing through dark and narrow streets, and traversing squares,—in which Buddhist pagodas, with their many-armed images of *Mahadevi*, *Indra*, and *Parvati* alternate with the Brahminical temples† that rise tier above tier,—we at length found ourselves at the other extremity of the town.

The gate is, like all the other gates of the city, a simple, tall, white arch, with a large eye painted on either side; indeed every entrance is, according to Chinese fashion, adorned with these horrid eyes surrounded with red borders. On the flat roof above the gate, stands a slender iron dragon, with a tongue a yard long, exactly of the form usually represented by the Chinese.

The dwelling of the British resident is about a quarter of an hour's ride beyond the town, in the centre of a beautiful park, on a little eminence, and its white Gothic buildings, although somewhat faulty in style, have an extremely picturesque effect, rising among tall fir-trees,

* Menu, the lawgiver of the Hindoos, enumerates the articles of which the offerings to the manes of deceased ancestors should consist, and which, when the ceremony had been duly performed, were to be eaten by the Brahmin and his guests: among these is the flesh of the rhinoceros.—Tr.

† The creeds, deities and superstitious rites of the Nepaulese are no less diversified and intermingled than their tribes. While the Brahminism of the majority of the population is looked upon by the natives of Bengal as corrupt in the extreme, the Buddhism of the remainder is not unmixed with divinities, rites and customs borrowed from the Pantheon and the sacred books of the Hindoos.—Tr.

with the snowy Alpine range in the back ground. We found the interior of the house very roomy, but so permeable in every part by the open air, that it appeared to us scarcely habitable in this spring-like and, to say the least, temperate weather. The fire was never suffered to expire on the hearth during the first eight days; for the thermometer very frequently stood, about sunrise, at ½° (33° Fahrenheit) or even at the freezing point. At noon, with a cloudless sky, the temperature mounted again to from 20 to 22° (from 77° to 80°.) Continuous rain was a rare occurrence; on the other hand, about seven o'clock in the morning, dense mists often rose, which lasted during the whole day.

The town of Cathmandoo stands not far from the lowest point of the valley, at the spot where the Bishmutty flowing from the north-west, and the Bogmuthy from the north-east, unite their waters. On the opposite side of the Bogmuthy, at the distance of about a mile from Cathmandoo, lies the second city of the valley of Nepaul, LALITA PATAN, which is said, in days of yore, to have surpassed its rival in size and importance. The greatest extent of the valley is from east to west; its highest level is in the north-western part, its lowest in the south, at the point where the Bogmuthy flows out of it. One of its most remarkable features is the natural terracing of its steep sides, which has been extended and improved by art, the most rugged and abrupt declivities having thus been transformed into gently sloping terraces, along the whole extent of which however it is necessary to pass in order to reach the mountains, from whatever point the ascent may be undertaken.

On the third day after our arrival, (the 12th of February) the ceremony of our reception by the Rajah took place. His elephants were sent to convey the Prince and his suite. We were conducted to the usual reception-palace,—a sort of court-house; but were not admitted to the proper "*Durbar*,"—the Royal Residence; the interior of the latter however is said to be very shabby, and even its exterior is by no means imposing.

The large wooden building, in which the reception took place, has certainly no resemblance to a palace. It contains dark staircases, and rooms filled with dust and with old armour. The audience-chamber is on the third floor. Two rows of chairs were placed at the sides, and a couple of sofas against the wall at the end of the apartment. The dirty yellow hangings were but partially concealed by old and very bad French engravings, and portraits as large as life, among which I remarked a Napoleon with cherry cheeks, and the whole succession of the Rajahs of the last century, as well as many of their kinsfolk, all painted, after the flat and rude manner of the Chinese, by native artists. Coverlets of white cotton served instead of carpets. No display of wealth or magnificence appeared, save in the costly and brilliant costumes of the Rajah and of his courtiers and household.

Upon the divan to the left side of this presence-chamber, sat the young Rajah (he is only sixteen years of age) and beside him his father, the deposed sovereign: both have quite the air of rogues,—the young Rajah even to a greater degree than his father. If his face had not that disagreeable expression, which he has heightened by the habit of distorting his mouth and nose abominably, he might, with his large black eyes, his long, finely shaped, aquiline nose, and his small, delicate mouth, have been reckoned very handsome. Young as he is, his actions prove that the opinion formed of him from his outward man, is not an erroneous one. He appears to have every quality best fitted to make an accomplished tyrant. The father, a man of milder disposition,—has still many adherents; but, fortunately for the country, the real ruler is Martabar Singh.

Both Rajahs were not only magnificent in their apparel, but literally overloaded with gold, gems and brilliants.

The divan on the right-hand side was occupied by the Rajah's three younger brothers, boys of eight, ten and twelve years of age. The two elder ones are already married.

The Prince sat on the side row, next to the Rajah, and, as I took my seat at some distance and on the same side, I could, to my great regret, follow but little of the conversation. Meanwhile, it afforded me no slight amusement to see how Martabar Singh made a point of showing off his power, as he now rose, now again seated himself: for all those present, even the members of the Royal Family, are obliged to stand up the instant he rises; there was therefore an incessant rustling up and down, and he took care moreover to give occasion for perpetual bowings and salutations.

At the conclusion of the audience, presents were distributed; various and costly furs, Chinese silken stuffs, and beautiful weapons. My turn too came to stand up and to receive a fur dress made of otter's skins, a poniard, and a "*khukri*" in a gilt scabbard. The Rajah touched my hand, which honour, graciously conferred on me, I was instructed to acknowledge by a low salam, while Martabar Singh threw the gifts over my arm.

The following day we visited a very ancient place of pilgrimage, in the neighbourhood of Cathmandoo,—the celebrated sanctuary of SAMBHUNATH. It stands on one of those isolated sand-stone hills, of which several rise in this plain, apparently unconnected with the surrounding ranges of hills, though their formation is identical. This monument of antiquity,—a bell-shaped structure, from fifty to sixty feet in height, above which tower the twelve stories of the gilded temple,—is surrounded by trees of great age and of immense size. A flight of nearly three hundred steps leads to the summit of the hill on which it stands. At the upper end of the stair lies, upon a stone pediment, the thunder-bolt of INDRA,* a thick gilded staff, seven feet long, terminating at each end in a sort of sceptre-crown, the form of which reminded me of the French fleur-de-lys. In the vicinity of the great sanctuary, there are various other temples, containing inextinguishable fire, and a multitude of figures of Buddha. Pilgrims from Bootan, and Fakeers, flock in numbers to these sacred shrines; we saw also on the day of our visit, a procession of young maidens ascending the height; they had decked their hair with the red blossoms of the rhododendron, and were themselves for the most part not without beauty.

Another sanctuary, of Brahminical origin, named PASUPATINATH, rises upon the summit of a similar hill. Its doors are of massive silver, and its architecture, which in other respects is by no means remarkable, abounds in gold. The interior was full of monkeys and of young cows. The former, of the Rhesus species, *(Inuus Rhesus)* which here, equally in Buddhist and in Brahminical fanes, is treated with the greatest partiality and respect, and inhabits the groves around every temple.

The sanctuaries of HANDAGONG were the objects of our excursion on the 16th, as was on the 17th the ancient temple-city of BHATGONG, distinguished, in former days, for the learning of its priests; in the latter we did not find much to interest us.

I became acquainted with the animal creation of the valley of Cathmandoo by means of a great battue,

* The Jupiter of Brahminism.—TR.

arranged by Martabar Singh, on the 13th and 14th of February. Two regiments were called out, to tread down the jungle, and the birds were so much alarmed by the noise, that many of them rushed against the drivers, as if robbed of their senses, and were thus caught by the hand. Great numbers of them were also set upon by the Rajah's trained hawks. The Prince received specimens,—living and dead,—of all that this chase afforded; so that, for three days, I was engaged in stripping and preparing the skins of the victims, assisted by two servants who performed the coarser part of the work. A few Civet cats, beautiful Nepaul pheasants, thrushes, woodpeckers, parrots, &c. &c., were numbered among the booty.

After witnessing, on the 19th, a grand review of the Nepaulese troops, with their artillery and their elephants, we availed ourselves of the permission graciously vouchsafed us, to see something of the interior of the country by making a tour to the valley of NOYAKOT, to which no European has penetrated for many years past. The Minister's stout mountain ponies were prepared for our use; and, accompanied by Captain Ottley,—whose presence, from the delicacy of his constitution, rather impeded than facilitated our progress on the journey,—we started on the 20th of February.

We soon quitted the lowest part of the valley of Cathmandoo, and gradually ascended the terraces of alluvial soil, through which the four branches of the Bogmuthy to the north-east, and the three of the Bishmutty to the north, have hollowed out deep clefts. In many places we found cuts of more than 200 feet in depth, affording admirable opportunities for studying the strata. The banks between the streams are most carefully divided, from the lowest to the highest point, into terraces, varying from two to four feet in height according to the elevation of the ground, and every inch is rendered available for cultivation. This gives to the valley the appearance of an immense amphitheatre, these terraces forming the tiers all round.

Here and there, in the steep ramparts that enclose the valley,* I counted upwards of fifty different strata, consisting of beds of clay of the most various colours, alternating with sand,—fine and coarse,—which, like the clay, is more or less intermingled with mica, and also contains larger fragments of mica schist and of granite. In the layers of blue clay, kidney-shaped lumps of black charcoal, and a species of clay abounding in *humus*, are found in great quantities; those of the latter are known by the name of *Konkar*,† and are used as manure on the fields.‡

* Those writers best acquainted with the great valley from which our author was thus ascending, agree in supposing that it was formerly a lake, which gradually deposited the alluvial matter that forms the different substrata of the plain. The extent of the lake, Dr Buchanan Hamilton informs us, may be everywhere traced by that of the alluvial matter, above the edges of which generally appear irregularly shaped large stones, which, having rolled down from the hills, had stopped at the water's edge, as is usual in the lakes of hilly countries. The remembrance of the lake is preserved in the mythological fables of the natives, both Brahminical and Buddhist, tradition affirming that one of the gods, with a blow of his scimitar, cleft the mountains, and that the Bogmuthy forthwith issued through the gap, which now forms its narrow gorge. While the lake existed, the two hills of Sambhunath and Pasubatinath must have appeared as islands in the midst.—Tr.

† Ritter, in his "*Erdkunde*," (Asia, vol. iii., p. 67,) gives this name as "*Koncha*." From the experiments he has hitherto made, it appears probable that they are the beds of *Infusoria*.—Editor.

‡ Dr Royle, in describing the geology of the great Gangetic Valley, says that in most parts calcareous particles are intermixed with the sandy soil, and with the substratum in which clay predominates, assuming in many places the form of spongy cavernous nodules, remarkable especially from their being so abundant as occasionally to give the appearance of the surface being covered as with a fall of large hail-stones, and forming the extensively diffused *Kunkur* formation of India. That of Nepaul is described by Dr B. Hamilton as a black substance resembling clay, and constituting a large proportion of the alluvial matter, approaching very near to the nature of turf, and much intermixed with leaves, bits of stick, fruits and other vegetable exuviæ, the produce of plants similar to those now growing on the neighbouring hills. He says it is called "*Koncha*" by the Newars, who dig it out in large quantities, and apply it to their fields as manure.

The first town we reached was BALADCHI, a place distinguished by its many temples, and its great traffic in spices and dyes; it is situated on the western range of hills,—the boundary of the principal valley,—about three hundred feet above the level of Cathmandoo. More interesting is the village of DARUMTALLA, on a sharply projecting tongue of ground between two deep branches of the Bishmutty.

In an hour and a-half we arrived at CHITPOOR, the last village of the valley of Cathmandoo, of the whole of which it commands an extensive, though not particularly beautiful view. Blocks of granite and of gneiss in great numbers cover the ground; yet gneiss does not occur *in situ* till the cliffs, from 300 to 400 feet above that level, where it is in conjunction with mica schist. The path, although much trodden and enlivened by numerous bearers, pilgrims and fakeers, is yet very bad, and quite impassable for any beast of burden. For a considerable distance it skirts the western side of a chain of hills that extends from north-east to south-west. We were obliged to cross three or four branches of the Bishmutty, before reaching the foot of the KAULIA PASS.

Here agriculture has, on every side, taken complete possession of the land to the extermination of all wood; even to a great height on the Kaulia Pass, we found capital soil, everywhere laid out in terraces: the whole western side of the chain of hills of Darumtalla is richly supplied with water, springs and purling brooks abounding in every part, though the absence of trees might lead one at first sight to suppose the contrary. In six hours we gained the head of the pass and our night's quarters,

He adds, that the rivers that pass through this Koncha have washed from its strata another harder and blacker substance, but still having so strong a resemblance to it that it is called "*Ha-Koncha*" by the natives, who suppose it to be decayed charcoal; an opinion, the truth of which however seemed to him incompatible with the great size of some of its masses.—TR.

—a bungalow, erected by Mr Hodgson, at a height of two thousand feet, near the summit of the mountain-peak. Unfortunately the shades of evening prevented us from enjoying a full prospect of the chains of mountains. Of the Himalayas, we saw only the DHAYABUN group, still irradiated by the crimson glow of sunset: all the others were wrapt in clouds. Early in the morning of the 21st of February, the most glorious and enchanting landscape burst upon our view, that imagination could picture in any highland scenery: a boundless ocean of gigantic snowy mountains, towering one behind the other on the clear horizon; four distinct ranges were visible; the peak of Dhayabun in the north-west seemed almost to vanish amid so many other giants: but lo! in the north, while we were gazing at the huge GOSSAINTHAN its eastern surface caught the bright glow of morning light. Now again our attention was attracted to the W.N.W., where a sharp and lofty summit seemed to pierce the very skies, its three needle-like peaks, one after the other, illuminated with the most exquisite crimson tints. We could hardly venture to believe it the DHAWALA GIRI itself; yet, according to its position, it could be no other.

Our maps, the compass, and the testimony of several old men, soon removed all doubt. Who could have imagined that a distance of thirty German miles* could thus shrink into nothing? It was an overpowering impression, filling the soul with awe. The realization of a perpendicular altitude of a German mile,† there it stands, like a giant spectre, and in vain does the astounded beholder seek for similes whereby to shadow forth the sublimity of the spectacle: I can only say that the outline of the

* Upwards of a hundred and thirty-eight English miles.—TR.

† Mr Hamilton, in his account of Hindostan, gives the height of Dhawala Giri (or the White Mountain) as exceeding 26,862 feet above the level of the sea. Dhayabun, he gives as 24,768, and states that it is visible from Patna, a distance of 162 geographical (about 186 statute) miles. Dr Wallich marks the height of Gossainthan, 24,740.—TR.

Alps of Switzerland, so deeply engraven in my memory, now shrunk into comparative insignificance, and as it were vanished into nought.

At sunrise, I found all the eastern and south-eastern slopes covered with ice; our thermometer meanwhile had sunk, at half-past six, A.M. to 3½° (40° Fahrenheit) although a little while before, it had been standing at 5° (about 43–4° Fahrenheit).

As we scrambled down the steep declivity of the northern side of the Kaulia, we marked the rolling vapours, resplendent with every gorgeous tint of purple and of red, gradually filling the depths of the vallies below. Thick bushes of fragrant Daphnes clothed the cliffs, till, after a descent of an hour and a half, we reached a table-land, on the north-east side of the Kaulia, a thoroughly Alpine stretch of prairie-ground. The chieftain of a tribe of Bhooteas,* surrounded by his wild retainers, all clad in most singular garb, had there pitched his camp. Farther down, the path presented quite an animated scene, from the multitude of bearers, of whom the larger proportion were females, laden with heavy burdens,—the varied products of the sultry valley of Noyakot†,—pine-apples, oranges, betel-leaves, sugar-

* Mr Hamilton, in his "Description of Hindostan," informs us that, besides the countries which we call Thibet and Bootan, the Bhooteas, through the whole tract between the rivers Cali and Teesta, occupy the Alpine region adjacent to the snowy peaks of the Himalayas on both sides of the mountains, called by the natives of the South, Bhote. Thus this race is scattered through the mountain-regions on the borders of Thibet, afterwards visited by our author. The principal support of their country is its mines and numerous flocks of sheep, goats and cattle; the quantity of grain raised being inconsiderable. The higher Bhootea villages in the tract between the rivers Cali and Dauli are entirely deserted in winter, all access to them being prevented by the snow, from October to May. This singular race is of Tartar origin, and preserves a striking resemblance in language and personal appearance to the Chinese Tartars of Thibet, and a great veneration for the Lamas; and, though their religion is much mixed with Brahminism, they are regarded with hatred by the other hill tribes, as cow-killers, and, as such, outcasts of the worst description.—TR.

* Mentioned by other writers as being two thousand two hundred feet

cane, and the garlic so highly prized in Cathmandoo, all carried on the back, and supported by a head-band across the forehead. Our road lay through a succession of hamlets surrounded by fields, whose enclosures were formed of Spurge *(Euphorbia antiquorum)* with stems often as thick as a man's thigh.

The terracing is here carried out even upon precipitous chasms and deep ravines; in many places, the terraces are three times as high as they are broad, and the inventive skill of the mountaineers has made them serve the additional purpose of stables for the cattle. Horizontal poles are stuck in, so as to project from the upper edge of each terrace-wall, and mats are thrown over them; under the sheltering cover thus provided, the whole herd is made to stand, in regular order. The next day the stable is moved up to the tier immediately above: and thus the trouble and expense both of building stables and of manuring the land are dispensed with.

We found ourselves, after much ascending and descending, in a lofty forest, the first we had met with on this side of the valley of Cathmandoo. It consists entirely of umbrageous trees; *Erythrina*, *Shorea*, *Bauhinia*, &c., with an underwood of *Carissa* and *Justicia*. The soil is a compact red clay with a large admixture of mica; cliffs of mica-schist and gneiss occurring but rarely. At length we slid down an almost perpendicular declivity, from eight to nine hundred feet in depth, overgrown with thick bushes, at the foot of which we found ourselves on the rocky bank of a little stream, whose name we could not ascertain, but which was distinguished by the pale green hue of its clear waters. We followed its course till the point of its confluence with the BALOO TADI, whose channel is less rocky, though the banks continue very steep. The

lower than that of Cathmandoo, and uninhabitable during the hottest season, from the prevalence of the Ayul.—TR.

bed of the latter is sandy and almost entirely flat; a fourth part only of its surface was covered with water, all the rest being cultivated land, and chiefly laid out in sugar plantations. A few miserable straw huts, and a potter's oven standing in the open air, in which water-jars, formed of a beautiful micaceous clay, were undergoing the process of baking, over a fire fed with the favourite fuel of Nepaul—cow-dung—were the only signs of habitation that presented themselves, upon the road which finally led us to the real TADI river,—a broad and beautiful, though very shallow stream. Flowing down from the north-north-east, it unites itself, just beyond the spot where it receives the waters of the Baloo Tadi, (Little Tadi) with the TRISOOLGUNGA.

On the other side of the Tadi, rises the mountain of Noyakot. The warm climate of the lower part of the valley here, produces a vegetation totally different from that of the plain of Cathmandoo. At the foot of the mountain, which is richly wooded, we found a beautiful species of Bamboo,—also the *Butea frondosa*, the *Feronia*, (Elephant Apple) and other *Aurantiaceæ*,—several varieties of the fig-tree, (*Ficus infectoria, latifolia*, &c.), among which was one unknown to me, with beautiful dark-red fruit; and higher up, a shady wood, consisting of various species of *Laurus*, intermingled with many varieties of *Grewia, Bauhinia*, &c., &c.

Without turning aside to visit the city of Noyakot,*

* Noyakot, (New Fort) the key of Nepaul Proper on the Thibet side, is remarkable as having been, in 1792, the ne plus ultra of the victorious Chinese arms, though situated within only 26 miles of Cathmandoo, and 60 of the British territory in the Bengal Presidency. The motive which led the Celestial Empire to hazard so bold and so remote a campaign was vengeance against the ambitious Gorkhas, who, having in 1768 conquered Nepaul, had turned their arms against the Grand Lamas of Lassa and Teshoo Loomboo. The result of the Chinese invasion was, that the Rajah of Nepaul concluded a treaty on ignominious terms, and became nominally tributary to China, though it has ever been the wise policy of that empire, as of our own, to leave Nepaul in its independence.—TR.

we immediately ascended the steep mountain to the sanctuary. The umbrageous forest soon came to an end, and the heat became most oppressive, until, at the end of an hour's climb, we gained the summit and the temple that crowns it. According to a rough estimate, its elevation above the vale of the river may be between three and four thousand feet.

This mountain is no solitary peak, but rather the last and the most pointed summit of a ridge which rises to a much greater height, and stretches far towards the north,—the MAHAMENDEL. Two separate shrines are situated on this hill of Noyakot; the lower one, the access to which is by means of a flight of steps somewhat exceeding one hundred in number, is the larger of the two, and contains a multitude of strange and grotesque figures of animals: it is rich in wood-carvings and votive offerings, weapons and vessels formed of metals of every sort, but the whole is filthy beyond description. The upper one is much smaller, built almost entirely of brick, and devoid of all ornament: the low story of wood, on its plain and lofty substructure, is the only part adorned with beautiful carved windows, and displays, as does also the roof, considerable taste. Between the two sanctuaries stands the *Durbar*, a royal palace of small size and built of brick, but singular and striking in its appearance, and surrounded by pleasure-grounds dignified with the name of gardens.

The magnificent view of the valley of the Trisoolgunga is the best reward which this mountain offers to those who scale its heights; and its temple structures, with their gilded roofs, form an incomparable foreground. But, alas! the beautiful valley and the city that lay at our feet, were objects unattainable by us. The limits of our tour were fixed; we returned as we had come, and saw on our way, at the foot of the mountain, the splendid edifices of the "*Great Durbar*," architectural monuments, quite unique in their style. The wood-carving of the windows seems as imperishable as the hard bricks of flaming red of which the whole is constructed. In the extensive garden of this palace we saw very large beds of pine-apples. The banana flourishes here without culture or care.

Towards evening we set out on our toilsome march, retracing our steps towards the capital. Our continued and severe exertions were however so richly repaid, that for a long time the weariness of our limbs was altogether forgotten. Before the sun sank to rest, we had gained a commanding height, from which we enjoyed a full view of Dhawala-Giri and Gossainthan, bathed in burning tints by the deep effulgence of the parting orb. The prospect of those thousands of ice-clad pinnacles, now glowing, now fading, in every variety of brilliant or of exquisitely delicate hues,—afforded us an enjoyment beyond the reach of comparison, but which left an impression that nothing can ever efface.

While the shades of approaching night were fast thickening around us, our path was by no means free from danger; however, we arrived without any misadventure befalling us, at the little bungalow on the Pass of the Kaulia, where we rejoined our travelling companions; and on the following day we returned by the same route we had followed in coming, to the city of Cathmandoo.

The days allotted for our sojourn in the kingdom of Nepaul were fast drawing to a close. A visit to Martabar Singh in his own palace, and a farewell audience of the Rajah, were the points of interest in the latter part of our residence in its capital. Our leave-taking was celebrated by a thoroughly Nepaulese entertainment, which consisted in cutting off the heads of a number of huge buffaloes, with the peculiar weapon commonly used here for that purpose,—a short but extremely heavy sabre, curved inwards, and sharp on the inner edge,—known by the name of "*Kora*." After the most distinguished personages of the court had displayed their skill in decapitation, Martabar Singh himself doffed his gorgeous robe,—woven of peacock's feathers and silk,—seized the short sabre, sprang forward with the greatest agility and grace, and fetching a tremendous blow, hewed down a young buffalo on the spot, cleaving its whole body asunder, by a stroke of the "Kora" immediately behind its shoulder-blades!

To-morrow we shall depart from this most interesting city, following the same route by which we penetrated into Nepaul, to re-enter the flat plains of British India, and to visit Benares and Delhi.

SEVENTH LETTER.

SUGOULI—TIGER-HUNT—PALANQUIN JOURNEY—BENARES—ALLAHABAD—THE INDIAN PLAINS—LUCKNOW—ENTRY INTO THE CITY—BUILDINGS—PALACES—THE NABOB OF OUDE—THE RESIDENCES OF THE ENGLISH—NATIONAL MANNERS AND CUSTOMS—DANCING GIRLS—MOSQUE OF IMAUM BARRY—TOMBS OF THE ROYAL FAMILY—BAZAARS—ROYAL GARDENS—THE NABOB'S STEAMER—BREAKFAST WITH THE NABOB OF OUDE—THE ROYAL FAMILY—SINGULAR DISHES—ANIMAL FIGHTS—PALACE OF FAROOK BAM—HUNT—COMBATS OF WILD BEASTS—THE ARTIST BEECHEY—GIFTS FROM THE NABOB—PARTING FESTIVITIES—JOURNEY TO AGRA—HOUSES IN AGRA—THE TATTIES—MANNER OF LIFE OF THE BRITISH RESIDENTS—SOCIETY—BHURTPOOR—DELHI—ARCHITECTURE OF DELHI—PALACE OF THE GREAT MOGUL—TOMB OF HUMAYOON—TOMB OF NIZAM UD DEEN.

DELHI, *2d of May* 1845.

WE arrived at Sugouli, on the 1st of March, *via* Bheemphed and Hethaura. At that place we remained for several days, on account of a tiger-hunt, which it had been arranged should take place in the neighbourhood. The Bettiah Rajah had sent twenty elephants for that purpose; ten more had been placed at the disposal of the hunt by the Rajah of Nepaul. These preparations made, we set out for the forests, in company with several English friends, lovers of the chase, who had joined us at Bissouli; and day after day, the hunt was carried on with indefatigable zeal.

On the second day, a tigress was beat up, with her whelp; the latter was shot dead by the Prince, and the mother was likewise wounded, but she did not charge, and finally escaped in the thick jungle. In the course of the following days, several wild boars, axis-deer, (*Cervus porcinus,*) a civet-cat, and several peacocks and jungle-fowl were brought down; but not one tiger was even seen: we wearied our elephants in vain.

At length, on the last day of the hunt, (the 8th of March) the drivers roused a large and powerful tiger, where we should least have expected it, in a field of Cajan. There was in its appearance none of that grandeur which I had expected: it walked away softly, slowly and clumsily, like a dog that has had a good cudgelling! A piece of marshy ground retarded its escape, which was soon rendered impossible by a shot in the leg. The next ball entered the heart, and the tiger fell dead upon the spot.

It was a mighty beast: from the snout to the tip of the tail it measured about eleven feet, and a very sufficient load it was for the elephant that bore it off the field. I had great difficulty in preventing the natives, through whose villages we passed with our booty, from plucking out all the hair of the beard; in a short time one side had actually been plucked bare, and nothing now remained but to tear out the hair of the other side myself to remove the possibility of its being stolen. On account of the great heat, the skin was taken off, with the assistance of several butchers, that very night, that we might secure it in all its beauty, and carry it off with us as a trophy of the chase.

We were now once more in the flat country, and, as the journey was to be performed after the usual fashion in palanquins, a separation of our party must needs take place. I travelled in the second detachment, with Mr Fortescue; and setting out on the 10th of March, we proceeded *via* Gorucpoor and Azimgur, and reached Benares at the end of a four days' march.

BENARES is in my opinion the most beautiful of all the Indian cities we have hitherto seen. It extends along the banks of the noble river, forming a wide crescent of majestic buildings,—countless mosques, minarets, pagodas and palaces. All these splendid edifices are of a remarkably beautiful red sand-stone, found in quarries near the city. The motley inhabitants, whose real numbers have scarcely been ascertained, move and jostle on, the live-long day, in the crowded streets, and on the banks of the Ganges, which are almost every where provided with broad flights of steps,—"*Ghauts*,"—to enable the pilgrims to descend with ease and comfort to the margin of the sacred stream. No other city that I have seen presents as lively a picture of the mode of living of the people of India, their manners and their customs, as Benares. How poor and monotonous in comparison of it is that great metropolis, Calcutta, so often extolled by the English,—wedded to all their home luxuries,—because, forsooth, roast beef and pickles, and everything that appertains to good living and to "*comfort*," may there be had in abundance, to their very heart's content!

The heat is to be sure great enough in Benares; we had to endure a temperature of from 25° to 26° (89° to 91° Fahrenheit) on our way hither; and even in the airy tent pitched in the garden of the house in which we are lodged,—the residence of Major Carpenter,—I should feel disposed to give myself up to quiet contemplation, did not time forbid any such luxurious indolence. Musquitoes too are super-abundant here, to the no small detriment of our night's repose.

The few days of rest in Benares passed rapidly away in sight-seeing, among the ancient and very remarkable mosques and temples of this far-famed city. We quitted it on the 19th of March, and half a day's journey brought us to ALLAHABAD, a city much resorted to as a place of pilgrimage. At seven o'clock A.M., on the 25th of March, we entered LUCKNOW, (the natives pronounce it *Lachno*) after traversing, in our palanquins, the weary plain that extends from Allahabad, and passing through the town of CAUNPOOR, spending Maundy Thursday, and Good Friday itself, *en route*, as heathen among the heathen.

The plains in this part of India have a singularly dismal aspect: the carefully cultivated fields of oil plants, ricinus, barley, spelt and other kinds of grain, here make way for a sandy waste, destitute of all traces of vegetation; or for a hard, parched, clayey soil, from which every green blade is removed as fast as it springs, by the destroying hand of the grass-cutters; this desolating work being in these parts a profitable trade. Trees are a rare apparition here; it is only in the neighbourhood of the mud-built hovels clustered into wretched villages, and of the filthy towns surrounded with mounds of rubbish, that an occasional group may be seen,—mangoe-trees, intermingled with Acacias and with Peepul trees,—under whose shade travellers,—Moslems or Hindoos,—have pitched their tents. The brown, half-naked Hindoos, crawl and squat together beside their rude buffalo-carts, while the Moslems, clean and neat in their apparel, with their ample and flowing garment of white muslin and the characteristic turban, sit cross-legged in front of their tents, smoking their hookahs, surrounded by a circle of naked children, and of women wrapped in large shawls, of whom nothing is to be seen save the black rings painted round their eyes, and their feet, loaded with ornaments of gold and silver. These people are unmoved by the groans or the measured and doleful cries of the palkee-bearers; they scarcely condescend to bestow a glance, much less a salam, on the stranger, as he inquisitively peeps forth from within his palanquin.

Such groups as these present however the only variety that can tempt the traveller, on his sultry and weary way, to clear his eyes of the thick dust, to rouse himself from his lethargy, and to look abroad. Petty annoyances are as unfailing a feature in the history of his journey as ennui itself: now a pole of his palanquin breaks, now one of his luggage-bearers *(Bangiwalla)* has disappeared, or again, he arrives at a station, where perhaps not a single palanquin-bearer, or at any rate not half of the number he has paid for, is forthcoming. Nothing remains in such a case, but violently to belabour, with stick or fist, these miserable creatures, whom dire necessity has long accustomed him to regard as half brutes. Sometimes indeed it may suffice to bestow a severe reprimand on the first that can be got hold of, upon which the recreants almost always suddenly make their appearance, and the refractory forthwith jog on their onward way. Blows serve to interpret, as well as to enforce, those unintelligible phrases which unluckily too often occur; for Hindostanee is not easily acquired by Europeans: we are however studying most diligently, each one seeking to outstrip his neighbour. As I was at the head of the second detachment, my scholarship was often in requisition. What a desperate case am I in, when doomed to listen to interminable discourses from the "*Moonshee,*" and other authorities, not comprehending a single word, and scarce daring to indulge the hope that these worthies take it for granted that I understand them perfectly!

On the 25th of March, we had alighted from our palanquins at five o'clock in the morning,—for we travel on, night and day without intermission,—to take our morning walk, and run a race with our palkee-bearers. Not imagining ourselves in the immediate vicinity of the city of Lucknow, we had not changed our usual travelling guise,—loose trowsers of thin red silk, with only a shirt and a "*solah*"* hat,—when, to our utter amazement, at day-break, we found ourselves in the narrow

* "Solah" is the name given to the pith of the cotton-tree, of which are made hats calculated to afford shelter from the burning rays of the sun.—W. Hoffmeister.

streets,—then peopled only with dogs,—of a suburb of that great city. The clay-walled hovels, with their outer coating of cow-dung to exclude the moisture, soon came to an end, after we had passed through the last of several large gates of Saracenic architecture, with painted arches. Brick houses, entirely open on the ground floor, with shops and workshops, at this early hour still occupied as bed-chambers, formed, within the city-gate, wide and regular streets. Here and there appeared a building of greater size, and of semi-European aspect. Another gate, larger than the preceding ones, presented itself at the extremity of the great street through which we had proceeded; beside it was drawn up a detachment of soldiers, with red jackets and iron morions, but wearing, instead of trowsers, the simple white cotton handkerchief hanging about their legs. One of the veteran officers felt himself called upon,—in his great zeal to imitate European civilization,—to run up behind us, most respectfully desiring to know our names. So unreasonable a demand we had never yet met with in India, and Mr Fortescue seemed inclined to reply by brandishing his stick. I contented myself with informing him in a most confidential manner, that my name was "*Sechs und sechzig sechs-eckige Hechtskopfe,*" ("*Six and sixty six-cornered pike's heads*") upon which, after repeated and unsuccessful attempts to pronounce the name, in the course of which he nearly dislocated his tongue and his jaw-bone, he retired, grumbling and indignant; for neither Sanscrit nor Persian could furnish the necessary sounds.

After a quarter of an hour's march, the aspect of the city changed. Large and lofty houses, plastered over with yellow or white shining stucco, formed an unbroken line on either side of the street; numerous mosques, and minarets of ingenious and spiral form, rose amid edifices of thoroughly European appearance. Domes with gilded summits, and white open balustrades round the terraced roofs of noble palaces, increased in number as we penetrated further into the interior of the city; yet its architecture, though elegant and magnificent in a style of its own, is not of pure and correct taste. Thus, for example, we passed an edifice of extraordinary size, where the rules of art would have required a great number of tall windows in front. The spaces for them indeed were there; but, as no Mahometan likes to have any towards the street, they were all, on both stories, completely walled up. Something however being necessary to break the dismal monotony of the solid masonry, each niche intended for a window was, with truly Oriental bad taste, filled up with figures as large as life, representing men of every age and every rank, painted al fresco in the most gaudy colours. Picture to yourself a house with sixty large windows ornamented in this manner! The one above described is a "*Mehalla*" or harem. The part of the city which we last traversed consists entirely of government offices and royal palaces.

But now, at a turn of the street, we were met by a troop of armed horsemen at full gallop, who were driving the foot-passengers out of the way with great clamour; next followed a company of the infantry body-guard, with red uniforms and silvered halberds, to clear the way more thoroughly still. We found ourselves in the midst of such a crowd and tumult, that it became necessary to brandish our sticks, and make vigorous use of our elbows. A frightful din, caused by a military band, consisting of fifes, drums and cymbals,—the men bedecked in most strange costumes,—increased the Oriental character of the scene, and heralded the approach of some person of high dignity. This advanced guard was succeeded by three huge elephants, with brocade trappings over their heads, and silver howdahs upon their backs. Accustomed to such processions, we did not dream of anything extraordinary, least of all, at this early hour, of the immediate proximity of the Nabob of Oude. A corpulent man, with immoderately bloated cheeks, and of extremely phlegmatic appearance, enveloped, cap-à-pie, in gold tissue, and mounted on a tall white charger of Cabul breed, was seen riding in the midst of a troop of showy lancers, handsome, well-made men, with yellow uniforms, blue caps and enormous boots. It proved to be none other than the Sovereign himself. We had however in the throng no opportunity to look more closely at him.

The street soon widened into a spacious square; a beautiful and verdant lawn and rich wood appeared before us on the other side of a lofty free-stone arch. Passing through this gateway, we entered a sort of park, at the farther extremity of which are several large, yellow roughcast buildings. Flat roofs with massive balustrades, lofty colonnades surrounding plain quadrangular boxes, and carefully closed jalousies, characterized it as the dwelling of the British Resident; for this form of architecture is universally adopted for the habitations of the English throughout India, from Ceylon to the Himalayas, being indeed rendered almost necessary by the sultry climate.

We had reached our goal, and Mr Shakspeare, the British Resident, gave us a most friendly welcome in this his chateau. The Prince and his companions had arrived the day before; we were all delighted to meet again after a separation of four or five days, such as often happens in the palanquin travelling of these lands, and mutually to recount the adventures of our journey. Our kind host is himself a bachelor; but three or four other English gentlemen are resident at Lucknow with their families; and in this little circle we could clearly mark the pleasure caused by the arrival of foreign guests, as introducing a little variety into their dull and monotonous life. The stiff and aristocratic tone that prevails among the fashionable society of Calcutta, does not reign here; consequently the drives, pleasure parties and evening entertainments, which were of daily occurrence, were most cheerful and agreeable. Music was all the fashion; the most trifling performance seemed to give universal satisfaction; no voice was so poor or insignificant, as not to be exerted with pleasure, to display its owner's skill in the tuneful art, by pouring forth some simple melody; no piano-forte so discordant as not to enable one to shine by striking up a few hackneyed waltzes.

After a two o'clock *tiffin*, our second repast, no less substantial than the first designated by the English name *breakfast*, of which we had partaken at ten o'clock, we proceeded, in the equipages prepared for us, to make acquaintance with the wonders of the city. We saw it in its most brilliant aspect, for it happened to be a festival both with Hindoos and Mahometans, and a countless and motley multitude in festive attire was crowding the streets, and the square in front of the great mosque of Imam Barah. It must be remembered that Lucknow is a city of nearly a hundred thousand inhabitants, and that the Moslems have a peculiar propensity to indolence and lounging, especially on feast-days, when all labour is positively prohibited.

There they sit, all in a row, neat and clean in their muslin garments, the rose-coloured turban on their heads, squatting upon the broad marble balustrades, in grave and solemn repose. Their high head-dress marks them as Mahometans. The Hindoos are moreover seldom seen with those beautiful Damascus poniards, with thick ivory handles and golden tassels, stuck in their girdles. These Moslems are plainly the dandies of the place. Their slippers of gold embroidery, with long, turned-up points, testify still further to their opulence and their love of finery.

Here, a crowd of screaming, raging Hindoos,—for they are incessantly quarrelling,—is gathered round a hideous fakeer. The servant of the gods, condescending to exhibit his skill in profane art and tricks, is actually balancing a sword upon his nose! Two diminutive youngsters, likewise fakeers, with faces painted white, and high caps of gold paper, are dancing in a circle around him. Farther on, a yellow Himalayan bear is performing his antics, amid a throng so dense, that the animal's grotesque movements are scarce visible to passers-by.

From within a tent at no great distance from us, issues a sound of horrid, nasal singing. The cadences and trills,—to add force to which, both hands are held before the mouth in a most ungraceful manner,—would, if but correctly in tune, have by no means an unpleasing effect. I know the melody; it is an extremely pretty one; were it sung without that dreadfully harsh, nasal twang, I could fancy its being really charming. The words are, "*Tasa be tasa no be no,*"—a Persian song of Hafiz; indeed most of the national songs are of Persian origin, for in ancient times the Persians were the poets whose province it was to provide lays for the whole country: now, alas! even their muse is silent.

The lovely songstresses whose strains had reached our ears, now appeared amid the throng. A rich and flowing drapery of red muslin enveloped them from head to foot, in its thousand folds: its airy texture was resplendent with spangles of gold and silver; large gold rings were passed through their right nostrils, and three or four others through each of their ears. Their arms,—which appeared from time to time as they gracefully moved the ends of their long robes backwards and forwards, now winding them closely round their figures, now again loosely unfolding them, turning and circling in elegant gyrations,—were adorned with thirty or forty bracelets of gold, silver, and many-coloured enamel; and even their feet, which occasionally, in the stamping movement of their measured step, peeped from beneath their long, loose, silken pantaloons, displayed broad silver bands fastened above the ankle and hung round with bells of the same metal, whose tinkling marked the cadence as they moved. Each toe was moreover adorned with a sort of signet-ring of silver. These singing or dancing girls, "Bayadères," who never fail to appear at every festival, every audience, and even every serious and important proceeding among the great ones of the land, are most popular, both among Moslems and Hindoos; and their dance,—if the turning to and fro without moving from one spot can be called dancing,—is, as well as their singing, known in India by the name of "*Natch.*"

Our four outrunners, or "*Chobdars,*" bearing long silver staves, the badges of their office, had great difficulty in opening a way for us through the crowd, to the entrance of the great mosque. This gate, known by the name of "*Rumi Desum,*" is a large arch, with elaborate and tasteful decorations of stucco on either side. In the centre, above the arch, the attention is attracted by the emblem of the Nabob of Oude, two gigantic fishes. The great beauty of these, as well as of other Indo-Moorish architectural chefs-d'œuvre, consists especially in the neatness and correctness of the execution. The lofty white façades produce a pleasing impression, and no offence is here taken at the fact, that the adjoining buildings form, on one side an obtuse, and on the other a right angle, with the main edifice; or that a multiplicity of arches and numberless turrets to the right, are made to correspond to a straight and simple wall to the left,—symmetry being a thing never aimed at here.

The IMAUM BARRY* is one of the largest and most remarkable mosques that I have seen in India. Its vaulted hall is a hundred and seventy feet in length. The whole edifice is majestic in its simplicity; gold and silver are not here lavished in the same degree as in other similar structures; yet the general effect is far more vivid than that of the ancient mosques of Cairo, which the niche-work of the fretted gate-ways, and the scolloped designs of the sculptured ceilings strongly recall to my mind. Nor did I ever see in Egypt minarets as beautiful as those of this mosque: they are fluted from top to bottom, and enriched with exquisite wreaths.

The grouped buildings of the mosque, irregular as they are individually, present altogether a charming and fairy-like picture; the whiteness of the front is finely thrown out by the fresh verdure of the garden, enriched with pomegranate trees and Persian roses in full flower. In the interior of the lofty structure stands a sepulchral monument, containing some relics. It is of great size; somewhat in the form of a tower-like cabinet, overlaid with thin plates of gold, and decorated with pearls and precious stones; in the lower part of it are the turban and Koran of the deceased. The curious are only suffered to look in from afar, although generally the Mahometans of India are not nearly so bigoted as those of Egypt, no such thing as putting off one's shoes being ever spoken of, nor free access into their holy places ever denied.

We also visited the burial-place of the present Royal Family, a wonderfully fine work of art, for Moslems spare no expense on their sepulchres. The dwellings of the living may indeed be filthy and scarcely habitable,

* The Imaum Barry has not, however, like the mosques of the Egyptian Sultans, a halo of antiquity to add romance to its magnificence. It was built between the years 1780 and 1784, by the Nabob Asoph ud Dowlah, the first sovereign of Oude who made Lucknow his capital.—TR.

provided only the departed are lodged in splendour. The entrance to the royal tomb is a lofty white gateway, surmounted by a cupola, and from its appearance the stranger would never expect to find a place of sepulture within. In the first court, surrounded by buildings, fountains are ever playing in beautiful marble basins, encircled by myrtles, roses and cypresses; palm-trees grace each corner of this garden, on every side of which glittering turrets and walls of dazzling whiteness rise amid the fragrant and shady bowers. The balmy air of evening was loaded with the perfume of roses and jessamine, and the deep azure of the vault above formed a striking contrast to the whiteness of the domes and the corners of the roofs, still illuminated by the last rays of the setting sun. A brilliant light shone through the arched windows of the lofty Moorish hall, under the marble gateway of which we now passed.

If the entrance court and external appearance of the burial-place produce an indescribable and magic impression, the charm is somewhat broken in the interior, where the eye wanders, distracted by the confused mass of incongruous yet brilliant objects; the tone of feeling caused by the first general view being, meantime, unpleasantly disturbed. The inner space, from its overloaded magnificence and unbounded profusion of gold and silver, pearls, gems, and all the valuables the East or the West can afford, had rather the appearance of a retail shop or of a fancy glass warehouse, than of the resting-place of the dead. Glass cupolas, and candelabras of every variety, may be seen standing in dozens, pell-mell upon the ground; lustres, ten feet in height, of bright and many-coloured glass, brought hither from England at an immense expense: and among these are deposited many trophies, swords and other weapons, of the finest Ispahan steel. The glare of the innumerable lamps so dazzles the eye, that it is difficult to find the principal thing among the multitude of other objects of interest.

Here, stand a couple of tigers, as large as life, formed of pieces of green glass, joined together with gold, presented by the Emperor of China. There, the attention is arrested by a silver horse, five feet high, with the head of a man, and the wings and tail of a peacock,—the steed sent down to the Prophet from heaven. Another horse, carved in wood, is an original likeness of the late Nabob's favourite charger. Vases, bronze figures, marble statues of moderate size, plans of the city and of the palaces, painted upon a gold ground, and a thousand other toys and trifles, were gathered together in this extraordinary place.

At length however amidst all this chaos, we discovered the tombs themselves; enclosed within massive golden railings, and canopied with a baldachin of gold, filigree-work, pearls and gems, large and small, lavished upon them. Besides the father of the reigning sovereign, who lies buried in the principal tomb, several of his wives repose on either side of him.

Dazzled by the brightness of real and false diamonds, we quitted the sepulchre, and mounted the elephants, which were waiting at the gate to convey us, at their heavy trot, to the old part of the city, where, from our lofty seats, we looked down on many and varied bazaars, all clean and neatly kept and lighted with very pretty lamps. Most pleasing pictures of domestic life were seen as we returned, on the balconies and through the open windows of the second stories, with which our howdahs placed us upon a level. Seldom does an opportunity offer of looking into the interior of a family circle so as to get a peep at real home-life among the Hindoos. The narrow streets here seem formed expressly to afford such a peep: many a beautiful lady was seen, before she had time to throw away her hookah and betake herself to flight, for "*Johnny Hatee*" (the elephant) marches on at a furious pace.

On the 26th of March, we set out in carriages, at five o'clock in the morning, the only hour at which the heat can be endured, and drove to the royal stables on the opposite bank of the Goomty. We there saw nearly two hundred horses of the greatest value, each standing ready bridled and attended by two "*syces*" (grooms) in splendid attire. Most of these noble steeds were of Arab race, but too fat from over-feeding to be beautiful, for they are never mounted; they stand there merely to be looked at.

The gardens of several of the royal palaces on the banks of the Goomty, remarkable for their tasteless magnificence, formed the more distant object of our excursion. The summer-houses of these pleasure-grounds are built in half French, half Moorish style; their large and heavy roofs supported by many slender and feeble columns. A kind of white stucco called *chunam* is the substitute for marble, and the wood work of the walls is painted grey or white. Never, even in the smallest of these pavilions is the warm bath wanting, and but seldom the private mosque, which I can only compare to a child's toy in appearance. The centre of the garden is usually occupied by a marble tank, in which many fountains are playing, and cypresses alternate with roses in embellishing its margin. The water-works are very tastelessly modernized; soldiers in red jackets, sheep, crippled dogs and lions, all spout forth water in the most wonderful manner!

The bowers and flower-beds are, in the hot season, owing to the great drought, in a poor condition, in spite of their being every morning inundated by means of multitudes of small canals; which, along with the straight paved walks, produce a very stiff effect in the general aspect of the grounds. In addition to this a mania prevails at Lucknow for placing marble or plaster statues, as large as life, at every turn and corner, without the slightest regard to the choice of figures, which seems to be left to the discretion of the sculptor. He copies the most antiquated French models, the originals of which have been out of date for many a long year, and manufactures, for a very reasonable price, shepherds and shepherdesses, British soldiers, Neptunes, or it may be Farnese pugilists, or dogs, lions, and sundry other beasts. Among them all I espied busts of Jean Jacques Rousseau, D'Alembert, and Napoleon, standing on the ground amid the fauns and the monsters of Indian mythology, all gathered together in the most perfect harmony to defend a flower-bed! What marvellously enhances the brilliant effect of these works of art, is a discovery which certainly is worthy of notice in Europe, viz. the custom of painting the hair, eyes and feet, (whether bare or shod) with a thick coating of lamp-black. The Venus de Medici appears to wonderful advantage in this improved edition!

The piece of water usually forms the uniting link between the larger summer-house or kiosk and a small wooden pavilion, which, destitute of all ornament save a neat balcony, is only intended as a point from which may be commanded, at one glance, the prospect of the whole long row of fountains playing in the reservoir.

Little furniture, beyond a few divans, is to be seen in these garden palaces; on the other hand, the walls of the apartments are decorated with a number of old French copper-plate prints, such as make their appearance at sales by auction, with the inscriptions below, "*l'Etè*," "*Modestie*," "*Innocence*," &c., promiscuously arranged among the productions of native artists, water-colour daubs of favourite horses, and dogs or pet monkeys, belonging to the Potentates of the Kingdom of Oude!

When the traveller has seen one of these gardens, he has seen them all; what I liked best in them was the continual supply of exquisite bouquets of roses, which the gardener never failed to present with a deep salam. We visited two or three such gardens, all belonging to the king; the first was quite enough to satisfy me, and I rejoiced when we were once more seated in our carriages and on our way to see the state-steamer, which his Majesty has caused to be built for his own use. It lies in the Goomty, and as that river is but small, the dimensions of the vessel are proportionably diminutive, and elegant. The Prince's arrival on board was greeted by a protracted salute, such as almost to make us repent of having risked the safety of our ears, since the boat herself did not offer much of interest.

She contained two handsome saloons, the sides of which were fitted up with divans covered with velvet and brocade. Here again was to be seen a selection of wretched, gaudily-coloured French engravings, as well as a variety of musical clocks, which, in accordance with the Indian notions of music, were all made to play at once. One saloon was appropriated to the Nabob, the other to his wives. More singular and characteristic was the sight of a curious gondola lying alongside the steamer; in form, it exactly resembles the ordinary representations of the whale swallowing Jonah, and like them, it rises almost entirely out of the water, which it merely seems to touch below.

The afternoon of the same day was occupied in visiting several mosques; we saw, among others, that of *Saduth Ali Shah*, the grandfather of the present king, which differs but little in the main from those we had before seen.

By far the most interesting day of our residence in Lucknow was the 27th of March, on which his Majesty gave a *déjeûner* in honour of the Prince. At nine o'clock, we were waiting, all in our best, for the arrival of the Nabob's son, by whom the Prince was to be presented. He did not come,—but, instead of him, came the news that he was indisposed, and that some time must yet elapse before he could arrive. It was rumoured that he had taken rather too much opium!

One half-hour after another passed away; at length a noise was heard in the court and in the garden. His Highness appeared, accompanied by the Minister, a tall, lank-looking man with a shrewd and cunning face. He was deadly pale, his eyes rolled with a restless and vacant expression, and his fat puffy cheeks hung flabbily; the lofty gold turban,—formed almost exactly like the crown of Charlemagne on a pack of cards,—harmonized ill enough with the haggard air and listless countenance; pearls, rubies and emeralds were glittering upon it, and a magnificent diamond clasp fastened the bird of Paradise that waved above his brow. A gorgeous robe of gold brocade, strings of pearls about his neck, diamond ear-rings, a sash of the most exquisite Delhi work, trowsers of gold tissue, and peaked shoes bordered with gold, completed the splendid apparel, in which the corpulent scion of royalty, leaning on the arm of the sharp and lean, but no less superbly attired Minister, slowly and heavily dragged his lazy steps along.

The usual ceremony of the theatric embrace was duly performed, and after a somewhat short and monosyllabic conversation, we entered his Majesty's state-carriages, which were waiting for us. On arriving at the court of the principal palace, which was enlivened by military groups of every variety, we were popped into palanquins of silver, and thus carried up the first flight of steps. Even on reaching the landing-place, it was almost impossible to stand upon one's own feet, so great was the throng of bustling attendants, the "*Khidmutgars,*" "*Soobadars,*" and whatever else their various offices may be called,—one and all endeavouring to make way for the coming guest, and thereby, one after another, stumbling and falling in the mêlée. If, in India, at an ordinary dinner-party of forty persons a hundred different servants are required, you may form some idea of the number in attendance on this grand occasion.

The long table was already set, and soon his Majesty appeared, grave and dignified in his demeanour, and surrounded by his suite, all glittering with gold. His entrance was proclaimed in a clear and sonorous tone by various officers. The King is a tall, stately person, of enormous embonpoint; his apparel resembled that of his son, except that it was yet more splendid and more richly ornamented with diamonds. He was accompanied by another of his sons, who, though still more corpulent, much resembled him. The physiognomy of the reigning family is expressive rather of good nature than of shrewdness or talent, if indeed character can be expressed at all in such a mass of fat! How different were the portraits of their ancestors, even of the father and grandfather of the present Nabob! In their features power and energy are strongly marked, while the living faces around us bore the stamp only of luxurious enjoyment, and of a life of indolent pleasure.

The numerous company was distributed in such a manner at the long table, that on one side sat the Royal Family, his Royal Highness Prince Waldemar, the grandees of the state, and the King's household; while all the English guests, with their ladies, took their places opposite to them; a strangely mingled assemblage! At first the heat was suffocating, because the punkah could not be set in motion until the Nabob had taken his seat. At length the signal was given for commencing the operation of eating. The Nabob graciously condescended to send each of us a large plate of "*pillaw,*" a dish consisting of rice dyed yellow, with abundance of grease and of pepper, and boiling hot besides; in cool weather it may probably be a very pleasant sort of food; here, in the most oppressive heat, the very sight of the smoking platter threw us into a perspiration! The Mahometan grandees opposite to us sat stiff and motionless, without touching a morsel of food; we, on the contrary, tasted several dishes, of which we highly approved; most of those at table were however by no means palatable, owing to the superabundance of colouring matter, of spices, oil, and gold and silver froth with which the curious and artistic pyramids of mutton and rice were richly loaded. The ladies seemed to follow our example in the matter of appetite, and seemed perfectly at their ease in the midst of the heterogeneous company around them: I was fortunate enough to sit next to one of them, who made a point of ordering, in a tone quite as if she were at home, each individual thing to be handed to her that could tempt the dainty palate; and thus I had an opportunity of doing full honour to the cuisine of His Majesty of Oude.

Exactly opposite to me sat three most lovely little boys,—the younger Princes,—in whom I could see clear marks of a good appetite, and of the eagerness with which they longed to attack the ragouts that stood before them. Their heavy golden turbans seemed to be no less an oppression to them than the moderation they were constrained to observe. The King, on the other hand, was in a most merry mood. He himself helped Prince Waldemar, and did the honours of the beautiful delicacies of Indian confectionary. Flower pots were set upon the table, the flowers, twigs, leaves and soil in which, were all eatable, and when they had all been devoured, the flower-pots themselves were demolished in like manner; again, on breaking off the pointed top of a small pasty, which he caused to be handed to the Prince, out flew a pair of pretty little birds,—which playful surprise threw the corpulent Nabob into an immoderate fit of laughter.

At the end of the déjeûner, ice was actually served; it may well be termed a luxury here, in every way, for it can only be obtained by an artificial process; nevertheless, refreshing as it was, we were delighted when the company rose from table, and we were once more permitted to exchange the close and sultry atmosphere of the saloon for the open air.

The combats of wild beasts were now to commence. We were conducted to a gallery, from which we looked down upon a narrow court, surrounded by walls and gratings. This was the arena on which the exhibition was to take place. Unluckily the space allotted for spectators was, on account of the great number of English ladies present, so circumscribed, that we could find only a bad standing-room, and one moreover in which the glare and heat of the sun were most oppressive: however, the spectacle exhibited before our eyes in the depth of the battle-field, was of such a nature that all discomfort was soon forgotten.

We there beheld six powerful buffaloes, not of the tame breed, but strong and mighty beasts, the offspring of the *Arnees* of the mountains; measuring at least four feet and a half in height to the back, with huge and wide-arching horns, from three to four feet in length. There they stood, on their short, clumsy legs,—snorting violently, and blowing through their distended nostrils, as if filled with forebodings of the approaching danger. What noble animals! what strength in those broad necks! Pity only that such intense stupidity should be marked in their eyes!

A clatter of sticks, and the roar of various wild beasts now resounded; to which the buffaloes replied by a hollow bellowing. Suddenly, on the opening of a side-door, there rushed forth a strong and formidable tiger, measuring, I should say, from ten to eleven feet in length, from head to tail, and about four feet in height. Without deliberating long, he sprang, with one mighty bound, into the midst of the buffaloes, and darting unexpectedly between the redoubtable horns of one of the boldest champions, he seized him by the nape of the neck, with teeth and claws. The weight of the tiger nearly drew the buffalo to the ground: a most fearful contest ensued. Amid roars and groans, the furious victim dragged its fierce assailant round and round the arena, while the other buffaloes, striving to liberate their comrade, inflicted on the foe formidable wounds with their sharp and massive horns.

Deep silence reigned among the audience; each spectator watching, in breathless suspense, to mark the issue of the combat and at the same time the fate of a few unhappy monkeys which, constrained, as if in mockery, to witness the bloody scene, looked down, at first, with indescribable terror, from the tops of their poles, but, when these were violently shaken by the horns of the buffaloes, fell down as if dead, and lay, extended at full length, with the utmost resignation expecting their end, without making the least attempt to avert it.

Two other tigers, somewhat inferior in size, were now, with great difficulty, driven into the battle-field, while the struggle still continued. Nothing however could induce them to make an attack in any quarter: they paced slowly round the scene, rubbing themselves, cat-like, against the wall as they moved, whenever the buffaloes,—which without regarding them, were ever and anon goading their adversary with their horns,—approached nearer to them. But now the dread tiger received a thrust upon his ribs, which forced him to quit his hold: he fell with violence and then slunk timidly into a corner. Thither he was pursued by the buffalo,—rendered furious by his mangled neck,—and was made the butt of many a vengeful blow and thrust, while he merely betrayed his pain by the hideous contortions of his mouth, not making the least movement in self-defence.

Fresh actors now appeared on the scene; two Himalayan bears of different species, were,—though not without most arduous exertions,—forced into the fight, to the very point whither the tiger had retreated. Many a wound inflicted by sharp claws, and many a rude box on the ear, were now interchanged, amid fierce growls and roars. Blood was streaming from the face of every combatant. While all were furiously engaged in one tremendous mêlée, the wounded buffalo, which meantime had been occupied with one of the half-dead monkeys, renewed his attack, drove them altogether in a heap, and did not desist from his infuriated assault, until the wound of an adversary's claws had torn a great part of the skin from off his muzzle.

A universal exhaustion now prevailed: the first tiger lay as if dead, save his horrible grimaces; the others, lame from their wounds, hobbled from one corner of the arena to the other; the bears too maintained a most peaceful tranquillity, so soon as they ceased to feel the sharp goading sticks of the keepers.

It was truly a savage and horrid spectacle, but not the less entertaining for the ladies and gentlemen! however only that unhappy buffalo lost its life, in consequence of its wounds; the tigers are all yet living, one only having had a rib broken. The Nabob keeps sixteen powerful tigers in his menagerie, all destined for this sort of spectacle.

We now quitted the gallery, to betake ourselves to the plain, near the Goomty, which had been prepared as a fresh theatre, and where a stand had been erected from which we were to witness the continuation of the dreadful drama in an altered form. There appeared as successive combatants,—rams, antelopes, and elephants:

every living creature is here trained for the fight, even the partridge and the quail.

The elephant-fight was, as may be easily imagined, the most magnificent scene of all. Two huge champions were selected, and, after being rendered frantic by spices and brandy, were led up towards each other. At first, for some time, they stood, face to face, in perfect stillness; then suddenly they took a short run, and rushing with tremendous violence, thrust each other backwards and forwards, with their strong tusks and entangled trunks, as if in a fearful wrestling match, till the very earth shook beneath their feet. Their "*Mahouts,*" or drivers, who sit upon their necks, remained, to my amazement, in their places during the whole struggle, which they even appeared to direct.

Suddenly one elephant slightly drooped his head; the other pressed him backwards, and finally put him to flight. At full trot, the stronger elephant pursued the fugitive. The usual issue of such a retreat is, that the victor, on making up to the vanquished, bites off his tail; to prevent which, squibs and rockets are thrown in between them; on this occasion, that device failed, for the victor,—who, as we could see when he ran past us, had had one of his tusks broken off, from the root of which streams of blood were flowing down into his mouth,—was quite beside himself with rage.

The fugitive now in an instant unexpectedly turned towards the river; whereby a multitude of spectators, who had no other way of escape, were forced to rush into the water. We could yet for a long while see the two combatants chasing each other to and fro, till at length, they both vanished among the bushes in the distance.

During all this time, jugglers, ring-fighters, wrestlers and dancers, had never ceased to exhibit the best performances of their various wonderful arts, and the rams continued to fight with each other on this side of the river, while the elephants were wrestling on the other. Even camels they attempted to put into a state of fury, and to provoke to single combat: they are said to carry on a regular wrestling with necks and legs, and to have a most ludicrous appearance when thus struggling; however, on the present occasion, every endeavour to incite them to it failed. They foamed and groaned, but, in spite of all the tugging hither and thither with ropes, they still would not engage in the fight.

During the whole of these entertainments, the royal personages, the grandees of the court, and the English officers in full uniform, were sitting together,—a motley assemblage,—till at last the yawns of his Majesty gave the signal for breaking up.

On the evening of the same day, after the extreme heat was over, we visited one of the grandest palaces, that named "FURROOCK BAM." It contains an immense suite of apartments, all painted in very dark colours, and with very few windows. The walls are hung with worthless pictures, the tables and consoles are loaded with musical clocks, Chinese automatons, and objects of art from every nation and every clime.

In this palace, we saw several thrones, which, taken together, contain more gold and precious stones than could be found in many a large city in Europe. A few of the little diamond roses having been knocked off by the bayonets of the soldiers on duty; no less a sum than two lacs of rupees (L.20,000) was expended in repairing them. Yet with all their costly magnificence, these monuments of former days can boast no real beauty.

From the court in the centre of the palace are seen handsome balconies and several neat façades, which however are not correct, according to the rules either of Moorish or of Indian architecture: much of the old-fashioned French style prevails throughout.

On the opposite side is a far more spacious court, adorned, in the middle, with a large marble tank. The "*Mehalla*," or Harem, receives its light from this court, as does also another side-wing built to correspond to it.

A hunting party was arranged for the following morning, the 28th of March. We set out very early, mounted on elephants; the king had sent his chittahs,* his hunting lynxes† and his falcons, in order to exhibit every variety of field-sport known in this land. In the first place, herons, woodcocks and fowls were turned out, and then set upon with falcons: next, civet cats were set a-running, and caught by the lynxes. Lastly, the chittah was brought up to act its part; seated, blind-fold, upon a cart drawn by oxen, it was driven along behind a herd of antelopes, until we had approached within about sixty paces of a party of three of them. The head of the wild beast was then uncovered, whereupon, crouching low like a cat, it crept up to within half that distance, then springing upon its prey with few and easy bounds, it seized first one and then another of the little band by the throat with lightning speed.

The antelope with its elegantly twisted, spiral horns, its graceful form and cream-coloured hue, does not much exceed in size a large ram: it lives, in the parks near this place, in a half wild state; as does also the Nyl-Ghau,‡ a large animal, of a slate-gray colour, with sloping backs and short horns, and equal in point of size to an ox. Several of these creatures trotted by, close to us.

* A species of long-legged *Leopard* from Thibet. Schreber mentions the same animal under the name of "*Gepard*."—W. Hoffmeister.

† The *Felis Caracal*,—a species of small Lynx.—W. Hoffmeister.

‡ The *Antilope picta* of most naturalists, but designated in Dr Royle's work on the Himalayas as the Antilope Hippelaphus. Its size is usually described as between that of an ox and that of a deer.—Tr.

A new edition of the fights of wild beasts,—though of a less sanguinary character than the last,—was arranged, to be exhibited on the same day for our entertainment. Among other single combats, was that of an ass and a hyæna, which has obtained great celebrity in the East, as a spectacle diverting in the highest degree: to me it appeared that the custom of baiting against each other animals so heterogeneous, which in the course of nature never come into contact, far less into collision, with each other, savoured much more of cruelty than of amusing sport. Both animals are held with ropes, and thus drawn forward until they are made to touch each other; then the ass kicks and stamps, and even endeavours to bite, while the hyæna contents itself with opening its fierce mouth tremendously wide, without doing much injury to its foe. This nevertheless is called a fight.

The combats between antelopes were, on the other hand, an extremely pretty sight; consisting in wrestling, and pushing backwards and forwards, in the course of which the graceful antagonists perpetually strive with their long horns to turn each other's heads to one side.

The people of this country also avail themselves of this mode of fighting to catch wild antelopes by means of tame ones, a noose, weighted with lead, being fastened to the horns of the tame animal: in the course of the fight those of the wild one become entangled in the noose; the trained antelope, immediately on feeling that it is drawn tight, stands still to prevent the escape of the prisoner thus caught.

Large black rams also appeared as combatants, and thrust each other round the arena most lustily: their horns were polished to a shining smoothness, and their fleece was all shorn with the exception of a shaggy mane; which gave them a most comical, somewhat lion-like appearance.

On our return, we paid a visit, in his studio, to the artist *Beechey*, an Englishman, who, from early youth, has been in the service of the king of Oude. He has painted many a capital picture; but the climate, so often injurious to European constitutions, seems to have weakened him much.

On arriving at the palace of the British Resident, we found there the minister, sent by the king as the bearer of several rich presents: precious stones, richly ornamented sabres, and other weapons, with blades of Ispahan steel, rich and brilliant scabbards, and superb hafts. *Hakeem Sahib*, as I am here designated, was presented with a huge illuminated folio volume, the cover of which was adorned with beautiful arabesques painted on a gold ground. It is a rare Persian manuscript, containing the heroic poem of the renowned Hafiz,—"Shah Nameh,"—rich in fine and delicate miniature paintings, all executed on a gold ground, and exquisitely illuminated throughout in blue and carmine.

A pleasure party to one of his Majesty's country seats, now almost deserted, concluded the sight-seeing of this busy day. The most enjoyable part of the excursion was our homeward row on the Goomty, in the Nabob's splendid gondolas; and Arndt's song, "*Was ist des Deutschen Vaterland*,"—sung with clear voices, sounded not amiss as the notes died away amid *Amjud Ali's* gardens of roses. Unfortunately however the rosy fragrance was, in consequence of the burning of several corpses on the banks of the river, strongly mingled with other and less welcome odours.

Several banquets yet followed during the latter days of our residence at Lucknow; one dinner-party was at the house of Colonel Willcocks, whose beautiful observatory and astronomical instruments were of the deepest interest for me.

The most splendid fete was that given by the king on

the 1st of April. At four o'clock, his Majesty's cavalry lancers were already filling the garden and court of our quarters; at five, the cannonade commenced, and an uninterrupted salute was fired till seven. At about six o'clock the Heir-apparent and the Minister arrived in their carriages; the former was, on this occasion, free from the intoxicating and stupifying effects of opium, and appeared almost handsome. The usual ceremonies took their course; I also was obliged, in my turn, to go through the theatrical embrace, which really, after a little practice, is not a very difficult matter; only it is very necessary to be on one's guard against remaining suspended to the person who performs this salutation, by the buttons of one's coat being entangled in the labyrinth of his gold chains and pearl necklaces, which happened to me with Martabar Singh, at Cathmandoo. During these salutations flourishes of trumpets were sounding from without, and three bands of various musical instruments were carrying on their performances all at once. Amid this dreadful din, which was rendered more deafening still by the continued thunder of the artillery, we drove to the king's palace, in the Royal carriages, accompanied by a numerous escort of lancers in yellow uniforms.

The great court of the palace, and the tank in its centre, in which the fountains play, were brilliantly illuminated with small Chinese lanterns. On arriving in the great hall, we were received by the Prince, for the King sent his apology on the score of illness, having something the matter with his foot. There was in this spacious saloon, a crowded assemblage of varied and gorgeous costumes, and the host of richly apparelled domestics was yet more numerous than on former occasions. It was not without difficulty that we could make our way to the table, which was prepared in a horseshoe form, in the great hall, and at which we took our places for dinner: the dishes were all cold, and many of them by no means palatable, however the excellent claret and champagne were all the more prized.

The King's buffoon and several dancing girls now made their appearance, and commenced their usual performance, accompanying it with singing. The buffoon danced in the character of a lady, with frightful contortions of his whole frame, and afterwards appeared in various other travesties,—among the rest, disguised as an old man, carrying on his back a palanquin, in which a lady was seen reclining. Next began the "*toasts,*"—Prince Waldemar, the King of Prussia, the King of Oude, and the Princes his sons. Fine speeches, and long ones too, were made upon the occasion. Mr Shakspeare spoke for a full half-hour. The "*hip, hip, hip, hurrah!*" seemed to afford great amusement to the grave Mussulmans, who, without tasting a drop, sat gazing and listening in mute wonder, scarcely able to comprehend what it all could mean.

The dinner was succeeded by a brilliant display of fire-works, which lasted till the night was far advanced. Long rows of human figures, and animal forms of various sorts, were burning in magic fire; lofty palaces of wood and paper, shone, burst, and were scattered in flames; and, more beautiful than all the rest, rose some twenty or more air-balloons, which, having shot up to a great height in the air, showered down sheaves and nosegays of fire.

In the garden behind the palace, shone in giant letters, formed of lamps of many colours, the inscription in English, "*Prince Waldemar of Prussia.*" The fête was terminated, after the echo of the last cannon had died away, by the ceremony usual here, of throwing a chain of silvered metal round the neck of every guest, whether lady or gentleman.

Thus then, we bid farewell to the splendour and the

pleasures of the court of his Majesty of Oude, and to the beautiful city of Lucknow. The Prince started on the 2d of April, and Mr Fortescue and I followed next day. On the 4th of April we passed the ruins of the ancient and celebrated city of CANOUGE,* and after an uninterrupted march of three days and three nights, we at length found ourselves in the magnificent city of AGRA.

It is situated on the south-western bank of the JUMNA, *(Yamuna)* and presents, when the first distant view of its many beautiful domes and minarets meets the eye of the traveller, a most wonderful and striking picture. The surrounding country can boast no beauty; indeed, since passing through Allahabad, or even since our visit to Benares, we have traversed one continued arid and desert plain. The harvest is past, and the few fields in which any cultivation is to be seen,—and scarcely a third part of the land is used for any sort of agriculture, —bear parched and unlovely crops of *Ricinus*, with its short and stumpy stems, vetches, or herbs used in dyeing. We miss the opium cultivation here, and since leaving Lucknow, we have seen no more fields of barley or of spelt.

This is the most unfavourable season for seeing the environs of Agra, which, for the distance of some miles, look like one vast heap of rubbish. The *Acacias* alone, with their tender verdure, resist the fatal and desolating west wind, which often blows with great violence, bringing with it a heat so fearfully glowing, that the

* A place of great renown in the remote eras of Hindoo history, and described as having been at one time the proudest of all the Indian capitals. First humbled in 1018, when its sovereign tendered his submission to Mahmoud of Ghizni, it was spared by that great conqueror, only to fall a speedy prey to other and less distant foes; since the early part of the 11th century, it has never regained its former power and splendour, and it has now for ages presented only a mass of ruins, sufficient from their extent to mark its imposing size, while fragments of temples, mausoleums and sculptures, prostrate amid desolate jungles, fail to preserve even a vestige of its beauty or magnificence.—TR.

thermometer rises, at about 2 o'clock P.M., in the shade, to above 33° (106° Fahrenheit)! Several trees of the Acacia tribe, such as the beautiful *Acacia Serissa,* and the tree from which gum Arabic is procured,* occasionally gladden the eye, and fill the air with a delicious, spicy fragrance. Beside every spring too, even here, is a group of the ash-like *Sumach,* but no grass, no herbaceous vegetation of any kind, is to be seen,—not a single flower nor a single butterfly. Blueish-green thistles and caper bushes form the only clothing of these undulating hills, the tombs of ancient greatness and magnificence. The prevailing colour of the soil is, almost universally, a reddish gray, or a blackish tint; but scarce in any spot is its original formation to be traced, for recent débris are heaped over the ruins of remoter date. The highways are the only features of the landscape that tell of habitation and civilization; and it was certainly the first time in my life that I hailed with delight the sight of a road grown smooth from long and frequent thoroughfare, a welcome object however, in these white and dusty plains.

We entered Agra on the 7th of April, rejoiced at having hitherto escaped the noxious effects of the hot season in this climate, and not less so, to find a shelter from its intensity in the ingenious construction of the dwellings here. It is difficult, in the temperate climate of our German home, to form any conception of the burning heat of a tropical sun. When in Agra, tempted by the artificial lowering of the temperature in the interior of our residence, we ventured, after mid-day, to take a short walk along the street, the sensation caused by first meeting a rushing stream of air heated up to 34° or 35° (109° or 111° Fahrenheit) was most startling. The pain

* The *Acacia Arabica,* the gum of which is used in India, and exported thence as a substitute for the real gum Arabic, the product of the *Acacia Nilotica* to which it is however very inferior.—TR.

felt in the nose resembled that caused by excessive cold, and a sort of shivering ran down the back. We were involuntarily impelled to betake ourselves to running, in order to reach the cool atmosphere of the first Tatty, or of the nearest shades. Immediately on re-entering, after such an exposure to the heat, any inhabited apartment, or, I should rather say, vault,—for all the rooms are very lofty, and surmounted by domes, and light is admitted only by a small sky-light,—one is in danger of being struck with apoplexy, for a current of cold air flows upon one from all sides. A pair of bellows is at work, noiseless but ceaseless, behind each door; and over the heated crown of the entering guest,—which nevertheless he is constrained to uncover,—the weighty punkah is moved backwards and forwards so vehemently, that every hair is made to fly loosely about his head. At any rate, there is no doubt that to go out before evening is by no means advisable; coup-de-soleil or fever may not indeed be very frequent, but cough, catarrh and toothache, are the ordinary evils that result from such imprudence.

It is interesting to observe how inventive the necessities of the climate have here made man. How varied and ingenious are the methods he has devised in the internal arrangement of his domestic architecture for obtaining relief from the oppressive heat!

A house, such as the wealthy and distinguished British residents here occupy, is generally a structure of considerable height, but of only one story, of a horseshoe form, with a colonnade in the centre: windows are altogether wanting; and the only doors are in the side walls opening into a corridor, and screened by double hangings,—coverlets of cotton cloth, thickly wadded,—beneath which every one that enters must bend, and thus creep in. The sitting-rooms in the side-wings of the mansion receive their light from above, or else through small bath-rooms, in which jars full of water are continually standing, and which have but one external entrance, and that closed up by means of a tatty-frame, kept always moist by having water poured perpetually upon it. All rooms, that lie towards the west, are cooled by an apparatus of this sort; for the sultry west wind is changed, by the rapid evaporation of the water,—caused by the current of air flowing in,—into an agreeably cool, and even occasionally into a cold breeze: it is therefore much easier to produce a moderate temperature within the dwelling when this hot wind blows, than when every breath is hushed, even though the heat in the open air may then be less intense.

The so-called "*Tatties,*" to which I have already repeatedly alluded, are wooden frames, of the size of the door; upon which thick bundles of the roots of Ivarancura Grass, (*Andropogon Ivarancura*) bound together in close rows, are fastened down with thin bamboo; the whole resembles in miniature the walls of briers and thorns at a salt-work. These roots are extremely porous, and rapidly absorb the water, which speedily evaporates, causing a very peculiar smell, which at first is most unpleasant, and even produces headache and a feeling of stupor, but to which habit soon reconciles the stranger, and for which he even frequently acquires a real passion.

The central, and by far the most habitable part of the house, is a spacious rotunda, with a very lofty roof, which however is flat, so that the vaulting of the different apartments into which it is divided does not interfere with their symmetry. This part of the building is surrounded by a wide corridor, in which various machines for cooling the atmosphere are stationed like pieces of artillery. Several of these, with their broad, wind-mill-like wings, somewhat resembling mill clappers, are turned without intermission, and the current of air thus caused, finding its way into the room through small double tatties, produces a most grateful effect. The ever-active punkah is in motion at the same time; even by night it is never suffered to rest, as it serves the double purpose of creating artificial coolness and of driving away the musquitoes, for even gauze curtains cannot be tolerated here during the excessive heat.

Another most agreeable contrivance in these houses is the bath; a large tank of water with marble steps. This luxury is not however universally to be met with; and I was often obliged to content myself with having a few pitchers of water poured over my head, which a servant on whom this office properly devolves,—the "*Bihishtee*,"—is ready continually to replenish from his goat-skin vessel. This man has, as may be imagined, a most important office, and is ever and anon replenishing empty water-jugs and jars, or supplying thirsty water-bibbers. His assistants are several huge oxen, which relieve him of the hardest part of the work, by pacing down an inclined plane beside a deep well in the garden, to draw up thence the huge barrel.

The water for drinking is cooled either with ice, or, when that is wanting, with saltpetre; in the more ordinary degrees of heat, the porous vessels formed of red clay, ("*Gailas*") prove sufficient to accomplish that object, their efficacy being increased by wrapping them in wet cloths. These earthen jars are manufactured in all parts of India, and both their elegant forms and the large admixture of mica in the clay of which they are made give them a remarkably pretty appearance.

The making of ice is practicable only in elevated situations, in early spring, and even then, only when the wind is blowing from certain quarters. It is carried on in large clay pans, which are placed on finely chopped straw; the small fragments of ice, formed in them, are carefully gathered up and packed closely and firmly together; and each member of the joint-stock companies, formed for that purpose at Benares and at Agra, receives on certain appointed days, his portion of ice, according to the number of his shares.

The manner of life, where every thing great and small is so artificially regulated, differs essentially from that usual among us at home. The open air is only to be endured till about nine, or at latest ten o'clock; an Englishman at least will never leave the house after that time of day. German constitutions, fresh from Europe, are not easily injured by the heat; I have frequently remained at my drawing, in the open air, till eleven o'clock, without suffering in consequence, although the danger of such an exploit was depicted before me in the most vivid colours. It is an inherent part of the English character, to maintain stedfastly a belief once established; no one therefore ventures to go out of doors after nine in the morning, or before five in the evening; while, on the other hand, it is held to be quite allowable, and indeed a matter of course, to make a most substantial meal three times daily, and to drink a quantity of strong ale and fiery wine, as though no danger could possibly be apprehended from that quarter. In my opinion it would be abundantly safe to take a little more exercise, even during the extreme heat; indeed, with a table so luxuriously supplied, it might doubtless be a most wholesome practice.

As soon as the sun has risen, the Indian traveller according to established custom enjoys whatever is worth seeing of the beauties or curiosities of nature or of art; then takes his bath, and makes his toilet for breakfast; this repast ended, he repairs to the lady's music-room, regales himself with a little music in her company, and carries on some conversation touching the respective merits of Italian and German composers. The pianoforte is unfortunately almost always out of tune, and in no very brilliant condition, as rust commits its ravages among the chords, in spite of the cover with its wadding three fingers thick. After this, those who have time to spare, devote a few hours to slumber. About one or two o'clock the company re-assembles in the dining-room for a second meal, which is followed by another short sleep, —an afternoon "*siesta*,"—on rising from which, at five o'clock, carriages and saddle-horses are found in readiness for the usual airing. The heat is even then very oppressive, and the west wind covers equipages and cavaliers with a thick coating of gray dust, so that leisure for the bath and toilet before dinner is no slight luxury. The party sit down to table at seven o'clock; several ladies are usually present, among whom the individual partner whom he is to hand to the dinner-table is always pointed out beforehand to each gentleman of distinction.

There was seldom any lack of society; for sociability, interrupted during the day by the overwhelming heat, receives a new impulse in the cool hours of evening; and in fact, this custom of late dinner-parties is one with which the stranger willingly complies, as being very well adapted to the climate. But what shall I say of the frequent and, even in the hottest season, so dearly loved balls? Dancing is carried on with passion, and with perseverance too; and it is even at these same balls that the greatest number of persons is found assembled, since the invitations are less rigidly select than those for the dinner-parties. There, may be seen figures the most singular and grotesque; European ladies, whose youthful bloom has passed away, with their grey hair "*frisés a la paysanne*," making most laborious endeavours to dance what, as if on purpose to annoy us, they here call "*Polka*;" beside them, youthful belles, perhaps not more than thirteen or fourteen years of age, with all the "*pretension*" of maturer dames, not unfrequently even with artificial brightness glowing on their cheeks, whose natural roses fade early indeed in this torrid zone.

The roses however may be tolerated; but when, in order to conceal somewhat of Indian blood, which sheds a faint tinge of bronze over the skin, a coating of white of egg mixed with chalk is carefully laid on, then the arts of the toilet have really, according to European notions, been pushed a little too far; and I should have held this to be mere calumny, had not a nearer look of more than one of these artificially made up "dames blanches" convinced me of the reality of the thing. The life of feasting and revelry in the city of Agra, was, on the 13th of April, once more exchanged for the hot and dusty palanquin.

We next proceeded to Bhurtpoor, at which place we arrived on the 16th, and where we spent five most interesting days with the Rajah. He has, in gratitude to the English, to whom he is indebted for his elevation to the throne, built a palace for his friends, quite according to English taste in its architecture and arrangements. It contains all manner of "*comforts,*" which can render life agreeable in this country, apparatuses for refrigeration, ice-pans, a large tank or bath on the second story, and an excellent cellar, well stocked with claret and champagne. In this palace we resided during our stay at Bhurtpoor, sallying forth early every morning to the chase of the *Antelope* or the *Nyl Ghau.* During the hot hours of the day, we occupied ourselves with drawing, painting and reading, and with preparing the skins of the slaughtered victims of the hunt. The Rajah got up for our entertainment, besides the various field sports, wrestling-matches, in which we witnessed wonderful feats of strength; the usual fights of elephants, of tigers, of antelopes, and of rams, were also here again exhibited.

The most considerable place on our road from Bhurtpoor to Delhi, was Muttra or Mathura, where we were most kindly welcomed, and most hospitably and agreeably entertained by Mr Thornton, an uncommonly pleasing English gentleman.

Delhi,—the ancient seat of the *Great Mogul,*—was the ultimatum of our day's journeying on the 26th of April. It is a large but melancholy-looking city; its environs a complete desert, covered with the wreck of former grandeur. Our residence here was rendered more unpleasant by the circumstance of our being quartered with an old gentleman who did as little as he possibly could for his guests. His horses were but once put to his carriage, and that at a time when, as he well knew, the Prince had gone out; the door of his splendid marble bath was never unlocked, and indeed it was only after we had quitted his abode, that we were made aware of its existence. We were obliged therefore, in order to visit the very remarkable ruins of the ancient edifices of Delhi, all of which are at a considerable distance from the British station, to mount the elephants which belong to Government. In the heat of this climate, the peculiar and uneasy motion of being rocked on an elephant's back, and the glaring sunshine, were most irksome, especially on our return, for although we started for our sight-seeing at five in the morning, we never found it possible to be at home before eleven.

There are monuments here of a very ancient date, which in point of interest fully equal the Pyramids of Egypt. The remains of a gigantic mosque, begun on too grand a scale to be completed, present an image of the bygone magnificence of ancient Delhi. One minaret is yet standing; it is two hundred and fifty feet in height, and measures sixty-five paces in circumference; three hundred and ninety-eight steps conduct to its summit. It is fluted externally, and its stories consist alternately of red sandstone and of white marble, a combination often met with in India.

Far more ancient than the "*Kootub Minar,*"—as this great tower is called,—is a pillar of cast metal, bearing Sanscrit inscriptions, which rises to the height of forty feet from the ground, while its shaft and base are said to be buried for an equal depth beneath. Timur caused a cannon to be fired at it; but the ball made an impression without injuring the column. The spot on which it stands, is surrounded by the ruins of a Hindoo temple, which this primæval and mysterious monument, concerning whose origin there is a lack of all satisfactory information, has outlived.

I must also mention the palace built on the banks of the Jumna, by *Shah Jehan,* which on the 1st of May, we visited in company with Mr Metcalfe. It stands without the city-gate, and is enclosed by ramparts, from five to six feet in thickness, and fifty feet in height. Its shining walls of red sand-stone are visible from a great distance, and the vast space within their circumference forms quite a city of itself.

The gates of the palace are semicircular projections; the walls are fluted on the top, and fortified with a multitude of low turrets. A vaulted passage "*Chatta,*" which has only one opening, in its centre, leads from the gate, in the semicircle of which the sentinels are stationed, to the first court, distinguished by the name of "*Noubut Khanah.*"* In this court are the royal stables. The second court, "*Devani Am,*"† which is the largest of all, surrounds an open hall the front of which is supported by nine arches of sandstone inlaid with marble. A third handsome gate leads from this court into the third one, "*Devani Khãs,*"‡ in which is tho marble hall, where in days of yore, stood the peacock-throne of the Great Mogul. Its roof rests on columns of solid marble, and the pavement is formed of the most precious stones,

* i. e. Place of the band of instruments. † i. e. Public Hall. ‡ i. e. Special Hall.—Tr.

among which I observed cornelians of great value. On one of its side walls, stands the Persian inscription in large characters of gold, "*If Paradise ever existed on earth, it is this, it is this, it is this!*"

The marble gallery, or rostrum, on which the Great Mogul was wont to step out to address the people, is also here shown. The walls are inlaid, throughout, with Italian mosaic-work of various marbles: the apples, pears and cherries, represented on a ground of black marble, in these works of art, as well as the oft-recurring goldfinches and bulfinches, afford most conclusive evidence as to their European origin.

On the left side of the hall is the private mosque, also of marble, called *Motee Musjid:* it is small and simple, but built in a very beautiful style. On the right side is the present Palace of the Emperor, where he lives, surrounded by his many wives. The gilded roof of this edifice still remains, while all other similar ones have long since vanished.

In the garden beside the Palace, is a marble bath, the magnificent mosaic pavements of which are covered with perfectly carpet-like designs. Unfortunately it is in an extremely dilapidated condition; and its floor covered with thick dust, old rubbish and fragments of marble seats and divans. A superb tank with an enclosure of sea-green composition, and an extraordinarily beautiful rosette, formed of cornelian and blood-stone, in its centre, was half buried beneath the rubbish; in addition to which one of the Imperial barbarians had caused a large box filled with earth to be rolled over it on iron-bound wheels, to serve as a target for the display of his skill in archery.

The noble arcades that surround the court, are, for want of repairs, falling, one after another, into ruins; the finely sculptured balustrades of the marble halls are gradually disappearing; and tattered remnants only of the large awnings which afforded shade in former days, now hang from the roofs. Yet this shadowy potentate is in the regular receipt of a pension, the amount of which exceeds that of the annual income of the Queen of Great Britain, and which is intended to maintain the palace in good repair. No good is done with it all; the numerous parasites and useless idlers at court embezzle three quarters of the whole sum, while the fourth is consumed chiefly by the countless host of wives who people the Harem.

Early on the morning of the 2d of May, mounted on ponderous elephants, we rode through a part of the city, passing by the Fort. The object of this expedition was a visit to the tombs of the Baberide Emperors, which are about four miles distant from the town. The soil is covered with the ruins of ancient Delhi, scattered amidst solitary mimosas and fig-trees.

The walls which enclose the magnificent burial-place of *Humayoon*, are in a half dilapidated state; the outer gate only, built of imperishable red sandstone, is still in very good preservation. An interval of about a hundred paces,—originally probably a garden, but now used for the cultivation of tobacco,—separates the main building from the surrounding walls. The former has a broad façade, numbering seventeen arches, including the central one which serves as a gate. The sixteen others are built up, with the exception of small square doors left in them as entrances to the vaults. The whole edifice forms a perfect square, containing sepulchral cells on each side, the total number being sixty-eight. On ascending the stair, we reached a spacious platform, the foundation on which rests the principal part of the structure, viz. the tomb of *Humayoon* himself.

This tomb is a large octagonal tower, consisting of three stories surmounted by a dome, altogether rising to a height of sixty feet; with eight smaller towers clustering around it. It was erected by *Humayoon*, the father of *Akbar*, about the year A.D. 1540: it is simple, but noble in its style of architecture, and, considering its antiquity, in excellent preservation.

At a still greater distance from the city is the mausoleum of the renowned saint *Nizam ud Deen*. Before arriving at it, we were obliged to traverse a whole city of tombs; small sepulchral edifices of mosque-like form rose around us, as far as the eye could reach; on every side ruined domes, open vaults and columned remains, mark the sites of ancient temples. At length, on arriving in front of a lofty gray wall, a low door was opened to admit us, and within, we beheld the welcome verdure of several leafy trees. A narrow court leads, through a second entry, to a large tank surrounded by galleries and by various temple-like structures. Here a number of priests and of fakeers volunteered to throw themselves down from the points of the domes, if only we would suitably remunerate them; which however we begged to decline doing.

The sanctuary itself, a marble structure of wonderful beauty and elegance, stands in another court, under the shade of fig trees. Its inner walls are decorated with numerous Arabic inscriptions, in characters of gold; and the ceiling is hung with silken drapery; however, though we saw all this, we were, as unbelievers, not permitted to see the coffin of the saint. A priest now drew near, bearing in his hands two small earthen vessels; while he opened their lids he uttered these words, "This is the gift, offered to all, to the poor as well as to the rich, to the King as well as to the meanest subject." Thus saying, he presented to us part of the contents of his little pot,—a sort of small confectionary, or "*sucrerie.*"

In the vicinity of this peculiarly sacred spot,—for *Nizam ud Deen* was a holy Sheik,—are several sepulchral monuments of singular beauty, which, somewhat more in accordance with our European style, consist of simple sarcophagi, surrounded by finely sculptured open screens of marble. Here is to be seen the tomb of *Jehan Ara ("Jahara,")* the daughter of *Shah Jehan*, as also that of *Moodjewadje;* again, a third, surrounded by a very lofty enclosure of marble, is erected to the memory of *Gengri Medrih Baba*, son of *Akbar Shah.*

A temple-like quadrangular edifice, with a flat roof, stands near to, yet isolated from, this vast and splendid city of the dead. It consists of twenty-five small contiguous arches, five in each row; the outer ones supported by double, the inner by single columns: the intervals between the outer pillars are filled up, to the level of the capitals, with gratings of elegant arabesque design. The material of this edifice is a yellow sand-stone: it contains, within, the marble sarcophagi of the mother, sister and brothers, of the individual by whom it was erected,—*Khan Asim Khan*,—who is said to have been a foster-brother of Humayoon.

One of the grandest architectural monuments is the ancient and mighty fortress of *Shere Khan,—Purana Killa,*—which we visited on our way home. Its strong and massive towers and ramparts, although much dilapidated, are tolerably well patched up with brick, so that no considerable breach now remains. Of the four gates, three are built up; at one of these, we observed elephants, sculptured in marble, sunk into the red sandstone walls of the side towers.

After making a great circuit, we at length arrived at the only gate which still affords access to the interior; and beheld within, to our amazement, a number of houses, standing side by side: a whole village is enclosed within the circumference of the walls, which measure, I should think, not less than from eight to nine hundred paces on each of the four sides. Several ancient buildings, worthy of note, yet remain standing in this spacious interior. The first is a tall, octagonal tower of red sandstone, without a dome and flat-roofed; it bears the name of "*Shere Mundul,*" and is said to have been built by *Shere Khan* as an airy summer residence. Steep stairs lead to the two upper stories, which are surrounded by external galleries, and decorated, within, with beautiful painted ceilings, and mosaics of blue and yellow glazed sandstone. Another is the wonderfully beautiful mosque, attributed to *Ghoree Allah ud Deen.* It is one of the flat mosques, of inconsiderable depth, and consisting of but one simple structure. The front is adorned with five large portals, the arches of which are of nearly horse-shoe form, the middle one, which is the principal entrance, having but little to distinguish it from the others. The central vaulted hall is very lofty, but its dome is flattened; the niches opposite to the doors of the entrance contain remarkably beautiful marble frameworks, filled with splendid arabesques.

From this wonderful fortress we proceeded to visit that of *Feroze Shah,* whose sand-stone monolith,—*Feroze Kotelah,*—is visible at a great distance, rising above the venerable walls around. It is surrounded on every side by a mass of small arched structures raised one above another, and bears numerous inscriptions, those near its base in Hindui, those higher up in Sanscrit characters.

Our ride back to the city I cannot certainly number among the pleasant features of our expedition; for the sun, having already attained a high point in its course, spread a scorching glow through the atmosphere. On returning to our quarters I was obliged, with the utmost despatch, to make ready our trunks for an early departure; for to-morrow we are to quit Delhi, and to proceed, *via* MEERUT, towards the cooler regions of the Himalayas, with the intention,—should the Chinese authorities put no hindrance in our way,—of penetrating through the mountain range, by one of the frontier passes, into Thibet.

EIGHTH LETTER.

MEERUT—MOORADABAD—THE TARAI—THE BROKEN PALANQUIN—THE FOREST—MALARIA—KALI DHUNGI—VALLEY OF THE NIHAL-GUNGA—FOREST VEGETATION—HOONUMAN APES—PASS OF GHAGER—NAINETHAL—ABUNDANCE OF WILD BEASTS—THE LAKE—ECLIPSE OF THE MOON—KOSILA RIVER—TEMPLE OF DORA—THE VALLEY OF KOTELAL—SMELTING HUTS—VALLEY OF THE RAMGUNGA—LUSHINGTON'S BUNGALOW—ADH BADRI—PASSES OF TILLEKANNI AND KHONKALA—DHUNPOOR—THE SANGHO—DURITHAL—THE HIGH-PRIEST OF KEDARNATH—OKIMUTH—THE SPRING AT GAURIKUND—THE FAKEER—TEMPLE OF KEDARNATH—PASS OF TSORIKHAL—VIEW OF THE SNOWY MOUNTAINS—PAWALI DANDA.

PAWALI DANDA, *20th of June*, 1845.

WE have been quickly transported from the burning desert of the plains to the cool heights of the mountain range. Even at Meerut, where we arrived on the 3d of May, and took up our abode in a handsome English hotel, "the Albion," we found the heat much less oppressive. The weather was warm indeed, but the thermometer at noon did not rise above 25° (89° Fahrenheit). About two o'clock in the afternoon a fearful storm burst upon us; the sun was darkened by clouds of yellow dust, whirled high in the air, until at length a violent tropical shower fell in torrents which, gradually relenting in their fury, ended in a soft spring rain.

The air was mild and pleasant in the extreme, when, on the 4th of May, we proceeded on our farther route. In the evening we reached the banks of the Ganges, and crossed its stream near the sanctuaries which bear its name,—the *Gunga Deval.* During the night we accomplished a considerable part of our journey, so that early dawn found us approaching MOORADABAD, the last station before reaching the mountains. A carriage, drawn by four horses, met us a few miles from the town, and conveyed us, at a rapid pace, to our destination. *Mr Wilson*, a most amiable and agreeable man, welcomed us to his house, and entertained us at a splendid dinner, after which, the heat of the day being past, we continued our journey, along an extremely pleasant road, and, having double relays, we advanced with great speed. A small village, at the boundary of the low forest region,—the *Tarai*, so much dreaded on account of its malaria,—was our first halting-place.

Horses were in readiness to convey the Prince, Count von O—— and Mr Wilson without delay to the foot of the mountains. Count von der G—— and I were to follow immediately in the palanquins, which had been sent forward from Mooradabad. This was not however destined so to be. To our no small annoyance, we now found our palanquins, already grievously the worse of their four months' journeyings, heavily loaded on the top with flower-pots and water-jars, the weight of which much retarded our progress. My medicine-chest made my vehicle, at any rate, sufficiently weighty; and now the addition of the ponderous pitchers caused its every joint to crack. Accordingly, I had scarce fallen into my first slumber, when a loud crash suddenly awakened me, and I rubbed my drowsy eyes only to gaze at my broken palanquin! The bearers, dismayed, stood still; I alighted, and found, alas! that the pole had given way,—an injury which ropes and fastenings were unable to repair.

There I sat, in the dark and dreary solitude, completely at the mercy of a set of lazy, knavish men, to whom I could not even make myself intelligiblo. Even in this extremity, violent measures proved successful. After first wreaking my vengeance on Mr Wilson's water-pitchers, I seized the first bamboos that could be found, and with their help the ponderous and ricketty machine was once more set in motion. Arriving in safety at the nearest village, we roused a "*Mistri*," or joiner, from his repose: a crowd of idle folk gathered around, while, with most provoking slowness, he bored holes, for which he had no nails. When at last the nails were procured, screws were wanting; and to wind up the catastrophe, the oil failed, and we were left in darkness, of which the bearers availed themselves to make their escape. In short, it was past one o'clock before we resumed our march. Even then, in spite of these repairs and of my fatigues, I was obliged to make the best of my way alongside the palanquin, on foot.

When day dawned, we were entering a forest; gigantic trees,—*Saul* and *Sissoo,*—and bushes of *Volkameria*, richly interlaced with creepers, excluded all view by their dark and impenetrable foliage. A narrow path only had been cut through them, and it was often blocked up by huge stems of fallen trees, an obstruction which in some places had been cleared away by fire. The sun was now more vertical, and the heat more overwhelming; the humid, sultry, oppressive air,—the "*Ayul*,"—seemed like a weight of lead. Towards eleven o'clock, we reached the station of KALI DHUNGI at the end of the TARAI district, and there found the first detachment of our party, who had been waiting for us since five o'clock in the morning. Refreshed by a breakfast which we had ourselves cooked,—during which the unfortunate palanquin, after a second break-down, again made up to us,—we mounted the highland horses, "*Ghoonts*," which were standing ready.

Some six miles or so we wound along the broad, but almost dry, channel of the NIHAL-GUNGA, which, though often a considerable river, dwindles, during the hot season, into a scanty brook. Its bed is overgrown with dwarf bushes of Mimosa and Bauhinia, and strewn with rolled fragments of quartz-rock and of grauwacke-schist. Our road next climbed the rugged acclivities of hills of feruginous clay and gypsum, and after this beginning, our ascent was steep and continuous. The tiny stream, which we crossed and re-crossed, brings with it a quantity of lime, which covers all the pebbles in the shape of calcareous spar.

We now left behind us the desolate heights,—covered with boulders,—of the lower hills; and gained the verdant and lofty summits of the second range, at least four hundred feet higher. A current of cooler air here met us, a delightful contrast to the heavy and insalubrious atmosphere of the valley; here roses were blooming, and syringa-bushes shedding their perfume, while delicious yellow raspberries and the berberis with its large blue berries, invited us to feast on their refreshing dainties.

Upon the ridge of a bare hill, stand the few straw-built huts of the village of SIMORIA. Near this place, our attention was attracted by a strange-looking, high frame, much resembling a gallows, from which hung twisted chains, assuming, at a distance, the form of a gibbeted skeleton. Swinging is, in these parts, a mode of worshipping the gods, practised by the pious Hindoos with as much devotion as I witnessed in the Nepaulese while they were turning their prayer-wheels! Various indeed, are the ways that man has devised to reach heaven; but I never should have dreamod of any people attempting to swing themselves into its precincts!

We were now drawing near to the chain of the GHAGER mountains, and ascending a succession of beautiful hills, rendered more charming by the noble pines, *(Pinus longifolia)* that crowned their summits, and by the roses, barberries, red-blossoming pomegranates, and fragrant syringas *(Philadelphus* and *Deutzia)* which clothed their sides. Gorgeous wreaths of a species of clematis were twining around the hawthorn bushes, among the tall stems of apricot and cherry trees. Our mountain steeds clambered up many a steep path, over travelled and polished masses of clay slate, ere we reached the head of the pass, where the forest becomes thicker, with stems taller and more massive, and consists chiefly of lofty oaks, *(Quercus tomentosa* and *semecarpifolia,)* whose gnarled branches form a thick bower of foliage.

Herds of Hoonuman monkeys, *(Semnopithecus Entellus)* were making every bough tremble, as they precipitated themselves with bold springs from one tree-top to another. This animal, in face, bears a strong resemblance to an old man; it is, in this part of the country, peculiarly pale in its colour, often indeed perfectly white; and its black face, its long beard, and thick tuft of hair over the eyes, give it a most extraordinary appearance. In point of character however it has certainly been the object of vile calumny, being described as extremely malicious; whereas it throws neither stones nor cudgels, but contents itself with making a grimace from its lofty seat, as it looks down in conscious security. To clap one's hands suffices to put to flight a whole herd; a sudden rustling and crackling is straightway heard among the branches; on every side the venerable oaks are seen to shake their massive tops, and the large, white creatures, with their long tails, dart swiftly through the air, passing from tree to tree, without ever missing their aim. The Bhansh Oak is apparently their favourite tree.

The ridge of the pass,—full of precipitous ravines, abrupt declivities, and deep clefts cut by the rushing torrents,—is richly wooded. Here flourish the maple, the ash, the box, the poplar, the horn-beam, the walnut and the apricot tree. The underwood consists chiefly of syringa, and of two most odoriferous kindred shrubs, worthy of being the distinguished ornaments of a European garden; while the deliciously elastic mountain breeze, balmy from the fragrance of numerous flowers, refreshes and invigorates the traveller after the toilsome ascent. Lilies of the valley, strawberries in blossom, and ivy, with a beautiful variety of white melilot, and many other familiar plants, reminded us of our German hills.

But now the descent began; soon however we were again climbing an abrupt acclivity, and in a quarter of an hour we espied, between the green oaks and luxuriant rhododendrons, which formed a frame for the picture, the dark and glassy surface of a lake, deep in the valley at our feet. A retired group of four stone-built houses and three lowly cottages, clustered together under the name of NAINETHAL, stands on the margin of the lake, amid groves of splendid trees, on a spot where, but a few years ago, the bear, the leopard, and the Jerow deer, reigned undisturbed. We dismounted, and, winding through a deep dell, arrived at the dwelling of Mr Lushington, who received us in the most friendly manner.

The forest around this place still abounds with wild beasts: on the preceding day a leopard had seized the dog of our next-door neighbour, close to his house. On the cliffs of the surrounding hill, two species of antelopes, (*Antilope Ghoral* and *A. Thar*) one called "*Ghoral,*" the other "*Surow,*" find their rocky home. The barking of the small Muntjac deer,—here known by the name of "*Kacker,*"—often echoes from crag to crag; while the larger Jerow deer,—called "*Saumer*" in the plains,—is also not unfrequently met with. Within a quarter of an hour's walk from this place is a spacious cavern, the bear's retreat; no bear was however at present to be seen, and unluckily the den is too deep for its inmate to be driven out by the fumes of sulphur. Even the tiger seems to fix upon this mountain region as its favourite haunt, and much is he dreaded among its retired dwellings, on account of his bold and plunderous sallies. Not far from Nainethal, four months since, one of these latter beasts of prey lay in wait upon the pilgrim's path, and tore to pieces no less than ten or twelve travellers. It is a remarkable fact that this animal, apparently unaffected by any difference of temperature, is fully as dangerous in this elevated region, on the verge of eternal snows, as it is in the flat and sultry plains. I have even been assured that, in the Punjaub, the tiger's foot-prints have not unfrequently been found in snow.

"NAINETHAL" signifies the lake of *Naina*, the latter name being that of a renowned heroine. The lake lies between lofty cliffs of black limestone on the one, and loose deposits of argillaceous schist on the other side: its depth is very considerable; the plumb-line proved it, in several places, to be from sixty to seventy-five feet. Near its centre is a shallow spot, which, from the adjacent mountain summits, shines with emerald hue. The narrow end of the lake is towards the south-west; the north-eastern extremity is broad, and is the only place where, for a short distance, its margin is flat, scarcely raised above the level of the water. According to the measurements of Colonel Everest, its height above the sea is six thousand three hundred feet, and its circumference three miles and one third. The calcareous spar, which appears on the highest point of the surrounding rocks of clay-slate, the greenstone-trapp, detached blocks of which lie upon its western side, and the broken, indented form of its shores, would lead to the conclusion that this lake is of volcanic origin. Three others are situated in the neighbourhood, within a circuit of from ten to fifteen miles.

Our stay in this charming valley was prolonged from

day to day, as the provisions necessary for our further wanderings in the mountains could only be procured,—and that not without many delays,—by a mountainous and circuitous route from ALMORA. I thus enjoyed abundant leisure for collecting botanical and zoological specimens. The chase afforded us one *Ghoral-Antelope*, which the English call *Chamois*, and several specimens of various species of deer, and of pheasants, the skins of which I was busied in preserving. The bears did not vouchsafe to show themselves; leopards we saw indeed in abundance, but not one was slain, the nature of the rocky ground rendering it impossible to pursue these swift-footed creatures. The insects were but few; I found however a considerable number of butterflies on the Syringa bushes: chiefly of the species *Hipparchia* and *Lycæna*, also one *Euprepia*, of most brilliant colours, all bearing a striking resemblance to those familiar to us at home. It might indeed naturally be expected where so many shrubs and flowers are perfectly similar to those of Germany, that the insects which appear among them should coincide with those of that country.

On the 23rd of May, we observed a total lunar eclipse, during which the natives made a most fearful noise, howling and beating the drums, to drive away the dragon from the moon! Shortly afterwards, on the 27th, we were to start from Nainethal, furnished with seventy-four coolies, eight horses, four tents, and a whole flock of sheep for food. The appointed day arrived; but a tremendous thunder-storm burst upon us, with deluges of rain which inundated the whole place, and such was the rush of water that cascades were leaping down the side of every hill into the lake. At length, towards nine o'clock, the rain ceased: and after breakfast we mounted our horses, and, having despatched the coolies in advance, bid farewell to the lovely Nainethal.

We began our journey by scaling a mountain ridge; after which followed an abrupt descent, on rugged, winding paths. The Bhansh-oaks soon came to an end, and we found ourselves in a thick wood of firs, which filled the air with balsamic fragrance, while it rendered our path extremely slippery by the fallen needles of its foliage. From an elevated projection we commanded an extensive view of the mountain, vallies and glens: the spot was even pointed out to us, which was to be our next day's halting-place.

The boundary of the Nainethal district is here marked by a large heap of stones. The path leads, for some time after having reached the base of the hill, along the dry channel of a stream overgrown with raspberries and barberries; soon however we were obliged to quit it, as it was impracticable for horses. We passed through several villages of neat, clean houses, roofed with slate: beyond the last of these, the road turns off to ascend the acute angle of a narrow ridge, thickly wooded with pear-trees. On reaching the edge of this hill, we saw before us the glen of the Kosila, and after a toilsome descent, we arrived at the banks of the river, which, swollen by the late rains, was here about eighty paces in width, its greatest depth being three feet. On the opposite bank lies Boojan, a hamlet of some twenty houses, surrounded by a verdant coppice of Sycamore, Mango and Pomegranate-trees. Here we pitched our tents, dismissed our coolies, cooked our supper, and reposed from the fatigues of the day.

At eight o'clock A.M., on the 28th, we proceeded to ascend the valley of the Usigacka Nuddy, a tributary stream of the Kosila. Rugged precipices of argillaceous schist, clothed with scanty vegetation, rise on either side, above this narrow glen, which contains several small mills of very simple construction. To my amazement, there appeared here, at an elevation of four thousand feet above the sea, a few solitary palms, *(Phœnix humilis)* one of which, near the village of CHUKOLA, I should estimate to be at least thirty feet in height. Passing by an opening in the valley, which disclosed to view high cliffs of mica-schist and of black clay-slate, we climbed the rounded ridge of a naked hill, to the village of TIPOLI, which stands in a little circle of well cultivated fields. The ascent here becomes very difficult, on account of the height of the artificial terraces, and with the exception of the little sanctuary of JOOLEGA DEBI, it presents no object of interest. A march of four hours brought us to the spot where we were to bivouac, among tall pine-trees, on a gently sloping hillside. The headmen, "*Pudwaries,*"* of the two adjacent villages, THANDA and DIULI, had, with many of their kinsfolk, received us at the latter place, and they now followed us to our encampment.

Next day, the 29th, we crossed the GAGAS river, and passing through several pleasant villages, proceeded to the valley of DORA HATH. Our attention was here directed to a multitude of small temples, close to a grove of palms probably planted by the hand of man. These sanctuaries are said to have been erected, seven hundred years ago, by the RAJAH OF KOTHAUR, who dwelt here during one year, and completed one temple, or "*Deval,*" on each day of that period. These buildings have the appearance of diminutive towers of various heights; quadrangular below, but terminating above in a pyramydal form, and surmounted by a knob or ball on the pointed top. In front there is a small opening, protected by a very small portico resting on four pillars.

A far more stately and remarkable monument is the temple in the village of DORA *(Dwara)*, an edifice of considerable size. The main building, which is half dilapidated, is quadrangular, and adorned with sculptures of very dis-

* Petty collectors appointed by Government.—TR.

tinguished merit. Unfortunately the base,—which represents elephants, closely crowded together, and seen in full front with their heads projecting,—has been grievously defaced by Mahometan zealots; above it is a row of figures, both male and female, but not one of them many-armed. In the interior are several half-demolished sculptured figures, executed in demi-relief. This ancient monument is overshadowed by a Butter-tree,* *(Bassia butyracea)* and by groups of palms *(Phœnix sylvestris)*: close beside it, is a fine spring, covered by a subterranean passage of solid masonry.

Another temple, a Brahminical shrine still inhabited by priests, stands at no great distance. The most considerable of its buildings is a *Deval* of great height and of extreme antiquity, which stands in a court surrounded by walls painted red and white, adjoining which are two small wooden temple-halls. This sanctuary is dedicated to the *Mahadeo*† of KEDARNATH, and many pilgrims, shrinking from the length of the journey to the latter shrine, make DORA HATH the end of the pilgrimage.

The succeeding days of our travels led us,—as we followed the valley of the KOTELAL, which springs from the base of the lofty DUNA GIRI, a gently sloping and broad-ridged mountain,—through a comparatively level tract of country richly cultivated by its industrious inhabitants. The vegetation is monotonous in the extreme:

* The produce of the *Bassia butyracea*,—the Butter or Ghee tree of the Almora and Nepaul hills,—is described by Dr Royle as of a delicate white colour, and of the consistence of fine lard, but without any disagreeable smell; it is highly esteemed as a liniment in rheumatism &c., and when used by natives of rank is frequently impregnated with some fragrant attar. The fruit ripens in August; the kernels, about the size and shape of almonds, are easily extracted from the smooth chestnut-coloured pericarps, when they are bruised and rubbed up to the consistency of cream, and subjected to a moderate pressure in a cloth bag. The oil concretes immediately on being expressed, and retains its consistency at a temperature of 95°.—TR.

† *Siva*, the Destroyer, the deity peculiarly venerated throughout the mountain region, is believed, under the appellation of "*Mahadeo*," to be enthroned among the most inaccessible precipices of the Himalayas.—TR.

a few Balsams, Raspberries, *Bauhinias*, and here and there a *Gossypium* were all that I observed. We crossed the RAMGUNGA, into which the Kotelal flows: the former river is about eighty paces in width, and its channel, which is filled with pebbles washed down in quantities, may perhaps be about as wide again. On its banks we saw mines, from which rich iron ore is procured in abundance; the smelting huts are situated close beside them, near the confluence of the Kotelal and the Ramgunga. High-piled heaps of slags were pointed out to us, and small hearths, not larger than that of an ordinary kitchen, on which the ore is smelted. The huts immediately adjacent, had been very recently burned down, and were still smouldering. We also found mining operations carried on, close to a little village consisting of straw huts, in the valley of the KATCHERRI, which running for a time parallel to that of the Ramgunga, and enclosed by tame, and somewhat bare hills, contains very rich and beautiful meadow lands, watered by a mere insignificant rivulet.

We availed ourselves of this opportunity of seeing the very primitive operations of the smelting carried on here. A pair of bellows, with a mouth piece fastened on by cement, leads down into a small pit, rudely constructed of stone, under which a space has been hollowed out which is connected with the shaft above by an air-hole: in the upper part, the pounded iron-stone is mixed with an equal quantity of charcoal, and brought to a state of glowing heat: the slags sink down through the air-hole, and the welded iron forms into masses, which are from time to time drawn out and hammered.

The whole of this level creek among the hills, which forms the valley, is known by the name of SHIMOLTEKA; the pass of PONDUAKHAL, by which we ascended from it, rises to some eight hundred feet higher. After crossing it, we once more reached the RAMGUNGA, and thence proceeded along its left bank, often at a great elevation above the river. A multitude of pilgrims, chiefly women, coming from KEDARNATH, here met us; they declared themselves to be natives of BUNDELCUND, and the women were all clad in garments of dark blue cotton, bordered and tricked out with red. The elderly matrons greeted us with shouts and screams, while the young maidens ranged themselves in a line, turning their backs to us.

A forest of Rhododendron and of various species of Oak bestowed on us its welcome shade, and a few solitary pines appeared upon the opposite ridge.

Near the little village of Agoor, where we again descended to the water's edge, a precipitous face of rock of greenish blue stone caught my eye; the mouths of three different shafts, and a great quantity of lumps of ore and slags made it evident that a copper-mine was worked at that place. The beautiful, green cupriferous schist is worked in a simple manner, exactly similar to that we had witnessed in the iron-works of the valley of Katcherri. The ore is smelted, by means of charcoal, with an alloy of limestone broken down into it; but here the slags are brought up above, as the crucible,—if indeed a hole of half a foot in diameter, built in with unhewn stones, can be so called,—has no outlet whatsoever. With the greatest difficulty we obtained permission from the men in the huts to see their proceedings, and examine a few pieces of their metal, which they produced most unwillingly, being evidently afraid that we had some design of robbing them.

A most agreeable night's quarters awaited us on the evening of this day, the 1st of June, in the bungalow of Mr Lushington, which stands on a beautiful lawn, with its little garden, a sequestered nook in the midst of lofty, forest-clad mountains,—altogether a charming scene. The neighbourhood reminded me strongly of many landscapes in Switzerland, and this European character struck me the more from the presence of the numerous ornamental plants so familiar in our own flower-beds,—wall-flower, hearts-ease, carnations, roses and coreopsis.

From this spot forward, the banks of the Ramgunga are so steep and high, that we could but seldom see the river; lovely dells, their rippling brooks overgrown with beautiful ferns, and often enlivened by cascades, interrupt the monotony of the way, which lies generally through a thinly planted wood, consisting of Oaks and Pear trees, with underwood of roses and barberries. In the bottom of a deep lateral glen, I saw for the first time, the Æsculus (Horse-Chestnut) trees in full blossom, as tall as ours, but with narrower leaves; I also remarked a few solitary Walnut trees.

At length the dark forest became more light, the valley more open, and in the distance we descried our tents and the temples of ADH BUDRI, rising beneath the shade of tall Mulberry-trees. Our encampment lay near the sanctuaries, but about eighty feet lower down; close beside a sweet little stream,—the NARUNG, also known here as the ADH BUDRI NUDDY,—abounding in trout and in little waterfalls. Ascending the river through the glen, on our next day's march, we found that its banks soon became higher and more rugged; the rocks, clad on the height with a scanty vegetation, descending almost perpendicularly to the margin of the water, a declivity of eight hundred feet.

Here we gradually bid farewell to the rounded, gently sloping hill-tops and carefully cultivated terraces, which had hitherto characterized our landscapes; and entered upon mountain scenery marked by bold grandeur. The geological formation is schistose sandstone, and frequently also compact sandstone assuming the form of smooth cliffs; in a few particular spots, grauwacke-schist of dark colour, and some actual laminated slate are found,—but these are more rare. Crossing a hill, we entered a district watered by another stream, the valley of the KURSALI NUDDY, great part of which is thickly wooded; higher up this river, the path winds along its banks, crossing and recrossing from side to side, and ascending as if by steps. It was peculiarly difficult at the village of KIRSAL: there the abrupt declivities of the mountains are naked and desolate; a few giant trees only remain to mark what the forest was in days of yore, ere the destroying flames annihilated its glory.

Two passes,—the TILLEKANNIKHAL and the KHONKALAKHAL,—were crossed in one day's march, on the 4th of June. Before we gained the summit of the first, we were struck by a great change in the vegetable world around us: the forest became more and more dense; Walnut trees, Horse-Chestnuts in full flower, Oaks, Willows, and a species of Mulberry-trees, constitute the higher wood, the under-growth being entirely of roses. The PASS OF KHONKALA is about five hundred feet higher, and bare of wood on its highest ridge.

What a glorious prospect should we have enjoyed from this height, had not the whole atmosphere been filled with vapour! We could distinguish at such a depth below as might well make the beholder giddy, the large village of DHUNPOOR; but the surrounding summits were all veiled from our view.

The ground was covered with beautiful flowering plants,—melilot, white anemone, and several varieties of columbine; and lower down, a species of strawberry new to me, bearing a profusion of fruit, the delicious flavour of which is a great contrast to the *Fragaria Indica* with its yellow blossom and tasteless fruit, which we have invariably met with hitherto.

We descended by frightfully steep and rocky paths to the spot where our tents had been pitched, near DHUN-

POOR, where we did not arrive till eleven o'clock at night. The village is beautifully situated, and consists of neat, clean, stone houses, roofed with slate. It was however standing empty and desolate, the inhabitants having all gone, as we were informed, to pursue the "*Tikahdar*," —or village magistrate,—who had run away with the public funds committed to him; according to another report, the "*Tikahdar*" had refused to pay the workmen their full half of the profits of the copper-mines which form the principal source of revenue in this place; in consequence of which, we were assured, the men had refused to work, and had even quitted the mines.

I visited one of these copper-mines, the entrance to which is formed by a natural cavern, with numerous chasms and crevices. I was obliged to slide across a narrow bridge, which, without the protection of any hand railing, spans an apparently fathomless abyss. Splinters of resinous pine served as I descended, to shed some light on my path, and to spread great terror among the multitudes of bats and of a species of *Cypselus*, roused by this sudden intrusion on their solitude. The shaft,—or rather hole, for it is only a little more than a foot in diameter,—descends abruptly, and is besides so dirty, that I resolved rather to abandon all further investigation, than to penetrate, creeping quite flat on my face, through so narrow and uninviting a passage. The miners, I am told, lie upon their backs, and knock off the stone containing the ore, with a hammer.

Our day of repose at DHUNPOOR, the 5th of June, was devoted to the chase, which brought us a young musk-deer, and a Jerow-deer. Meanwhile, the village population, whom the presents bestowed on them had inspired with some measure of confidence, appeared in greater numbers; still however it was a difficult matter to bring together a sufficient troop of coolies. It could only be accomplished by means of the violent measures employed by the foreign *Putwaries*.

From this place we proceeded, along the valley of the DUDEGAON NUDDY, which, higher up, before its confluence, at the village of Sedoli, with another small stream, bears the name of the Sedoli brook. Many trees of the *Coniferæ* order appear on the mountain heights; *Taxus*, (Yew) of tall and noble stems, especially predominates. The rocky banks of the DUDEGAON are frightfully steep and wild: we quitted them before reaching the spot where that river flows into the ALACANANDA, and followed the course of a small stream, the Diuleh, which, falling over a deep and rugged declivity, unites its waters also with those of the Alacananda. The roaring of the latter, a turbid stream of a greyish yellow colour, which forces its narrow way through lofty cliffs of blackish-grey argillaceous schist, may be heard at a great distance.

A "*Sangho*," or rope-bridge, leads across, not far from the village of BAMOTH, situated on the right bank. These bridges, in universal use among the mountains, consist of two strong grass ropes, tight stretched across the river from side to side, to which are suspended, so as to hang perpendicularly, short grass ropes, not thicker than a finger, bearing transverse pieces of wood, fastened at right angles to their lower extremity; over these horizontal sticks, are laid lengthways, split bamboos, which, properly speaking, form the bridge. As its width is scarcely one foot, and these bamboos do not afford a very substantial footing, the passenger, who ventures to traverse this primitive suspension-bridge, must be free from all tendency to vertigo.

Our horses were obliged to swim through the stream, a rope being fastened round their necks, by means of which they were drawn over to the opposite bank. They all passed safely through the water, although the current is strong and rapid, and not less than a hundred and fifty feet in breadth. The transport of our tents and baggage was attended with no less difficulty: we followed, bringing up the rear. On the opposite side, the path climbs an abrupt ascent, constantly tracing the brink of the rocky precipice, here formed of pure sand-stone, which overhangs the Alacananda. At first, for about a thousand feet of the acclivity, we met with palms, *(Phœnix humilis)* loaded with richly flavoured dark blue fruit resembling dates.

Turning towards the north-east, we soon reached the glen of the KUNEGAR, which river flows between a thicket of woody bushes on the one side, and a range of cultivated terraces on the other. The reckless burning of grass and of underwood, and the barking of the large trees have dreadfully devastated the forest here, as in many other places. We found, encamped among the bushes, at the highest point of the glen, a troop of *Bhooteas*, from Neetee, who were carrying several hundred-weight of salt, stowed on the backs of sheep and goats,—their beasts of burden. These goats are very large, strong-built animals; for though laden with twelve "seers," or twenty-four pounds, each, in saddle bags across the back, they advance with an active and sprightly step.

Not far from the village of POKRI, which stands very high, and is surrounded with copper-mines, we met the *Putwario*, and a number of the inhabitants, all in white apparel, who had come out to receive us. A bungalow, situated on the summit of the hill, afforded us a most agreeable shelter, and we were obliged, by the heavy rains, to make a halt in it for one entire day. On the following we entered the pass of SIHALEKHAI, beyond the village of MATCHKINDA. The head of this pass is clothed with a very fine wood of noble mossed oaks, yews, bay-trees and willows: here, for the first time among the mountains, we met with bamboos; the luxuriant green sward was richly adorned with beautiful *Orchideæ,* a species of very fragrant *Polygonum,* and a profusion of strawberries. A second pass, the KHALLIKHAL,—or MUCKWAKHAL, for every place in these parts has more than one name,—which we ascended, after crossing the JAUMENIGHAR brook, proved a most toilsome climb; the path being slippery from the decayed leaves thickly strewn on it. The only habitations we passed were those of the miserable hamlet of DJUDE, (DUDE) beyond which, from our encampment at CHOBEDA, we caught the first view of the glorious snowy peaks of Kedarnath in the back-ground, shining in silvery splendour against the deep azure of the firmament, and appearing, from the effect of contrast, to be quite near us.

Our Hindoo attendants were not slow in availing themselves of the permission previously granted, to repair to the sacred spot of TUNGNATH, about three miles farther eastward.

The following day, the 11th of June, after descending by very steep and difficult paths, winding above the banks of the AGAS-GUNGA, we reached the lovely and mirror-like lake of DURITHAL, which lies at a great elevation. After making the circuit of its waters, we espied, beneath the summit of the overhanging ridge, a tent, in front of which sat a group of people clad in yellow silk and richly bedizened. The High-Priest of Kedarnath had come to this place to meet the Prince, and present his salutations, and he now requested to know whether he might have the honour of waiting upon His Royal Highness, and in what manner. Soon afterwards, his approach was heralded by the sound of a frightful kind of music, produced by long, trumpet-like wind instruments. After half an hour had elapsed, the High-Priest himself appeared; a handsome man, in the prime of life, with noble features marking him as a Hindoo of the purest race; he distributed a multitude of presents, consisting of pastry, confectionery, Cashmere shawls, yak-tails, musk, and a bowl full of rupees. His magnificent attire presented a curious contrast to our simple travelling guise.

Following him, we proceeded next day to Okimuth, descending at first along a sharp ridge, from which we obtained a general view of the valley of the Agas to our left, and that of the Cali-Gunga to our right; the latter studded with villages, and rich in terrace cultivation: before we were aware of its vicinity, Okimuth lay at our feet in the deep valley.

A large quadrangular edifice, with a Deval standing in the middle of a court surrounded by galleries, contains the dwelling of the high-priest. He received us at the door, touched the Prince's hat, as if to bestow a blessing upon him, and led us across the court, into an open hall, where a divan and two chairs were placed, on which we took our seats. Before the conversation began, two small canes were handed to each of us; the ends of them were wrapped in cotton, and steeped in a most exquisite perfume, a mixture of sandal-oil, and green otto of roses. The High Priest spoke very quickly, and with much animation, and seemed delighted with the present of a ring which he received in return for his fragrant gift; his hands trembled, as he added it to the many others on his little finger. He appeared, when we took leave, somewhat embarrassed, as to whether he should hold out his hand by way of salutation or not. This hesitation recalled to my mind Martabar Singh, with his hearty embraces: we have, by the bye, but recently received the intelligence of that illustrious person having been murdered at the instigation of the Rajah of Nepaul.

We soon proceeded on our journey, and, below Okimuth, reached the banks of the wild CALI-GUNGA, which, roaring and foaming, dashes on between its rocky banks.

A very loose and tottering "Sangho," formed of slender bamboos bound together with grass ropes, spans its angry whirlpool in the wildest part, at an elevation of from forty to fifty feet. At MASTA, we entered the glen of the MUNDAGRI, which river we afterwards crossed, at a bridge beyond NARANKOTE, a sacred spot, marked by a temple of great size. In the neighbourhood of a small village, in the valley of the Mundagri, I saw for the first time a *Deodara Cedar (Pinus Deodara)*; it had probably been planted there. Our party was, from this point, increased by the addition of an Englishman, who lives in these wild mountain regions, by the chase of musk-deer, which he finds a lucrative occupation. He is a delicate, almost feeble-looking man, on whom the invigorating effects of mountain-air, or of the life of a hunter, are not at all perceptible; in short, by no means the Nimrod that we had fancied him. Above JILMILPUTAM, the Mundagri, here a wild mountain torrent, makes a great bend; its banks become more and more rugged, in some parts rising in precipitous cliffs, to the height of more than a thousand feet. It receives, just at this turn, the waters of the BASSUGHI NUDDY. At this point too, we beheld the magnificent falls of the latter river; their deafening thunders, reverberating in the narrow glen, seem to make the very air tremble. I should estimate the lowest leap of the foaming waters, to be about a hundred and fifty feet in depth; broken in several places into angry spray, they rush down this mighty precipice with tremendous roar.

Higher up, the path, which climbs a steep ascent, becomes narrower, and soon consists merely of steps, from which we cast a shuddering glance at the raging torrent dashing along its rocky bed, at a fearful depth below. The glen is closely hemmed in by frowning ramparts of gneiss rock, which are too rugged at their base for any vegetation, but are clothed on the ridge above with Rhododendrons, Bhansh Oaks, and Pines. For some time, our path continued along the edge of the precipice on the right bank of the Mundagri; at length it wound down towards the margin of the stream: a quarter of an hour more, and we beheld before us, not far from the river, the far-famed temples of GAURICUND.

A multitude of pilgrims had gathered round the sacred springs of this spot, where, amid many ceremonies, they perform their ablutions. A basin of twelve feet square, with three gradations of depth, receives the water of one hot spring, TOPTACUND, which flows down from it in copious streams, by brazen conduits. Here we witnessed several singular bathing scenes. The temperature of the spring is 41°5 (125° Fahrenheit) the devout pilgrims, therefore, could not come into contact with its sacred waters without experiencing a certain degree of pain, the female bathers especially found the heat decidedly too great for their softer skins. They popped in alternately, first one, then another foot, without venturing a leap; many, even of the men, betrayed their pain while in the water by a most doleful mien. Others again displayed great heroism, standing in the centre amidst the bubbling of the fountain. One fakeer stepped in, without moving a muscle in his face; remained in the water fully three minutes, then rubbed his whole body with ashes, and, shortly afterwards, without having put on his clothes, was seen squatting in the cool evening air. What an enviable impassibility! I entered into conversation with this man regarding his mode of life. His expressions were as follows: "I left Juggernauth, my family property and home, and followed the god, by whose inspiration I was moved to wander hither. For twenty years I have been a fakeer. The god has ever given me all that I could need. The god has likewise kept me from being sensitive to cold, preserved me from suffering the pangs of hunger, and, when sick, raised me up again. In winter, the god must needs send me something in the shape of a mantle, something wherewith to clothe myself; yet, if it be not so, he will not suffer me to sink under the chilling blasts!"

When the pilgrims have at length contrived to perform their three prescribed immersions, their garments are next washed in the holy water, amid continued prayer. Among them may be seen men and boys running up and down at the edge of the basin, without the least idea of devotion, simply to wash their feet, or to cleanse various goods and chattels in its sacred fountain; gun-barrels and lamps were being cleaned in it; nevertheless, I was not permitted to descend to its margin, to estimate the temperature of its holy source. It is distant only about fifteen paces from the Mundagri, into which river the basin empties its descending stream, which forms a hot marsh on the bank, where, in spite of a temperature of 36° (113° Fahrenheit) nettles and docks thrive to perfection. Sixty paces from the first basin, and somewhat farther from the river, is the second spring,—a cold one, known by the name of GAURICUND. Its temperature is 17° 7, (about 72° Fahrenheit); the water is far more strongly impregnated with carbonate of iron than that of the hot spring: its basin is also resorted to by the pilgrims for bathing.

On the 16th of June, we arrived at the great object of pilgrimage, the templed shrine of KEDARNATH, renowned for ages on account of its peculiar sanctity. There the sacred corpse of Vishnu is said to have been deposited, after having been, when in the form of a bull, seized and put to death by the "*five Pardiks*" or holy brethren.

On leaving Gauricund, we had still a height of five thousand feet to scale before reaching the Temple, and therefore started early. The weather was bright and serene; and ere long, the sun's burning rays were striking down on our toilsome path, which, often not more than a foot and a-half in width, continued to wind along the ledge of rock. A new plague here presented itself in the shape of an innumerable swarm of small stinging flies,—*Ceratopogon*,—which crawled within our raiment, and covered the whole body; it is certainly the only kind of fly that practises this mode of attack: their stings are very malignant, and we continued to feel them for several days.

We proceeded up the glen of the Mundagri, the depth of which is at least twice as great as that of the "*Rosztrappe*" in the *Harz Mountains*. It is but seldom possible to see the river, although the hollow roar of its successive waterfalls never ceases to sound in one's ears. The declivities and the points of the gneiss cliffs are covered with noble wood: primeval oaks, with foliage of most singular form, from whose jagged boughs hangs down a sort of long, white moss, while rich ivy, and beautiful festoons of the vine, twine around their venerable stems; walnut and horse chestnut trees in freshest verdure, and the latter in the full glory of its blossom; maple and hazle-nut trees of great size, with bays and many other trees unknown in the forests of Germany, all intermingled in motley masses. Higher up, the wood becomes comparatively stunted and scanty; rose-bushes and willows chiefly predominate; tall trees gradually become rare; the *Taxus* only, which here supplies the place of the fir, still shoots up, and stands forth a full-grown tree among the stunted bushes. Ere long, forest trees, whether tall or dwarf, are no more seen, save in the depths of the glen below; roses and bushes of a species of syringa, of most powerful fragrance, are the last, but not the least lovely shrubs that crown the steep.

A beautiful cataract, broken into several falls, rushing over a precipice of some hundred feet in depth, riveted our admiring attention, before we reached the last pilgrims' resting-place,—BHIM ODIAR. Immediately beyond that station, the glen rises considerably; the path however continues much on the same level, so that we soon found ourselves beside the Mundagri. Here we came to the first bed of snow, the length of which I should estimate to be not less than eight hundred paces; it is covered with erratic fragments and large blocks of stone. A vast avalanche has formed a vault over the river. Murmuring rivulets trickle down on every side from their sources among the beds of snow which fill the hollows; their steep banks often obliged us to make great circuits. Beside one of these little streams, I suddenly perceived a most unpleasant smell, which at first puzzled me; but soon I observed, close to the channel of the water, a little white spot; and, scrambling to it, I discovered a sulphureous spring, gushing forth from beneath a large mass of rock, and filling the air with a potent smell of sulphurated hydrogen.

From this point forward, arboreous vegetation yields to a luxuriant Alpine flora: *Rhododendron*, with parched and unadorned stalks, *Fritillaria*, *Iris*, and *Potentillas* and *Anemones* of various colours, clothe the steep sides of the acclivities and their lofty summits.

Scarcely conscious how far we had advanced, we suddenly found ourselves at the valley where, encircled by frowning precipices, and embosomed amid lofty mountains, stands the sanctuary of KEDARNATH. In the background, to the north-north-west, the valley is bounded by huge heaps of "*débacles*," formed of brownish gray snow mingled with stones, piled up and towering into hills of ruins; to the right of these rises the glorious peak of KEDARNATH,—twenty-one thousand, five hundred feet above the sea. Undaunted by cold and fatigue, we forced our way through three fields of snow,—a most arduous achievement,—to the rock from which devout pilgrims, offering up their lives as a sacrifice to the deity, were wont to cast themselves headlong. On this elevated point, the air was rarified to such a degree that we all suffered from headache, and I was even seized with vertigo, though walking on level ground. The rock rises abruptly to a height of some six hundred feet above the beds of snow, and a waterfall,—the source of the Mundagri,—rushes down the steep, and vanishes beneath the snow-bed, from which the incipient river emerges at some distance lower down.

On a gentle eminence in the moorland bottom of the valley, surrounded by a profusion of beautiful flowers, and especially of the most lovely auriculas, of deep violet hue, stands the far-famed temple of Kedarnath. It is upon the whole well built, but has no marks of great antiquity: of the original structure, not a vestige now remains save its basement,—built, according to tradition, by the gods themselves, and a few ancient, much decayed capitals of pillars, which lie scattered around, half sunk in the moor. The sanctuary was erected in its present form, by the High Priest of Okimuth, only three years ago. Its façade has a narrow flight of steps, not more than ten feet in height, and a door in the centre, flanked on either side by a niche,—that on the left hand being occupied by the figure of a *Hoonuman*,—that on the right by the *Chuprassy* of *Mahadeo;* above the latter, in a diminutive niche, stands the flute-player of the god,—*Kirkissi*,—while the corresponding small niche on the left hand remains empty. A little spring, with a sort of tiny house built over it, rises at the distance of about a hundred paces beyond the temple; farther off, on the eastern declivity of the mountain ramparts which enclose the valley, is another spring, named RETICUND, strongly impregnated with carbonic acid. Its temperature is 4° 5 (41° Fahrenheit); several others, situated at no great distance from each other, higher up among the mountains, are of a heat not exceeding 3° 3 (39° Fahrenheit).

The valley in which the temple stands has an elevation of eleven thousand eight hundred feet above the sea: its width, measured across the Mundagri, which divides it longitudinally, is about four hundred and eighty paces. The lower hills which advance in front of the mountain range on either side of the valley, are probably mere mounds of débris, accumulated by the constant sliding down of masses of snow: they give a peculiar character to the whole scene.

We spent the night on this elevated plateau; the air became cold and keen, and towards morning the thermometer was standing at 5° 5 (44° Fahrenheit). About eight A.M., on the 18th of June, we quitted this wild and romantic solitude by the same path which had led us thither; before reaching Jilmilputam however, we turned to the south-west, and traversing a forest of noble oaks, gained a projecting point among the mountains, whence we commanded a magnificent prospect of the Kedarnath group. The sharp line of demarcation between snows and forests was, from this spot, clearly distinguishable. Opposite to us, separated by the glen of a little stream, lay the pretty village of TIRJOOGHI, near which we selected a most suitable and tempting spot for our encampment.

After holding a long consultation as to how we should proceed, and by what path enter the territory of the RAJAH OF GURWAL, no coolies being here to be had, we at last resolved to retain those who had hitherto accompanied us, and, turning north-west-ward, we immediately struck into the depths of the forest. Here and there we found an isolated space, where, in the heart of the wood,—there partially destroyed by fire,—the oval-spiked, or fox-tail amaranth, (*Amaranthus Gangeticus*) here used as grain, had been sown among the ashes. Broad slopes covered with ferns alternate with pieces of ground thus cultivated, or with the forest, with its tall and sturdy stems. The path, slippery with roots and fallen leaves, offers no easy ascent; as far as the head of the pass of TSORIKHAL, the wood continues to increase in the luxuriance of its vegetation, and even on the summit, it excludes all view. To our left, beside the path, a large tiger-trap had been set, consisting of a deep pit, with a portcullis formed of several heavy trees joined together, and weighted on the top with stones. A prop is placed below it, as in a mouse-trap; which is very easily moved by means of small pieces of wood; and to this is fastened, within the pit, a living goat. The portcullis closes, instantly upon the tiger seizing his slaughtered victim. The animals known among the natives here as tigers (*"Sher"*) are, in fact, almost invariably leopards.

A second pass, yet higher than the first, and after it three other mountain ridges, yet remained to be crossed, ere we arrived, in the middle of the wilderness, at the ruins of a bungalow, standing on a narrow and uninviting strip of ground, surrounded by thick jungle. The rich carpet of mosses and of ferns of most elegant form, was glistening with drops of heavy rain. Beyond this spot, the trees become dwarfed, and the oak gives place to the rhododendron and the birch.

Never before had the giant mountains to the north appeared so completely to pierce the very skies, as when seen from this point, where a deep and wide glen lay at our feet. Like crystal palaces of ice, they towered into the air; to our right, the PEAK OF BUDRINATH, with its immense slopes of smooth and shining snow; to our left our old friend, the PEAK OF KEDARNATH. Sharp and clear were the outlines of these bright summits,—pencilled against the azure sky,—and difficult would it have been to decide which was the more beautiful of the twin pair. Two beds of snow,—bordered with lovely, pale rose-coloured auriculas, and primroses of bright sulphur yellow and of delicious fragrance,—must needs be crossed; after which, scaling a steep rock of mica schist, the surface of which had been reduced by disintegration to a somewhat soapy consistency, we gained the summit, the crowning point of all these lofty passes. Here we again beheld the glorious snow-capped peaks of the higher Himalaya range; but it was only for a moment; the next instant, glittering icy needles alone towered above the dense mass of vapour, at such a height, that we might have deemed them an airy mirage, had we not, but a few seconds before, been gazing upon the entire chain, down to its very base.

We wandered on, along the ridge of this pass, for full two hours, till at length we descried, to the south-west, our tents pitched on the crest of a distant height. Memorial stones beside our path, and a fakeer whom we met, marked it as the pilgrims' route to GUNGOTRI; it was broad and smooth, and led us through a lovely valley richly wooded with oak, to our resting-place, PAWALI DANDA. The Rajah's coolies were awaiting our arrival. An overhauling of our baggage, along with the necessary repairs of our trunks, and the paying off of bearers and other attendants, made a day's halt indispensable. Our horses too were discharged for the present, as supernumeraries, great part of our further route being impracticable except on foot; and Simla being their appointed rendezvous, they were sent on by another road. To-morrow we are to proceed towards the sources of the Ganges. Our first stage is to be to the glen of the BILHANG; the "*upper route,*" in favour of which we had at first decided, being reported impassable, from its bridges being broken down.

NINTH LETTER.

THE COOLIES—DEPARTURE FROM PAWALI DANDA—GOWANNA—RICE CULTIVATION—KEDARAKHAL—GEWALI—MUSK-DEER-SNARES—LEOPARDS—CHANNEL OF THE BHALE GUNGA—PINNAREE—THE PASS OF KOOS—FORESTS OF CONIFERÆ—VALLEY OF THE BHAGIRATHI (GANGES)—ROPE BRIDGE—BITHAREE—BIVOUAC AT GODH-GADH—FALLS OF THE BHAGIRATHI—BRIDGE—SOOKHEE—FIRST CEDAR FOREST—DHERALEE—CONFLUENCE OF THE JAHNAVI AND BHAGIRATHI—MUSK-DEER—THE MONAL PHEASANT—CHANNEL OF THE BHAGIRATHI—GUNGOTRI—THE TEMPLE—RETURN—VIEW OF THE SNOWY PEAKS—THE NILUNG-BRIDGE—VILLAGE OF MOOKBA—ITS HOUSES—BEE-HIVES—AGRICULTURE—APRICOTS—PREPARATIONS FOR FURTHER JOURNEY.

MOOKBA, ON THE BHAGIRATHI; *7th of July*, 1845.

WE are now penetrating deeper and deeper among the mountains, and it is becoming more and more difficult to procure the number of coolies requisite to expedite our baggage and our tents. The villages, or rather hamlets, are few and far between; and the inexorable severity with which their miserable inhabitants are pressed into our service by their "*Putwaries*" or district magistrates, often makes me shudder. The wages of the bearers are very low; not one man could be obtained to act in that capacity without open violence; for each has his field or his trade, from which he must be torn away by the compulsory measures of the Putwarie, and of his "*Chuprassies*" or armed underlings. Thus necessity constrains us to lay aside all considerations of reluctance or of remorse, and to witness, day after day, the hardships of those poor creatures, as, panting and groaning under their heavy burdens, they toil up the steep and rugged paths. Our troop of coolies has dwindled down from seventy-four,—our suite on starting from Nainethal,—to about half that number: yet, even now, it is no easy matter to procure a sufficient supply of provisions in this poor country, notwithstanding that the people live most frugally, going through a whole day's hard work, on the strength of a handful or two of barley-meal or of wheaten flour. The victuals are transported on sheep, each having a small saddle on its back: of course no very weighty burden can be laid on so weak an animal; the usual load does not exceed eighteen or twenty pounds.

A strange rumour had spread among the people in the dominions of the Rajah of Gurwal, to wit, that the Prince was preceded by a host of three thousand military, carrying fire, devastation and pillage, wherever they went. With the utmost difficulty were the terror-stricken populace convinced that the plundering army, and the splendid court with its golden pageantry, all consisted merely of a few pedestrian travellers, clad in simple attire, and followed by their luggage-bearers. Our party has unfortunately been diminished by the loss of one most useful member,—the Prince's personal attendant,—who, being seized with repeated attacks of the nature of cholera, probably caused by the sultry air of the valleys, was left behind. His place was taken by the aforementioned English hunter, who is intimately acquainted with all the windings, the ups and downs, and the narrow passes, of these mountain roads, and is moreover well versed in the "*Pahari Zubaun*," or language of the mountaineers, a dialect unintelligible even to our interpreter.

We quitted our resting-place of Pawali Danda on the 21st of June. It was cold,—8° 3, (50 Fahrenheit)—and very wet, and an autumnal-looking mist concealed all the landscapes, as we descended into the glen of the Bilhang. Deep in its recesses lies the village of Gowanna, consisting of two parts, known as "*Mutegaon*" and "*Mullegaon,*" or "*upper*" and "*lower:*" our tents were pitched close beside it, on a small, isolated hill, round which the river winds, raging and thundering as it makes the bold sweep. Rice is largely cultivated near this place: the young shoots, but just transplanted, and arranged in neat spiral or zigzag lines in the fields, give the valley the appearance of pleasure gardens laid out in the Dutch style. I was struck by the singularity of this mode of culture in the rice grounds throughout the glen of the Gowann-Nuddy. The effect produced by the tender, velvety green of the young rice was most beautiful; the plant was one of the species called "*Basmutty,*" which is very highly esteemed in the plains. The fields lie in the deep hollow of a channel, where of old the river was wont to flow; in a few days, the proper season will have arrived for damming up the main branch of the stream, and thus diverting its waters for the purpose of inundating the young crops. The Rice harvest is here the second in the year; wheat and barley have already been reaped and brought in, and the stubble plucked up by the roots and burnt. I observed, here and there, on the rocky masses of gray gneiss, large cavities hollowed out in their flat tops. On these, the rice, when ripe, is separated from the husk by means of threshing.

A very frail and tottering bridge led us, on our next day's march, across the stream. The path up the glen from this place forward, is scarcely practicable, owing to the steepness of the rocky ramparts, covered with huge blocks of stone, and overgrown with alders, turf and vines. The ascent is abrupt and long-continued; our first breathing-place was the summit of the Kedarakhal pass, far above the limits of the growth of trees. In many places, we could scale the black surface of these loamy acclivities, softened by the heavy rains, only by dragging ourselves up on all fours. My measurement gave for the summit of the pass, a perpendicular height of ten thousand, five hundred and eighty feet, above the level of the sea.

On the descent of the opposite slope, vegetation begins with *Rhododendron campanulatum*, next follows a thick forest of maple with underwood of buckthorn, and a species of pear-tree, *("Poppemull")* with very large heart-shaped leaves, folded up in the centre, giving the tree a most singular appearance: a species of bamboo extends up to the highest limit of arboreous vegetation. Occasionally also, in the heart of this lofty forest, we came to insulated pieces of open ground, overgrown with tall herbs, chiefly *Rumex acetosella*, (sorrel) *Spergula nodosa*, (knotted spurrey) *Lamium*, (archangel) and several umbelliferous plants, but they were of such luxuriant growth, that we could scarcely see over their heads. These mountain prairies are often upwards of two miles in length. Lower down, are interminable fields of strawberries; and in the last place, we were obliged to pass through a dense forest of bamboos, before reaching the cultivated lands of the little village of GEWALEE, where we found crops of tobacco, cucumbers, and various species of millet.

On the 25th of June, we crossed the deep glen of the BHALE GUNGA, and beyond it, a wooded pass, the name of which we could not learn.

Bears and other wild beasts, abound in this part of the country: we met a man who had lost his nose, and were informed that he had been thus maimed by a black bear of the species so common here. Several musk-deer snares were laid close beside our path. They consist merely of a young tree, bent downwards; to the top,—which is wedged in between two little pieces of wood on the ground, in such a manner that the slightest touch will make it start up into the air,—a strong noose is fastened, and the whole is carefully concealed with leaves and twigs. A closely interwoven fence on each side leaves only a narrow passage. As soon as a musk-deer, in passing, touches the wedges, the tree-top, with the noose attached to it, flies up with a jerk, and the animal is taken. *Monal Pheasants*, and even leopards, are said to be caught in these snares. The last mentioned animal, of which there are great numbers in these regions, possesses great peculiarities. It seems to delight in paths trodden by human beings, and imprints with its claws, deep furrows on the bark of the trees near them in every direction; five parallel streaks on the stems attract one's notice continually, the central one beginning somewhat higher than the rest, which would not be the case were they the marks of a bear. These leopards appear to seek out, as particular favourites, trees of soft bark; for every stem of the *Rhododendron Arboreum* which had attained a tolerable degree of thickness, is covered with these furrows on every side.

After a forced march of seven hours, in which, on a broad meadow-land, we passed two small lakes, MUSSARNAG and MUSSARINAGGIN, we reached the channel of the second BHALE GUNGA; the latter part of the journey being performed by slipping along, and gliding down steep declivities after the fashion of the "Montagnes Russes;" for the bamboo canes closing over, and the fallen leaves of the Bhansh oaks strewn upon the clayey path, render it nearly impassable. We were obliged to help ourselves forward with our hands from one bamboo to another. The Bhale Gunga, which unites itself with the other stream of the same name, near the large village of KATHUR, is only ten or twelve paces across, but rapid and impetuous, and so deep is the ravine cut by its rushing waters, that it appears mantled in darkness amidst the magnificent foliage of the surrounding forest, consisting of maple, ash, beech and walnut trees. Among the various species of oak, the "*Mohroo*" *(Quercus dilatata)* was distinguished by its thick globular fruit, in size equal to a small apple, of a gray or reddish-brown colour, and growing on a very flat cup, which does not fall off with the acorn.

Below the village of PINNAREE (also called *Pinsaree*, or *Pinnawur*, according to the people we happened to ask;) we pitched our tents beneath the shade of a beautiful walnut grove. The trees were loaded with nuts, which however on account of their extreme hardness, and the difficulty of extricating the kernel from its shell, are little esteemed. These nuts are quite round, and when broken, spring into four pieces. We are told that there is another species, with thin-shelled fruit, which is cultivated in these parts.

The race of inhabitants here, as in Gewali, is large and strong: the men have thick black beards, and wear loose garments and trowsers of brown wool; the women studiously kept themselves out of sight. The houses of the village, situated higher up on the hill-side, are neat and clean, built of stone, with a flight of wooden steps outside, and a paved landing-place before each threshold. The village is surrounded by fields of red Amaranth.

Our first march on the following day led across a pass, ten thousand five hundred feet in height, on the other side of which we entered the valley of the Pelang, a deep lateral glen, running into the valley of the Pillgaon. The path was still through thick forests, in which I was struck by one huge hazel-nut-tree, with a stem equal in thickness to that of an oak. Ere long, we reached the banks of the rapid Pillgaon itself, over which a bridge had just been thrown, a work of mountain architecture, such as is in common use here. The trunks of three trees had been laid across the wildest part of the stream; railing there was none; besides which, the long stems of the trees, unsupported and flexible, vibrated in the centre, with a most unpleasant swinging motion.

On the 28th of June, from the sharp projecting ridge of a high mountain, beyond the PASS OF KOOS, which rises to an elevation of ten thousand, seven hundred feet, we caught the first view of the VALLEY OF THE GANGES, with the villages of Reital,—among them Malla and Bitharee,—to the south-west Sioochee, Gursollee, and several others, situated on an extended and apparently treeless slope on the right bank of the river. The contrast seemed to heighten the rich and beautiful effect of the thick wood through which we threaded our way on the descent. Here the Coniferæ begin to predominate, and among them are trees of incredible size and height; one "*Morinda*" Fir *(Abies Pindrow*)* measuring six feet in diameter, and rising to a height of, I should say, not less than two hundred feet; a *Taxus* (Yew) of five feet in diameter; and other similar giants. Lower down begins the "*Roi*" Fir *(Picea Morinda)*, which likewise attains a wonderful circumference. Even the *Spiræa*, and the *Xylosteum*,—of which latter one species struck me amid the lofty and massive forest,—are here arborescent. The "*Roi*" Fir much resembles our Red Fir; it has very thin and pointed leaves, half an inch in length, and its boughs grow at a right angle from the stem, while those of the "*Morinda*" Fir *(Abies Pindrow)* hang downwards. The leaves of the latter spring two from one sheath; they are two inches in length, and of a shining dark green on the upper side.

But now the forest became less gloomy; soon we found ourselves once more in the region of bamboos, and the sound of rushing water announced to us the proximity of the sacred stream, although we were still at a height of several thousand feet above it, and unable to catch even a glimpse of its course. The last abrupt de-

* Perhaps more commonly known as the *Pinus Khutrow*, of Royle, or the *Abies Smithiana* of Loudon. See Appendix I.—TR.

scent, which led us to its margin is covered with long, hard grass, on which we were perpetually sliding, and in some danger of slipping down from top to bottom of the smooth declivity, without anything to break our fall. In the valley of the BHAGIRATHI,—as the Ganges is here called,—we were surrounded by a vegetation entirely different from what we had before seen. All the rugged cliffs are clothed with grape-vines; in the midst of their climbing tendrils are thick bushes of *Aurantiaceæ*, *Berberis*, *Cissus*, and a species of Raspberry with gray fruit of most delicious flavour.

A simple rope, formed of thin strips of bamboo twisted together, and stretched across the river, which is about fifty paces in width, serves as a bridge. On this rope rests a crooked piece of wood, to each end of which, one is fastened by a strong cord round the waist. A signal is then given, to wind oneself across the rope with hands and feet, which is at first a tolerably rapid mode of transit, as one proceeds down an incline, but all the more difficult on the other side, so much so that it requires great strength and violent effort to reach the end of the rope and to set foot on terra-firma. Five hours passed away before all our baggage was conveyed across in this manner. Our tents were pitched upon the farther bank, which is neither steep nor very lofty; and in spite of the great heat, we enjoyed a tolerably undisturbed night's rest, as the stinging flies (*Ceratopogon*) were not nearly so numerous as they had been at the former stations, where not one of our party could close an eye, on account of their attacks.

The banks of the Bhagirathi in this valley consist of a white stone, the component parts of which are quartz and feltspar intersected with black mica. At the spot where the rope spans the river, two large masses of rock advancing on either side, contract the channel considerably: the waters dash up against them in furious and roaring breakers, like the waves of the sea against a rugged beach. I was particularly struck here by the extraordinary colour of the stream: it has an opalized appearance, caused, probably, by the fine shivers of mica which float in it.

A fresh troop of coolies was here engaged, who, unlike what we had met with on former occasions, displayed the greatest willingness to enlist in our service; because a "*Tikahdar*" was granted them, *i. e.* a man appointed to superintend and lead them, and support them in all their rights; notwithstanding this however a long time elapsed on the following morning, before we were actually in motion. The path is steep, but as well made as could possibly be expected in such a district. The greatest delay we met with was the numbers of little rivers and brooks, the first of which we crossed at the village of BITHAREE below Reithal: each of these made it necessary for us to scramble down by steep paths, like flights of steps, from rocks often not less than a thousand feet in height, to the water's edge, and straightway to climb up again to an equal elevation opposite, exposed all the while, to the burning rays and scorching glare of a vertical sun. *Lämmergeyers** and black crows were hovering and circling around us; but very little was to be seen in the way of either plants or animals. Parched, withered pines, of the species *longifolia,*—standing in mournful solitude, their attenuated forms casting no shadow,—serve only to render the slippery path more smooth and slippery still by their fallen foliage; some small primroses, scattered singly, the white *Cyperus*, a few ferns, and long, parched grass, compose the entire flora of those slopes where any soil is to be found.

* *Gypaetus barbatus,* bearded vulture-eagle. It is so rare a bird, and so unsocial in its habits, as to be considered a precious capture even in those countries where it most inhabits. Rare as it is in all countries, it is the inhabitant of many,—from the Pyrenees and Alps to the steppes of the Siberian deserts.—TR.

The rocks rise precipitously on either side of the river, and few villages are seen in its vicinity, as most of them are higher up. In some places, the dip of the strata on the one bank is diametrically opposed to that on the other; the colour is no less different, one being black, the other white.

After a march of nearly five hours, we arrived at our resting-place, beside the rivulet of Godh-Gadh. Above us lay the village of TIARRI, mentioned by Hodgson as TEWARRI. The river UAR,—which Hodgson incorrectly calls the SAAR,—flows down from this little place, and falls into the Ganges, and a little lake, bearing the name of RANAL or NAGH, lies at a distance of five or six miles.

Our path, next day, the 30th of June, continued without much variety, beside the Ganges; gentler slopes,—clothed with "*Cheel*" Pines, *(Pinus longifolia)* Rhododendron, Bamboo, and Indigofera,—alternate with deep cut glens, in which mountain torrents rush down between steep and rugged banks. The rocks below, on the edge of the Ganges itself, are covered with a species of climbing fig, while the bed of the stream is full of stems of fir, swept down by the current.

Higher up, a hollow thundering roar, resounding from afar, reminded us that we were approaching the falls of the Ganges. With great difficulty we scrambled over the loose boulders down to the river, to obtain a nearer view of them. There are several falls, one above another. The first, a sheet of water, about eighty feet wide, rushes over a precipice of only sixteen feet in depth; on the left side indeed the fall is even somewhat less; but the falling mass, rebounding against a sunken rock beneath the dark surface of the pool below, rises again into the air in a vast pillar of water. The second fall is rather deeper; the third is the greatest, being at least thirty feet deep. Every thing around is wrapt in a veil of vapoury spray, and sprinkled with the finely attenuated drops from the mighty body of water, whose thunders cause the very earth to tremble. Several rapids and falls of inferior depth occur higher up the stream, where, hemmed in by frowning cliffs, to a gorge of no more than twenty feet wide, it forces its onward way with tremendous violence. The wild music of the stream,—its deep hollow murmurs, or loud and angry raging,—henceforward our constant companion, had the effect of making us habitually speak to each other in a high and screaming tone; at night, notwithstanding my weariness, its ceaseless clamour resounding in our tent,—almost always pitched close to its brink,—not unfrequently banished sleep from my eyes.

Immediately before our next halting-place, we crossed, by a bridge formed of trunks of trees, to the left bank of the river, where, on a small piece of level ground, we found a half ruined bungalow.

Lofty granite cliffs and high banks of débris, through which the Bhagirathi has cut its way, made our march on the 1st of July sufficiently difficult and fatiguing. In one place, where our path led close beside the water, we saw a precipitous face of rock a thousand feet high, which the calcareous springs that trickle down over the whole extent of its surface from top to bottom, have covered with a fretwork of yellowish white calcareous spar. Fallen blocks of loose calcareous stone upwards of two feet in thickness, are lying in the sand of the river; the water of the springs, which falls in numerous little cascades, has an unpleasant astringent taste, and is slightly impregnated with carbonic acid.

For some time the newly repaired path continued along the edge of the stream; it was so loose, that in some places it gave way beneath our feet: it led us down to a bridge of beams, a very fragile affair, and, as usual, without rails or parapet, in spite of which it appeared to me far preferable to the simple rope; for it is easier to reconcile oneself by habit to the swinging and tottering of the long trees, and to the sight of the deep abyss beneath one's feet, than to the desperate situation in which one is placed in sliding along the giddy rope.

Just beyond the confluence of the LUNEGADH river, which rolls its golden sand into the Bhagirathi, we were obliged to pass over mounds of rubbish, caused by the fall of an immense mass of rock, which took place eight years ago. Large blocks, from ten to twenty feet in thickness, are piled above each other, towering to a height of three hundred feet above the river. The path over these is a most laborious, scrambling ascent; walls of rock are to be scaled which rise nearly perpendicularly, and in many places, where the smooth stone offers no firm hold for the foot, long narrow planks of cedarwood, their ends propped up with stakes, are laid along its edge. A wood of small extent, consisting of willow, poplar, mulberry and elm trees, and a few scattered "*Roi*" firs, occasionally ornamented by the climbing tendrils of the vine, extended along our path till we arrived at the slope on which lies the village of SOOKHEE. Higher up, we were exposed to the scorching rays of the sun; here and there only, a beautiful group of walnut and apricot-trees cast a welcome shade, before we reached the cultivated fields of amaranth and of wheat.

The village seemed like an abode of the dead; we saw only a few solitary men, with rope-baskets on their arms, spinning wool; and ugly women, with clumsy turbans, and dirty brown woollen jackets and trowsers. Our encampment lay in the centre of the village, which consists of some thirty well-built wooden houses. Several of these have two or three low stories; the windows are mere small holes, and the roofs consist, like those in the Valais, of strong, rough planks. The building materials are for the most part furnished by the *Deodara Cedars* that are carried down by the river. A tree with steps hewn in it leads up to the first floor, where the entrance into the principal apartment is through a door just high enough to admit of a man creeping in, bent double. Dark bed-chambers and store-rooms occupy the space beside it.

Beyond the neat little village of JALLA below PURALI, we reached the beginning of the first forest of Indian Cedars *(Cedrus Deodara)*. It is in part destroyed by fire, but noble trees yet remain in it. The *Deodara* is the most beautiful tree of the fir tribe that exists in any part of the world: it shoots up with a tall, straight, taper stem, often a hundred feet in height, and not unfrequently forty feet in circumference. The branches grow in stages, at regular intervals, and spread out like overshadowing roofs. They are adorned with thick-set, upright cones. The leaves, strewn in abundance upon the ground, choke all vegetation.

We crossed on wavering cedar-tree bridges, the broad SEANEGADH, *(Sian)* and the largest of all the many tributary streams of the Bhagirathi, the GOOMTY, and, finally, the HERSILE *(Hursil)*; beyond which last we passed over the Bhagirathi or Ganges itself. Here the Cedar forest ceases, and is succeeded by the Roi-Fir.

The wood gradually becoming less dark, we soon perceived in the distance the village of DHERALEE; almost at the same moment, we came within sight of that of MOOKBA, lying over against it, upon the rugged steep which forms the rampart of the valley. After a march of four hours, we arrived at the former place. A tower, of six stories, serves as a fortress, as we are informed, to protect the village,—consisting of small neat wooden dwellings, resembling Swiss cottages,—from the sheep-stealing hordes. Above Dheralee, we crossed an elevated mountain ridge of granite, beyond which the cedar forest begins again. Even on the rugged precipices that overhang the river, towering like huge battlements, a solitary Deodara has here and there struck root, and rears its noble and shapely form.

We here saw, but did not pass over, a "*Sangho,*" which, swinging at a height of about seventy feet above the Bhagirathi, leads the NILUNG path across its stream. The name of "*Sangho*" is here applied, not only to the platform or suspension bridges, but to the tree-bridges above described, by one of which, four hours afterwards, we crossed the BHAIROGETHI,—the parent stream of the JAHNEVI or JAHNAVI. A trunk of a tree with steps hewn in it, leads down to several flat masses of rock at the edge of the raging stream, which forces a narrow passage,—scarce twenty feet in width,—through the frowning cliffs; two other trees, joined together by means of unhewn pieces of wood laid across them, form a very rude and nervous bridge, which, to add to the difficulty, inclines downwards from one bank to the other at a most formidable angle. Through the gaps in this primitive structure we looked down upon the dark waters rolling at a depth of sixty feet below. Close beside the bridge, there lies a stone, of oval form, about one foot long, and painted red. It is neither more nor less than the body of the god, here worshipped under the name of *Bhairam!*

Our camp, though not very conveniently situated, afforded a magnificent prospect of the wild and broken glen, covered with shattered masses of rock, and of the picturesque confluence of the BHAGIRATHI and JAHNEVI. The two rivers unite their waters just at our feet; each seems to repel the other with its wild waves. It is a desolate and savage scene: the path, beyond the bridge, is quite in character with it, winding up the lofty steep in zigzags, now on giddy flights of steps, now again on tottering planks, laid across chasms and deep abysses. We now crossed the base of the DEKANI PEAK, where we again found ourselves in a wood of splendid cedars. Here lies the sanctuary of *Bhairam*, who is worshipped as the god of the river; it is surrounded by heaps of stones, and by flags, or rude streamers, fastened to sticks, set up on all sides by the devout pilgrims. The aged *Zemindar*, who had been appointed by the Rajah to attend upon us, did not forget to avail himself of the opportunity of displaying his piety by setting up his tiny banner.

Here and there we perceived a strong odour of musk, marking the track of the *Moschus moschiferus*, commonly known as the *Thibet Musk*, and said to abound in these parts; for it is a beast of the forest, and loves the wild rocks and cliffs. The cedar forest in particular is its proper home. Recent tracks of bears were also observed in abundance; these seem to be tolerably peaceful animals, feeding principally on the pods of the leguminous plants, and in autumn on the fruits that drop from the trees. The locusts also, which fall upon the fields of snow, they seek out and devour voraciously.

I saw few birds, except one species of partridge, and the Monal Pheasant.* The latter is a splendid bird, of the size of a small turkey-cock, with shining plumage of dark blue and metallic green. Again and again did we hear its cackling cry, as it started and winged its upward flight; again and again did we mark the dazzling brilliancy of its feathers, shining through the branches of the Deodara Pines.

* Or "*Bird of Gold*,"—the *Lophophorus refulgens*, or Impeyan pheasant. It is described by Mr Wilson as "ornamented with a handsome crest; the feathers of the neck long and loose, like the hackles of a cock. The colours of the plumage, so exceedingly brilliant from their metallic lustre, and so variable, according to the direction of the light, or the position of the spectator, that they cannot be described by words,—purple, green and gold being the prevailing hues." An attempt has been made to transport them to England, but they died on the passage. Were it repeated it might probably ere long succeed, for they endure cold well, though impatient of great heat." —Tr.

Each hamlet, each open space, each steep ascent, has here its name, which lives in the mouth of many a pilgrim. On one spot a desolate chaos of shattered rocks was pointed out to us, where once a village stood: it was overthrown by the fall of a mountain, which swept it away, leaving not a trace behind.

We passed several small streams, which flow into the Ganges from its left bank,—the SIURIGADH,—MIANIGADH,—and BOODDIGADDI,—before reaching the last and greatest of its tributaries, the KEDRA-GUNGA, at Gungotri. The Bhagirathi itself is more and more confined between the projecting rocks; when we first descended to its waters, they spread over a broad channel, at least eighty feet in width; here, they are again and again forced to wind through a rugged and deep-cut passage, hemmed in to a breadth of no more than twelve. At one place, a mass of rock has formed a natural bridge over it, close beside a lofty wall of everlasting snow. Here and there, its waters are hidden under beds of snow. Immediately below Gungotri however, the stream is broader, notwithstanding which it flows, even there, with tremendous fury, and keeps up a continual hollow thunder, by rolling huge stones and masses of rock along its wild and rugged channel.

We had almost reached the level of the water, ere we beheld before us the low and unimposing temple of GUNGOTRI.* The deep and savage ravines, with their

* Until a comparatively recent period, this region was unexplored by any traveller, save some wandering Hindoo devotees. Mr J. Fraser, who visited Gungotri in 1816, was the first European who penetrated thither; he ascertained the elevation to be 10·319 feet. Even among the devout Hindoos, this pilgrimage is considered an exertion so mighty as to redeem the performer from troubles in this world, and to ensure a happy transit through all the stages of transmigration. The three pools,—*Surya* (the Sun) *Coond*,—*Vishnu Coond*,—and *Brahma Coond*,—are said to be of pure Ganges water, unpolluted by any confluent stream. The water taken from hence is drawn under the inspection of a Brahmin, who is paid for the privilege of taking it, and much of it is carried to Bengal and offered at the temple of

black pools and raging torrents, their naked perpendicular cliffs and magnificent vistas of distant mountains, we had now left behind us; the rocky heights which bound the glen on either side are still indeed high and steep enough, and crowned by jagged ridges and sharp summits, but these are overgrown in many parts with cedars and birches; and the principal feature which we had expected would add the sublime to this landscape,—the splendid back-ground of snowy peaks,—is altogether wanting, being shut out by the overhanging rocks around.

The scene presented before our eyes is by no means that picture of awful desolation, which we had gazed on before, on our way hither, in those boundless ranges of snowy mountains, towering in every variety of bold outline, which seemed as though they were fresh from the creative hand of some mighty volcanic power. Those gigantic, needle-like peaks of ice, or softer, conical, snowcapped summits,—those clear and polished crystal bulwarks, with their attenuated and projecting edges, sharp as that of the warrior's blade,—those towers and battlements with their thousand pinnacles,—reposing on a broad basement of solid rock,—which we had seen before so near and so distinct that the boundary of eternal snows

Baidyanath. The ascent of the sacred stream is, beyond Gungotri, of extreme difficulty; it was however accomplished by Captains Hodgson and Herbert, who after ascending an immense snow bed, and making their second bivouac beyond Gungotri at a level of 12,914 feet, found the Ganges issuing from under a very low arch from which huge hoary icicles depend, at the foot of the great snow-bed, here about 300 feet in depth: proceeding for some thousand paces up the inclined bed of snow, which seemed to fill up the hollow between the several peaks, called by Colonel Hodgson Mount Moira and the Four Saints, and geometrically ascertained to vary in height from 21,179 to 22,798 feet, they obtained a near view of those gigantic mountains described by our author as seen from Mookba. As Colonel Hodgson justly observes, "It falls to the lot of few to contemplate so magnificent an object as a snow-clad peak rising to the height of upwards of a mile and a half, at the short horizontal distance of two and three quarter miles."—Tr.

seemed like the border of a vast white drapery, dropping its ample folds over the gloomy cedar forest,—this again, casting its sable mantle around, concealing the features of every form, save the naked, arid cliffs,—itself traversed by broad bare stripes, marking, like giant's tracks, the resistless and all-destroying course of a rushing avalanche,—the roaring stream in the depth below, with its countless rapids and its foaming cataracts;—all, all are wanting here. In a word, I must confess that I had expected something more at Gungotri than two half-ruined deal houses, a diminutive temple, and a few ancient cedars, torn and battered by the storms. As to distant landscape, nothing of the sort is to be seen.

The temple, a small stone structure destitute of all external ornament, measures scarcely forty paces in circumference, including the whole surrounding wall. Fakeers may be seen squatting around it on every side, under the projecting cliffs. A few poplars, birches and sturdy cedars, stand near the sacred edifice. It is necessary, before permission can be obtained to enter the shrine, to bathe in the holy stream. The water of the Ganges has, however, here a temperature of only 3° 2 (39° Fahrenheit) rather too cool for me at least to be willing to join the rest of the party in their dip; especially as I was informed that there was nothing to be seen within the temple except a small silver image of *Gunga*, and a few rude stone figures.

Siva and *Bhairam* are the gods, and *Gunga* the goddess, to whom the sanctuary is dedicated; *Ganesa* is merely an accessory object of adoration.

Ministering at this place of pilgrimage is a most lucrative occupation for the priesthood: its duties are at present performed by an aged priest, to whose family the sacred charge was committed by the Rajah; he accompanied us hither from Dheralee.

On the 6th of July, we descended from these rocky heights, favoured by clear and lovely weather; thanks to its bright and glorious influence, we enjoyed the prospect, to the north-east, of the RUDRU HIMMALEH, here also named SITPURIKANTA,—piercing the skies with its icy needles; and farther southward, when these, far surpassing the rest in height, had vanished from our eyes, we could yet gaze on the smooth and sharp-crested UDAGRIKANTA. The last must be the "*Ironside Peak*" of Hodgson; it rises high into the air, in the form of a single polished icy mass, with a bold indented ridge. Towards the south-west appeared, through a deep cut in the outline of MIANIKANTA, a smooth, rounded, snowy summit of wonderful beauty and clearness, covered on all sides with immense glaciers. Unfortunately it soon disappeared behind other nearer heights. One castellated, conical mountain, rising apart from all the others, not far from the DEKANI PEAK, was pointed out to us as "BHAIRAM JUMP."

We now recrossed the dangerous bridge of Bhairamgath. From the summit of a lofty cliff, we cast a lingering glance on the JAHNAVI GUNGA (also called *Jahni* or *Jahdi*) and on its impetuous neighbour, the BHAIROGETHI,—the meeting of their wild waters being here visible at our feet,—and then bid a long farewell to the thunders and the picturesque fury of the wild mountain streams.

An hour and a half brought us to the precipitous chasm across which the NEELUNG bridge is laid; the river is here some thirty paces in breadth, and hemmed in between perpendicular banks; the bridge, formed of three very thin beams, spans its dark pool at a height of seventy feet. The path, after crossing it, winds up the steep ascent to a wooden gate, which to the pilgrims coming from *Jalla* and *Mookba* marks it as that leading to *Gungotri*: another, stretching away to the northward, leads into Thibet.

From one part of our road, where, for a short distance, we emerged from the cedar forest into an open country, we again commanded a magnificent view of the peaks of the highest Himalayahs on every side; UDAGRIKANTA, RUDRUHIMMALEH, another mountain of conical form, perhaps identical with MOIRA, and in the direction of Dheralee, far over the heights that mark the river's course, the lofty CHOORIKANTA. This last is by no means a sharp peak; but rather appears like a very corpulent figure, and its heavy summit like a night-cap.

The pure granite continues as far as the vicinity of MOOKBA; there we again met with a schistose formation for the most part greatly disintegrated. There too, the little streamlets, bright and limpid, which rush in beautiful cascades from the rocky heights, first afforded us that pure and precious beverage of which we had been so long deprived; the water of the Bhagirethi being utterly undrinkable, and that of the Jahdi, which is a little better, extremely difficult to procure.

In the village itself, on a sunny terrace paved with stone, we pitched our tents. An open space such as this, serving the purpose of a threshing-floor, while it has all the air of a market-place, is usually to be found in the centre of each village, and is here called "*Joka*" or "*Patang:*" the inhabitants assemble on it every evening, and amuse themselves with dancing and singing.

Groups of pretty childen, with gentle countenances, were playing in front of the houses; the women on the contrary, clad in their coarse, stiff, woollen jackets, and thick, clumsy turbans, are frightfully ugly. The men, with their tall, well-made figures and stately beards, have a warlike air; their caps, stiff and pointed, resemble Macedonian helmets; and their woollen garments, of thick and unpliant texture, a suit of armour.

I here saw many of those houses which Hodgson calls "five-storied;" they might just as well be dignified by an enumeration of twelve stories; for they are constructed of a considerable number of beams, laid across each other, the interstices being built up with stones. Between every two cross-beams a narrow slit is left open, the only inlet for the light of day. The two higher stories are those in which the family apartments are placed; in these may be seen occasionally a couple of tiny windows, like those of a dove-cote: the side opposite to the entrance is also often ornamented with a balcony. In many of these tower-like cottages, a gallery runs all round, close beneath the roof, which is nearly flat, and formed of smooth planks, over the seams of which are laid triangular listels, to prevent the rain from penetrating. As neither posts nor sleepers are employed in this architecture, wooden cramps are, in very high houses, fixed on the upper part, for the sake of securing greater firmness, extending over, and holding together, three or four transverse beams. Chimnies I never saw: the ground-floor, over which the first story usually projects, contains the stalls for cattle and the bee-house. The latter occupies one whole side of the house, in which the window slits are walled up, leaving only fly-holes for the bees on their lower edges; all the rest is closed with cow-dung. The entrance to this apiary is on the opposite side from that to the dwelling-house, and it was with the greatest difficulty that I obtained permission to cross its threshold, as the people were afraid that I might take possession of their honey. I found within, a perfectly dark chamber, three feet high, in which, resting on a low wooden stand, are the bee hives, a sort of square tubes formed of four planks, connected in front with the fly-holes and open behind towards the dark room. When the honey is to be taken out, which is done in July or August, a fire of cow-dung is made in this little chamber, the smoke of which drives the bees out by the fly holes; they soon return however and build anew.

Beside every dwelling-house stands a small, square, wooden hut, generally not so much as six feet in length, and the same in height, with three stakes before its entrance. This is used as a store-room; its door is opened and closed by means of a large piece of iron, shaped like a sickle, which serves instead of a key.

The agriculture here is the same commonly prevalent throughout the country of the upper Ganges. Some of the cedars are burnt down, and thus, in the most simple manner, a portion of the dark forest is converted into land fit for cultivation. The mighty stems of these venerable trees do indeed, by their thickness, bid defiance to the annihilating power of the devouring element, but the husbandman, taking no further trouble about clearing away the stumps, merely sows among them a species of red *Amaranth*, the leaf of which is used as a vegetable *("Lal Sag")* and its seed ground into meal *("March")* for making bread. The corn harvest, barley or wheat, is here but just beginning, and a second crop is not yielded, or at any rate only in remarkably good soil. Rice does not succeed here, but three different sorts of millet, (Kaoni, Kodha, and another,) are cultivated in its place.

Apricot-trees are planted in great numbers for the sake of their fruit; almost invariably, in the centre of the village, may be seen a grove of them; it is not the same tree which we cultivate, but the wild apricot-tree, which maintains an inverse ratio between its own growth and the size of its fruit. The tree grows tall and sturdy, like an apple-tree, often measuring three feet in diameter, while the fruit, on the contrary, although very plentiful, is not larger than a cherry. There is also a second variety of apricot, which grows lower down, near Reithal; its fruit is of the size of a small plum, with a perfectly smooth skin. The peach-tree likewise grows wild every where in these parts, and bears a similar fruit, small, but of an agreeable, sourish flavour.

Here at Mookba, all our preparations have been made for our further journey, across the nearest frontier pass, that of the NEELUNG, into Thibet. Stores of meal and rice, and pack-sheep for their transport, have been purchased, and an agreement has been made with the necessary number of coolies. It is indeed rumoured that the head Mandarin of the district which we shall first enter, has given orders to break down the bridges in the neighbourhood of the border villages; but we put no faith in such reports. Hitherto, we have been received with good-will every where, excepting perhaps those villages where, on account of their scanty population, the raising our troop of coolies proved, at harvest-time, a great oppression; in all other places, the people have been delighted with the opportunity of earning a trifle, and at the same time of satisfying their curiosity, as they had full leisure and facility, on the march, for contemplating those strange beings, whose appearance was so unlike anything they had before seen.

TENTH LETTER.

DELAYS CONCERNING DEPARTURE FROM MOOKBA—IMPOSSIBILITY OF ENTERING THIBET—DEPARTURE—VALLEY OF THE HERSILE—BIRCHES—USE OF THEIR BARK—FOOLAL DAROO—WILD SHEEP—VALLEY OF THE GOOMTY—SNOW-BEDS—BAD ENCAMPMENT—SOURCE OF THE GOOMTY—FIELDS OF SNOW—MOUNTAIN-SICKNESS—PASS OF LAMA KAGA—DANGEROUS DESCENT FROM THE PASS—DO SOOMDA—GLACIER OF THE BUSPA RIVER—VALLEY OF THE BUSPA—ERRATIC BLOCKS AND MOUNDS OF LOOSE STONES—VILLAGE OF CHETKOOL—ARCHITECTURE OF ITS HOUSES—COSTUME OF ITS INHABITANTS—AGRICULTURE—DEPARTURE—RUGSAM—BEAUTIFUL FOREST—SUNGLA—THE MOOKDIAR AND HIS SON—THE PRAYER CYLINDER—PASS OF HARUNG—MEBUR—THE URNS—MANNER OF OBTAINING CEDAR-OIL—FEMALE BEARERS—VALLEY OF THE SUTLEJ—ROGEE—BARUNG—AVALANCHES—NEOZA PINES—POOAREE—LAMA TEMPLES—THE LAMAS' HYMN—ROPE BRIDGE—KONGHEE—THE TEMPLES—THE CHOPAL—KOTEE—EXTRAORDINARY FISH POND—HUGE CEDARS—DAK ROAD—TRAFFIC IN WINE-GRAPES WITH SIMLA—MILLS—BUNGALOW—TEMPLE AND CHOPAL.

CHEENEE, 28*th of July*, 1848.

OUR departure from Mookba was, owing to shameful intrigues, delayed from day to day. Our provisions were not forthcoming; our coolies became refractory, and at last openly declared that they would not go to Neelung; the whole village was in an uproar; much was said about treaties and agreements, according to which no foreigner durst set foot on the pass; it was positively affirmed moreover, that the Rajah had given peremptory orders that no one should be suffered to cross the frontier. In short, so many obstacles presented themselves, that His Royal Highness at length resolved, instead of penetrating by way of the Neelung Pass into Thibet, and advancing by a road which traverses that country into Kunawur, to proceed directly to that province by one of the mountain passes.

Who would have imagined that our afore-mentioned companion, the English Nimrod, during all this vexatious and disgraceful business, would be secretly acting a part in the game, and, while publicly appearing on our side, privately, behind our backs, doing his utmost to oppose our plans. He was dismissed forthwith.

In high indignation, after innumerable difficulties and negotiations with the coolies, we at length quitted the village of Mookba on the 11th of June. The "*Tindal,*" or superintendent of the coolies, was dismissed,—then again engaged, and once more sent away on account of his impudence. At length, about one o'clock, our train was in motion; but, when only an hour and a half had elapsed, at our halting-place, in the valley of the HERSILE, not one of our coolies would move a step. Meantime, we had learned by spies that two village chiefs from Mookba, and our dismissed "*Tindal*" had laid a plot for instigating them to a unanimous rebellion, and to a midnight flight. Accordingly, two hours afterwards, these three men arrived, and we watched them as they winked and nodded to one after another of the coolies, endeavouring to carry out their insidious designs. A bold and sudden interference on our part however, defeated them entirely; the two village chiefs fled; but the Tindal was taken captive, and thoroughly humbled by means of a well-merited castigation. He gave us very fair words, and confessed the whole of the shameful intrigue. As his attendance was of no small use to us, we retained him, taking however the precaution of binding him with ropes every evening for some time. To prevent all possibility of the coolies making their escape, the bridge over the Hersile, which we had crossed in the course of the day, was broken down through the night, so that every homeward path was cut off. On the following morning therefore the full troop was mustered, and during that day's march we advanced considerably.

During the early part of it we had a most toilsome climb in crossing a high mountain, on the other side of which we reached the valley of the GOOMTY. The whole of the eastern declivity of this steep ridge is clothed with a dense forest of cedars; higher up, on its very crest, we ascended above the region of that tree. The wood here becomes less dark, and the ground is covered with large patches of grass mingled with strawberries and *Cheiranthus* (Wall-flower.) The two ridges, which bound the valley of the Hersile, are of equal height, the only difference being the extreme richness of the woods of cedar on the left bank. The path on the descent leads in a slanting direction, northward, into the parallel valley of the *Goomty.* On this side the cedar-tree ceases immediately below the crest of the mountain, and is succeeded by the birch ("*Bootch*" or *Bho*,) appearing singly, intermingled with *Philadelphus,* (Syringa) Roi Fir, and various kinds of raspberry, afterwards in large masses forming a thick forest. The appearance of this tree is far more beautiful than that of our birch; for even the oldest stems, of which however I did not see any exceeding one foot in diameter, retain their beautiful bark, which, though rough and full of fissures, never loses its whiteness; in young trees it has an almost silvery effect. The leaf is much thicker and rounder, and has a shorter point than that of the European birch. The bark,—known by the name of "Bhojputtra,"—is used as a writing material which is procured in a very simple manner; a longitudinal incision is made upon the smooth, branchless stem of a half-grown tree, and the separate coatings of thin bark are stripped off singly with great care. Six or seven of them are fit for use, but the outer ones are the best, being thinner and more thoroughly bleached. Pieces as large as three feet square are sometimes obtained in this manner.

We were now, on the left bank of the Goomty, once more climbing a steep ascent, and crossing a multitude of small rushing torrents. Many a smooth acclivity, overlaid with masses of travelled granite, added to the difficulty of the path. From the top of one of these we caught our last glimpse of the Ganges; then the forest grew thicker, and the ground more level. Hazel-nut trees, from three to four feet in diameter, were, with the birches, the most prevailing wood. The former are here called "*Sheroli*," and bear short, rounded, thick-shelled nuts. We marked the traces of the plentiful nut-harvest,* which the mountaineers had recently gathered in. A species of juniper,—"*Taroo*,"—from the berries of which an intoxicating drink is prepared, forms the underwood. After threading our way along one of the principal lateral glens, we halted upon a meadow covered with rich grass two feet in height, at a lovely and enchanting spot named BUNKARA. But even this resting-place did not satisfy us: we quitted the pleasant shade of the birches, and descended into the glen of the BOOTOO GADH. It is a rapid stream, full of rocky débris. Its icy-cold water reached up to our knees as we waded through. Immediately after crossing it, we scaled an abrupt and boulder-covered height; half way up, we reached the region of Alpine prairies clothed with tall grass and beautiful umbelliferous plants. One of these latter (the "*Eiallach*,") is remarkable for its extremely spicy fragrance. Its sappy stalk is commonly eaten, and has a most agreeable flavour.

Our tents were at last pitched on one of these eleva-

* So abundant indeed, that hazel-nuts form an article of Himalayan trade, being sold in the bazaars of Hindostan under the name of "*finduk*," and not unfrequently subjected to expression for the oil largely contained in them.—TR.

ted prairies above the limit of arboreous vegetation, which here gives place to an Alpine flora only at a height of eight thousand feet. Our encampment was surrounded by a perfect garden of sweet flowers,—splendid Anemones, beautiful varieties of *Potentilla*, *Epilobium*, *Lilium*, *Aster*, and, somewhat higher up on the rocks, the exquisite sky-blue *Papaver Alpinum* of the Himalayahs. A lofty but gently rising mountain ridge, from which murmuring brooks innumerable trickle down, bounds this stretch of meadow-land, the name of which is FOOLAL DAROO. We had scarcely taken up our quarters there, when there appeared, on the sun-lit hill at the foot of which our tents lay, a large flock, at least eighty head, of wild sheep ("*Bhural*").* They were sprightly, active creatures, leaping merrily about; among them were some rams with large and powerful horns. Not long afterwards, we observed a second, somewhat less numerous, flock, grazing still higher on the mountain pastures; they seemed to have no shyness, and allowed the sportsmen to approach close to them. Unfortunately, not one was killed, and the report of the guns, which doubtless they had never heard before in their wild home, put to flight the whole flock; swift as the wind they vanished behind the crest of the ridge.

These animals, for which I had hitherto sought in vain, live close to the boundary of everlasting snow, and only visit the lower regions from time to time. They have a very thick, reddish brown fleece, with black shaggy wool on the breast, and horns twisted spirally, which, in the older rams, are inclined far outward. The Prince told me that he had seen one ewe, which had a lamb beside it, make the most tremendous bounds to drive away an eagle that had attacked its young one.

We were much favoured by the weather at this place;

* Mentioned by some authors as the Asiatic Argali, or, *Ovis Ammon*."—TR.

the air was clear, and, after the sun had set, we saw the peaks of the snowy mountains still glowing in the lingering radiance; soon however it became sensibly chill.

The height of this spot, obtained by thermometer, is eleven thousand two hundred and seventy-two feet above the sea.

Early on the morning of the 13th of July, we set out on our march, amid heavy mist,—the thermometer not above 5°8 (45° Fahrenheit). Bare, treeless ridges, clothed with slippery grass, and abruptly sloping Alpine pastures, on which we wound up in zigzags, not venturing to face the steep, rendered the ascent a most fatiguing one; to add to our troubles, the mist was so dense that our coolies lost sight of each other, and finally, a continuous rain increased our toil not a little, by the difficulty of advancing through the tall, wet grass, or upon the smooth, argillaceous soil. We scrambled up and down on the lofty masses of débris, forced, in the intervening hollows, to wade through the many tributary streams of the Goomty, keeping that river itself constantly to our left hand; neither bridges, nor even trunks of trees to supply their place, are found here. The water of these streams is icy cold, and often flows so rapidly that we had difficulty in keeping our footing as we passed through.

At length, after sliding down an abrupt declivity consisting of crumbling clay and loose fragments of granite, we reached the first bed of snow, which covers the Goomty for the distance of several miles. We crossed over it, and proceeded, on the surface of the snow, along the right bank of the river. The snow-bridges of the smaller streams having fallen in, we were soon obliged to return to the opposite side; there our path, after traversing several mountain meadows, wound up to a great height, scaling a rocky acclivity.

We were perpetually sliding back upon the wet grass,

and a full hour of tedious climbing had passed away, ere we arrived, half-way up the hill, at the base of an overhanging precipice of granite, which, although the level space below was limited enough, afforded some slight shelter to our party from the ice-cold rain. We halted here. Our naked coolies cowered around us, shivering and their teeth chattering from cold. It proved however actually impossible, with our coolies and baggage, to pass the night on this platform of only ten feet square. There was not room sufficient to allow of pitching our tents, and not a spot was to be found in the neighbourhood bearing the most distant resemblance to level ground,—nothing but rugged acclivities and precipitous cliffs on every side.

Count O——, meanwhile, had gone in search of a better resting-place. The wind was every moment becoming colder and more piercing, and our limbs more and more benumbed; and still no messenger arrived to announce the discovery of an encampment-ground. Thus an hour passed away in dreadful discomfort and suspense; at the end of that time one of the guides returned, to conduct us to a spot which he had at length found.

It was nearly dark from the heavy rain; we stumbled on,—following our guide, over the almost impassable mountains of débris,—so stiff from cold that, when we slid down, it was scarcely possible for us to rise up again, and our benumbed hands almost refusing to grasp our much-needed mountain poles. At length we reached the spot selected as our resting-place, a somewhat less steep declivity, above the deep glen of the Goomty's parent stream. Our tents were pitched as well as could be managed, but the rain poured through them on all sides. Before our camp-beds could, with the help of large stones, be set up, another hour and a half had elapsed, and we had not yet got rid of our drenched clothes. As to establishing any thing like a comfortable abode, such a thing was not to be dreamt of for this night; and the wood we had brought with us was so thoroughly wet that it would not ignite. At length, after many vain attempts, a feeble flickering flame rewarded our perseverance, and, cherishing it into a small fire, we boiled our own chocolate, the cook being ill from the cold, and incapable of doing any work: but neither chocolate nor brandy,—in which last we indulged more largely than usual,—succeeded in thoroughly reviving the natural warmth of our frames.

I was scarcely in a state to make any measurements of height by the thermometer, however the result of my calculations, such as they were, was an altitude of eleven thousand, seven hundred and nineteen feet above the sea.

The night was passed by no means in the most agreeable manner. At length however morning dawned, and the rain ceased. We now perceived that we were on the right bank of a large river, bridged over by beds of snow. It is the central parent stream of the Goomty; the confluent on the right-hand side descends from the "*Snow Lakes.*" There also a path leads across; but it was not selected for our course, being reckoned the longest and most difficult. I was unable to obtain any accurate information as to what these snow lakes really are; we probably lost a great deal by not visiting them.

A bright and serene day, with a sunshine most welcome at such an elevation, favoured our ascent of the pass which now lay before us. We soon arrived at the snow-bridge over the rapid river, beyond which we ascended without intermission over a naked waste, covered with travelled blocks, among which an argillaceous schist, with a ferruginous tint, chiefly predominates, though with a copious intermixture of fragments of quartz and of granite.

As for plants, a very small remnant of soil, on the margin of the numerous rippling brooks, is all that is left for them. This narrow border is adorned with dwarf yellow Potentillas, and Ranunculuses; while the stones are clothed with mosses and with black-edged, yellow lichens.

Not a living creature is to be seen in all this death-like solitude; no feathered songster enlivens, with his joyous warbling, these desolate and rugged cliffs, nor these wild wastes, whose dreary expanse is broken only by huge erratic blocks. From time to time indeed, I watched the flight of a few beetles, but their monotonous hum soon died away in the silent air, leaving only a more intense feeling of solitude behind.

At the end of one hour's march, we had already reached the first broad field of snow; before entering upon it we had to ascend a hill of travelled stones, from which we obtained a bird's-eye view of the broad valley through which we had just passed. To our right and left lay extensive moraines, those dirty glacier masses, loaded with argillaceous and stony fragments.

We now proceeded to traverse the immense and shining field of snow. In many places it was so soft that we sank in it up to our knees, and a most fatiguing march we found it. The ruined heaps of a fallen and shattered rock rise like an island in this ocean of snow; we halted upon it to rest ourselves and gather new strength.

The confluent of the Goomty, whose course we were following, had long ere now disappeared beneath immense glaciers and masses of snow. Only in some few spots, where deep crevasses and formidable chasms were to be cleared, we heard the roar of its waters in the unseen depths below.

We overcame however all these obstacles, and reached the further end in safety; but a long and toilsome ascent yet remained to be accomplished, before we could gain the summit of the pass. We were forced to scale the precipitous wall of a vast glacier, while the wild wind was continually pouring down upon us showers of small stones, from the lofty, needle-like pinnacles of rock which, weathered and worn by friction, towered on our right from amid this sea of ice. At the end of four hours, the Prince, the guide and I gained the culminating point, without suffering much from the difficulty of breathing, and the feelings of indisposition caused by the "*mountain sickness.*" A naked pyramid, consisting of broken masses of white granite, domineering high above all around it, forms the apex of the mountain; making a wide circuit round a towering crest of snow, we scrambled up to its base. It consists entirely of huge rocky débris, and fragments of from three to four feet in diameter; water was trickling down on all sides, although there was no snow lying upon its summit. From this point, our guide pointed out to us the path followed by the English traveller, Mr Bailey; it lies farther westward, tracing the course of the western tributary of the Goomty. The point on which we stood, on the other hand, had never yet been trod by any European explorer. According to my measurement, the head of this pass,—the name of which is LAMA KAGA,—is fifteen thousand, three hundred and fifty-five feet above the level of the sea; the conical apex rising above it, I should estimate to be at least from three to four hundred feet more.

Nearly an hour and a half passed away before the van-guard of our troop of coolies, with their load of baggage, arrived at the head of the pass. They were in a deplorable condition, and suffering, as was also our interpreter Mr Brown, from headache, which they described as intolerably severe. Anxiety, debility and sickness are the other symptoms of the disease, known here by the name of "*Bish,*" poison, or "*Moondara.*" Travellers among these mountains, ascending within the limit of eternal snow, are generally attacked by it. It showed itself among the coolies even half-way up the pass. They take, as an antidote, a paste prepared of the small sour apricots ("*Choaroo*") which I before described, the kernels being bruised, and mixed up with it; it has an unpleasantly sour taste, from which it derives its name of "*Khutai.*"

When, after long delays, the whole train of coolies was at last assembled at this point, the guides, who meanwhile had been exploring, with a view to our onward march, returned with the assurance that it was impossible to advance farther in the same direction, recent avalanches having formed a perpendicular precipice of from five to six hundred feet. We satisfied ourselves, by ocular demonstration, of the truth of their assertion; the snow-field had fallen off abruptly towards the hollow on the opposite side. How then were we now to descend, with our half-dead coolies, into this profound abyss? No expedient remained for us, but to clamber in a westerly direction, over the cone, and thence to endeavour, by traversing frightfully steep banks of snow and ice, to effect a descent.

We set out on the march, and had scarcely gained the highest point, when a chill and soaking mist, gradually changing into a violent hail-shower, enveloped us in a gloom so dense, that the pioneers of our long train were altogether cut off from the rest.

Everything however conspired to make us earnestly desirous of reaching the foot of the mountain with the least possible delay; for the day was already on the decline, and it would have been utterly impracticable to pursue, amid the perils of darkness, a march itself so replete with danger. As little could we, without risking our lives, spend the night on these heights. Our guides, themselves apparently anxious and perplexed, were urged forward with the impatience of despair.

We arrived in safety at the base of the first snowy steep; but here we found that the lowest, and unfortunately also the most abrupt declivity consisted of a smooth mass of ice, upon the existence of which we had by no means calculated. We forthwith began, axe in hand, to hew steps in it. It was a painfully tedious operation; and, while engaged in our fatiguing labour, we were obliged, hanging over a giddy abyss, to cling fast with our feet and our left hands, lest we should lose our hold and slide down to the bottom. This did indeed all but happen to the Prince himself; his pole however, furnished with a very strong iron tip, checked his fall. I too slipped, and darted down to a considerable distance, but fortunately, with the aid of my "*alpenstock*," I contrived, in spite of its point being broken off, to keep myself in an upright position. Thus the Prince and I, accompanied by the guides, arrived prosperously at the end of the ice, and reached a less dangerous surface of snow; but not a creature had followed us, and the thick rimy snow that darkened the atmosphere prevented us from casting a look behind, towards our lost companions and attendants. One of the guides was sent back in quest of them; and it turned out that the coolies had refused to descend by this route. Neither money nor cudgelling seemed now to be of the least avail.

At length the snowy shower somewhat abated; the curtain of mist opened for a moment, and we descried, standing in a line on the crest of the ridge, from which we had descended an hour before, the whole array of coolies. Not one of them could muster resolution to venture upon the icy way; they looked down in despair. When they perceived us standing below, a few of the most courageous,—urged on by Count O—— with voice and stick,—at length agreed to follow in our steps. They got on pretty well as far as the smooth icy precipice; but here several of them lost their firm footing and slid down the steep descent with their heavy burdens on their backs. It was a frightful scene, and, to all appearance, full of danger, not one of them however met with any injury; even Mr Brown, whose shooting descent from the highest part filled us with terror,—as he slid down a distance of at least a hundred feet, into a crevasse, in which he was apparently engulfed,—was at last brought to us safe and sound with the exception of considerable excoriation and torn raiment. It cost half an hour, however, to hew a long flight of steps for him in this icy wall. During all these proceedings, which occupied more than an hour, the Prince and I were standing at the foot of the declivity, up to our knees in snow, exposed to a freezing blast and to incessant sleet, but most heartily were we rejoiced, when at length all our people were gathered around us, without one broken neck or limb. The coolies had latterly given up the attempt to scramble down the fatal precipice of ice, and had glided down "*a la montagne Russe*," abandoning themselves to their fate.

The remainder of our downward way was through half-melted snow, and unattended with any considerable danger, until we arrived at the top of a mound of travelled blocks about three hundred feet in height, by which we must needs descend, to reach the glen below. Here our coolies seemed to lose every spark of courage; some howled and wept aloud, others threw themselves prostrate, with their faces on the ground. What was now to be done? Who could have brought himself, in such circumstances, to have recourse to blows with these poor, suffering creatures? Our last expedient, to bring them to their legs again, was to relieve them of all the baggage, each one of our party carrying a share of the load on his own shoulders. It was no very arduous undertaking, for the most ponderous article,—to wit, our tent, —we had been under the sad necessity, as it had become thoroughly wet and very heavy, of leaving on the summit of the ridge. This good example produced the desired effect; the bearers advanced immediately, and, —with the exception of a few who were extremely ill,—at a more lively pace; thus the joyful prospect opened upon us, of reaching a night's quarter below the limit of perpetual snow.

This glen is choked up by a glacier, covered with a great quantity of travelled stones,—many-coloured schist, resembling sandstone, of every shade from a deep purple to a yellowish red, and often not unlike rotten wood. The side ramparts of the glen have a worn, broken, desolate air that makes one shudder. We proceeded down a gently inclined plane, traversing now solid, or partially melted snow,—now masses of ice,—furrowed with deep fissures and fathomless chasms. Streams of water had worked out for themselves channels on its surface, and were murmuring along at our feet, while we could catch the hollow roar of rivers in the depths below. I was much struck and surprised here by the sight of multitudes of dead locusts, strewn in masses on every side; they must have lain there since last year, if not longer, for I sought in vain to recognize in them any one distinct colour.

After about an hour and a half, we reached a turn of the glen, where, gliding down a wall of ice covered with fragments of stone, we at last set foot on terra firma. This was the terminal moraine of the glacier, and we now perceived the river, about thirty feet wide, which, after flowing on beneath the superincumbent mass, rushes out furious and roaring from its vast prison, by a low-arched glacier-gate. We followed its course, along the left bank, on which here and there bridges of snow yet remained. At length, at a second turn of the glen, the cliff-embosomed valley of BISSAHIR suddenly lay stretched before us in the rosy illumination of a splendid sunset, the snow-capped peaks veiled in an airy drapery of mist and golden vapour, through which their clearly pencilled summits shone forth in peerless majesty.

We had now arrived at our resting-place. It lay in immediate contact with a large glacier, which leaves but a narrow strip of open ground, on the left border of the valley, and once more conceals the river, which, lower down, bursts forth anew in two broad streams, whose waters however are soon re-united. The place is named, on account of the meeting of the waters, Do SOOMDA. Our guide could give us no information regarding a place called *Barsini*, which, according to our maps, must lie at no great distance. The dwarf cypresses and willows afforded us from their long roots, which creep far under the blocks of travelled stone, a sufficiency of wood for fuel, with which we lighted a cheerful blazing fire; and thus it was not till the shades of night had fallen, that we felt the want of our tent. Our night's rest was certainly not the most agreeable, as we were obliged to cower round the fire cheek by jowl with our filthy Hindoo attendants.

The following day, (the 15th of July) was spent at our halting-place, for the sake of fetching down our tent from the head of the pass. It was brought down so completely frozen together, that it was scarcely possible to set it up.

We were now compelled in the first place, on starting the following morning, to make a circuit to the source of the impetuous BUSPA,* as there was no other means of gaining the opposite bank. We were therefore forced

* Buspa is the name given to this river in the maps; our guides called it *Kerzom Nuddy*.—W. HOFFMEISTER.

to bestow all our skill and pains on cutting out a path for ourselves, across the towering glacier from which it rises. Each one gave a helping hand in the arduous labour of hewing out steps and transporting the baggage. The passage occupied three hours, and was not without danger, especially on the highest spot, beneath which the main branch of the *Buspa* rages along; for there the loose blocks of stone might so easily have been dislodged from their positions on the polished heights of ice, that we could descend from the many little eminences only again "*à la Montagne Russe.*" Soon after we had crossed this glacier, the rain recommenced; the people most to be pitied as suffering from its effects were the unfortunate bearers, who had to carry the tent, heavy with accumulated moisture. After an hour's march over level wastes of débris, we were detained by a new obstacle. A rapid and greatly swollen stream, flowing down from the lofty beds of snow on the right bank, cut off our path. We spent three hours in traversing the rugged mounds of loose blocks which form the ramparts of its little glen, before reaching the snow-bridge, which spans it higher up; having crossed it, we returned down the other side to the edge of the *Buspa*. It was not possible to transport our tent by this route; we were obliged to float it through the stream by means of ropes, and what little of it the rain had yet left dry, was in this transit completely soaked. The eight coolies too who had the charge of carrying it, were dragged through the river in a similar manner.

The valley now became wider, and the bed of the river flat and sandy: to counterbalance this improvement we found ourselves in a perfect net-work of little brooks, in wading through which, the rushing, ice-cold waters often reached up to our knees. They all belong to one group of springs, the name of which is NITTAL NUDDY. We crossed a larger brook by means of a hastily constructed, very frail bridge, formed of trees found on the spot. Beyond it the valley expands to a width of several thousand paces, bounded on either side by gently sloping hills: the snows on their summits were yet unmelted. Endless heaps of mountain-wreck, extending along these parallel ramparts in wild and sterile desolation, give to the scene a character of awe-inspiring melancholy. The bottom of the valley, along which we were proceeding, consists of a level bed of clay, clothed with fresh and verdant grass. One spot, where the river makes a bend, and a lofty impending precipice offers some shelter from the wind, appeared to us perfectly adapted for a comfortable encampment.

On the following morning also, (the 17th of July) our path was at first easy and pleasant, lying through beautiful meadow land: soon however the scene changed; the narrowed glen was now hemmed in between steep acclivities covered with débris and crowned with savage frowning rocks, broken into dark clefts and furrows. The snow and ice have committed fearful ravages here; the mountain summits appear as though all the mightiest powers of nature had vied with each other in the effort to shiver them into fragments!

We scrambled up the steep bank overhanging the river; suddenly, we beheld at our feet a yawning abyss, nearly a thousand feet in depth, apparently excluding all prospect of advancing farther. Evidently a huge mass of rocky wall had here given way, and precipitated itself into the deep below. It seemed impossible to descend without endangering our lives, for in no part did the rock afford a spot, on which to rest one's foot. A chamois would have found it a perilous path! But what was to be done?—we must find our way across. The guide first made the experiment, placing his foot warily on stones that projected here and there; we followed, one by one, with great caution, and actually reached the base without a single accident, although the fragments, constantly detached from the mass of loose blocks, were rolling down under our feet, and every gust of wind hurled down upon us showers of small stones.

No form of rock among the mountains can be so difficult and irksome for the traveller to scramble over, as this loose erratic débris, in which granite, schist and pebbles, all conglomerated with very loose earth, form lofty mural precipices of the most treacherous kind. Rocks, be they ever so steep and high, may, if one is not a victim to giddiness, be scaled or descended in safety; but on heights such as these, where all firm footing fails, where each projecting stone yields beneath one's tread, and rolls down with stunning velocity, every scramble is a most hazardous adventure.

The conveying of our baggage down the side of this chasm cost us great labour; we were once more forced to leave our tents behind us, now saturated and more heavy than ever with rain.

The worst part however was yet to come,—a mound of boulders, along which we scrambled, at a height of some four hundred feet above the river, constantly exposed to the danger either of shooting down into the stream with the loose blocks, or of being buried beneath the perpendicular walls of crumbling stone and clay, which threatened to give way at the slightest touch.

How thankful were we then, once more to set foot on a beaten path, how enchanted to welcome the first birchen bushes! There yet remained indeed a great number of narrow deep-cut glens, where mountain-torrents must needs be passed either by throwing across them bridges, formed of trees dragged to the spot with great toil, or, where no wood was to be found, by wading through; these hindrances were however more time-consuming than dangerous.

Our attention was now directed to some cattle grazing

on an Alpine pasturage in the distance; below that wild prairie, we were assured, lay CHETKOOL, the frontier village of BISSAHIR. We reached the first pasture-land, but still no trace of inhabited regions or of the proximity of human beings was discoverable. The tracks of bears only,—seen here in great abundance,—and the yellow-beaked crows hovering above us, reminded us that animal creation was not extinct. At length we marked rose bushes beside our path, and on winding round a bend of the river, the first trees appeared,—Cheel pines *(Pinus longifolia,)* and Roi firs, *(Picea Morinda,)* presently we descried in the distance the tower-like, wooden temple of Chetkool. Rich fields of green wheat upon the lofty terraced banks we gladly welcomed as symptoms announcing that the village was now near, and, before darkness had over-spread the scene, we had gained the height and the hamlet that crowns its summit.

Chetkool is a pleasant village, surrounded by terraced rocks, adorned with emerald crops of wheat. We already marked the thoroughly Chinese character of the architecture, both of the temple and of the houses; and in fact this place has much intercourse with Thibet. Its temples are dedicated to the Lama-worship. That beside which we pitched our camp, stands upon a basement of stone, and has a broad portico, supported by beautifully carved wooden pillars; a quantity of wood-carving, especially dragons' heads, adorn the corners of the roof, and a number of the twisted horns of the *Bhural* sheep are hung upon the walls. In front of the temple stands a smaller edifice, resting on nine pillars, and containing an idol-figure which on our establishing ourselves beside it, was withdrawn. The houses, about twelve in number, are almost all built of wood, the narrow interstices only, between the beams, not broader than the beams themselves, being filled up with stones: the roofs are flat. On one side of the building, the trunk of a tree, with steps hewn in it, leads up to a balcony with a balustrade of varied and fanciful wood-carving. From it is the entrance to the family apartments. Most of the dwellings have a sunk story, with small, low doorways, probably leading into the store-rooms.

On the balcony of the first floor, we usually saw the women sitting, for here they do not conceal themselves, as is the universal custom throughout the valley of the Ganges. Their costume is a very singular one. Besides the round felt hat, they wear, fastened on the back of the head, a large bush of red wool, below which hangs a profusion of thick plaits, not indeed of hair, but of this same red wool. It is a species of peruke, similar to that worn by Fakeers. A wreath of everlastings is twined round the hat. A web of woollen cloth, of home manufacture,—red, brown, or white,—is thrown over the left shoulder, twice wound round the upper part of the body, and then twisted, on the back above the waist, into a knot, from which it hangs down like a scarf, in drapery reaching to the ankles. A brass clasp of very peculiar form confines the ample folds on the left shoulder, while the right is left uncovered. The lower end of the web, laid together in many plies, is bound round the waist by means of a girdle, and covers the rest of the figure. The whole dress is no less dignified and becoming, than it is elegant; it were impossible to conceive a finer effect produced by such simple means. It bears some resemblance to the guise of a French shepherd in olden times. The physiognomy however is here marked by thoroughly Tartar features; the women are, for the most part, extremely ugly; but among the men we remarked a few, who, with their long flowing black hair and noble beards, were tolerably good-looking. The men alone spin the wool, and go about, as at *Mookba*, spindle in hand, with their little basket on the arm. The women devote themselves to agricultural labour, and to the tending of the cattle. The breed of this place is a cross between the woolly-tailed *Yak* ox, and the common Indian cow; a pretty race of animals, rather high in the nape, and of a black colour. What a delicious treat for us once more to enjoy a drink of new milk!

The cultivation of the fields is carried on with the utmost care; they are all inclosed with low stone walls, and the soil is excellent. Two kinds of wheat *("Chog"* and *"Gehong,")* buck-wheat, *("Madua")* a species of cabbage, *("Sheaia"),*—possibly *Brassica napus*, to which at least it bears a great resemblance,—are the fruits of the ground here cultivated. Here and there also, we saw crops of tobacco; but the greatest part of the fields is occupied with buck-wheat, the green blades of which are used as a vegetable.

We remained at this place during four days; unfortunately, during all that time, the rain never ceased; once only did we behold the lofty, snow-capped peaks, which, rising in the back-ground of the valley, add such beauty to the landscape. At first we had the fairest prospect of penetrating hence into Thibet; the guide was already engaged, and a store of provisions ordered to be laid in; but the timid irresolution of the village chief frustrated the whole plan. The people altogether are not to be depended upon; while encouraging us by the smoothest words and the best promises, they were, behind our backs, using every endeavour to hinder the execution of our designs.* Accordingly, when at length the long-expected coolies and the provisions were, at least

* The disappointment experienced by the prince and his party on this and similar occasions, and which was not caused by the mere doubt or intrigues of a village population, is explained by Dr Royle's account of the system pursued towards travellers in these regions. He says, "the crest only of the passes can now be visited, as every one is prohibited from crossing the frontier for fear of exciting the jealousy of the Tibetian authorities, and disturbing the trans-Himalayan trade of the province of Kemaon."—Tr.

in part, collected, we were obliged to content ourselves with casting a longing look up the valley, along which stretches the path leading into Thibet, to all appearance neither a dangerous nor a difficult one.

Our own path, on which we proceeded on the 22d of July, led us between green fields of buck-wheat, down the right bank of the river, on which the *Cheel*pines (here called "*Limm*") begin much later than on the opposite side, being probably dispossessed of their pristine domain by the encroachments of agriculture.

After the second hour's march, the path descended to a considerably lower level, nearly that of the river, whereas before we had been at a height of several hundred feet above it. The only stream of any importance which presented itself on our path, was the LINGNARA, which we crossed about half-way to our station, the village of RUGSUM, a small place, consisting of some twenty houses, situated in the midst of damp meadows. The Buspa is here contracted in its channel, and has a great fall; our bivouac was close to its banks, on an open, verdant meadow, about a hundred feet above the water-fall. I calculated,—by the point at which water boiled,—that the elevation of this spot must be nine thousand, seven hundred and fifty feet.

The clear, brilliant weather of the following day enabled us to enjoy the extensive prospect of the mountain ranges to the southward, crowned with icy peaks and needles. Our path was at first difficult from the accumulated masses of huge granite blocks, often connected together by bridges. Further on, we entered into the shade of a beautiful forest of Cheelpines and poplars; the cedars also once more appeared, though singly and scattered, beyond the BURSEN NUDDY. They here bear the name of "*Kjelmáng.*" At one place, where the valley trends round a projecting cliff which advances far into its hollow, the granite gives place to a gray gneiss, which, higher up the crags, is more and more mingled with mica, passing at length into mica schist, but this is only for a very short distance, after which the white granite re-appears.

A charming wood of apricot and walnut trees, beneath the shade of which lay scattered a number of solitary huts, made us aware of the proximity of the village of SUNGLA, round which agriculture has extended its sway over a wide and fertile domain. We arrived there after a three hours' march. A "*sangho*" leads across the river,—here about ninety paces in width,—to the further bank, on which the village lies, which is large, and built in a very pretty style; the houses, which have chimneys and flat roofs, being richly decorated with wood-carving. On an open space in the centre of the village, stands the temple, thoroughly Chinese in its appearance, surrounded by a columned gallery with decorations carved in wood, evidencing taste and skill in the art, the points of the roof projecting and curved upwards. Neat, clean and pretty as this village is, it did not, from our encampment on the opposite bank, produce as picturesque an effect as Chetkool, the beautiful back-ground being wanting here.

Sungla is situated upon a lofty terrace, which, jutting out at the foot of the mountains, is cleft, by the brooks which flow down from them, into four separate parts. Farther down, on the same side of the Buspa, but on a level much higher than that of Sungla, stands upon a projecting rock the village of KAMERO.

A walk through Sungla brought us into close contact with the inhabitants. The leading people among them had assembled for the evening on the open space in front of the temple. Among them were the "*Mookdiar*" or village chief, and his son, both distinguished by the elegance of their attire. Trowsers of blue and white striped cotton, drawn in tightly above the ankles, a long coat of white woollen stuff, with skirts turned back, and trimmed at the bottom with a border of red, a broad belt, elegant shoes and a brown cap, form their neat and pretty costume. The women wear a dress exactly similar to that already described at Chetkool, only prettier and finer in every respect. A small, singular-looking building, standing close to the temple, with a roof remarkable for its far-projecting, dragon-shaped points, contains two chests, with staves for bearing them: these reminded me by their form, of the scripture description of the Ark of the Covenant. Another edifice, standing farther back, attracted our attention by the wonderful paintings on its interior walls; representing, in pale brown and gray colours, symbolical figures of various sorts; the fish and the dragon occur repeatedly. On the path from the village to the "*Sañgho*," stands a tiny house of prayer, rudely constructed of stones: a flag is stuck up on its top, but within, it contains only a niche, in which is placed a "*prayer-cylinder.*" This little machine, which in form is exactly like a coffee-roaster, covered with hide, and resting on a moveable axle, is called a "*Manneh*, or, "*Lamake Manneh.*" The passers-by may frequently be seen to stand still before the little oratory, and diligently to turn the cylinder, thus performing their devotions. In like manner they may be often seen to pass rapidly through their fingers strings of wooden beads, of Chinese workmanship, a species of rosary used in prayer.

We quitted Sungla on the 24th of July, not very early, for it was a misty morning. Our path lay at first along the banks of the Buspa. We passed over the waters of a chalybeate spring, which gushes forth from under an immense block of granite, between fields of "*Phapur*," or "*Madua*," (species of *Fagopyrum*). The thick fog excluded all view, so that, on reaching the summit of a conical mountain, named STELLINJOOTIPAH, we could only see the grand outlines of the snowy peaks, peering dimly through over against us. The way was rendered toilsome by the numerous rocky chasms, where mountain torrents had cut their deep passage through the heights. After each one of these clefts we had a considerable ascent; three of them we had to cross before reaching the foot of the pass of HARUNG. We ascended in the first instance a spur of that mountain, distinguished by the name of TOKA: the partial opening of the mist occasionally revealed to us the fine view which it commands, extending over the pass of BRUANG, the towering snowy mountains on the other side of the river, and a number of small villages in the nearer distance. On the highest ridge of the pass, we found a small level space, almost entirely surrounded by pyramids of stone, for the most part of very complex architecture, and furnished with projections which serve as seats. This plateau is covered with a luxuriant Alpine flora, consisting of sky-blue poppy, red and yellow potentillas, beautiful grasses, and rhododendron.

We now descended in a north-easterly direction, into a thick forest, which begins with *Pinus longifolia*, and *P. excelsa.* Some six hundred feet lower down, a new species of pine mingles with these, remarkable for the extreme shortness of its leaves, and known here by the name of "*Koorooz;*" it is the *Abies Webbiana*, closely allied to the Silver Fir. Three hundred feet lower again, appears the *Morinda Fir, (Abies Pindrow)* occurring however only singly. Immense *Deodara Cedars* stand here and there in the midst of them; and at length, beyond the village of MEBBAR, or MEBUR, which lies at the foot of the mountain, these last are grouped into a magnificent grove.

This village stands upon an eminence above the SUTLEJ, not far from the place where it receives the waters of the Buspa; however, to obtain a view of the former river, we were obliged to pass over a rocky height partly overgrown with bushes.

Not a living soul was to be seen in the village: the very fields seemed lifeless, though rich with crops of barley and "*phapur*" in full ear. The "*Mookdiar*" was however at length found, and dragged home by force. He made many apologies, and ended by supplying us, to the best of his ability, with meal, rice, butter and milk. The temple-court, surrounded by an open colonnade resting on six pillars, served here, as at Sungla, for our bivouac. Not far from our tent stood a species of altar, surmounted by ram's horns and an urn not unlike the monumental urns of the ancients.

I had often before this been struck by the appearance of these urns, portly in their proportions, rudely formed of clay, painted white, and covered over with a roof. It is exceedingly difficult to obtain any information as to their meaning and use: the people, when we questioned them, were unwilling to give an account of the matter, and their replies were ludicrously evasive,—as for instance, that "the boys had made these urns," &c., &c. It is probable that they are intended to represent some sort of Lama incarnation.

The sons of the "Mookdiar" of Sungla, who had accompanied us hither, now exhibited to us the process of obtaining the very highly valued cedar oil. Resinous cedar-wood, cleft into many small pieces, is carefully squeezed into a new round pot, in such a manner that nothing can fall out when the pot is whirled round and round. It is then turned upside-down over a copper bowl set in a little pit, every opening being filled up with small stones and moss. Round about the pot, a heap of billets of wood is piled up so high as entirely to cover it, and kept burning for fully two hours. Next morning the little pit is opened, and the copper vessel removed, in which the cedar oil is found to have gathered, in the shape of a thin liquid substance resembling tar. It fetches a very high price here, and is used as a medicine, internally and externally, in cases of intestinal disease and in eruptions of the skin.

There was at this place a lack of coolies, and many things required to be put in order, for which reasons we did not set out on our march very early on the morning of the 25th of July. A number of really pretty young girls were standing in readiness to transport our heavy baggage; at first we hesitated about accepting of them as bearers; however, we were assured that such was the custom here. So, reconciling ourselves with a good grace to so agreeable a change, we acquiesced in the appointment of this extraordinary retinue, which, particularly as contrasted with our former troop of filthy coolies, savoured not a little of the romantic. A few of these damsels had very beautiful eyes, and their characteristic costume,—the long cues of hair with the bushy tuft of red wool, the small, brown, felt cap lined with red, stuck in a most coquettish manner on one side, the graceful drapery, with the peculiar bunchy knot behind, and the shining brass ornament fastening the folds on the clothed shoulder,—set off their beauty to the best advantage.

We proceeded through a tall wood of cedars and Cheel pines, in which we enjoyed, at several points, an open view of the Sutlej roaring at a great depth below. On the lofty bank opposite, appeared the village of ROGEE, built, like a swallow's nest, at the top of a nearly perpendicular precipice, five hundred feet in height, with cultivated terraces, covered with corn, situated on ledges so dangerous that it seems as though no mortal could set foot on them without sliding down into the abyss. The bank on this side is not inferior in elevation, but less steep, and partly clothed with grass. We descended, at some distance farther on, from the high ridge, chasing, on our way, a herd of *Rhesus monkeys,** neighbours we had not seen for a long while; they were plundering the noble cedars.

At a turn of the path, the first "*Neoza*" Pines (*Pinus Gerardiana*†) met our eyes; they are trees of large and bending boughs, with pale leaden grey stems, and leaves springing three out of one sheath. Their round, pale green cones are of the size of an infant's head; those of last year are still hanging among the young and tender ones, which will not be fully matured till two months hence.

The country in the neighbourhood of the next village, BARUNG, is lovely and enchanting indeed; a warm spring air was breathing around us, and beautiful trellised vines were crowding upon the apricot trees that shone in the full glory of their ruddy fruit. The flat roofs of the high houses were covered with piles of apricots, about to be dried and prepared as "*Khutai.*" The inhabitants were ever and anon bringing in fruit newly shaken off the tree, and they gave us *carte blanche* to take as much as we chose. The rosy-cheeked maidens who were bearing the load, tumbled them, with liberal abundance, into our hats.

The same neat, but stiff costume prevails among the women here, which we observed some time ago at *Mook-*

* The *Papio Rhesus*, or "*Bhunder*" of Hindostan, and the *Semnopithecus Entellus*, or "*Hoonuman,*" already described by our author, and well known as the sacred monkey of so many eastern lands, are remarkable as being the only species of *Simia* known to be migratory in their habits. They pass the hot summer among the heights of the Himalayas, where they have been known to gain an elevation of more than 10,000 feet, and descend to the plains before winter. The Hoonuman is even said by some travellers to have succeeded in accomplishing the passage of the great mountain barrier, and to wander occasionally into the extensive table-land of Central Asia.

† The seeds of the *Pinus Gerardiana* are mentioned by other travellers as forming (though probably not at the season in which our author visited the Himalayas,) a principal article of food of the inhabitants of Kunawur. —TR.

ba. The men are good-looking, tall and of stately bearing.

This village, which appears to be of great size, lies in the heart of the *Neoza* pine region. About half-an-hour's march beyond it, we marked the traces of a vast avalanche, which had obstructed the whole lateral glen, and dammed up a small river, which flows into the Sutlej. The whole side of the mountain, far above, is denuded of its rich forest, and the valley is blocked up with a mound, fifty feet high, formed of many thousand sturdy trunks and youthful stems, not a few of which have been snapped off in the middle. I recognised among them Cheel pines, birches, poplars, and, most numerous of all, Deodara cedars. Beneath this layer of forest-wreck, which is conglomerated with earth and loose stones into a mass of some ten feet in thickness, there still lies a bed of snow, forty feet deep. We crossed over this mound to the opposite bank. On the side on which Barung lies, an impetuous brook, rushing down over the snowy rubbish, has made a deep cut in it, thus enabling one to see how completely the whole is interspersed with stems of trees.

After crossing the avalanche, we descended, along that side of the little river, to the banks of the Sutlej, which here flows over a sandy channel full of loose pebbles: the water is yellow and turbid. These sandy banks seem to be the favourite home of the *Neoza* pine, a species met with only in a very limited region. The *Neoza* is, in comparison with the other giants of the mountain forests, but of inconsiderable size; its sturdiest stems not exceeding a foot and a half in diameter. It lacks also the beautiful slender top of the other Himalaya pines; nevertheless, it is a pre-eminently handsome tree; its smooth, silver-gray bark,—which never transforms itself into a rough outer coating,—and the large, elegantly formed, pale green cones, with which its branches are loaded, give it a strange, yet peculiarly beautiful air.

At the end of about four hours we reached the base of a granite cliff, from the top of which a rope is stretched across the Sutlej, to serve as a bridge. We climbed the height, and saw the "*Cheena*" *(Panicum miliaceum)* fields and vineyards of the village of Pooaree extended before us. We passed along a rich bower of vines, adorned with clusters of grapes of prodigious size, to an open green sward, bordered with tall poplars and hazel nut trees. Unfortunately, neither grapes nor nuts were ripe; but what an aromatic air, what a lovely valley!

The situation of Pooaree, embosomed amid vine-clad hills, where many a tall stem, loaded with rich foliage and exquisite grapes, has been trained into a shady bower, is romantic in the extreme. The village occupies the only bare and unfruitful spot in the neighbourhood, a bold rock jutting out into the bed of the Sutlej, on which it is perched at a height of a hundred and fifty feet above the river's deep, dark pool. The high houses, neatly built of beams, with intermediate stones, stand so near each other as to leave only very narrow lanes between; their upper stories are adorned with balconies, and their doors guarded by long chains, which can be drawn tight and held firm by those sitting upon the balcony. At the entrance of the village stands a great Lama-Temple, with its small, pillared structure close beside it, in which are kept the kettle-drums, and a sort of enormous trumpets,—instruments used here in religious ceremonies. Large prayer-cylinders, "*Mannehs*," are seen in every place; here they are made of wrought copper, and covered with Lama characters. Here too, we again saw, in great numbers, those white, rude, loam-built domes or urns, before which, as Lama worshippers, the inhabitants perform their devotions.

We are told that written rolls from the grand Lama are placed within them; they are here called "*Chosden,*" or "*Chokhden.*"

The surrounding fields are well cultivated; the crops of "*Cheena*" and "*Kaonee,*" (species of *Panicum*) are not yet ripe for the harvest. The vine is used in a singular way, an intoxicating drink being made by boiling the juice; it is called "*Rak,*" and has a very peculiar sweet taste, somewhat like grape-brandy.

From the top of a cliff, over against Pooaree, we enjoyed, for a long while, the pleasing view afforded by the groups of neat houses surrounded by smiling vine-bowers and verdant corn-fields,—the frowning rocks in the back-ground, crowned on their summits with dark cedar-forests,—while the light clouds flitted across the silvery peaks of *Raldung, ("Reildang")* in the far distance, and we were refreshed, after our day's fatigues, by the soft and balmy breath of evening. Already the valley was veiled in twilight, when the Lamas (Priests) of the temple appeared, with their long red mantles thrown round them in imposing drapery, and commenced, in honour of the Prince, a strain of melancholy singing; first, a leader gave forth the melody, as if intoning a Latin prayer; then the whole chorus, consisting of four other voices, joined in chanting the response, as in the "*Responsorium*" of a Roman Catholic church. The scene produced a wonderfully grand and solemn effect. It was long before we could summon resolution to quit this enchanted spot; and we did not return until a very late hour to the shady walnut trees under which our tents were pitched.

Our next day's march (the 26th of July) began with the tedious passage of the Sutlej, here ninety paces wide, which was accomplished by means of the rope-bridge. We were bound by a woollen rope to the crooked piece of wood, and thus we moved slowly along to the opposite shore. We managed the matter tolerably well ourselves, but the transport of our baggage after this fashion occupied an immense time. It was most piteous to see the unhappy sheep,—our yet living victuals,—hanging by only one leg, and thus drawn across the raging stream. A large dog too, which ran up to us at Barung, and has followed us ever since, was sent across in the same manner, amidst tremendous howling; scenes which caused, as you may imagine, abundant laughter. The impudence of one of the coolies was however no matter of laughter to me; for I saw, from the other side, without any power of interfering, that he was coolly cutting off the new rope from my tin trunk, and pocketing it; the distance was so great that, though I could distinctly see the proceeding, it was impossible to recognize the thief's face.

When the whole of the baggage was safely deposited on the farther bank, and stowed once more on the backs of our coolies, we ascended a steep height, under the rays of a scorching sun. We saw, after this, only a few vine-bowers, beside a small village on our left hand; then all was débris of gray argillaceous schist, along which we could scarcely trace our path. As I had advanced far beyond the rest, and found myself in perfect solitude, I began to fear lest I should have strayed from the right way, and accordingly I descended the steep up which I had just climbed; to my annoyance however, I was obliged to re-ascend it straightway. On the summit, we found an ancient wall, screening a village, the houses of which are so low and flat-roofed, as not to be visible until one has approached close to it. The name of this place is KONGEE. Here the vineyards entirely cease; in their stead, the terraced fields,—enclosed with apricot-trees, loaded with ripe fruit,—are laid out in crops of the finest wheat, just beginning to exhibit a golden tinge.

The most considerable edifice at Kongee, is the "*Deval,*" or Temple, of that peculiar style of architecture, universally prevalent in the higher mountain districts, which are peopled entirely by Lama worshippers. High walls surround a quadrangular court; contiguous to it, but without windows, are the actual temple buildings, with flat slated roofs, supported by elegant pillars of cedar-wood. During Divine service,—if such a name can be bestowed on the chanting of the priests,—the interior of the temple is illuminated with lamps. The people themselves take no further active share in the matter, and indeed, with the exception of the turning of the prayer cylinders, I have witnessed nothing like a religious ceremony among them.

In the middle of the court stands a diminutive wooden sanctuary, of thoroughly Chinese architecture which in the Kunawur district bears the name of a "*Chopal.*" It is open on all sides, and contains a space of from fifteen to twenty feet square, the height being generally about fifteen feet. From eight to twelve elegantly carved, square, wooden pillars support a broad over-hanging roof, with four corners in the form of dragons, or other monsters of wonderful device, turned upwards and furnished with wooden bells. The floor is just sufficiently raised above the ground to allow of one's sitting comfortably upon its edge, and altogether the building affords a convenient resting-place for travellers, sheltering them at any rate from rain; and we were never hindered from taking possession of it; whereas the temples are invariably closed against foreigners. In the temple-court at Kongee stands a large baldachin of red silk, an abundance of gold and silver tinsel is hung round it, and on its highest point, waves a large *yak-tail.** With-

* The English call this article of luxury "*cow-tail.*" One would fancy, from such a name, only the greasy whisk of our own domestic cows. This, however, is the bushy, white tail of the *Yak-Ox,* which is in universal use

in, there seems to be not an article save the silver vessels of the temple.

Beyond this place, we had yet an ascent of more than a thousand feet, before we reached the next village, which stands almost on the crest of the ridge. Our path lay between hedges of white-flowering *Spiræas*, merging into a long shady avenue of apricot trees. This terminates at the village of KOTEE, one of the most charming that I have seen in this mountain region. A spacious lawn, surrounded with gigantic hazel-nut trees, and carpeted with luxuriant, velvety turf, now opened upon us; on a little raised platform to our left hand, stood the neat, pretty houses of the village; to our right stretched a water-course, bordered by a rich enamel of varied flowers, and soon losing itself among the thick bushes, which enclose the fields, for the irrigation of which it is afterwards divided into numerous little channels.

Close to the hazel-nut grove, rises a lofty wall with a neatly fluted border, and a gate of Chinese style, covered with a slanting roof of large slates. I entered and found an open space, in which was a tank enclosed with stones. The jet-d'eau in the centre, and the stone border are much decayed; the water flows into the basin from a fish's head of bronze, still in good preservation, opposite to the entrance. The friendly, pleasing inhabitants, who, full of curiosity, gathered in great numbers around me, were unable to give me any information regarding this secluded and extraordinary spot; moreover, I unfortunately understand but very little of their language. I could follow just enough to discover that the innumerable fishes, swimming in the tank, are fed daily by them, but never eaten. Doubtless this reservoir must, in former times, have been connected

throughout India at the tables of people of any distinction, as a weapon of defence against flies.—W. HOFFMEISTER.

with some sanctuary, and the feeding of the finny race here must have had some religious signification. Although this is now forgotten and lost, yet the village population engage in the employment with great zeal, because it was the custom of their ancestors. Many such inexplicable and singular practices are to be found among the mountaineers, and the only answer that I could ever obtain, by way of enlightening me on their origin and meaning, is, that they do it "*for God's sake.*"

These fishes are however also interesting in another point of view. The streams that flow down into the Sutlej from the wild, broken, rocky glens, rise for the most part amidst snow, have a very short course, and contain no fish. Everywhere, when I made inquiries on the subject, I received the reply, "*There is no fish here.*" Even in the Sutlej, no one ever thinks of fishing, and it is said that no fish can live in its waters up to the point where it issues from Thibet. Whether that statement is correct or not, I cannot pretend to decide, but at any rate the perpendicular rocks which rise from its margin, and only at a very few spots leave any access to the stream, are undoubtedly not favourable to fishing. Whence then have these isolated fishes been brought to this place? They were of two species; as far as I could distinguish their appearance, one belonged to the carp tribe; in all probability, they may be yet unknown to us, however it was utterly impossible to get possession of even one specimen of them.

While I was reflecting on the possible origin of this fish-pond, the rest of the travellers arrived, and we now refreshed ourselves with the beautiful apricots, offered to us with great politeness by the hospitable villagers. They quietly allowed of our selecting the best fruit from among their heaped-up stores, or beating them down from the trees. A multitude of pretty children,—clad only in little shirts, made of wool and very short,—were jumping and playing around us; many women also, with pleasing features, appeared in their usual costume,—the head covered with the small felt cap rolled up at the edge, and the bush of red wool on the nape of the neck. The huge brass brooches, of the singular, spectacle-like form, are never wanting, and here, as at Chetkool, serve to fasten, on the left shoulder, the single long piece of woollen stuff which forms their garment.

We soon reached the advancing corner of the first range of hills, some two thousand feet above the level of the Sutlej; the path proceeds pleasantly, lying between fields of wheat and of barley, and apricot trees loaded with fruit. The numerous groups of inhabitants enticed to the path by curiosity, led us to suspect the proximity of another village, though we could not see its houses.

After the ascent of a considerable hill, we again entered the Cedar forest, which, in a region eight or nine thousand feet above the sea, is almost invariably met with. In this part it is thinly scattered, and numerous Cheel pines are interspersed among the Deodaras. The great number of villages in this district must have interfered much with the denseness of the forest; on the other hand, there are some individual stems of immense circumference, though of no great height. We measured several with pack-thread, and found one twin tree to be thirty-six feet in circumference, and many others were very little less.

Our path,—here very steep, and rendered slippery by the fallen leaves of the cedars,—soon led us above the wooded region, and we found ourselves upon a well-made and carefully kept-up road, the *dák-road* to CHEENEE. It has been made, for the distance of at least a hundred miles, across the roughest mountain country, by a company of British merchants, simply on a speculation, for the sake of carrying grapes with the greatest possible expedition to Simla, from the few places where they are successfully cultivated; they arrive at that station fresh, and in excellent condition. A contract has been entered into with the authorities of the district, according to which the grapes are packed by people appointed for the purpose, and transported from one village to another. Each station is fixed, and the Dâk has scarcely arrived, when the Mookdiar makes his appearance with fresh coolies, ready to forward the grapes without a moment's delay. Thus they travel on from village to village, till they reach Simla. The baskets, in which they are carried, are long dossers, or back-baskets, pointed at the lower end. Cotton is sent up the country for packing them; in this the grapes, gathered not in bunches but singly, are packed in alternate layers. When they come to table at Simla, they have by no means the tempting appearance of a handsome, full-grown cluster, but rather resemble gooseberries; an immense quantity of them is however disposed of.

In this grape trade, to which the Rajah of Bissahir presents no obstacle, a single English merchant is said to realize, in the course of each season, a profit of four hundred pounds sterling, and the demand for grapes is greater than the supply. It is strange that the Rajah knows all this, and yet it never occurs to him that he might carry on the traffic in this article with the low country on his own account, by which means he would make much larger gains, as the grapes are his own property.

On this levelled road, still bordered for some distance with detached groups of pines and cedars, we advanced at a very rapid pace, so that within half an hour, the village of Cheenee presented itself before us. Well contrived water-trenches extend on every side down the slopes, for the purpose of irrigating the numerous cultivated terraces, or of turning little mills, called "*Pandcheckies.*" The latter are at present in full activity. A "*Pandcheckie*" consists of a tiny house, scarcely large enough to admit of two persons standing in it. The water rushes with great violence from a wooden conduit, upon a wheel which moves horizontally, its broad felloes being placed obliquely like the wings of a windmill. The rudely fashioned axle bears, at its upper end, the circular mill-stone, which is kept in constant motion by the revolving of the wheel. In these mill-boxes,—for houses one can scarcely call them,—may generally be found an individual of the fair sex, busily engaged in removing the flour, and in pouring in the corn. The water-channels, formed of cedar-wood, are manufactured with extreme care. At the places where our road crosses their course, they are interrupted, in order to leave a free passage; but the current of the water is so rapid, and its impetus so great, that it shoots from one conduit to the other in a strong, unbroken line, like a ray of light, which struck me as a most singular appearance.

We had now gained an open height, commanding a view of the left bank of the Sutlej. Behind the chain of mountains which rises from its banks,—in the rugged defile of which we could yet recognize the ruinous avalanche and the masses of snow which we had so recently traversed near Barung,—appeared heights, treeless indeed, but clothed with fresh verdure: above them rose the outliers of the Raldung group, piercing the very skies with their eternal snows. Unfortunately a shroud was wrapped around the highest summits, for a storm was advancing towards us. How magnificent the contrast of the dark cedar forests, the alpine pastures of tender green, and the white dazzling snow!

In the fore-ground, to our left, rose a smooth rocky hill, its summit covered with numerous heaps of ruins, apparently the remains of an ancient fort. A peaceful-looking structure in the midst of these, is marked by the many flags and streamers waving on long poles to be a Lama temple. The sloping front of this projecting rock, a face of granite, is smooth and naked from top to bottom, rendering it impracticable to scale the hill on that side. We turned its right flank however, and found ourselves presently under the shade of a row of large poplars and melia trees. A wide expanse of corn-fields lies behind them, near the village, which here extends on our left hand, upon the gently sloping acclivity of the hill, almost to the temple that crowns it. In the centre of a verdant meadow, we descried a really stately looking bungalow; on closer inspection however, it was discovered to be in so dilapidated a condition, that it would have been hazarding our lives to remain in it. It was erected seven years ago, at the expense of an English traveller; but this part of the country is so little frequented that nothing has been done since to keep it in repair; the inhabitants of the place have moreover robbed the untenanted structure of all superfluous ornament, and of every little bit of iron that was not too firmly fixed to be removed, and its windows of every atom of glass. Our tent was therefore pitched on the emerald turf close beside the deserted bungalow. We little thought that we had fixed our bivouac so near the grave, in which an Englishman was buried but a few weeks ago. Two sportsmen, in their passion for the chase, undertook a tête-á-tête expedition into the mountains from this place, for the sake of hunting wild goats. One of the two,—the most renowned hunter among the mountains,—fell sick on the return, expired the second day, and was, with great difficulty, interred by his companion in this sequestered spot.

Scarcely had our tent been set in order, when the storm burst upon us with awful violence; the crash and roll of the thunder was tremendous, and so shook the air, that a multitude of avalanches detached themselves from the snowy mountains, and, with a rumbling thundering noise, forced for themselves new paths to the old established piles of snowy débris, on the other side of the stream. The rain poured all night long from the heavy clouds, and we should have fared much worse under the perforated roof of the bungalow than in our tent. Towards mid-day, the sky began to clear. I availed myself of the favourable moment to climb to the highest point of the hill on which Cheenee stands. It was a matter of more difficulty than I had anticipated, for every where one house stands close to another. I was constrained to creep through, between the cottages, along narrow passages, often terminating in most filthy corners. More than once I found myself, on the flat roofs of the houses, exposed to the danger of stepping into the air-holes, for chimneys they have none. The houses are half excavated in the rock, the fore-part only projecting beyond, and the roofs, level with the edge of the terrace above, are quite covered with the same kind of soil as that of the hill-side, so that I could often distinguish only by the hollow sound, whether I was treading on firm ground or on the top of a house. Adjoining to the village is a wilderness of hemp,—ten feet high,—and of stinging nettles, through which, with much trouble, I made my way to the top of the hill. Here I perceived that the edifice which, from below, we had supposed to be a temple, was only a Lama residence. It is painted white, and the verandah in front, with its broad, overhanging roof, yellow: several very remarkable specimens of wild goats' horns of great size were nailed up round the doors.

There was little else to be seen here; the river-valley is not in sight, and the village, of which nothing was visible but the flat roofs, covered, in great part, with dried or rotting apricots, appeared to great disadvantage. On my return, I was repeatedly in danger of falling through a crazy roof; and my sudden apparition, as I descended from ledge to ledge, caused great alarm among the many notable dames engaged in their domestic occupations. At length I found myself in the principal open place of the village, where stand the larger "*Deval*" and a "*Chopal*" with very beautiful wood-carving. The roof of the latter is terminated, at each corner, by a large wooden bird with spread wings, and the usual decoration of bells. The pillars too of this venerable sanctuary, are of skilful and elegant workmanship. There is a particular caste, or rather a subordinate class of the priesthood, who devote themselves to the execution of this wood-carving. Differences of caste, such as exist among the Hindoos, are unknown here; nevertheless, the son of a Lama becomes a Lama in his turn. All the other inhabitants of the village on the other hand, are, with the exception of the "Mookdiar," equal to each other in rank, and all are bound to serve as coolies, whenever the Rajah commands them. In the plains of Hindostan, on the contrary, none but the lowest castes perform the duties of bearers; seldom indeed does a Brahmin make up his mind thus to demean himself; and when he does, he never fails to demand a higher payment for this condescension, because he is a Brahmin.

I had but just returned to our encampment, when the rain began to pour down with renewed fury. How is it that people maintain that the whole of UPPER KUNAWUR lies beyond the rainy zone? I do not think one could possibly witness, during the rainy season, in the plains, or among the lower and plain-ward range of hills, a more complete and tremendous down-pour, than what we have experienced during the last two days, in this mountain region. Unfortunately this unfavourable weather excluded all view; the glorious Raldung group was constantly shrouded; and besides this disappointment, the chilliness of the atmosphere compelled us to have recourse to our costumes of felt, similar to those of the mountaineers, lest, being prevented from taking exercise, we should be frozen in our tents!

Cheenee was the place where we had hoped to find our horses awaiting us for our further journey; but one only of the "*chuprassies*" who had been despatched with them from Gowanna, made his appearance; he alleged that he had left them all in the lurch to come on more quickly to meet us with part of our baggage. He was immediately sent back, to bring the horses. In all probability he had been endeavouring to advance his own interests by this manœuvre, for it is impossible to place confidence in any of these Hindoos, when they are left without surveillance. They are all rogues, and never fail to pilfer when a good opportunity offers.

The unintermitting rain and the necessary improvements and repairs in our wardrobes and our shoes, detained us,—nolens volens,—at Cheenee until this day, (the 28th of July) and a few days of repose are far from being unwelcome, after our forced and toilsome marches. Meantime, it is now firmly resolved that we are to start to-morrow morning, rain or no rain, and to trace the Sutlej, ascending its course as far as we can possibly penetrate.

ELEVENTH LETTER.

NON-APPEARANCE OF THE HORSES AND BAGGAGE—WANDERING LIFE AMONG THE MOUNTAINS—AGRICULTURE AT CHEENEE—VILLAGE OF KOSHMEE—PANGEE—WALK THROUGH THE VILLAGE—VIEW FROM THE ROOFS—PECULIAR SITUATIONS OF THE MOUNTAIN VILLAGES—MODE OF PREPARING APRICOTS—THE ZEMINDAR—TOBACCO-SMOKING—THE COOLIES—LAMA URNS—PRAYER-STONES—INSCRIPTIONS UPON THEM—HAMLET OF JENGERA—EMBASSY FROM THE RAJAH OF GURWAL—ERRENGKHAL—VIEW OF PURKYUL—MONUMENTAL STONES—LIPPA—THE TEMPLE—COOLIES' SONG—LABRUNG—ANCIENT TOWER—KANUM—DOMESTIC ARCHITECTURE—INHABITANTS—LAMA HOUSE—GREAT TEMPLE—THE CHIEF LAMA—VALLEY OF THE SUTLEJ—THE RIVER RUSKALONG—ARCHITECTURE OF THE BRIDGES—CHASOO—DANGEROUS PATH BESIDE THE SUTLEJ—KORA—COSTUME OF THE INHABITANTS—THE NAMTOO BRIDGE—DUBLING—PLEASING INHABITANTS—DUBLING—KABA.

SIMLA, *10th of September*, 1845.

WE are now at last in our haven of rest, the British convalescent station of SIMLA. During three months we were cut off from all communication, for the post never penetrates into the regions through which we were wandering. Almost the whole of our mountain journey,—a few days at the end of May and at the beginning of June forming the only exception,—was performed on foot; a distance amounting at the lowest estimate to a hundred and eighty German miles.* In the plains, this would not have been anything very considerable, but you must keep in mind that heights of fifteen thousand feet,—more than the elevation of Mont Blanc,—presented themselves on our path; and that frequently after marching a short distance early in the morning, to pre-

* 720 English geographical, or nearly 829 statute miles.—TR.

pare us for our breakfast, we had, as soon as it was over, to ascend a snow-capped mountain.

The non-appearance of our horses, which had been sent round by a nearer way, and of our heavy baggage, of which we were also disappointed at Cheenee, caused the lack of sound shoes and untattered apparel to be painfully felt. We soon consoled ourselves for the want of our horses, having now been long inured to pedestrian travelling: our torn coats too, and jackets,—out of which our elbows were peeping forth, and in which their own original colour was less easily recognised than that of the vegetable and geognostic productions of the regions we had traversed,—were still capable of rendering us some service; but shoes without soles, on sharp rocks and stony ground, were almost more than human nature could endure without repining. However, since, among the mountains as in the plains, cows never die any other death than that of old age, leather is a rare article, and we were constrained,—after the soles, patched and cobbled with our own hands, had shared the fate of all their predecessors of the shoe tribe,—to march forward in sandals such as are worn by the mountaineers.

Luckily they were in very good keeping with the rest of our apparel; for we had been driven by necessity to accustom ourselves to the costume of the mountaineers ("*Pahari*,") consisting of a short dress called "*Bakoo*," —like a sort of coat-of-mail, or loose smock-frock, of raw, white wool,—and wide trowsers bound tight above the feet. Both are confined by a worked, woollen girdle. The small, brown, felt cap, with rolled-up border, deficient, not so much in suitableness to the heavy rains and chilly air, as in neatness and elegance, completed our attire. Often were we constrained to spend our days of rest in washing our own linen, and in mending our tattered raiment; and we engaged more willingly even in this occupation, than in the tedious and distasteful labour of cobbling our shoes!

In spite of these trifling discomforts, I must certainly vote these mountain wanderings to be the most interesting portion of our whole tour. We have endured many fatigues and hardships; have slept week after week under the shelter of dripping tents; travelled on for whole days in half-melted snow; stood up to our knees in ice-cold water, to construct, with hands frozen and benumbed, hasty bridges across rushing streams; scaled acclivities on which a goat or a chamois might have become giddy, and subsisted the while on the stringy flesh of rams or goats, and hard sea-biscuit, or tough "*Sheppatty*," (cakes of barley-meal) to which,—the greater part of our stock of wine having been lost,—a mouthful of brandy was found an excellent accompaniment.

Meanwhile, our good spirits and good humour were inextinguishable; indeed no serious cause of disquietude ever occurred, or at any rate, we had no time to dwell upon grievances.

Our last steep ascent for the day accomplished, and a spot selected for our encampment, our first concern is to fix our tent. Each one sets his hand to the work, and in a few minutes the tent is pitched; our cloaks are unrolled, our blankets spread, and thus our night's quarters are prepared. But there stand, expecting their pay, the whole troop of coolies; the poor fellows must not be kept too long waiting for their hard-earned pittance. Many a rope must be unbound to get at the money, and forthwith tied up again in dexterous knots, the substitute for a lock and key. Suddenly, I bethink myself of my beautiful gathered plants; what a pity that they should be left to wither! The paper too, saturated with moisture, must be laid out in the sun to dry. To release from suffering the various living creatures, swarming and sprawling in all manner of bottles, and to file them on needles, is likewise a duty that admits of no delay. While I am occupied with it, numbers of people gather round me, with imploring gestures. One points, moaning, to his stomach; another brings a sick child, and without more ado lays it silently at my feet; while yonder group are carrying hither an unfortunate man with shattered legs. There is no time to lose; not a moment to linger among my zoological treasures: I must at least show my willingness to afford relief, even where I cannot give a remedy; and alas! how rarely can an efficacious remedy be provided in such haste! Yet it would be hard indeed to send away with worthless or fatal advice these poor people, who have come from their far-distant homes confidently anticipating their cure from the "*Bara Doctor Saheb!*" When the wonder-working medicine has, at length, been rummaged out of the deep and closely-packed chest and duly dispensed, and the bandages applied,—though not without making large holes in the remains of my linen shirts,—I begin to think of indulging in a little repose. But lo! a sudden torrent of rain threatens destruction to the plants I had but just prepared for my *hortus siccus:* I hasten out to rescue my treasures. Thus the rest of the day slips away; darkness comes on with swift and unlooked for strides; and, as evening closes in, our simple repast is devoured with voracious appetite. Scarcely have the dishes been removed, when the conversation dies away, and our eye-lids drop heavily; but no! hence lazy sleep! my journal must be written before the vivid impressions of the day have faded from my mind. A solitary candle,—sheltered from the draught of air by an ingenious paper bell, lest it should be too often extinguished,—sheds its faint and murky light upon my work. In what a poetic mood must I then indite, in what interesting and witty language clothe my descriptions of the adventures we have gone through or the scenes we have beheld! At length, I am free to sink down on the hard couch of coarse, scratching, woollen stuff; and refreshing enough would be my slumbers, if the incessant blood-letting, occasioned by gnats and stinging flies, and other little hostile animals of the sucking or stinging kind, would but suffer the dreamy doze to merge into a sound sleep. After a short rest, morning dawns; a noisy menial enters, and unmercifully pulling away the bed-clothes, compels me to throw on my apparel, yet damp from yesterday's rains. The tent vanishes no less quickly; and we are left to stand shivering in the chill morning blast.

But to return to the province of KUNAWUR, from which I despatched my last tidings of our peregrinations.—

After our four days of rest at Cheenee, we started on the 29th of July, amid continued rain, and retraced our steps for some distance, towards Kotee, on either side of the dâk-road, which we quitted before long, lay the wheat and barley fields of the village of Cheenee. It was harvest time, and the rain was doing fatal havoc. For the most part, we saw only the women occupied in field labour; they move in a row along the narrow terraced fields, cutting off the ears with short sickles; one man and several children following to bind them together in bunches. The stalk is left standing almost entire, and afterwards either burnt down or ploughed in. The terrace is next irrigated, and the second crop sown, consisting of "*Phapur*," (Buck-wheat) "*Kaonee*" and "*Cheena*" (millet) "*March*," (Amaranth,) or peas and beans. During the reaping of their corn-harvest, they all sing in chorus a melancholy tune, ending with a long sustained note, while part of the chorus resume the melody.

The agriculture in the environs of the village soon gives place to the cedar forest, into which we penetrated on quitting the dâk-road. Clouds of heavy mist were resting on the mountains, new masses ever and anon rising from the river-glen and rolling slowly upwards to the region of everlasting snow. The cedar forest becomes more and more dense and gloomy; and solitary *Neoza* and *Cheel* pines are intermingled among the giants of the forest, which have almost monopolized the mountains of Kunawur.

The diminished darkness of the wood betrayed, after we had journeyed on for an hour and a half, the proximity of a village: we descended to it by a steep stair, leading down a considerable declivity. Its name is KOSHMEE. Several clear rivulets ripple through it, and a variegated carpet of flowers,—beautiful blue *Campanulas*, *Spiræas*, *Delphiniums*, and *Dianthuses*,—is spread around the cottages. Here, for the first time, I saw oxen used in agricultural labour; they were yoked to a very simple plough, made entirely of wood.

We had scarcely passed through the fertile district attached to Koshmee, when the rain began anew, penetrating even through the tall thick cedars, whose broad boughs, like spreading roofs, overshadowed our path. After some time, we found ourselves overlooking a deep ravine; immediately above a fine water-fall, we saw our appointed resting-place, PANGEE, situated on the same level on which we were standing, but with the stream flowing between us. An abrupt descent through a wood of *Neoza* pines leads to the bridge; but after crossing it, our real toils commenced. It seemed as if the steep acclivity of slippery granitic fragments would never come to an end, and we were repeatedly deceived by the scattered and isolated groups of houses, which we mistook for the longed-for village: still we were not actually at Pangee.

At length we reached an avenue of Hazel-nut trees; thick hedges of raspberry loaded with scarlet fruit, and balsams of various species, growing beneath their humid shade, had reached an immense size. Walls and houses of loftier architecture now marked that we were drawing near to the village itself. It consists of three distinct parts, situated at different heights on the hill-side; that which we entered was the highest and most considerable. We pitched our tents beside a tower-like building, ornamented with the horns of the "*Bhural*" and of the "*Iskin*:"* the rain was still pouring in torrents. The stem of a tree, with steps hewn in it,—the ordinary kind of stair here,—leads to the door of this tower, which is used as a magazine. Between it, the temple, and a newly erected small house of cedar-wood,—which serves as a depot for the instruments of the temple, trumpets seven feet long, drums, and kettle-drums,—lies an open space, with a "*Chopal*" in its centre, of which last our attendants immediately took possession. Those who could find no room in it, sought shelter under the verandah of the temple, accessible only by climbing; others took refuge in the tiny drum-house, where they killed time by sundry first-rate performances on the tin instruments and the huge drums. Doubtless they were better off there than we under our wet tent, sitting on our cloaks, which were drenched through and through.

Fortunately, towards evening, the sky cleared up, so that we were able to take a walk through the village. A narrow lane runs round behind the temple, to a small garden full of apple-trees, ("*Paloo*") and from it again to the sordid, filthy streets of the village itself. As the houses here also are built into the terraced rock, it is not difficult to reach their flat roofs, and, leaping from one to the other, to gain a general view of the place. The house-tops were covered with apricots, which, in this weather, so little fitted for drying them, had in great part become a mass of putrefaction, making the earthen roofs extremely slippery.

* The wild goat is here called "*Iskin*."—W. HOFFMEISTER.

A most inviting ladder led us from the roof of one of these houses down to the court below. This edifice, the most stately into the interior of which we found our way in these parts, is decorated with a lavish profusion of wood-carving. Windows there are none; their place is supplied throughout the upper story by a wainscoting of open work, the perforations of which represent bouquets of flowers, and monsters of most various device. The cock appears to play a principal part among the figures in this tracery; and also stands conspicuous over every door, and on the corners of the roof. Some of the male inhabitants made their appearance, by no means displeased at our intrusion. To carry on conversation with them was no easy matter; however, I gathered from what passed that one of them was a huntsman. He gave me some interesting information regarding the wild animals of the neighbourhood, particularly the "*Iskin*," and assured me that no bears are ever found here. He was most desirous of accompanying us as huntsman; instead of this plan, we proposed that he should sally forth on his own account to the wild-goat chase, with the understanding that we should pay him a handsome price for every skin with horns.

We mounted to several other roofs after this; a scramble which was richly rewarded by a most enchanting view of the valley and the scenery beyond. Every where in these parts there may be seen the same dark cedar forest, the same smooth face of granite rock, the same snow-capped mountains, and the same wildly storming, roaring river; yet every landscape presents so much variety in the grouping, so much fresh charm, that it seems as though one had never seen any thing similar to it before: thus we found it here also.

Immediately below the village, at a frightful depth,—two thousand feet at least lower than the point on which we stood,—the Sutlej makes a bold sweep among the frowning crags. From time to time the thunder of its waters resounded even to this distance. Waterfalls leap down into its vortex from the opposite bank, shining like streaks of silver amid the sable woods. High above the gloomy forest region, we perceived a little village scattered among verdant terraces, on the face of a rugged, and prodigiously lofty cliff.

It were impossible to describe the strange effect produced by these rock-built villages, when seen from a distance: they seem to hang among the crags, like swallows' nests under the eaves of windows. The narrow paths, by which their inhabitants ascend, appear like a vein of coal on the face of a smooth precipice. One can scarcely believe it practicable, in such situations, for men to till, to plough, to carry on labour of any sort, without tumbling,—plough, oxen and husbandman,—into the deep abyss. Yet there these simple mountaineers establish themselves, and pass the rest of their days overhanging these chasms, the mere crossing of which seems a break-neck adventure. A water-spout, a snow-drift, or an avalanche, might annihilate dwellings and fields by one fell sweep.

The appearance of these bold eyries is however on nearer inspection somewhat different from what one had expected; there is in fact a sufficiency of firm ground for the building of half-caverned houses, for the laying out and cultivating of terraced fields. On the other hand, the villages on the opposite cliff appear from this side no less critically balanced, and their access no less impracticable.

The village, whose picturesque position as viewed from Pangee led to this digression, is named Poorbanee. Its roofs appeared red and yellow, from the huge piles of apricots, which form the principal source of wealth and one of the chief articles of food of the inhabitants, who subsist during the winter on fruits, either boiled with flour or grits, or eaten raw. The apricots have by no means an unpleasant flavour, when half-dried; but if, when laid out for desiccation, they are on the contrary drenched by the rains, the whole heap passes into a state of vinegar-like fermentation, in which it emits a most abominable smell; all sweetness and aroma are irrecoverably gone, and nothing remains but an elastic, brown mass, mixed up with the kernels, and covered with a thick powdery crust.

From the nauseous sour taste which the fruit has in this form it derives its name of "*Khutai;*"* a peculiar flavour, resembling rhubarb, is borrowed probably from the flat roofs on which it is spread, which consist of a layer of loose earth or of loam, beat firmly down on a sub-stratum of birch bark. This covering is softened and opened up by the soaking rains, and mingles, in a disgusting manner, with the half-rotten fruit.

I cannot hazard any judgment as to the origin of this peculiar mode of roofing; possibly it may have been adopted for the facility it affords of construction and of repairs, and continued from hereditary custom; but to me these flat roofs, which in Europe are found only in southern regions, appear remarkably ill suited to a climate, where deep snow lies for three or four months of the year. On this point I was informed, in reply to my enquiries, that the snow is swept down from the housetops daily, and that its breaking through into the house is a very rare disaster.

Early on the 30th of July, in spite of the pelting rain,

* "*Khutai,*"—so called from the trans-Himalayan province from whence it is procured, Kathai or Cathay, the ancient name also of the northern part of China,—is the name of what is considered the best of five different kinds of "*Judwar,*" or "*Nirbisi,*" i. e. Poison antidote, from *Nir,* the privative preposition, and *Bis* or *Bish,* the celebrated poison: by this last appellation (*Bis*) the mountain sickness is also known, as previously mentioned by our author.—Tr.

which penetrated through our tent in every part, we prepared for our onward march. Our "*Zemindar,*"*—one of the most burlesque figures that can be imagined, exactly like Pantaloon in the pantomime,—was already bustling about in the greatest fuss, to drive, or rather to halloo forward, our coolies; for his sonorous bass voice is the best part of him. During our whole mountain tour, he was continually to be heard shouting and blustering; and evermore to be seen in a state of super-activity, as though our interests lay nearer his heart than words could tell; nevertheless, we were abominably ill provided for by him; for, in spite of his stentorian voice, he accomplished very little unless he was constantly watched.

The conceit of the man was really prodigious; he was vain in the first place, of his small foot, of which he made a perpetual parade in the most elegant, gold-embroidered ladies' slippers, courting admiration, and swallowing the most egregious doses of flattery, without a moment's doubt as to its being genuine praise; then of his moustachios, from which he carefully twitched out every grey hair; and lastly, of his snow-white garments of finest muslin, and his gracefully twisted turban. His vanity could fail not to meet with full many a rub from the heavy rains and the rough mountain-paths; and indeed

* The "*Zemindar*" is a civil officer, appointed by the Rajah in whose territories the traveller may be, to attend upon him for the purpose of procuring the requisite supplies of coolies and of provisions, settling the payments to be made for them, and selecting the best spots for encampments. He acts as negociator between the traveller and the natives.—W. Hoffmeister.—The explanation of these services being thus rendered by the Zemindar, we believe to have been, the desire of the Rajahs of Gurwal, Bissahir, &c.—to treat the Prince with the same respect he had met with in the Bengal Presidency. The duties of the Zemindar are not necessarily connected with the accommodation of travellers, of whom indeed there are very few in Kunawur, his position being that of land-holder, or collector of the Government rent or revenue in a village or district, with interests in the soil of various extent in various places.—Tr.

it was here peculiarly out of place. He loved to hasten forward some distance before us, that he might be able to smoke his pipe of tobacco at his ease, for which purpose alone he keeps two special servants; one to carry his large hookah, the other, a vessel full of water, ready to furnish a supply for it at any moment, for water is not always to be found here.

Tobacco-smoking is here, as in India, a universal custom: those who are unable to procure a hookah, even of the simplest form,—which consists of a cocoa-nut-shell with a small clay pipe fixed upon it,—supply the want by making a hole in the moist, loamy soil, to serve as a pipe-bowl; a pipe passes into it through the ground, the mouth-piece above being a stalk or hollow twig, through which they inhale the tobacco-fumes, with such violence indeed that they are often seized with fearful fits of coughing, and convulsive vomitings; for they swallow every particle of smoke. Those who have not already an aversion to tobacco-smoking, would certainly acquire it here, on seeing this most abominable form of it.

But to return to our departure from Pangee,—on the open space before the temple we found our coolies drawn up in array; among them a number of women in their finest gala attire, tricked out with necklaces of silver and tin beads. Many, almost children, were gazing with tears in their eyes at the last remaining burdens, by far the heaviest of all, which, as they had not pressed forward with sufficient alacrity to the distribution of the baggage, now fell to their share. However, as we took good care to prevent the lustiest fellow from marching off with the lightest packages, a more equitable division of the whole was soon effected, and harmony was restored; the wrangling and screaming ceased, and our long train moved on at a rapid pace, to the sound of singing. The steepest mountains alone interrupt this vocal strain; ever warbling, never resting, the coolies pursue their ceaseless march. From time to time only, they halt beside a spring, for they could not exist without water. To refresh their strength, they sometimes hastily prepare for themselves, with the aid of the crystal stream, a kind of dough made of coarse flour, which they eat raw; the hookah meantime passing from mouth to mouth. Generally, if our stage was not too long, the whole file arrived very soon after we did, at the night's resting-place; but the longer our day's journey, the more did they linger behind. Freed from their heavy burdens, coolies and coolias then seated themselves in a circle together, waiting patiently for their pay, which they never received until the last stragglers had reached the goal. Meanwhile, they passed the time in hunting for a certain little insect in each other's hair, an occupation in which they set to work with no less unceremoniousness than skill. This mutual service appears to be a peculiar mark of favour tendered by the fair sex to their male friends, and a polite attention of the latter to one another, supplying the place of conversation, somewhat as, in some circles of society at home, riddles and charades are given out, or a game of forfeits is played.

Not far from the village of Pangee,—the beautiful landscape of which was alas! entirely concealed in heavy mist when we quitted it,—my attention was again attracted by those curious, portly-shaped, loam-built urns,* marking the dominion of Lama-worship. They are rudely formed lumps,—urns, or bells, or whatever else they may be designated,—sometimes oval, sometimes spherical, measuring from two to three feet in diameter, and painted white on the outside. They stand on a basement of masonry two feet high, and are covered with a roof made of boards. I made repeated and

* Their name was, at this place also, variously pronounced; sometimes "*Chokhden,*" sometimes "*Chesden,*" with every intermediate gradation of sound.—W. HOFFMEISTER.

strenuous endeavours to discover whence they derive their origin; but to every enquiry as to their signification, I received the laconic answer,—"God;"—the same reply which invariably cuts short all investigations concerning their temples or other holy things. These urns are constantly met with on all the roads and in all the villages, and persons may be seen praying before them, as at the way-side oratories in Roman Catholic countries. That which appears to me the most likely to be true of all the contradictory statements made to me on the subject, is that they contain prayers written on scrolls, and signed by the Grand Lama at Teshoo Loomboo.*

In some places, these urns are constructed of stones; in others again, of a sort of basket work of twigs; but invariably they are plastered over with loam, and painted white. It was not till we advanced farther, that I saw them regularly arranged in rows of three, each urn having its own distinguishing colour; one yellow, one grey, and one white. In ascending the Sutlej, the first of these curious objects is met with not far from Cheenee, that place apparently marking the boundary of Lama-worship.

No less strange and mysterious than the *Chokhdens* are the "*Manneh Paddehungs*," which begin about the same place: they are piles of stones regularly put together, in form somewhat like long, narrow altars, the upper surface being covered with polished pieces of slate,

* Not the personage usually known as the *Grand* or "*Dalai*" *Lama*, the Pontifical Sovereign of Thibet, whose residence is at Lassa; but the "*Teshoo Lama*," protected and worshipped by the Chinese Emperors of the present dynasty. The description given of his capital, its temples and monasteries, by Captain Turner in 1783, indicates great spiritual power, but nothing like magnificence. The number of "*Gylongs*" or monks, in attendance at daily prayer in the great "*Goomba*," or temple, was said to amount to 3700, the nunneries being on an equal scale. Until the Nepaulese invasion in 1790, the territories of Teshoo Loomboo enjoyed unbroken peace, without the protection of any armed force. Since that date, the bonds of dependence on the Celestial Empire have been greatly tightened.—Tr.

each of which bears the following inscription in Thibetian characters, "*Om man neh padeh ho hung.*"* Some of these graven stones are perfect master-pieces of sculpture; others are merely scratched, as though they were the productions of children. With few exceptions, they are all engraved with the same characters: the above-mentioned syllables contain the initials of all the principal divinities of the pantheon of Thibet; however, even the priests could enlighten me only as to the "*Ma,*" which is said to stand for *Mahadevi*, and the "*Pa,*" which signifies *Parvati*. At all events, it is a very easy and passive mode of performing devotions; for the prayer is entrusted to a stone, which lasts as long as the life of the worshipper, and is preserved and cherished as a memorial of his piety, long after he has mingled with his kindred dust.

* Properly these words are,—"*Om Mane Padma houm.*"
"Oh precieux Lotus! Amen."
According to *Klaproth's* translation of "*Vigne's Travels to Cashmere,*" vol. ii. p. 331, where Wilson thus explains them. See also "*Nouveau Journal Asiatique,*" Janvier, 1831; and *Fokien's Foue-koue-ke*, translated by *Abel Remusat*, p. 118 and 136. *Padma*, the *Lotus*, is the symbol of *Vishnu*.—Ed.

These sacred and mysterious words are held in veneration not only by the Buddhists, or Lama-worshippers of Thibet and Kunawur, but by those of Bootan. Mr Hamilton mentions that in the latter country they are inscribed on most public buildings, frequently also engraved on the rocks in large and deep characters, and sometimes even rendered legible on the sides of hills, by means of stones fixed in the earth so as to form the letters, and of so great a size as to be visible at a considerable distance. They are moreover connected with another singular custom mentioned by the same author. He informs us that "a white silk scarf is an invariable attendant on every intercourse of ceremony in Bootan and in Thibet, and is always transmitted under cover with letters. The manufacture is of a thin texture, resembling that sort of Chinese stuff called '*pelong,*' and is remarkable for the purity of its glossy whiteness. This scarf is commonly damasked, and the sacred words are usually near both ends, which terminate in a fringe. The origin or meaning of this mode of intercourse has never been ascertained; it is esteemed of such moment however, that the Rajah of Bootan once returned a letter to the resident at Rungpoor, which he had transmitted from the Governor-General, merely because it came unattended with the bulky encumbrance to testify its authenticity."—Tr.

These accumulated masses of prayer-stones are regarded with the deepest veneration by the Lama worshippers, and increasingly so in proportion to their size. No one ever turns his left side towards one of these monuments as he passes by, but always studiously contrives to leave it on his right hand. For this reason there are always two paths made beside the little heaps, one for coming and the other for going. Just beyond Pangee, we were struck by seeing the first of these piles of stones. We did not find any again till we reached the other side of the pass, which we soon afterwards ascended.

The gradual rising of the mist permitted us to reconnoitre the position in which we were. We found ourselves proceeding along the edge of a hill, at an elevation of about two thousand feet above the river. An inconsiderable stream, the Keshem, which has cut a deep chasm in the hill, forced us to make a circuit of two hours, down into its hollow and up again: at length we regained the same level on the further side, after which we had a very toilsome ascent, by steps hewn in the granitic blocks. The pines and cedars gradually become stunted; at length they make way for cypresses *("Leoora")* and juniper, *("Taloo")* which cover the entire slope of the hill, on which our tents were to be pitched for the night. The place where we encamped was not indeed very pleasant or inviting, and moreover, it was abundantly exposed to the wind; but it was the only spot of level ground. Bushes of thorny, blueish-green juniper and dwarfed cypresses formed a thick copse all around; and a multitude of Alpine plants,—thyme, everlastings, campanulas, roses, and hyssop,—clothed the flat space, amid scattered fragments of granite.

Some two or three hundred feet below, we espied the glistening verdure of rich meadows. There is indeed no village there, but in that bright spot lies nestled the tiny hamlet of JENGERA, where a few shepherds dwell the whole year round; and where, at certain seasons, the flocks and herds scattered over the pastures of these hills, are collected together. A few cow-houses were the only buildings I distinguished. From this sequestered nook we procured new milk, a luxury to which, from this time forward, we were to bid a long farewell. We also purchased several kids, for we were obliged to spare our flock of sheep as much as possible, since, in the absence of all vegetable food except rice, one sheep was necessarily slaughtered every week.

On returning to our tents, after feasting on the glorious prospect of the peaks and mountains shining in the crimson tints of sunset,—the passes of HARUNG and BRUANG to the south, and RALDUNG to the east,—the emerald brilliancy of the insulated meadows, and the magnificent irradiation of the granite cliffs towering in the midst of dark cedar forests,—we were met by the announcement that an embassy from the Rajah of Gurwal, attended by a number of "*chuprassies*," had just arrived at our camp, bringing the salutations of his Highness, and moreover, a multitude of presents. We had long since quitted the dominions of that potentate,—which lie much farther southward, bounded on the north by the river Jumna,—and had pushed on among the Himalayas, without paying our respects to him at his residence, Tiri, upon the Ganges. He had fully expected a visit, and had contemplated honouring the Prince with a magnificent reception. Notwithstanding the disappointment of all his hopes however, this kind and hospitable Rajah persisted in despatching a great part of the presents destined for the Prince and his suite; selecting those that could most easily be packed, and sending with them a numerous escort. As our paths through the mountains were not easily to be traced, still less followed, his embassy had passed a whole month in wandering hither and thither, during dreadful rains, without being able to fulfil their commission, until at length, by a fortunate chance, they fell in with us in this wild solitude. The audience was deferred till the following morning.

When the appointed time arrived, the present-bearers made their appearance; for the most part officers of the Rajah's household-troops, arrayed in gorgeous turbans, and newly-washed flowing garments of finest muslin, with powerful broad-swords at their sides. Amid many ceremonies, after touching the Prince's feet with the points of their fingers, they spread the costly gifts upon the ground before us: an epistle, embroidered on Chinese brocade, was also delivered to His Royal Highness: how much did we regret that not one of us was able to decipher it!

The most worthy of notice among the presents were handsome Nepaulese poniards and "*Khukries,*" musk-bags, Nerbissi-roots,—a highly prized arcanum, believed to be a cure for every disease,—shawls of great value, and a skin of a Thibet Musk, which would have been an inestimable treasure, had not the *Dermestes lardarius* (Leather-eater) been so busy in its ravages during the long wanderings that it was almost falling to pieces. The bearers of these treasures returned home richly rewarded, and entrusted with counter-presents for the Rajah, and immediately afterwards, we followed our long since departed baggage.

Our resting-place near the cow-houses of Jengera was not more than from a thousand to fifteen hundred feet below the pass, which we now saw rising before us in its naked and rugged grandeur. For some time, we forced our way through the thick and thorny bushes of juniper and cypress, till at last we entered upon the actual ascent of the pass. The lower part of it is a steep and difficult mountain-path; soon however we reached a broad road through wild pastures, enamelled ith the most beautiful, fresh, Alpine-flora: here for the first time I saw gentianas, which I had missed on all our previous wanderings among the Himalayas, and near them, a rich profusion of red and yellow potentillas, dark blue forget-me-not, thyme of most aromatic fragrance, mint, and, last not least, hiding its charms under huge blocks of dark granite, that lovely cerulean Alpine-poppy of the Himalayas. Who could have imagined that those banks of primitive rock, so naked and desolate when viewed from beneath, would prove to be thus exquisitely adorned! But we had been no less deceived, owing to the clear mountain air, regarding the nearness of the head of the pass: the sun had risen far above the icy needles of Raldung, and its burning rays had become very oppressive before we gained the nearest height. We had imagined that the ascent of the whole pass,—the name of which is ERRENGKHAL,—was now accomplished, when suddenly we beheld its culminating point in the distance before us; for it was a mere out-post hill that we had climbed. During two hours more, we mounted higher and higher, on paths, most delightful certainly, and adorned with lovely Alpine flowers, but no less toilsome than charming.

But what a surprise awaited us on reaching the highest ridge! A single, sharply-drawn crest of white granite, destitute of all vegetation, (such are all the loftiest ridges of the Himalayas,—one cannot even walk along them), now rose before us; at one spot only there is a passage broken through it, a narrow opening like a sort of gate. The instant we entered this, the most magnificent Alpine panorama, beyond what fancy could have pictured, burst upon us: the mountains of the Chinese territory,—PURKYUL,—which we now beheld for the first time. How strange, how interesting, the thoughts that filled the mind on thus finding oneself, as it were, magically transported to the very gates of the Celestial Empire! Alas! we knew too well by former experience, how securely defended these were; so much the more ardent was our desire to penetrate the barrier! so much the more vivid were our imaginings of the beautiful and the wondrous enclosed within! The mellow violet blue of the long lines of hills towering one behind another, had something in it so mysterious, so enchanting, that the most intense longing to see them more closely, to perambulate them at our leisure, was kindléd in our minds. We did not then know how little they gain by nearer approach,—how, at last, that landscape which from a distance appears so attractivé, resolves itself into cold, naked, ruinous-looking rocks, crowned with everlasting snow. We afterwards reached these heights, and so far crossed their barrier, that we saw before us no more blue mountains, and even no more snow,—but only the monotonous horizon of that table-land of Thibet, which, most unpromising in its sterility and desolation, stretches far as the eye can reach.

On the highest point of this pass, we found, as usual, memorial stones, or rather monumental heaps, set up beside the road, to which every traveller adds his contribution. He who wishes to acquire a peculiar stock of merit, carries up with him a pole, on which he fastens a streamer, and which he then sets up on the monument, where many such flags already wave. Others content themselves with throwing a few flowers on these altars, and this, to please our attendants, I also did; for even on this lofty point, flowers are to be found without much difficulty, and I had loaded myself with so many, gathered by the way, that I had been forced to throw away part of my treasure ere now. One small umbelliferous plant, with whitish gray flowers, and most aromatic fragrance, is peculiar to this spot: the coolies, who fell upon it with great eagerness, called it "*Losser*" or "*Lasser*," a name which reminded me of the *Laser* of the ancients.* I had never seen it before except on our way to the sources of the Ganges, where I met with it at a height of six thousand feet.

The rocky mass of the pass is a micaceous formation, intersected by an extraordinary species of stone, consisting entirely of shining crystals, sometimes pale blue, and sometimes white. The path before us was a gradual descent; soon we once more obtained shelter from the violent wind, which had made our stay on the summit of the pass most uncomfortable. The limit of arboreous vegetation lies about six hundred feet below the ridge: the wood begins with trees and bushes of most singular

* This umbelliferous plant is referred by Dr Hoffmeister in his second Appendix to the genus *Astrantium*. It may very probably have been unnoticed by the few scientific travellers who have hitherto visited Kunawur; it is at least not noticed in Dr Royle's section on the *Umbelliferæ*, nor in Dr Lindley's notices of those of the Himalayas embodied in Dr Royle's work. By the kindness of that eminent botanist, Dr Greville, we are favoured with the following remarks. The Laser of the ancients was a gum-resin endowed with, or believed to be possessed of, such important properties that by the Romans it was valued at its weight in gold. This precious substance was the Sylphion of the Greeks, and the parts about Cyrene whence it was brought were called the "*Regio sylphifera.*" Amongst the many miraculous powers attributed to the Laser were those of neutralizing the effects of poison, curing envenomed wounds, restoring sight to the blind and youth to the aged. So highly was this drug prized, that stores of it were preserved at Rome among the treasures of the state, and Pliny says,—so great was its value, that Julius Cæsar, when Dictator, caused a hundred and eleven ounces which he found in the public treasury to be sold to defray the expenses of the first civil war. The plant was considered of such importance that it was represented upon the coins of Cyrene. There can be no doubt that it belongs to the natural order *Umbelliferæ*, and it has been successively referred to *Laserpitium Siler*,—*L. gummiferum*,—*Ligusticum latifolium*,—*Ferula tingitana*, &c. Viviani has described a plant in his "*Flora Libyca*," under the name of *Thapsia Sylphion* which, being found by Della Cella on the mountains of Cyrene, and resembling the representation on the coins, is probably the plant so highly valued by the ancients. The root is reported by the natives to possess valuable medical properties. It is clear, however, from the accounts of ancient authors, that there was more than one kind of *Laser*, and it is not improbable that spurious drugs were gradually substituted for the true one. The term has been considered a mere corruption of *Lacter*, and might represent the concrete milky juice of various plants. It is known that Assafœtida was at one time exported from Persia and substituted for it. The juice of the Assafœtida is used as a condiment by some Asiatic nations.—Tr.

shape and appearance, which I could not at all recognise, until my guide told me what they were; neither more nor less than birches, thus stunted and disfigured by storms and snow drifts. Here and there also, in moist spots, I remarked beautiful bosquets of rhododendron, of two very rare species, one with rose-coloured, the other with yellow flowers; both unluckily had passed the prime glory of their blossom. Five hundred feet lower down, we entered the region of the *cheel* pine, on a declivity covered with boulders of red granite, in which are traces of copper ore, in the form of copper pyrites or of azure of copper occurring among the rolled stones, or of a mountain green clay covering the rock *in situ*. It struck me as remarkable that on the northern side of the pass, the intermediate step between the birch and rhododendron and the lofty *coniferæ*,—viz., bushes of cypress and juniper,—is altogether wanting, as is on the southern side, the rhododendron.

Our descent was, for the space of an hour, through a wood consisting only of firs: not till we reached the point lower down, where the roar of the TIGAR river,* rushing deep below us, first met our ears, did we see any cedars, and even then only single trees; at the same time, golden fields of wheat appeared in the distance. Umbrageous trees,—oak and rhododendron arboreum,—compose the wood on the banks of the river. We soon saw, on its opposite side, the village of which we had caught a bird's-eye view from the height of the pass. Close to the place at which we crossed the Tigar, the granite ceases on both sides of the stream, as if suddenly clipped away, and is succeeded by a hard clay-slate, often passing into clay-ironstone, and a marked change takes place in the outline of the hills.

The vegetation here presents many forms familiar as home-friends: I observed *Leontodon* and *Malva rotundifolia*

* It has various names; on the maps it is called the *Leesa*.—W. HOFFMEISTER.

growing under the cedar-trees; and beside the margin of the river, large bushes of a species of *Ribes*, called "*Njangke*" by the natives: it bears a beautiful light red fruit, with a greasy outer coating, similar to that of the honeysuckle berry, from which it derives an unpleasant, turpentine-like flavour: in spite of this however, it is commonly eaten by the natives.

The first cultivated fields appear on the farther side of the Tigar, after crossing the "*Sangho*," which is thirty paces long. The lovely village of LIPPA, to which they belong, lies between terraced fields on the side of a lofty rock: we ascended to it by a very considerable climb. Here forest and thicket are alike wanting; the ground is clothed with a thoroughly southern flora, such as we did not see again before reaching the banks of the lower Sutlej. A wonderfully beautiful species of *Capparis*,—spreading its bunches of blossom and garlands of tender green, far and wide,—*Malva, Althea rosea*, and *Echinops* growing to the height of a man, with white or pale-blue flower-balls, form the splendid ornaments of the lofty slope. These soon give place to yellow wheat, and the young and verdant blade of buck-wheat, with which, after the barley-harvest, the terraced fields are cropped, each being inclosed with a wall crowned with a hedge of Clematis, filling the air with a most delicious perfume. Along these walls extends the path, which occasionally also serves as a water-channel for irrigation. Sometimes indeed, the water-courses may be seen suspended high above the road, resting on tall fir poles,—for the mountaineers bestow much industry on the irrigation of their cultivated lands, and are thorough masters in the art of planning and constructing their little canals and aqueducts. The river below is, moreover, divided into a complete system of small water-courses, each of which drives one of those small mills,—"*Pandzeckies*,"—which I have already described.

Thus by slow yet not tedious steps, our path at length led us to the village, which, quite according to the custom of our father-land, begins with a suburb of stinging nettles and sow-thistle. The temple, with the "*Chopal*" in front of it, stands at the end of the lower terrace; by far the greater part of the village being on the second one, immediately above it. We pitched our tents on the margin of a little rivulet which flows beneath the temple-lawn, our coolies taking possession of the "*Chopal.*"

This sanctuary appears new, or at least recently repaired: it is adorned with very pretty wood-carving, both on the corners of the roof and on the doors: the verandah, formed of the most beautiful cedar-wood, with tastefully flowered patterns in the carved work, has an uncommonly fine effect; not unlike,—though on a very small scale,—the ideal suggested on reading the description of the temple of Solomon. Hangings of many colours, flags and yak-tails, are combined in its decorations, and they are employed indeed in the ornamenting of many houses here. On either side of the temple stands a very ancient cypress,—the two largest stems of this tree, that I have ever seen; they are nearly destitute both of foliage and of branches, and have a grisly and haggard air.

Lippa is a most animated village. A multitude of inquisitive, good-humoured, merry folk, soon found their way into our tent; many sick persons too were carried thither, and I had enough to do in dressing wounds, applying plasters, and dispensing medicines. We saw here several Chinese from the interior of Thibet; among the rest, one fat and portly fellow, a smith by trade, completely equipped in his national costume, with his long cue of hair, and funnel-shaped cap, who repaired our guns and other arms with great skill. Not many of the women appeared; those we did see were well-made and pretty, clad in the same picturesque drapery we had remarked on the other side of the pass, with the same brass ornaments, which are here called "*Pitchoock,*" or "*Pitzoock.*" On the fair sex rests the whole burden of field labour and of domestic toil, while the men,—whose appearance is thoroughly Chinese,—saunter about, all the day long, smoking their pipes.

Towards evening, we visited the upper village, the approach to which is by a broad road. As the intervals between its houses are also on a wider scale than usual, it is not practicable to pass from roof to roof; many of the dwellings are distinguished by long flag-staffs, on the end of which yak-tails wave as banners; these, if we were rightly informed, are the houses of the priests. The lower story is, for the most part, of masonry; in its wall is a door with a round arch, opened and closed by means of the long chain with a padlock upon it: the upper story is of wood with the usual flat roof. Beside the houses are little gardens with luxuriant vine-bowers, apricot and peach trees, and apple-trees loaded with beautiful fruit. The inhabitants, especially the children, seemed much alarmed at our appearance, and fled, screaming, into their houses.

It was harvest-time, and the flat roofs, which serve for threshing floors, as do the trees for hay-lofts, were richly covered with wheat or with apricots. We could mark the merry gambols of many a group of little ones on the house-tops: how often must one and another tumble down from this airy play-ground! doubtless, the great number of cripples one meets with in these parts, must be attributed to this perilous custom.

Leaving the village to our left, we proceeded, after traversing several gardens, to reconnoitre a small edifice adorned with many flags: its appearance marks it as a temple or consecrated spot; it is a tasteful structure, with a slanting roof of slate; all the wood-work is varnished yellow, while the walls are painted white; beside it stands a colossal white "*Chokhden*," similar to those before described. Strange sounds from within the temple now fell upon our ears,—a deep murmuring, accompanied with the tinkling of bells: amid the still solitude and solemn twilight of the place, the effect was striking and mysterious in the extreme. We had not long stood there, gazing silently at the ever darkening shades of the river-glen, when the door opened, and an aged priest (*Lama* or *Lamba*) stepped forth, wrapped in a red mantle, thrown over the shoulder like the toga. He was followed by a woman, bearing a finely wrought copper pitcher with a silver lip, of perfectly Etruscan form, and several boys carrying large censers—a most picturesque group! The woman came after us, as we wended our way along a side path, to present us with flowers, having observed that we had ornamented our hats with the milk-white bells of a beautiful species of *Datura*.

Here again, I saw, among the decorations of the temple, wild-goats' horns of extraordinary size, and horns of the *Snow-Gazelle*,—which pass here for those of the female of the wild-goat,—as well as of the *Bhural*. We were told that bears are never met with here, nor indeed in the whole country on this side of Sungla: if this information be correct, the sharp line of demarcation, limiting the appearance of this wild beast, is very remarkable.

On the first of August, we were in full march before sun-rise; we were this day again to see the Sutlej, which, for the sake of cutting off a large angle of the road, we had quitted, two days before, at Pangee. For some time, we traced the course of a small stream, the Mangalung; afterwards, our path led us close to the second Lama temple, through fields covered with wild hollyhocks, of colours as varied as those in our gardens at home; next followed a steep ascent, accomplished for the most part by means of steps hewn in the many-coloured clay-slate. The ridge of the chain of hills, which extends along the deep and narrow gorge of Lippa, is thinly clothed with cedars; even from this height we could distinguish some few distant windings of the Sutlej, here called Sutteloosa. But we had a tedious climb before we gained the summit of the mountain, passing, as we ascended, through a small, solitary hamlet with an apricot-garden; numerous flights of wild doves were fluttering above our heads; the same species, which with us is kept tame in dove-cotes, here in all their primitive freedom; they afforded us an excellent dinner. On the highest point of this pass, which forms the wall of separation between two lateral valleys watered by small streams, we commanded an extensive bird's-eye view over a great part of the valley of the Sutlej, with the two villages of KOLA and PILLA,—the three separate groups of the snow-capped giants of Purkyul forming a glorious back-ground to the north. Immediately before us, lay wild and magnificent masses of broken rock, and desolate, sun-scorched mountains of débris, frowning, and naked save a few decayed and solitary pines. Behind us lay the smiling fields of Lippa; we could also trace, stretching far on the other side of the village, on the rugged, boulder-covered steep, the zig-zag path leading to a side-valley in which is the village of POSHOO. To the north-west, below a gloomy rampart of vast, shattered blocks, lay the Oasis of KANUM; but, as the depths of the lovely and fertile valley were as yet concealed from our view, the whole region wore an indescribably melancholy aspect, one mountain range rising immediately beyond another,—wave upon wave,—all bare, gray and monotonous. Nevertheless, this desolation has a peculiar charm, even though, above Kanum, not a single stunted tree, not a shrub, is seen to break the vast wilderness.

While, under the shade of the last cedar, I was feasting my eyes on this sublime prospect, there arose behind me a very melodious strain of singing. The chorus was a full one; a few voices began the air,—replete with sudden transitions and wild roulades,—and as its high final note approached, the other voices echoed the melody, while the closing note was still sustained. This artless song was so in character with the wilderness before me and with the dreamy thoughts and feelings to which it gave rise, that I listened to it with intense delight. The singers were none other than our bearer-train, consisting, for the most part, of maidens and youthful matrons from Lippa: I gave them a few coins, to hear more of their sweet warbling, and they sang from that time forward, the whole way down the steep descent, never hindered in the least degree by the heavy burdens on their backs.

Soon we had left the last thin, shabby copse behind us; before us stretched the gray and naked waste of débris, over which we were threading our tardy way; a few scattered and stunted bushes of roses, and of wormwood with its white parched stalks,—the true plant of the wilderness,—were the last traces of vegetation which the sun had failed to scorch from off the face of the schistose cliffs. At a turn of the path, we caught a view of several villages, surrounded by green bushes and fields of golden wheat; a narrow stripe of verdure runs down the mountain side near them, marking the course of a little brook, to which the groups of dwellings owe their existence. Springs of water are rarely found in these parts; we passed but one, which was instantly encompassed by the coolies, and for the time nearly exhausted.

The village of Kanum, the ultimatum of our day's journey, had hitherto, from its situation in the deep recess of the river's narrow gorge, been concealed from our view. At the end of another hour, the lower half of the opposite mountain-slope became visible for the first time, with its green trees and rich bushes, far below us; and at length the village itself appeared, though still at some distance. Immediately we bid adieu to the steep and naked wilderness of mountain wreck: apricot gardens rising above each other in high terraces clothe the slope, announcing the proximity of the dwellings of man; they belong to the village of LABRUNG, situated on the near side of the deep glen that separated us from Kanum. A large pile of "*Manneh Paddeh*" stones lies not far from its entrance, and as soon as we had rounded a projecting corner of rock, we were struck by the unexpected view of a grand and lofty building, a species of tower. It is built half of stone, half of wood, square, and with from ten to twelve stories; the upper part is very ruinous, and perfectly black from age and smoke. Its venerable and gigantic form has an imposing effect; the more so, as it occupies a bold and commanding position on the brink of a precipitous cliff, where detached masses of rock are scattered on every side. We had, ere now, seen many similar structures on the banks of the Bhagirethi, but few of equal size. They served, in olden times when the Chinese yet extended their sway over this land, as places of refuge for the population of the whole village.

The apricot-trees on the terraces were loaded with ripe fruit, and no one restrained either us or the coolies from shaking down and eating as many as we chose: they are here used as food for the cattle. They are not indeed of the finest kind, but yet abundantly sweet and juicy, and the refreshment which they afforded was a most salutary preparation for our renewed march; for we here observed to our consternation, that, in order to reach Kanum, we must make the circuit of the deep glen, and moreover clamber up a steep acclivity on the opposite bank of the river.

This fruitful valley forms a pleasing contrast to the dreary and barren heights among which it is embosomed. Avenues of silver poplars enclose each terrace; between them are richly-loaded apricot-trees, and yellow fields of wheat; and in the far depth below, among innumerable mills, green gardens of herbs, one behind another, along the margin of the stream.

We arrived before long at the beginning of the water-courses, which, often passing over scaffoldings from twenty to thirty feet high, convey the precious stream in numerous pipes and channels, from the most elevated point of the valley, to the highest of the cultivated terraces. Some thousand feet or so below Labrung, we crossed the rivulet, and wound up the opposite slope, by a most enjoyable path. Limpid brooks murmur on either side, fringed by rich and umbrageous avenues of silver poplars and apricot-trees; so that, while the mid-day sun was darting his relentless rays, we luxuriated in deep shade almost till we reached Kanum. It was in the desert solitudes of the Himalayas, that we first learnt fully to appreciate the gladsome blessing of clear streams. With exquisite delight we could have gazed for hours at the rippling waters, refreshing not only the parched tongue, but the eyes also, wearied by the ceaseless prospect of a chaos of stern and sterile rocks: often too, between the mountain villages, we could not only quench our thirst, but feast on travelled dainties; for multitudes of apricots floating down the current were fished out with the utmost ease.

Kanum is one of the largest villages which we visited among the mountains. The inhabitants of the remoter villages, far and wide, flock together here to make their purchases: articles of gold and silver, boots, woollen shoes, beautiful carpets and coverlets, and tasteful and ingenious wood-carving, are the products of the industry of this place: it also contains one of the largest Buddhist monasteries,* and two temples of considerable size, so

* The "*Gylongs*" or monks among the Lama worshippers, like the monks of the Roman Catholic Church,—to which the religion of Thibet is proved by the testimony of various travellers, and we may add of Dr Hoffmeister

that it may almost boast the dignity of a capital in Kunawur: the houses are built on terraces, like a flight of steps on the hill-side.

We pitched our tents on one of these terraces, a hundred paces or so from the village, close beside the great temple. A multitude of the curious soon crowded around us, and all manner of wares were brought and offered for sale; Chinese silken stuffs, silver hookahs, cloth boots, knives and poniards. All the different merchants began their dealings by making us a present, consisting of a sort of bad raisins handed on large brass dishes; the prices however which they asked for their goods were so exorbitant, that, in spite of their raisins, they were speedily driven out of our tents.

When the cool of the evening drew on, I ascended the hill to the village. The houses of the first row are very high, and constructed in a very singular and clumsy style, of thick cedar stems: the streets leading up to the second and third rows are narrow alleys, dark and filthy, and in many places closed above by the overhanging houses: doors and windows are most sparingly introduced; the former are guarded by a couple of long chains passing through a hole in the second story; while out of the latter is often seen peeping, not the human

himself, to bear in some points a singular resemblance,—renounce worldly avocations and family ties, and maintain strict ecclesiastical discipline, and a regular gradation from the Sovereign Pontiff down to the youngest novice. Among other features of Lama worship are, prayers for the dead, chanting of masses, the intoning of prayers, the perpetual burning of lights in the temples and sanctuaries, the tonsure, the celibacy of the clergy, holy water, relic worship, and the adoration of the queen of heaven. The name "*Lama*" is properly applied to the president of a monastery. The grand Lama is held by them to be an incarnation of their divinity. He resides at Lassa, and unites the regal and priestly dignities in his own person, the civil power being however almost entirely vested in the rajah or deputy, and in no measure, however small, shared by any inferior functionaries of the sacerdotal order. On the decease of the grand Lama, peculiar and mysterious invocations are carried on for three years; after which, the individual in whose person he is to re-appear, is said to be announced by inspiration to the ecclesiastical, and confirmed by the civil, powers.—Tr.

face divine, but the head of a horse or of an ass! That portion of the building which calls itself the ground-floor, is in fact scarcely ever more than the stone basement on which the house rests, and the first story contains the stalls for the cattle. It is only by night, or during the winter season, that the human inmates betake themselves to the dark chambers of the interior: in summer the roof is their usual abode, and indeed during the warm months they even sleep there.

Mounting a sort of henhouse-ladder, I reached the terrace immediately above, to which I was obliged to fight my way against several furious dogs. Here I found myself on a level with the roofs of the houses below; street and house-tops are here one and the same, and covered with the same layer of earth: in not a few cases when the door below is wanting, the only entrance to the house is from its roof.

On the top of one of the largest houses, I saw an aged man, in a brownish red mantle and a red cap, pacing up and down, and diligently threading his rosary backwards and forwards between his fingers, while a younger man and woman, both attired in the same hue, were spreading out the grain on the flat house-top. Other figures, also in red gowns, and not one without the rosary, were gliding about, bringing forward fresh sheaves of wheat. I at once concluded that this was one of the Buddhist monasteries, which I knew to exist in Kanum. The old man beckoned to me to approach, and I stood for a while looking at these people as they moved up and down; they were soon joined by several women clad in the same capuchin of brownish red. They were the brethren and the sisters of the monastery and nunnery, and the aged father was the Lama or President of the former.

I wandered on along several other roofs, everywhere received without the slightest shyness or reserve, and even gladly welcomed. One old woman, whose grandchildren I had been caressing, came to me in a very friendly manner, and discoursed to me at great length and with most voluble loquacity: the peroration of her address,—all the rest of which was utterly unintelligible to me,—being loud peals of laughter, in which all her neighbours of both sexes took part. In conclusion, the venerable dame presented me, amid many extraordinary gesticulations, with a bundle of herbs and vegetables from her kitchen garden. I endeavoured, as best I could, to make myself understood by her; but all my efforts only occasioned fresh bursts of laughter; for the language of these people is totally different from the Hindui, no less than from the Hindostani, being known as the *Kunauri* or *Milchan.*

I now bent my steps toward our tent, laden with various species of grain peculiar to this district, for the most part winter corn, bicuspidated barley, wheat of most remarkable beauty, &c. The summer fruits of the earth are peas, vetches, broad Windsor beans, turnips, and oleaginous plants.

Meeting my fellow-travellers on the way, I returned with them straightway, to visit a more distant quarter of the town: we found it all alive with industrious inhabitants, busily engaged in the labours of their harvest-home. They generally use, for carrying in the corn, large baskets, which they bear upon the back; much of it is however also brought in from the terraces on asses. One apparently prosperous and wealthy man,—probably a naturalised foreigner, for he wore a garment of white muslin, and a flat turban instead of the felt cap,—was looking down at the labourers from the roof of his house, giving them directions and imparting his commands. Another party was occupied in treading out the grain with horses, on a spacious threshing-floor, enclosed by a wall. This is the only service that horses are here required to perform; they are never yoked to any vehicle, nor made to bear a saddle: the wild and spirited animals are chased round upon the spread-out corn; a man with a stick hung with little streamers, and another with a long whip, were driving them up and down at a gallop. This mode of threshing makes a fearful dust, and the straw is trodden to nothing.

After wandering along several narrow, dirty lanes, between half-dilapidated walls, and dwellings ornamented with very ancient horns of the bhural and the wild goat, we reached the last row of houses, contiguous to which is a grove of tall juniper-trees. That tree here attains a height of from thirty to forty feet. A long line of sepulchral-looking monuments forms the boundary of this spot; among them stand several of the urns to which I have so often alluded,—one of a brownish yellow, one white, and one black, under the same roof: what these different colours signify, I failed in every attempt to ascertain.

Our attention was attracted by a large edifice at the extremity of the town: it is a hollow square, enclosing a small, open court. An old man with a venerable hoary beard, clad in the ordinary red mantle, and busily engaged in counting his rosary amid muttered prayers, came forward upon the roof and beckoned to us. He made himself known as a head-Lama, and promised to do the honours of the temple to which his dwelling is attached, as soon as he should have finished his devotions. Without much ceremonizing, we accepted his invitation, and, as a preliminary step, descended by the uncouth ladder into the court, to seize the favourable opportunity for seeing the interior of a Kunawuree dwelling. The ground-floor contains only store-rooms and cow-stalls: in the second story, which has a verandah about two feet wide, towards the court, we found an apartment which appeared to be the Lama's state-room, for it contained two rudely-worked chairs and a table;

articles of which he was exceedingly proud. Meantime he was so completely absorbed in his rosary, that he seemed utterly unconscious of our throwing open every door and window-shutter in his house. The plan of the building would have excited our admiration,—being upon the whole both pretty and judiciously devised,—had not all the details been so shabbily and unskilfully executed. Every door and window opens into the inner court. Upon the roof, and on the top of the colonnade which surrounds the court, are little gardens, filled with Iris, Datura, and Tagetes, which find abundant nourishment in the material of the roof.

When at length his prayer admitted of a pause, the aged Lama led us down into the court, by the trunk of a tall tree with steps hewn in it,—the only kind of stair I ever saw in these parts,—drew out a long wooden key, and intimated by a significant and mysterious gesture that we should follow him. The long key opened a large folding door at the bottom of the court, the entrance to the sanctuary or small temple, which, as a great favour, he was about to show us.

What strange and wondrous things did we see crowded together in this darksome hall! The light of heaven glimmers in only through an aperture in the ceiling, and through the open door, the sacred threshold of which we were not allowed to pass. The principal object is a large gilded idol, representing *Mahadeva* whom I should not have expected to find in a Lama temple. The image stands in a sort of shrine, with two open doors painted with golden stars and enclosed in a gilt border; its effect, in this magic and shadowy light, was most unearthly: it was almost the only object that could be distinctly recognized amid the surrounding gloom. A balustrade, hung with red streamers, enclosed the space round it; to its right, lay a multitude of strange instruments apparently of very ancient date,—huge-bellied brazen trumpets, with drums and kettle-drums of most various dimensions; to its left, a number of flags, a great bell, and divers coarsely painted figures of clay. At the first glance, the walls appeared hung with many-coloured paper; but when the eye had become accustomed to the lugubrious shades, we perceived them to be covered with small tablets of unbaked clay, about the size of ordinary Dutch tiles. They are apparently manufactured in a wooden mould, and contain diminutive figures of Buddha, in four different colours, yellow, red, grey and white. In many places, they had fallen off and were lying on the ground; of these the old priest willingly gave us as many as we wished to have; unfortunately however, these works of art are fragile in the extreme. Strange to say, with all his absorbing and long-continued prayer, the aged Lama displayed not the slightest veneration for his gods, but replied to our queries, and gesticulated amid great laughter, ever and anon sinking again into his devout abstraction: moreover, he had evidently reckoned with avaricious longing upon the money he received at parting.

Proceeding, in the twilight of evening, along another and a well-made path, beneath alder and poplar trees, we gradually descended to our encampment. Beside one of the water-courses, we found a numerous group of women, busily engaged in drawing water: they carry it on their backs in a peculiar kind of wooden vessel, constructed with great art of varnished wood, bound with iron hoops, and entirely closed at the top, like a barrel, except the bung-hole: a woollen cord, passing through several rings, serves as a strap for carrying it. Various other vessels of wood also testify to the expertness of the artificers: I saw plates and dishes of the most beautiful veined wood, delicately thin, and very neatly manufactured.

Already the sun had disappeared behind the lofty

mountains which form the western boundary of the valley; a full hour and a half passed away however, before night began her reign; during this interval, we had time enough to enjoy the glorious landscape of the deep valley below adorned with rich trees, and the rugged cliffs opposite, around Labrung, clothed with pine and cedar forests: the tall and ancient tower, domineering, at a height of a thousand feet, over the narrow glen,—the yellow corn-fields, and dark firs,—the long winding path by which, in the morning, we had threaded our way down the steep,—all conspired, in the mellow light of evening, to form a picture, of singular loveliness, in the peculiar blending of stern and smiling features, of bright and sober tints: it was abruptly severed from the heights on the Kanum side, by a ravine the depths of which were hidden from our view.

As the entrance of our tent was turned towards this magnificent highland scene, we enjoyed for a long while the delight of watching the exquisite succession of roseate and of purple hues, until, suddenly, the most clear and splendid starry vault was stretched above the scene, and nearer and more distant objects were alike shrouded in nocturnal gloom.

Our tent-bearers had been long on their march, on the following morning, (the second of August) before we could follow them. The Chief-Lama had announced his intention of honouring us with a meeting, promising at the same time, to exhibit the interior of the great temple, beside which we had encamped. Climbing up the stair-tree, we entered the building by a small, low door, which led us into a long and lofty ante-chamber, washed with yellow paint. On its longest side were doors opening into the temple itself. Here we were met by the Chief-Lama, a figure whose whole appearance and bearing were striking and majestic in the extreme: I felt as though I were beholding one of the philosophers of antiquity, Cato or Seneca himself. Picture to yourself an aged man of tall and stately form, wrapped in the long and ample toga of dark-red wool: his head uncovered, his snow-white locks cut short, while his long and hoary beard flows down upon his breast: the rosary suspended from his girdle, and under his arm a large book.* After saluting the Prince, he opened the doors, so as to afford us a full survey of the whole interior of the temple. Here too, the largest of the many images of the gods was a gilded *Mahadeo*, the other smaller ones being of stone or of bronze. To the right and left stood large, green, varnished cabinets, painted in gold, with a number of drawers, containing manuscripts: a multitude of mystic objects filled the remaining space. Unfortunately, it was impossible to make ourselves intelligible to our kind and venerable friend; for, besides the language of this district being unknown equally to our interpreters and to ourselves, his deafness precluded even the slightest attempt at conversation.

Would that I could yet have found among the living, the celebrated Hungarian sage, *Alexander Czosma de Körös,* who passed several years at Kanum as a hermit! We were often asked about him, for he is still well known in this mountain region by the name of "*Sikander Saheb.*"

We found here again the same clay tablets employed

* It is commonly asserted, as mentioned by Mr Hamilton, that the art of printing, that mighty engine of good and of evil, has from a very remote period been practised in Thibet, though so limited in its use by the influence of superstition, that it has not undergone any improvement. Copies of the religious books of Lama-worship are multiplied, not by moveable types but by means of set forms of the nature of stereotype, which are impressed on thin slips of paper of Thibetian fabrication. The alphabet and character are acknowledged to be derived from the Sanscrit. It is a general belief throughout Thibet, that the arts and sciences had their origin in the holy city of Benares, which, as well as other Indian places of pilgrimage, is much venerated and not unfrequently visited by the devout Thibetians. Although religious ceremonies of every kind are performed exclusively by the Lamas and Gylongs, the laity are not restricted from the study of their sacred books.—Tr.

in lining the wall; on each of them are six or seven figures of Buddha: they were distributed among us with the greatest liberality. With trembling hand the aged prelate closed the doors of his sanctuary once more, when he observed that we had derived, from the view of its inner wonders, all the edification that we desired; forthwith, after the farewell salutations, we proceeded on our journey.

It seemed as though the fields of Kanum had vanished beneath our tread, when, ere long, we found ourselves once more in a dreary, desolate waste. After a quarter of an hour's march, we re-entered the valley of the Sutlej; on its brink the path winds up from height to height. Few and faint are the traces of vegetation visible on those arid rocks; here and there only, a miserable-looking Neoza pine,—sad, leafless wormwood,—or a few stunted bushes of thorny *Astragalus*. Both banks of the river look as though they had but just issued from some fiery furnace: scorched and naked, the rude cliffs stand forth amid boundless masses of débris, which resemble gigantic heaps of ashes: Nowhere refreshing shade,—nowhere a trace of verdure,—the very water of the river, which laves the base of those high and rocky ridges at a great depth below, seems to have lost its fertilizing power.

It is an awful solitude: all nature is still and deathlike: to add to the wild melancholy of the scene, the acclivities are all so steep that not a single vestige of a path trod by foot of man is ever to be found. On the uncertain surface of those loose, shattered fragments, the wanderer's footstep leaves no mark behind. Blocks of stone and masses of rock, nicely poised, roll down beneath his tread. Woe to him that lingers there! With rapid and restless pace that brooks no tarrying, the traveller must pursue his giddy way,—ever forward, forward! lest he be precipitated, amid the falling wreck, into the deep abyss! The rattling and rumbling of detached stones was a music which accompanied us through all the long day. Some few parts of the rocky precipices were so abrupt, so polished by the attrition of constantly tumbling débris, that we were obliged to hew steps in them, before we could venture to pass on.

The sum total of the wretched plants that drag on a miserable existence on these sterile crags, amounted, during our first hour and a half, to only seven. One rose was actually to be seen there, and flowering even in this wilderness; the most frequent sign of vegetable life however, was a species of white worm-wood, so mean and wizened that from the opposite bank it was not to be descried.

Still we were ever ascending higher and higher; the burning sun and the depressing influence of a desert such as this, produced languor and exhaustion more speedily than an ordinary march. It was not till we had almost gained the summit of the ridge which separated us from one of the lateral vallies of the Sutlej, that some measure of brightness and of spirit enlivened us once more. There is, on the highest point, a spring,—the only one on the whole way,—the first sight of which was hailed by our coolies and heavy-laden damsels with shouts of joy: nevertheless its waters are very bitter, and strongly impregnated with copper. An abundance of copper ore is visible on the surface of the rock near this spot; carbonate of copper effloresces from the yellow-tinged clay-slate, and the ground is covered with calcareous spar and light calcareous stone. The moisture had however, notwithstanding this richness of the mineral world, called forth a somewhat more prolific vegetation. The *Epilobium* (willow herb) delighted me as recalling home, in spite of its being surrounded on all sides by prickly steppe-plants, dwarf Acacias, and a species of laurel-like Daphne.

We allowed our coolies time for refreshment and repose, and hastened forward to the head of the pass, which we gained after a short ascent. It is, according to usual custom, decorated with poles and many-coloured streamers. From this high point we distinctly saw the little river ROPA or RUSKALONG, which we were soon to cross: but oh! at what a tremendous depth! The path, scarcely distinguishable, runs down an almost perpendicular steep covered with mountain-wreck: now leaping, now sliding, we scrambled down: however, even at a distance of only eight hundred feet below the summit, the descent becomes somewhat easier; once more our feet found firm ground on which to rest, and numerous flowers,—*Asters*, *Delphinium* and *Papaver*, resembling our own, yet appearing in a foreign form,—clothe the less rugged spots. Half-way down the mountain, at a height of fifteen hundred feet, a beautiful forest of *Cheel* and *Neoza* pines commences; in it we found, occupied in hewing down a few stems, the thirty carpenters whom we had sent on before-hand to construct the bridge: they received a well-merited castigation, for they had been despatched with the Zemindar on the morning of the preceding day, so that the bridge ought to have been completed, instead of which they had loitered so long by the way that they had arrived only just before we did.

Meantime, leaving them to their dilatory proceedings, we descended the last thousand feet, where difficulties again awaited us, as the lower part of the mountain is very steep, and consists of smooth, yellow granite, and quartz-rock; our course was moreover frequently interrupted by precipitous chasms and gullies, cut by snow-torrents. The slope immediately on the banks of the river here, as on those of all the more considerable streams among these mountains, consists of perpendicular ramparts of great height, so that it was found utterly impossible to approach the channel of the river, far more to build a bridge: and not a trace of bridge-building was to be seen,—not a single tree had even been brought down to the water's edge.

There was here but one route by which we could descend. It consisted of the remains of an avalanche, which in spring had choked up the bed of the river, and had hitherto served as a bridge. Unfortunately this mass of debacles had recently fallen in, and one gigantic tower of snow was now left standing alone on either side; even these mighty piers of the quondam bridge had been partly washed away by the current at their base, while the glowing sun above, no less fatal a destroyer, caused the melted particles to trickle down their sides. We descended with great difficulty on these wet and dirty banks of snow, and when all was done, we found ourselves at the very margin of the river indeed, but without any means of transit across its rapid waters. We were constrained, on account of the distance from the wood, and of the difficulty of transport, to relinquish all idea of bringing down timber and beams for building; ropes of sufficient length too were wanting, and if we had had them, they must have proved useless by reason of the frowning crags on the opposite shore. At length a huge cedar-stem, torn down by the rushing avalanche, was disentangled, and one grand effort was put forth to drag it to the narrowest part of the stream; after long and arduous labour, in the course of which we were all drenched to the skin, and covered with black mud, we were forced to abandon this plan also; for the tree became deeply imbedded in the sand, and no power of ours could move it from the spot. In this dilemma, we at last learned that a better place for constructing a bridge was to be found elsewhere; for actually our pioneers had been too indolent even to obtain proper information regarding the locality.

In order to reach the spot pointed out to us, we were obliged to clamber up an abrupt cliff, then to ascend a steep acclivity, several hundred feet in height, and covered with loose fragments of rock, and finally, to scale a conical mass of granite, without the slightest vestige of a path. The slope of loose debris was expected to present the most insuperable obstacle: it proved otherwise; the blocks of stone did not yield beneath our feet, and when we reached the granite rock above, we found flat ledges and narrow fissures enough, so that, clambering up with hands and feet, we did at last gain the top of the cone, just in time to guide our coolies,—who were at that moment coming up,—to the right course by our shouts.

The second spot selected for the passage of the river, seemed, at any rate, less dangerous than the first; for although the stream, fifty feet across, dashes its raging billows through the narrow gorge, a solid pier presents itself in the midst of its eddy, in the shape of a huge mass of rock. If it be but possible to gain that point, all is safe; for it lies not very far from the opposite shore: unfortunately however, it offers no jutting corners, but presents, on the side towards which we descended, a smooth face of from sixteen to twenty feet in height. Without delay we proceeded to the work of building; there was no time to lose; for already, in the depths of this contracted defile, the shades of twilight were threatening to overtake us: each coolie must needs give a helping hand; stones were collected, and trees hewn down and driven into the bed of the river.

The work advanced more rapidly than I had expected. As soon as a few firm points in the stream had been secured, the rock in its centre was, with the assistance of a hastily-made ladder, speedily gained; from it a second rock was reached by means of a short bridge laid across, and thence the opposite bank itself was attained. At each hazardous spot, one of our party seated himself, to stretch out a helping hand to the *coolies* and *coolias*, and thus bring them safely across. After three hours of very arduous toil, the whole party and the whole baggage were on the further side. But we were still far from our station of Chasoo; a steep acclivity rose in front of us, and when, with much difficulty and fatigue, we reached its top, we found ourselves deluded, again and again, by a false hope, as, at each turn of the path, we expected to see the village immediately before us.

At length however it did appear,—like a green oasis in the rocky desert at our feet. What a refreshment for our weary eyes and limbs!

The last part of our descent was a well-made stair, of many hundred steps, hewn in the living rock. At its lower extremity, begin the apricot-gardens, vine-bowers and rich meadows. The village herds were returning slowly homeward as evening drew on,—a scene of rural charm seldom witnessed among these mountains.

CHASOO is a village of about forty houses, one of the most sequestered retreats to which we penetrated. Its dwellings,—one of which was given up to us for our night's quarters,—are neat and pretty. We pitched our tent on the flat roof, the coolies taking possession of the interior. The tops of the other houses, all equally flat, extend, in terraces, for at least a hundred feet down towards the smiling dale, where the lowest are concealed amid vine-clad bowers; on many of them, red and white flags and yak-tails, fastened to long poles, are seen waving in the air, while wooden "*Chokhdens,*" painted yellow, gray, or white, are placed here and there, by the way-side.

There was no lack of varied refreshment here; raisins, apricots and new milk, were brought in greater abundance than we could make away with; and the multitude of Chinese goods offered for sale gave evidence of a frequent and busy traffic with Thibet: a much-frequented pass leads hence through the mountain barrier to that country. The costume of the inhabitants, moreover, bears a close resemblance to that of the Chinese; some of the men even wearing cues of false hair. The purchases made from among the variety of wares of all sorts, were a piece of beautiful dark-blue Chinese silken stuff, and two silver tobacco-pipes: very pretty silver ornaments are also to be had here.

I regretted exceedingly that our stay at this place was so short; for in this remote river-glen, there are many rare and very remarkable plants, which never met my eyes again: however, we were on our march at break of day on the 3d of August, as we had a very long journey before us.

Instead of having reached better paths, we found ourselves, alas! immediately after leaving the little rivulet of Chasoo, once more in a wild and naked wilderness. Bare rocks of polished slate, now obstructing our path in the shape of large slabs or huge detached blocks,—now again, shivered into fragments and weathered almost to disintegration, forming vast mounds of débris, —were the only feature of the strange, chaotic scene around: gray, parched worm-wood, and here and there a dwarfed and crippled pine, alone marked that vegetation had not actually expired. Add to this, that our path continued uninterruptedly to ascend, though still never affording the slightest view; even the Ruskalong river, whose course we were following to re-enter the valley of the Sutlej, was hidden from our eyes; for we were too high up, on the rocky ramparts that hem in the stream, and its banks too steep and contracted. The view of the Sutlej, which burst upon us at the end of a two hours' march, brought little or no variety to the dreary landscape; for its yellowish gray waters flow on, devoid of anything like picturesque charm, between arid and monotonous rocks.

The only object which now by its beauty gladdened our weary eyes, was the magnificent chain of snowy mountains, which, on reaching the highest point of the ridge, where we began to descend towards the valley of the Sutlej, suddenly lay extended before us.

Our route continued along the banks of the river, in a north-easterly direction; we were some eighteen hundred feet or so above its waters, and yet so near the brink that we could cast a stone into its pools. But soon the few faint traces of a path disappeared; we followed our guide in silence, as he stepped forward, deeply imprinting his wary footsteps, and searching for unyielding spots of ground or firm and solid stones. Often we were obliged, in order to turn the flank of a smooth and perpendicular face of rock, to slide down several hundred feet; often again our way led us over the jagged edge of a projecting cliff, overhanging the deep and rugged gorge. In many places the only possible means by which we could advance, was to lie flat on our faces, and thus glide down, while the guide directed our feet, and another attendant held us firmly by the neck. Our "Alpen-stocks" were nearly useless, as we were forced to use both hands to help ourselves.

Thus sliding in every variety of posture, standing, sitting, lying prostrate, proving each stone before we ventured upon it, or,—when the pioneer with a bold spring had precipitated into the depth the entire layer of loose earth over which our course lay,—rummaging out, with the points of our poles, hollows in the wall of rock which might serve as props on which to rest our weight, we advanced in a most tedious and unpleasant manner; and the continual view of the open abyss, ready to swallow us up together with the rolling débris, was so overwhelming, that at each tolerably secure spot, we sank down faint and exhausted. The glare of the sun however soon drove on the weary traveller from his rest,—still forward, forward,—once more to attempt this hazardous exploit.

Those parts in which we had to scramble down over loose débris were decidedly worse than all the rest; for there, the stones, detached by those who followed, rolled downwards on the advanced guard of our party.

For six long hours our path proceeded after this fashion. How we one and all passed so prosperously over the dangerous spots,—the very remembrance of which still makes me shudder,—and still more, how the heavy-laden bearers passed over them without breaking their necks, is to me a complete enigma. It was one of the most arduous days of our whole travels, and one the perils of which I would not willingly go through again.'

We saw our day's goal for some time before us; but at the same time we saw also the whole length of road we had yet to traverse, extended in full view like a white streak along the blackish gray rock. Our toilsome, rope-dancing journey was still far from having reached its conclusion; the last bit was, however, far less formidable, and we marched forward in silent resignation, winding along a succession of projecting rocks and bold sweeps of the river.

One sharp and beetling cliff, an almost black schistose formation, whose funereal hue and shattered form completed the chaotic character of the scene, required the putting forth of our last energies to scale its height: the noon-day sun was glowing fiercely, the air was sultry and oppressive, and dark thunder-clouds were towering in the horizon.

To our great joy we perceived the north-eastern side of the pass to be somewhat less steep and desolate; there, at least, were some few grasses and parched steppe-plants. Before us to the north-east, lay the emerald oasis of the village of Pooa, our appointed resting-place, situated on a hill on the opposite side of a narrow glen traversed by a small stream. In the fore-ground, we marked another village, that of Kora, or Kor, at the extremity of a little plain, into which the north-eastern declivity of the pass juts out. The whole tract of land at our feet, rich with vegetation, appeared one uninterrupted garden, watered by many rivulets: high walls, surmounted by luxuriant hedges, form at once the boundary-line of the wilderness and the enclosure of fruitful corn-fields. Within two hours we reached the plain of Kora, and, overcome by fatigue, resolved to pitch our tents in this paradise. Thick, velvety turf, and the shade of very ancient apricot-trees, invited us to repose: we had only to touch the trees, to have showered upon us a redundant supply of ripe and delicious fruit; milk too, and cakes baked in the ashes, were soon brought in liberal profusion by the hospitable inhabitants. Beautiful butterflies and many other insects were swarming round the beds of flowers on the margins of the brooks, whereas, on yonder heights, I had seen not a trace of any living creature,—not a bird, not a lizard, not an insect of any kind. My entomological chase occupied me, in spite of my exhaustion, until, as twilight rapidly drew on, the tent arrived: it was pitched in the midst of the apricot-grove, and our dinner was speedily prepared.

We were soon surrounded by a throng of the inhabitants, attired completely after the fashion of Thibet. The profusion of amber ornaments, and the brownish red of all their garments, the thoroughly Thibetian complexion, the general use of boots and trowsers, even among the women, which prevails from this place forward, all mark the influence of the manners and customs of Thibet. The men wear skull-caps, sandals or high cloth boots, and a bread belt round the red vestment, in which are stuck a knife, a pipe, a spoon, and a number of other little articles. The only thing which distinguishes the women's costume, is the absence of the belt and the manner of wearing the hair, which, divided into numberless thin plaits, and interlaced with coral, shells, amber, and silver bells, hangs down like a sort of net-work upon the back.

The Tartar physiognomy is by no means very predominant; and although the noses are generally somewhat broad, and the cheek-bones large and prominent, yet I saw some faces which, in any country, would be acknowledged to be pretty and expressive. The figures are slender and yet athletic, resembling those of the inhabitants of the valley of the Buspa, near Sungla.

Through the evening, the whole population, having flocked together from far and near, sat in strange groups around our tent, perfectly satisfied with the simple permission to gaze to their hearts' content at the new and unwonted visitants. Whether we, in our semi-European costumes, appeared the more wonderful to them, or they to us, in their thick, stiff, woollen garb, tricked out with finery and hung with fantastic ornaments from top to toe, it were difficult to decide. The whole night long, these friendly people, ever wakeful, ever mirthful, bivouacked around their fire; a constant joyousness reigned among them, and their hours flew on amid laughter and singing.

Our departure, on the 4th of August, was, as had been our arrival on the 3rd, a universal fête. The path was enlivened by numbers of blithe and merry women, maidens, and children; and the male population escorted us as far as the river,—at least an hour and a half's walk,—and even there parted from us only one by one. The women remained on the vine-clad hills commanding our path, singing in clear but plaintive tones, "*Tantun ne re ho!*" which, I understand, signifies, "*happy journey!*" The kindly salutation was still heard resounding, long after the songstresses had vanished from our eyes.

We left the village of Pooa to our left hand; it lies at no great distance from Kora, and the vineyards of the two places, which clothe the lowest hollow of the vale, are all but contiguous, so that the whole landscape, as far as the Sutlej, seems like a continued fruit garden.

The river-glen itself, which we entered at the end of our second hour, loses, from this point upwards, much of its desert, chaotic character: the mural precipices rising from the water's edge are less steep and lofty, and the higher mountain-ridges recede further from the channel of the stream. Consequently, we here found some few green shrubs, and occasional solitary pines and juniper-trees; and even the grisly worm-wood, the ordinary clothing of the masses of loose stones, assumes a somewhat fresher hue.

In order to reach the left bank, we crossed the celebrated bridge of Namtoo, the only one on all this route: there are indeed but three bridges thrown over the raging Sutlej throughout the whole extent of upper Kunawur: this one derives its appellation from a place of the same name, which however is not situated upon our route. It is built of strong hewn beams, which must unquestionably have been brought hither from a distance of six or seven days' march. When this is taken into consideration, it may really be pronounced to be a wonderful work, and the merit of the Chinese, who gave a large sum for its construction, deserves to be recorded with high praise. In length, the bridge measures eighty-two paces: seven beams, laid longitudinally and parallel with each other, without parapet or rails, form the middle part, swinging at a height of some seventy or eighty feet above the stream. As all bridges, even the smallest, among the Himalayas, are stretched across the water at a great elevation, on account of its being regularly in flood in spring, so this one also is supported at either end, by a somewhat rude and primitive but most firm and substantial tête-de-pont; the descent to which, from the path along the cliffs, is by a steep flight of steps. Several layers of strong beams are fixed in a slanting position on the projecting crag, their lower extremities being well secured in the wall of masonry, while their upper ones advance boldly over the river. Upon the end of the longest and highest of these, the beams of the bridge itself are loosely laid, their other ends resting on a similar sub-structure on the opposite bank,—the most simple mode of constructing a bridge, so as perfectly to answer the purpose for which it is intended, viz., securing to the foot-passenger a safe transit; some caution however is necessary in the middle, owing to the violent vibrations of the long beams.

We proceeded, on the left bank, at first through loose gravel, which soon however again gives place to clay-slate; the soil is here intersected by numerous brooks, not, like those we had seen lower down, rushing over precipices in foaming cascades, but fertilizing the gentle slopes by their spreading moisture. Their channels are bordered by beautiful flowering plants; *Asters, Campanulas*, and a species of *Lonicera:* the juniper forming a tall copse, and here and there attaining the height of a tree.

After four hours' march, on tolerably level paths, we entered the deep dell of a rivulet which, at its junction with the Sutlej, forms in its valley a creek, some two thousand paces or so in width. To make the circuit of this, we ascended the lateral slope of the mountain, and immediately found ourselves within the cultivated lands of the village of DUBLING. This place must not be confounded with DABLING, which lies farther to the south-west: the district generally is one of the richest in this stony and unfruitful land.

The whole of the female inhabitants were, at the time of our arrival, busily engaged in the wheat fields; peas, millet, three varieties of barley, and a small, peculiarly well-flavoured Swedish turnip, called "*Njumah*," are also cultivated here: still however the great source of wealth is the apricot. That fruit grows in such lavish abundance that the flat roofs no longer suffice to hold the crop, the overplus of which is stored on the surface of the fields after the harvest-home; and every path and stile is rendered slippery by the numbers inevitably trampled down.

As we entered the village, the people, especially the women and children, assembled in crowds, and received us with loud shouts. These mountaineers of the Sutlej are certainly the blithest folk I ever saw, garrulous, unsuspicious and friendly, yet not troublesome by their importunate intrusions, like the natives of Chinese Thibet. Nevertheless they were not to be withheld from examining our goods and chattels and our every article of raiment, nor from prying even into our pockets,—each new discovery causing a fresh burst of laughter. Meantime, I thus enjoyed an opportunity of sketching many of the prettier women with their children; on seeing that I rewarded with a trifling coin the virtue of sitting still, they all pressed eagerly forward, although at first my mysterious designs had excited some anxiety.

The costume here is extremely curious: loose trowsers of their brownish-red woollen stuff, woven by the villagers themselves, form the principal part of it: a load of amber, ("*Poshoo*") glass beads and amulets, pendent in countless strings round the neck, and falling over the breast and back, is never missing in any female figure; equally indispensable are the long plaits of sized hair, which, to the number of forty or fifty, hang down the back, while the men adorn the head behind with a long, flowing tail, either of their own hair or of brown wool: the children and youths usually dispense with any such ornament.

The women are all distinguished by an uncommonly sweet voice, which often contrasts strangely with the broad, square face. Their singing is melodious, and their language too has a much softer sound than the "*Miltshan*" dialect of lower Kunawur, or the positively harsh one of Sungnum, called the "*Tebarskad;*" for here the *Bhootea* language is already spoken, which bears a great resemblance to that of Thibet.

While I was busily engaged with my drawing, the crowd had pressed nearer and nearer to me, and when I rose up, my last silk pocket-handkerchief was gone! It really pained me, on account of the pleasing kindliness of these people, to find myself disappointed in their honesty; but the love of stealing seems to be a main feature in the character of every Mongolian tribe. Among the high mountains of lower Kunawur, the traveller may leave everything he has, open and unwatched, without the slightest fear, provided only he is sure of the faithfulness of his own attendants.

In the evening we had a delightful walk through the fields: wherever we went, the villagers sought out and presented to us the ripest and finest apricots. Their dwellings, into which we obtained access without any difficulty, have, for the most part, court-yards inclosed within stone walls. In almost every court we saw the industrious inhabitants engaged in the labours of the harvest-season, with which they frequently unite the performance of strange ceremonies. I saw two women in one court winnowing corn, seizing the moment when the wind was in their favour: beside them stood a censer, round which, as often as a sieve-full had been shaken out, they circled three times with slow and measured step, strewing cypress leaves upon it, and waving over it a large bunch of cypress twigs, after which they resumed their work.

The houses rest on basements of masonry, and the ascent to the low door-way is by means of a stair-tree. One enters at once into a large room, the remaining space of the lower story being devoted to stalls for the cattle. The whole family, if not employed on the roof, may generally be found gathered together in this apartment, seated on boards. The women spin or wind the wool, to prepare it for the loom which, with a hand-mill, a few wooden bowls, and some vessels of earthenware, form the sum total of household furniture in this their public room. The indolent partners of their home pursue meanwhile their sole occupation,—to wit, smoking tobacco. In one wall of this room are the entrances to the gloomy dungeons which serve as bed-chambers. Unfortunately, these good people appear to have not the slightest idea of cleanliness. I could not resist leading one dear little, lovely, black-eyed boy to the edge of the brook, and washing his face, which extraordinary proceeding caused universal merriment and laughter. The little presents of pins and glass beads, packets of which I carried about with me, were received with joyous acclamations by young and old.

A tree with steps hewn in it,—sometimes indeed there are several such stairs,—leads to the upper story, or else directly to the roof. The former contains the store-rooms, at once granaries, and dépôts of dried pulse.

We perambulated the dwellings from the court-yard to the house-top, without the inmates manifesting any particular concern, the most they ever did being to laugh at our curiosity. It really did my heart good to find myself no longer regarded, as in the low lands of India, as a wild beast, whose impure touch would contaminate the abode and render it uninhabitable. The cringing, servile Hindoo of the plains, and of the lower range of hills, who will endure the grossest maltreatment in silence, says,—if one approaches too near his house,—quite openly, though with folded hands and head bending in deepest reverence, "Prince, *('Maharajah,')* 'Saheb,' thou wilt pollute the house of thy slave; have the kindness to depart!"

On our return, we found the tent, which had been pitched on a tilled field inclosed between hedges of syringa, decorated with flowers: a number of little children, bearing large bouquets which they had gathered for us, were waiting at the tent-door. All manner of fruit too,—currants, and a species of Cornelian cherry *("Munjili")* in particular, of an agreeable sourish taste,—were brought to us in abundance. Other little ones were busily providing our cooks with fire-wood, without making the slightest claim to remuneration for their kind offices.

The village of Dubling consists of some twenty houses, of architecture simple indeed but very much to the purpose. Many long stone dykes or piles of stone tablets, bearing Lama inscriptions, and well-preserved Chokhdens, testify to the piety of the inhabitants. Ranged beside the latter objects of superstition, I found small cakes of brown meal, in which was fixed a circle of small lighted sticks; grains of every variety of corn were also scattered among them: all this must certainly have some religious import: may it not possibly be intended as a sort of sacrifice?

The Sutlej is not visible from this place; we first caught sight of it again on the following day, (the 5th of August) after we had quitted the apricot groves and meadow-lands of the village. Very near our road lay the hamlet of DABLING, into which, misled by the similarity of its name, a portion of our troop of coolies had wandered on the preceding day; for, in the indistinct enunciation of these parts, Dubling and Dabling are almost identical in sound. At the latter place we remarked "*Manneh-paddehungs*" of dimensions such as we had never before met with: one of them is five hundred paces in length and six in breadth. Its upper surface is entirely covered with well-chiselled slabs of slate, several of which bear the usual inscriptions, in white characters on a red or a yellow ground.

We continued to thread our way close beside the banks of the Sutlej, whose waters are of a dark greenish yellow hue; the granite soon re-appeared, but only in detached fragments; the opposite rampart of the river-glen continued for some time to present a face of schistose rock; gradually however, the granite began to predominate, becoming at last a compact formation, with gray gneiss occasionally occurring in it, and intersected by numerous radii of blue zeolite.

The opposite bank is an almost perpendicular mural precipice, a thousand feet high, of gray granite, traversed by numerous veins of quartz from four to six feet in thickness, which cross each other in all directions. Each little snow-stream, after flowing gently down from the lofty rounded summits, suddenly plunges in one unbroken cascade from the edge of the rugged cliff into the dark, turbid waters of the river.

We ascended some eight hundred feet higher above the Sutlej, before we obtained a view of the vine-bowers and apricot gardens of the small village of Khab. The rumour of our approach had already spread even in this retreat: we had been described as giants with long, black beards; consequently, the inhabitants were waiting at the entrance of the village, on the tiptoe of expectation, to catch the first sight of these monstrous foreigners. Among them were many women in the red costume of China: they were decked out with a thousand different sorts of ornaments; amber and chank shells, lapis lazuli, turquoises, *("Jugate")* and opals, *("Njapchi")* all were hung about them as trinkets. Necklaces here often consist of many-coloured glass resembling agate, imported from Thibet. We were again presented with apricots and "*Khutai;*" garlands of flowers also, consisting of red and yellow tagetes and double hollyhocks, were lavished upon us.

The village is situated on a sharp projecting angle of rock, close to the junction of the Thibetian river LEE with the Sutlej, which is here called the GUHE. A woman led us through her farm-yard to a spot whence we enjoyed a nearer view of the confluence of the two streams. Each of them dashes furiously along between almost closing precipices of gray rock, forming by their collision a tremendous whirlpool: nevertheless, in spite of this tumultuous commingling, the separate colouring of their waters,—the yellowish green of the Guhé and the grayish blue of the Lee,—may be distinctly traced to a considerable distance. The rocky banks of the latter appear no less rugged than those of the Sutlej, and still more desolate.

Ascending through fields of wheat and "*phapur,*" we reached a grove of large and ancient Neoza pines; beneath their shade is a sacred spot, marked as such by the Lama inscriptions and patches of red paint on the detached masses of rock. Here we were once more greeted by the solemn salutations of aged, hoary-bearded Lamas, and presented by them with flowers, fruit and tobacco; marks of hospitality and respect for which they did not fail to demand some remuneration. In the evening we pitched our camp on one of the cultivated terraces of the village of NAMDJA *(Namgiah)*, from which we were separated by the dell of a little rivulet. In a field close beside us, the inhabitants were busily engaged in agricultural labours: the wooden plough was drawn by yak-oxen, which one man was guiding by the nose, while the other was directing the plough: the women and children following to hoe the ploughed ground, singing sweetly as they moved along. The *yak-ox*,—generally of a black colour,—is the ordinary domestic animal here. Those used for ploughing are ugly and short-legged, and hold their heads very low; the beautiful long silky hair hanging from below the belly is almost, if not entirely, wanting in them, no less than the bushy tail, which their avaricious owners commonly cut off, as an article of trade. The yak-ox used in riding is an infinitely handsomer animal; it has a stately hump, a rich, silky hanging, nearly reaching the ground, twisted horns, a noble bearing, and an erect head.

From Namdja we at length succeeded in crossing the frontier of Thibet; however, I must now conclude this epistle, which, unfortunately, I have been obliged to write in great haste. You will, at any rate, be able to form from it a tolerably distinct idea of the mode of travelling among the Himalayas, and a more or less vivid picture of some regions hitherto but little known.

TWELFTH LETTER.

NAMDJA—YAK-OXEN—DESOLATE REGION ON THE SUTLEJ—FRONTIER OF THIBET — VIEW FROM THE HEAD OF THE PASS—SHIPKEE—THE THIBETIANS—THIBETIAN PHYSICIANS — KJOK—VILLAGE POPULATION — RETURN — SANGHO OVER THE SUTLEJ—NAKO—ITS TEMPLE—THE IDOLS—LEEO—HANG—SUNGNUM—SINGING—VALLEY OF THE RUSKALONG—SALT TRADE—CHEENEE—MEROO—BEE-HIVES—URNEE—CHIGAON—HOUSES OF THE VILLAGE—THE WANGTOO BRIDGE—BEAUTIFUL FOREST—TRANDA—VEGETATION OF THE VALLEY OF THE SUTLEJ—SERAN—BATHING-PLACE—VISIT OF THE RAJAH OF BISSAHIR—VISIT TO HIM IN RETURN—GOORA—THE RAJAH'S SUMMER RESIDENCE — RAMPOOR—KOTGHUR—THE MISSIONARIES—NAGKANDA—SIMLA—ITS INHABITANTS—THE COURSE—NUMEROUS TRAIN OF DOMESTICS—HOTEL—VIEW OF THE PLACE—BAL MASQUE—CHURCH—FETE CHAMPETRE—DEPARTURE.

SIMLA, *23d of September,* 1845.

AFTER repeated unsuccessful attempts, His Royal Highness succeeded, on the 6th of August, in traversing the boundary of Thibet; not indeed at the place originally contemplated, but in a highly interesting part of the country; and thus we actually penetrated within the barriers of the Celestial Empire!

Four sturdy yak-oxen stood in readiness for us to mount their woolly backs; the baggage-sheep were saddled and packed, and a merry band of village dames and maidens, all clad in the loose red trowsers, were bustling about with the remainder of our luggage, amid incessant laughter and singing. The men, on the frontier and in Thibet, act as bearers only when forced to do so; and the whole burden of agricultural and of domestic toils they also leave to the women. It was a matter of some difficulty to gain a firm seat on the backs of our novel steeds, caparisoned with our Greek capotes by way of saddles; for they are very shy, and kick with their hind-feet, turning their heads round perpetually, as if about to gore their riders. About half-past nine o'clock, we set out on our expedition, leaving behind us the apricot-groves of Namdja, and thus bidding farewell to the last oasis in the desert of rocks and of débris through which the Sutlej forces its way.

Although our path appeared, from a distance, to be extremely dangerous, it proved quite sufficiently firm and level for our broad-footed yak-oxen, noble beasts with the thick, silky, white fringe under the body, and the bushy tail, both of which sweep the ground: but soon the steepness increased so much that these poor animals began to groan, or rather grunt,* in the most melancholy manner, and this unearthly music gradually rose to such a violent rattle, that,—driven rather by its irksome sound than by the discomfort of our saddleless seats,—we dismounted at the end of the first half-hour.

How dreary, yet how imposing, is the prospect of those rude, steep, rocky masses of shattered slate, between which the roaring Thibetian river thunders its dark yellow waves. Not a shrub, not a green herb to gladden the eye; as far as it can reach, nothing is seen but rock after rock, tumbled together in wild ruins, or frowning in stern crags, descending in deep and startling precipices, or towering,—if indeed the mist allows a glimpse of those stupendous heights,—into bold mountain peaks and lofty pinnacles, crowned with everlasting snow.

* From this peculiar sound the animal derives its name of *Bos grunniens;* by some naturalists it is designated the *Bos poephagus*. Besides the important article of trade furnished by the yak-oxen in their tails, which are sold in all parts of India as chowries, and as ornamental trappings for horses and elephants, and commonly used in Persia and Turkey for standards, dyed crimson and known under the name of horse-tails, they are valued by the natives of Thibet for their long hair, used in the manufacture of tents, ropes, &c., and for their rich and abundant milk.—Tr.

The narrow path winds, for several hours, along the ramparts of the gorge,—which consist of yellowish-gray débris,—at a level of from five to eight hundred feet above the channel of the river; frequently interrupted by deep and rugged hollows, constraining us to make great circuits. Beside the brooks,—which indeed are by no means numerous,—I found a number of interesting plants: the region of snow is also encircled by a belt of verdure; but unfortunately, beyond the compass of the snow-streams, this fresh vegetation abruptly terminates, and nothing is left but that parched, cheerless wormwood, and some few dwarf cypresses.

We were now mounting higher and higher: suddenly we halted on the brink of a perpendicular chasm, cleft in the rocky bulwark of the river-glen by the little brook Koopsung or Oopsung. We descended to the water's edge, a depth of from four to five hundred feet, by a steep flight of steps hewn in the living rock, a difficult descent, and more particularly so to our yak-oxen. This rivulet, which leaps down into the Sutlej in beautiful cascades, afforded us the refreshment of pure water, a circumstance worthy of note, since we found drinkable water only twice on this tour. In the hollow beside its margin we found, lying down to rest, a flock of Thibetian goats and sheep, laden with Cashmere wool ("*Lena*") and Shawl-wool ("*Uhn*") packed in sacks laid across their backs. We were now upon the great road leading from Ladak through Thibet.

Turning back on gaining the height on the further side of the ravine, we beheld the whole procession of female bearers, only then winding down the long stair. One plant after another here presented itself; at first only prickly steppe-plants, but presently roses, willowherb and gentians; for we were, while ascending higher and higher still, approaching nearer and nearer to the snow-line, and to the pass which defends the boundary of the Celestial Empire. The clay-slate, which had hitherto accompanied us, altogether disappears here, and makes way for a yellow granite, huge masses of which form the summit of the pass: between these, the ground is covered with a wide-spreading and thorny furze,—species of *Genista* and *Astragalus*.

From the top of an immense block of granite, we commanded, for the first time, a panoramic view of the plains of Thibet. Below us extended a countless succession of mountain ranges, each one loftier than the more distant one beyond; the last gentle wave of this mighty ocean of hills dying away, in the remote horizon, into a broad, straight line,—the first we had seen for many a long day; it was the elevated table-land of Thibet.

The wild and rugged character of the banks of the Sutlej had now passed away: and we here found its waters flowing between softly sloping hills, still however as naked and sombre, as monotonously gray, as those over which we had passed before: only in the depths of the little vallies did we here and there see a verdant stretch of flourishing wheat fields, and a group of flat-roofed houses enbosomed in an apricot grove: far as the eye could reach, no forest was to be seen. Yet these bare and desert ranges of hills had a beauty, a charm, which I know not whether to attribute to the exquisite radiance shed over them by the gorgeous illumination of the western sky, to the mysterious and spell-bound unknown that lay concealed beyond, or to the exciting feeling that we were on the very threshold of the Celestial Empire.

Our resting-place, the frontier village of SHIPKEE, was not yet visible; but we could descry three or four more distant villages, and could follow,—alas! with our eyes only,—a path winding across the barren mountain-ridges, into the interior of that hidden land. How much did I envy the lämmergeiers the freedom of their flight, as, poised in mid-air, they circled high above our heads!

To our left towered the majestic Purkyul, with its thousand sharp cones and pinnacles, like some gigantic Termites-hill: the greater part of it was covered with snow.

We descended from this commanding point by gentle zigzags, through tall bushes of furze, the home of a multitude of partridges and of small mountain-hares *(Lagomys)*;* and in two hours we arrived at Shipkee: the last portion of the way only was fatiguing from its steepness.

The village, built in the form of a semi-circle round the valley of a little rivulet, lies in the centre of a wood of apricot-trees, amid the tender verdure of rich fields, which, by means of skilful irrigation, are made to bear two crops yearly. The houses,—from twenty to thirty in number, and many of them very ruinous,—stand about two hundred feet above the river, which here bears the name of LUNG,—a name however which the natives seem unwilling to pronounce.

We had heard much of the rude inhospitality of the Thibetians; but nothing occurred in our own experience to confirm such a statement. We were suffered to carry on our proceedings undisturbed, while we set up our tent

* An animal unknown to scientific tourists among the Himalayas until a comparatively recent period: it was discovered by Dr Royle and named after him the *Lagomys Roylii*. To the Zoologist it is peculiarly interesting, as the other species of the Genus, from all of which it differs more or less, have been found only in Northern Asia and among the rocky mountains of North-West America. The length of the *Lagomys Roylii* is about nine inches: like most of the other animals inhabiting the elevated regions of Kunawur, Thibet, &c., it has a soft rich fur below the coarse outer hair. The former is of a blue-black colour; the latter dark-brown; and usually about an inch in length: the face is somewhat shaggy, and the ears are of a singular funnel-like form. By some travellers the *Lagomys* has been erroneously described as a tail-less rat.—TR.

on the roof of an untenanted house of one story; the long-cued, red-gowned figures only pressed forward inquisitively around us, and watched our movements with a smile. They were smoking their small silver pipes the while, or turning their prayer-cylinders; others, shaking their heads, were examining, with the deepest attention, the texture of our clothes, the buttons, knives, and utensils, —in short, every thing on and about us; and the women, clad in the same red costume, and tricked out with amber, brass and many-coloured stones, were standing a little farther off, laughing immoderately.

Notwithstanding the Emperor's mandate, which forbids the supplying of any victuals to foreigners under pain of being ripped up, these villagers brought us milk and apricots in as great abundance as we could possibly desire. By degrees, the whole population, men, women and children, assembled to stare and to laugh at the strange, unwonted intruders. The men are tall and well made, and have moreover, generally, agreeable features: still, the Tartar descent is betrayed by the broad cheek-bones, and the long oblique eye turned upward at the outward extremity. The difference between the population of Northern Bissahir and that of Thibet is scarcely perceptible; the features, the costume, and the manners and customs are the same, with this distinction only, that the inhabitants of Bissahir are friendly, merry, and yet modest; those of Thibet on the contrary, the most impudent, filthy, vulgar rabble upon the face of the earth: they cheat and chaffer like the Jews, and practise deception whenever opportunity offers.

The costume of both sexes consists of a caftan, a pair of loose drawers, and high cloth boots of motley patchwork; the women are marked only by their drawers being a little longer, and by their plaited cues of black hair, shining with grease, which hang down the back in a multitude of narrow cords, bound together with imitation-agates made of glass, innumerable shells, and pieces of amber. Round the neck they wear, besides amulets, from ten to twenty strings of lumps of amber, false stones, lapis-lazuli, and turquoises of great beauty. The men content themselves with one cue, which, to make it very long and thick, is interwoven with sheep's wool.

Among the numerous dignitaries of this little place, who without the slightest shyness forced their way into our tent, were two doctors, an elderly and a younger man. They intimated their earnest desire to make my acquaintance, and the elder one, by way of salutation, touched my brow with the points of his folded hands. Our conversation was necessarily somewhat monosyllabic, as neither our interpreter nor any one of our attendants could speak the language of Thibet. I understood only enough to convince me that these people are extremely ignorant, and physicians as it were by inspiration alone. One showed me his case of surgical instruments, which hung from his girdle; a long iron case, with a little drawer, beautifully inlaid with brass. It contained a number of lancets, or rather fleams, which are struck with a hammer to open a vein, a variety of rudely wrought iron knives, and a razor. He had set his heart on exchanging his instruments for mine, and for the sake of curiosity, I actually gave him one of my lancets for two of his fleams: he departed quite proud of his new possession.

Having positively ascertained that no Chinese official in the Emperor's service was here posted to hinder our progress, we proceeded the next day in our attempt to penetrate into the interior of the land.

We crossed several spurs of the ranges of hills, for the sake of reaching the nearest lateral valley, with its small village and gladsome brook; for where there is no water, the eye wanders only over arid masses of broken slate, with a sear and scanty clothing of thistles and steppe-grasses, thorny Astragalus and bushy Genista. All the villages are situated at a height of several hundred feet above the Sutlej.

Within three hours we reached the next village, KJOK, which had been visited by one European only, a long time since; smiling fields, and apricot trees bending beneath a load of fruit, encircle this neatly-built group of houses. On the flat roofs, we saw the women busied in threshing out the wheat, with flails exactly similar in form to those used among us in Germany,—whereas in Kunawur and in the valley of the Buspa, the grain is trodden out by horses or oxen driven forward over the sheaves. Even on the slope above Kjok, we found the usual slabs of stone with Lama inscriptions, the piles being here of great extent. From this place a steep descent of some four hundred feet leads to the terraced fields of the well watered valley, waving with rich crops of young and tender barley *("Njong")* and yellow wheat, *("Jaong,")* already partly reaped. Above the quartz rocks of the river-side precipices, there appears a deep stratum of very beautiful iron-ore, (hæmatite) which however, owing to the want of timber for fuel, cannot be turned to any account.

I was the first of the party to reach the village, which consists of some thirty scattered houses. I sought shelter from the overwhelming heat of the sun, beneath a spreading apricot-tree; but scarcely had I established myself there, to enjoy the luxury of repose, when the inquisitive villagers discovered my retreat, and gathered in troops to obtain a full view of this extraordinary apparition of a European: women in long drawers, and cloth boots with felt tops,—men in the red or white "*Bakoo*" with the broad woollen belt,—the elders of the village smoking their silver pipes. A couple of aged Lamas enlightened the rest on the subject of my descent and of my fatherland. My clothes and my pockets, my portfolio of plants and my boxes of insects, all were examined with minute attention and unshrinking importunity; and the very garments were well nigh torn from off my back; moreover, I am shocked to say that during all this overhauling, the fair sex decidedly manifested the greater impudence.

Meanwhile, the Prince with his companions had arrived, and straightway the process of inspection and manipulation re-commenced from the beginning. When they perceived that we had a mind to make purchases, they produced a multitude of strange wares,—trinkets, necklaces, pipes, &c.,—for all of which they asked the most exorbitant prices. Each man wears a brass spoon, a tinder-pouch, and a woollen sling with stones in it, hanging by his belt; the women have, in addition to these, a small pair of brass pincers, which they use for twitching out the hairs from their chin, and many other non-descript instruments besides. Willing as they were to part with their goods and chattels for money, however trifling the coin might be, their jealousy on other points was keen in proportion to their avarice: specimens of seeds and of various kinds of grain which I had collected were secretly abstracted from my pockets, and they could only be prevailed on to tell me the names of the river and the village, on condition of my not writing them down. One of the elders of the people, a fine-looking old man with a shrewd countenance, on my attempting to draw his portrait, flew at my sketch-book, and endeavoured forcibly to snatch it from me; when that measure of violence failed, he had recourse to the pathetic, throwing himself on his knees before me with gestures of deepest anguish, and seizing me by the beard.

This was the only means which I discovered on this occasion for distancing from our tents the uninvited guests; whenever their importunity exceeded all bounds, I assumed an attitude as if about to draw their portraits; instantly they fled, neck and heels, as if driven away by some evil spirit. Nevertheless I did succeed in committing to my sketch-book some few costumes.

The faces were, for the most part, of really frightful and repulsive ugliness,—the bridge of the nose deeply depressed,—the nasal stump scarce visibly protruding, —and the mouth very large and gaping wide.

The most hideous and filthy were the women, many of whom were spinning wool with the spindle, but without using the bowl as is customary with the women of Nako and Leeo.

We returned to Shipkee accompanied by two of the inhabitants of Kjok, who imparted to me, on our way, that the tablets of stone above described are paid for by the people of the village, that on solemn occasions the heads of families cause many such to be made, and that the Lama alone understands the art of engraving them. The inscription "*Om man neh pa deh hung*" is found unchanged here also, but sometimes repeated several times on one slab.

Our night at Shipkee was by no means of the most agreeable; till a very late hour we were incessantly disturbed by the intrusions of those impudent Thibetians, who boldly forced their way into our tent, always bringing some new article for sale. Moreover, to add to our disquietude, the gnats and other insects were most annoying, and allowed us scarcely any sleep.

Setting out at nine o'clock on the following morning (the 8th of August) to re-ascend the pass, we gained its height in two hours and a half, and arrived the same evening once more at Namdja. At that place, while I was sitting alone in the tent, a company of Lamas appeared, and straightway there arose the sound of soft and solemn singing. First one voice began by reciting,

—with alternately rising and falling cadence,—a sort of monologue; then the chorus joined in, with melodious voices and long sustained notes, in a somewhat high key. The whole strain reminded me of the anthems of the Romish Church with the amen of the chorister boys; and altogether, as an accompaniment to the strange figures in their picturesque red mantles and red caps with their yellow Lama insignia, produced a solemn and romantic effect.

From Namdja, we descended, by a steep path, covered with loose, rocky fragments, to the Sutlej, which we were now to cross. The "sangho" here, although spanning a stream fully thirty paces wide, is the worst we ever passed over; an old and tottering fabric,—fragile at the best, being woven only of willow branches and bass from various trees. In the middle of it, we were obliged to help ourselves forward almost entirely with our hands, the open frame-work of sticks which had served as footpath having fallen out: and, to add to the difficulty, it is so loose that, the two extremities being fastened to the opposite banks, it sinks suddenly towards the centre, forming a sharp angle.

Fresh toils awaited us on the further side, as we must needs cross the stupendous dam which here confines the course of the river,—a ridge of rocks, six thousand feet in height,—before we could enter the valley of the Leb. From afar, the path seems like a narrow stripe drawn upon a smooth wall, however we found it in reality less dangerous than those we had traversed on previous days.

At the entrance of the oasis on which stands the small village of Gimuth, *(Muth)* a number of Lamas again advanced to receive the Prince, with their choral chanting, said to consist of portions of the "*Tumshah,*" their sacred book.

Above this green spot we turned to the northward,

ascending a lofty pass by a difficult, but well-kept path. From this elevation we beheld the wide-spread tract of mountain wreck, stretching along the left bank of the Lee, in tame, undulating hills, and melting away in the dimness of a distant and undefined horizon. The path itself is covered with gray lime-stone. We marched on for eight hours before arriving at the large village of NAKO, situated in the midst of this steppe, at a height of eleven thousand, two hundred feet above the sea. Here apricots refuse to thrive, and no second crop of grain can be obtained. The agricultural produce consists chiefly of rape, (*"Njunkar"*) *"Phapur,"* wheat, barley, spelt and leguminous plants. In front of the village, which lies between huge granite blocks, is a little lake, surrounded by willows, the only trees to be seen in the neighbourhood. The costume is, upon the whole, the same as that of Namdja, except that the men wear no cues; and the women,—of whom I saw many spinning wool in the market-place, while others were seated, weaving busily at a primitive kind of loom,—wear, round the throat, a most extraordinary ornament, like a dog's collar, and round the waist a sort of bell-rope covered with blue glass-beads.

Before setting out for Leeo, we were conducted by the Lama,—a man still in the prime of life,—over the temple, an unadorned, square building, painted dark-red, which stands at the west end of the place. The lowly wooden door was opened to us without any difficulty, and we were permitted to enter. It is the only aperture by which light penetrates; consequently, the darkness of the interior was such, that it was not till we had gazed for some time that we could distinguish the various images of the gods, which the Lama was explaining to us. Over against the door stands, raised upon a pedestal, a small idol; a larger one is placed immediately behind it. The first image represents *"Lobun Patma;"*

his face is green, and he is clothed in stuff. The second or principal figure is called "*Dorjee Simba;*" over his head hovers the blue, winged and beaked "*Chakium,*" holding in his beak a string of pearls. To the right hand of these two, stands the yellow "*Nana theia;*" to the left the red "*Vinshin joongna.*" Further off, stands in a niche on the right, "*Thevadna,*" and to the left, "*Naburnangse;*" the complexions of the two latter are green and blue respectively. A quadrangular space, separated from these images of the gods by a threshold of large beams, serves as a floor on which to dry the blades of "*phapur,*" the food of the priests.

The walls are unfortunately in a very ruinous condition, but we could still distinctly trace on them a finely executed painting in size-colour, in which Chinese forms and Chinese taste are easily recognised. Rows of sitting figures with very expressive faces, are there represented; each figure is about six feet high, and surrounded by all manner of volutes and fantastic ornaments, in gold and various gay hues. The ceiling is also covered with Chinese designs in gilding, and ancient Chinese banners of bright colours are hung from the pillars of the middle aisle.

All the images of the gods are of some merit as works of sculpture, but unfortunately so covered, as indeed everything else is, with dust and dirt, as to make it evident that no cleansing hand has touched them for many a long year.

The Lama manifested endless uncertainty regarding the antiquity and the purpose of this sanctuary; moreover, he allowed us to take as many as we chose of the little clay figures of every imaginable Indian divinity, which lay heaped up together in a niche.

Over against this temple stands another smaller one, built in the same style, and of fully as great antiquity. The principal idol contained in it is the statue of a female divinity, standing in the middle wall: it is the goddess "*Doolma*:" over her the "*Chakium*" is again seen to hover, with its square, blue wings, and beaked head. Dragons with long probosces stand on either side, and small white elephants at the feet of the image. On her right and left are seated four figures, with faces of four different colours; their names were not mentioned to us. The Lama indeed stated them to be the servants of "*Doolma*," and alleged that they had no names. The remainder of the walls is covered with figures of Buddha.

Not a little dissatisfied with the indistinct explanations given to us by the Lama, we quitted Nako, and rapidly descended one declivity after another, to the banks of the Lee. Leaving the village of Maling to our right hand, we proceeded west-ward towards the bridge, a very beautiful and substantial structure of cedar-wood, which here unites the steep and rugged banks.

A quarter of an hour's march beyond it, led us to the village of Leeo. It lies two thousand, five hundred feet lower than Nako, reposing against the face of a projecting rock, which forms the angle between the little river Lipa and the Lee, and the highest ridge of which is a shattered, indented granite crag, crowned with the remains of ancient walls, encircling the summit, and apparently marking it as having been formerly the site of a fort. This rocky crest conceals at first the sweet sequestered village with its apricot-trees, and its beautiful, well watered and well cultivated fields. Crossing the Lipa, we ascended the height beyond, which forms a continuation of the lofty ridge on the opposite bank of the Lee, on which Nako stands. From the summit we once more commanded a view of the Chinese snowy mountains of Purkyul.

The vegetation on the loose masses of granite and of clay-slate, along which we were now marching, is scanty in the extreme, and the path unfrequented and desolate:

one single merchant, conveying his store of opium on the backs of several asses to Ladakh, was the only person we saw. At length, on entering the glen of the Chooling, we beheld, glistening before us, the golden and verdant fields of the twin villages of Sooling and Hangmat. Cavaliers mounted on finely caparisoned steeds, the first riding-horses we had seen for a very long time, now met us on the way.

Hang lies beyond the Chooling, and its wide-spread tillage covers a large tract of country. The view of these smiling fields, reaching far down into the hollow, was most refreshing to our weary sight, and formed a striking and agreeable contrast to the abruptly rising, limestone mountains, thickly strewn with loose débris, which, in comfortless sterility, bound the fruitful valley. With the exception of some few poplars, there is a total absence of trees; gooseberry bushes are met with on all sides, but their fruit only ripens at a very late season.

On the 12th of August, we accomplished the crossing of one of the most formidable passes, that of Hungarung, —twelve thousand feet high,—to the head of which we ascended by comparatively easy mountain paths, over acclivities covered with masses of travelled limestone. The descent on the other side, however, proved proportionably steep, as we scrambled down to the deep-cut glen of a mountain stream, to trace its onward course. Our path wound in a serpentine manner along the boulder-covered steeps, lower and lower still, till at last we saw lying before us the apricot groves and the deep hollow of the vale of Sungnum.

Sungnum is a considerable village, containing some forty dwelling-houses, and a great number of small store-houses, which appear like wooden boxes. A temple of somewhat recent date, and a multitude of Chokhdens, neatly wrought in wood, and placed beside the houses in groups of three,—grey, white, and yellow,—mark the zealous Lama-worship of the place.

We heard in this village exceedingly pretty singing. The women of Hang had also charmed us with several very pleasing melodies, which however, owing to their sudden transitions and modulations, and the habit of melting the notes into each other, are peculiarly difficult to recollect or to note down. One song which we had heard even at Lippa and at Namdja, had a more marked air than all the rest; they called it "*Soongnamook.*" Whether the name of the place Soongnum has any connection with the tune, I know not. It has three strophes, and while one division of the chorus sustains the concluding notes of the second, the other joins in with the third strophe. Occasionally also they repeat a strophe according to the character of the words they sing to it, which they vary each time at pleasure.

The tilled lands of Soongnum lie on either side of the little river Bonkioo; their crops are barley and "*phapur.*" The necessary purchases and other preparations for our further journey obliged us to rest one day at this place; we therefore pursued our peregrinations on the 14th along the valley of the RUSKALONG, passing close below a very elegant temple, picturesquely situated on the brink of the naked and commanding rock, not far from the little hamlet of Ruskalong. These "*Lama Devals*" are usually two stories high, and painted white, with the exception of the two balconies of the upper story, which are almost always black. The roof is painted red, and intersected by little grooves, formed like gutters; it is surmounted by several small, yellow-roofed, pointed turrets.

After the passage of the river, we again scaled a steep acclivity covered with loose slate, with here and there some few straggling Deodara cedars and Neoza pines,—

poor and dwarfish trees. Still the ascent continued, tedious and severe, and before long, we left all trace of wood behind us: bushes of honey-suckle and stunted cypresses bordered our path till we gained an elevation of ten thousand feet, when we found ourselves surrounded by a wide-spreading carpet of polygonum, blue geraniums, and dock, interrupted here and there by a desolate surface of broken rock, unadorned by a single plant. On the crest of the BENUNG pass, I found, to my surprise, Spurge growing in great abundance, exactly similar to our own,—the *Euphorbia exigua*. On the other side of this summit we caught a distant view of Kanum; and, proceeding in the direction of Labrung, along the naked top of the lofty mountain ridge, we reached our appointed camp at Tapung, still considerably higher than the latter village.

During the whole of this march, but more especially on the highest part of the pass, we had to fight against a violent south wind, and towards evening the atmosphere became decidedly chilly. The thermometer fell at eight o'clock P.M. to 7° (48° Fahrenheit). We saw on our way a flock of strong, large-boned goats, laden with salt, coming from Thibet, viâ Nako. In these mountain regions, salt is very highly valued as an article of trade. At Leeo I saw a woman who had, attached to her mantle, a little purse filled with salt. To my inquiry, what was contained in that little bag, she replied that it was full of "*Loo*:" these people give it to their children as we do sugar, by way of a dainty.

On the following day, we once more reached the banks of the Sutlej, where I was struck by the remarkable difference between the forest clothing of the mountains along that river, and of those on the other side of the Benung pass, although the geognostical formation continues the same. Here they are green with cypresses,

Neoza pines and cedars, and soon we entered a cedar forest, which was all alive with the loud chirping of a species of large *Cicada* (frog-hopper.)

After traversing the scene of this sylvan concert, we reached the banks of a small rivulet, the point of junction with our former road, which now led us the same evening once more to LIPPA. There I found, to my great joy, every one of the patients who had been brought to me on our first visit, perfectly cured. From Lippa we followed our old track across the ERRENG pass,—which seemed in the ascent infinitely longer than it had done before,—to PANGEE; and thence on the 17th of August, we proceeded, by way of Cheenee, on the dâk road down the valley of the Sutlej.

CHEENEE appeared, in the glorious weather with which we were now favoured, far more pleasant and inviting than it had done on our previous visit. Much of the snow which then covered the mountain had now thawed, and what remained was rapidly melting. We often heard the thunder of an avalanche though we never saw its course. The fields were already covered with the young and tender verdure of the second crop,—the blossoming "*phapur;*" and beautiful, ripe clusters of purple grapes,—the fruit of a long, oval form,—were bestowed upon us in lavish abundance both at Jengera and at Cheenee. The people were just then busily engaged in preparing the grapes for transport to Simla, and already large baskets were standing packed.

In the evening a procession, the distant sound of which we had heard for hours before, passed by our tent. A large ark, hung with drapery, on the centre of which towered a gigantic red plume composed of several yak-tails, was borne on the shoulders of two men; it was preceded by two trumpeters, labouring with distended cheeks to blow their unwieldy instruments, full six feet long; next to them marched drummers, beating hand-kettle-drums of various sizes; cymbal players, and several other musicians, with divers serpentine trumpets. We followed in the rear of the long train till it reached the temple, where the end of the ceremony consisted in the bearers of the ark raising it on high, and setting it in motion with vibrations of great violence, and of as bold a swing as the length of the staves would permit. The name of the divinity inhabiting the ark was variously reported to us; but "*Takoo*" seemed to be the prevailing designation. The people of Cheenee had been fetching home the ark,—their holiest shrine,—from another place, where it had been, for a considerable time, in a temple, united with other gods.

A total change had been manifest in the vegetation, ever since we had again set foot on solid granite, which, on this side of the glen of the Lesa, beyond Lippa, takes the place of the clay-slate. It seems almost as if the granite favoured the growth of the cedar and the fir. Wherever the declivities of this formation are not too steep and rugged, there may always be seen the sombre verdure of forests of *Coniferæ;* shooting up from the clefts of the rocks, the umbrageous, terraced foliage of the shapely Deodara, which, blending with the tender green of the cultivated fields, the smiling loveliness of the nestled villages, and the tumultuous career of the roaring Thibetian river deep below,—the windings of which may be distinctly traced from all the higher points,—gives to the valley a singularly picturesque character. Every treeless slope, every craggy summit is enamelled with an exquisite meadow flora, and the dell of each little rivulet is luxuriantly adorned with splendid flowering plants, *Germander*, (Forget-me-not) *Salvia*, *Spiræa*, and a variety of *Balsamineæ* and of *Umbelliferæ*.

On the 20th of August, followed by a train of forty-five coolies, we set out from Cheenee, to descend the valley of the Sutlej. Our march began with the ascent of a considerable acclivity, from which we enjoyed a view of the villages on the opposite bank, which we had formerly passed through,—Barung and Mebur; altogether a charming landscape!

Ascending by a rocky path, we were soon far above the region of trees: our way led us so far south-ward that we looked upon the confluence of the Buspa and the Sutlej at no great distance from us: the former river is not more than half as broad as that into which it falls.

Passing through the glen of many a mountain stream, —in which from time to time my attention was attracted by signs of tropical vegetation,—and scaling many a steep height, we arrived, after a seven hours' march, at the village of MEEROO. The culture of the vine is not attempted here, and the apricots are very bad; however, the surrounding district seems rich in corn, and I observed a super-abundant devotion to the nurture of bees. One small house was quite enveloped in swarms of them, and indeed I soon discovered that their lighting holes were in the first floor: the bee-hives,—which, on receiving permission to enter, I proceeded to inspect more closely,—consist merely of cells in the walls, about eight inches in depth by six in height, very insufficiently closed towards the interior with a sort of matted covering. The bees were buzzing through the whole house most peaceably, in the midst of the utensils and furniture, and of the inhabitants themselves.

We traversed, on the following day,—after passing the steep banks of the little stream Joola,—one of the most delightful regions imaginable, arrayed in rich vegetation, and affording numberless charms to beguile the way. Trees of spreading branches and leafy bowers were once more seen in greater abundance; we penetrated the deep recesses of a dense forest of horse-chestnuts and walnut trees, with tall and sturdy stems;

crystal brooks were murmuring beneath their welcome shade; and the tender, emerald turf was a refreshment of which our eyes had been too long deprived.

Soon after we had issued forth from the wood, we came in sight of the neat, flat-roofed dwellings of URNEE, built half of stone and half of wood, above which rises, in the centre of the place, the "*Deval*" with its two galleries, and the beautifully carved gable-end of its roof. This little village,—with its pretty, variegated houses, painted brown and white and richly ornamented with wood-carving, and the beautiful mountain landscape around,—has a very Swiss air: a few vine-bowers appear somewhat lower down on the near bank, which is clothed with beautiful trees, chiefly pear and apricot, alder and oak. The Sutlej, rolling along at a great depth below, abruptly severs this soft and richly-wooded slope, with its picturesque fore-ground and brilliant tints, from the bold precipices of the opposite mountain, which towers aloft in rugged grandeur, rendered more gloomy by the thick and sable forest of Deodaras. The grapes of Urnee were not yet ripe, while those of Pooaree, situated at a much greater elevation, had been gathered a week before: we had here reached the limit of the cultivation of the vine, and we were, at the same time, to bid farewell to the apricots; beyond this place not another roof ruddy with its stores of fruit is to be seen.

The bank along which we were now to thread our way beyond Urnee is but scantily wooded, and so extraordinarily steep that in more than one place we looked down an almost perpendicular precipice, at least a thousand feet in depth, upon the waters of the Sutlej. Following the narrow gorge, we descended the cliffs by a rough and stony path, to our resting-place at CHEEGAON (SIRGONG).

This is one of the most enchanting villages I ever

saw. Its lofty terraces rise one above another, in the midst of gigantic nut-trees, from a spacious and verdant lawn, which occupies the lowest spot and which we selected for our encampment. At the extremity of this open green, stands a tasteful "*Deval*" with beautifully carved galleries, and a conical, pointed roof; beside it a tall, tower-like edifice of five stories, the approach to which is by a flight of steps. All the houses of the village are cleanly and in good condition. We made our way into their interiors without ceremony; the inmates submitting to our impertinence with a very good grace, and leaving us at full liberty to do whatever we chose.

A ledge of planks, or a sort of wooden balcony without balustrade, surrounds the upper story, to which the ascent is by a primitive ladder-tree; but the entrance is at the opposite side, at the very furthest point from the stair, so that, to enter the family apartment,—which receives its only modicum of light through the door,—it is necessary to perform the circuit of the entire dwelling. In the first of these into which we pried, the neat and cleanly house-wife was engaged in preparing a sort of electuary or marmalade of peaches, (known by the name of "*Aruka*") while her spouse was busy kneading the "*Shepatty*" dough for those barley cakes which here supply the place of bread. A little band of pretty children crept away at the startling sight of foreigners, and seemed to shrink from us with extreme terror.

The houses here, as in many villages we had before seen, stand so near each other that the neighbours can step across from roof to roof; and the family groups might generally be seen assembled on the house-tops. The interstices between the houses are filled up with tangled hedges of hemp,—eight or nine feet high,—stinging nettles, and a species of gourd, called "*Tomba,*" —with a white blossom, and a juicy fruit about as large as an infant's head,—which luxuriates in rank profusion.

At the foot of the flight of steps which leads up to the highest terrace, we saw a young damsel diligently employed in pounding apricot-kernels in a wooden mortar: they are much used here, as from them is extracted a very fine oil with an agreeable flavour, resembling that of bitter almonds. This maiden had very pleasing features; and the miller-girls too, who were watching the small "*Pandzeckies,*" in which the millet ("*Cheena*") is ground, were really uncommonly pretty.

The vegetable world assumed a more and more rich and varied aspect, as we advanced lower and lower in the valley of the Sutlej. The tropical forms in these more southerly regions became increasingly manifest in the bamboos, the caper-bushes, the creeping fig-trees, *Bignonias, Dalbergias,* and beautiful and fragrant varieties of *Clematis.* Peculiarly luxuriant in this redundancy of superb plants is the vale of the rushing BABA, which river, on the 22d of August, we crossed by a sangho, not far from its junction with the Sutlej. A quarter of an hour's march beyond that point, brought us to the WANGTOO bridge,—the first structure really deserving the appellation of bridge,—and by it we crossed to the southern bank of the Sutlej. Magnificent indeed is the mountain scenery which here surrounds the wild and roaring river; its rugged and indented banks rise abruptly, bearing amid their rocky pinnacles a noble diadem of forests, while, in the back-ground,—forming a narrow vista between them,—extends the green and shady valley of the Baba.

We rested, after our fatiguing journey, in the village of NEETJAR; for the scaling of the steep mountain on the left bank of the river is no easy matter. Our next day's wayfarings (the 23d of August) led us for at least an hour, through a forest of oak and pear-trees, which, with its gorgeous profusion of flowering balsams and gloxinias, scattered over a velvet turf of liveliest green, seemed like nothing but the most richly adorned park. When this came to an end, the *Coniferæ,—Deodaras, Roi* firs, and *Cheel* pines,—again predominated in the sylvan scene that bordered our path. In the heart of the forest lies the village of PANG, with its beautiful and picturesquely situated temple. Among the trees of the wood are several of gigantic size: one Cedar we measured, and found to be thirty-six feet in circumference.

Beside the twin streams of the SOLDANG,—the banks of which are clothed with *Morus, Melia*, several beautiful species of *Dolichos*, and yellow-flowering *Orchideæ*,—we quitted the wood for a long and arduous ascent. On the other side of this mountain,—which is said to abound with bears,—we penetrated once more into the cool and shady recesses of the cedar-forest, in which we pitched our tents, immediately above the village of TRANDA. A violent thunder-storm, with deluges of rain, prevented our advancing further: it raged till about five o'clock. As soon as its fury was exhausted, we scaled one of the heights near our camp, from which we commanded a most glorious view of the extensive mountain landscape; the snow-capped peaks of Kotghur piercing the north-western sky with their sharp needles and serrated outlines; another range of pointed, silvery mountains, sublime in their stupendous height, extending far to the south-south-east; while, at a depth of fully fifteen hundred feet below our point of view, the Sutlej was rolling along its narrow gorge.

The freshness and luxuriance of vegetation continues unchanged in those parts of the river's wild defile which we traversed on the following day. The clothing of noble wood gives to the rugged mountains an air of richness and of life, and the emerald pasturage of every hollow glade and every level spot throws into the graver landscape gleams of brilliant and tender hue, while the countless torrents, leaping in beautiful cascades from the beetling precipices which form the ramparts of the glen, add grace and variety to the scene. The forest is by no means very thick, and there is a lack of under-wood, resulting probably from the conflagrations of the long grass before the rainy season; but this favours the exquisite and lavish verdure, which covers the ground wherever there is sufficient moisture, in many places so luxuriant, that we were buried in it up to the waist: the trees, maple,—ash, bhansh-oak,—beard-tree, mulberry, and rhododendron,—form a close and continuous bower, affording the most grateful shade; the path is bordered, moreover, by a thick hedge of amaranth, balsams, hemp, and a multitude of papilionaceous flowers: here and there a solitary fig-tree presents itself, and a species of yellow-flowering cucumber twines its elegant festoons over the tall beard-tree. Perpetually, throughout this day's march, we came to rocky grottoes in which cool and crystal fountains bubble forth amid a frame-work of various balsams, the blue flowers of a splendid gloxinia and the slender ears of a species of spurrey.

Immediately beyond the confluence of a small stream, —the CHONDA,—with the Sutlej, a lateral spur of the mountain ridge extends to the margin of the water; it bears the name of MANJOOTEE DANDA, and rises to an elevation of about two thousand feet above the river; its ascent is, however, not very difficult, as the path winds gradually up its flank. From the crest of this pass we looked down upon two small river-glens on the opposite bank of the Sutlej,—with their rippling brooks glancing in the sunshine,—and upon the lovely village of *Kyao*, while to the south-west, at a much greater distance, we could descry the loftier buildings of SERAN. The descent of Manjootee Danda is accomplished by gentle zigzags, and offers more than one picture of unrivalled beauty,—charming and sequestered nooks, where water-falls, grottoes, blossoming shrubs, and rivulets murmuring beneath the rich tracery of cucumber tendrils, or sparkling along a carpet of enamelled sward, exquisitely chequer the fairy-like scene.

In one of these dells we were met by an ambassador from the Rajah of Bissahir, leading an elegantly caparisoned horse, which he had been dispatched to offer to the Prince for his entry into Seran. His Royal Highness however begged to decline making a public entry, or being received with any ceremony.

A "*Deval*," and the Palace of the Rajah of Bissahir,—his summer residence,—were the first features of the town of Seran which caught the eye as we descended to it. The temple is an extensive edifice, surrounded by a gallery immediately below the overhanging roof; beside it rises the actual "*Deval*," a tall, white, tower-like structure, terminating in a truncated cone; it stands between the sanctuary and the abode of the Rajah, which is a simple and unpretending fabric, two stories high. Behind this range of buildings lies concealed the group of lowly dwellings, dignified with the name of Seran,—in reality, a miserable village, composed of a few half-ruinous, one-storied houses.

Tents were ready pitched in this place, affording ample room to accommodate us all. Before long, a crowd of the curious had assembled to gaze at us; young men and boys especially, flocked together in great numbers from every quarter. They were fine looking youths, with frank countenances: some of the older people also had an exceedingly pleasing expression. The "*Bakoo*," or smock-frock, the woollen drawers, and the broad woollen belt of the mountaineers, are no longer found here; and the flat, brown woollen caps are more rarely worn. The women are shy, and did not often make their appearance; their prevalent head-dress is still the same as in Pooaree,—the long plaits and bushy tuft of red wool behind the head,—but a white kerchief is here generally thrown over it. The long, party-coloured web of woollen stuff, fastened on the left breast with the Pitzook, or brooch, is also still the usual costume. The burden of labour and drudgery of every sort appears to be laid specially on the women; at least we almost always saw them going about with large baskets, —round, but tapering down to a point,—on their backs: almost every thing is carried in these baskets,—even water, which is, for this purpose, poured into huge brazen flagons.

We had scarcely established ourselves in our tents, when the Rajah sent a liberal supply of fruit for our refreshment,—beautiful forced mangoes, grapes, and unripe peaches, as hard as apples, for in this state it is the custom to eat them here. At the same time he announced his intention of waiting upon the Prince on the following day.

It was a lovely evening, but the heat in our tent was most oppressive; we therefore sought out a spot where we might cool ourselves in some limpid stream; a small brook, close to our camp, offered one of the most charming bathing-places that could be imagined. A pure and softly rippling rivulet which gushes forth among the rocky heights to the north of Seran, leaps in two beautiful cascades, over the jagged brink of a precipice richly clothed with creepers and coppice: each of these cascades is received into a little pool below: thick bushes of balsam, syringa, and gloxinia, surround these basins, whose clear, cool waters afford the most delicious refreshment. Near the spot where the streams from the two water-falls again unite, numerous monuments, in appearance resembling ancient tombs, stand beside the water's edge. The same figure seems to be represented on them all, a form clad in female attire, with the right hand uplifted; on some it was repeated six times, each time three figures in a row. I failed to obtain any explanation regarding the signification of these memorials of antiquity.

The following morning (the 25th of August) His Highness the Rajah kept us all very long waiting; noon had already arrived, when we at last heard the sound of trumpets and of drums, announcing his approach. The Sovereign appeared on foot; a small, decrepit man, clothed in violet-coloured silk, with morocco-leather boots of the same colour, and a huge and most unshapely cap of gold tissue: he was led forward by the Vuzeer (*"Bujeer"*) and another exalted dignitary, both arrayed in white.

Count von O——— and I advanced to meet him; the Count took his left, and I his right arm, and so, amid the acclamations of the people, and the loud shouts of *"Maha Rajah," "Maha Rajah!"*—we proceeded to the tent, where, already, the presents sent by His Highness as precursors of his visit were deposited on large brass dishes. Our camp-beds, with Indian shawls thrown over them, served as divans, on which the Rajah and his suite immediately reclined. Our interpreter, Mr Brown, translated questions and answers at a brisk rate, and the conversation flowed on with vivacity and zest; for the aged Rajah, however dulled and enfeebled in his outward man, displayed no lack of life and quickness in his mind and language.

Among the presents was a piece of Russian leather, which has thus the opportunity of making the great round and travelling back to Europe! There were also several singular weapons, and webs of silken and of woollen stuffs, musk bags, and the highly-valued Nerbissi root.

The same ceremonies took place at the departure of the Rajah; however, he very politely declined our further escort, not without symptoms of secret uneasiness.

After dinner the Prince returned his visit. The Vuzeer came to conduct us to the palace. Passing through a half-dilapidated gateway, surrounded by an eager throng of inquisitive spectators, we entered the great court, over which was spread a baldachin. A grand yet simple entrance leads into the interior of the palace, an edifice distinguished by the severe and unadorned style of mountain architecture. Three elegant silken sofas were placed in a circle; behind them and on either side, stood hosts of courtiers clad in white, with drawn "*Khukries*" (short sabres) in their hands: a few only were marked as heralds by the insignia which they bore,—the long, gilt staff, separating at the top into two curved points. The counter-presents now offered as an acknowledgment of those received,—in compliance with the oriental etiquette of exchanging gifts,—were accepted, apparently with great satisfaction, by the Rajah. He conversed for a long while with the Prince, and expressed a great desire to obtain information concerning the position, size and state of our native land, as well as to know the name of every sovereign in Germany; on all which subjects it was no easy matter to give his Highness an intelligible reply. He refused, through the medium of his "*Bujeer*," to allow us to see his palace; excusing himself on the plea that "the gods were in it," and only granting us permission to be conducted round its outer gallery.

Altogether the audience was a highly interesting scene, and one of peculiarly oriental character. By the crimson light of an exquisite evening sky,—a rarity in this part of the country,—we wended our way back to the tents.

As we quitted Seran the next morning, after a night of incessant rain, the whole of the river-glen was hidden by a vapoury shroud. We soon reached the end of the plain of Seran, and descended a declivity of some fifteen hundred feet to the channel of the MAGHELADGADH, which we crossed by a bridge. During the steep ascent on the opposite bank, we suffered greatly from the heat, which was so oppressive that we could scarcely breathe. A few trees,—chiefly mulberry, with an underwood of *Grewia* and *Carissa*, interlaced with the rank tendrils of many a vine,—afforded a scanty shade; but their poverty seemed but to enhance the beauty of the forest of noble oaks above, which, broken only here and there by the cultivated lands surrounding the numerous villages, continues as far as GOORA.

The Rajah has certainly displayed good taste, in causing a country-seat to be erected here; for it is a most enchanting spot. We selected, as our encampment-ground, the court which lies inclosed between this new palace and the temple.

As the former is still unoccupied, there was no one to ward us off, nor even to deny us access to its inner apartments. The building is a perfect square, with a small entrance, leading immediately into a spacious chamber probably destined for the domestics of the household, in which there is a projection covering the actual entrance to the interior of the dwelling. In the centre of the whole is an open space, with a tank, surrounded by a neatly carved gallery of cedar-wood, from which small doors lead into the dark bed-chambers, and larger ones, elegantly ornamented with wood-carving, into the apartments of greater size: the second story is laid out on exactly the same plan. The rooms are low, and do not exceed twelve feet in length, by from five to eight in width. The broad gallery which surrounds the second story on the exterior side, is not yet completed. It is covered by the overhanging roof, which is of black slate. Opposite to this country-house stands a large, handsome temple, with a wide and very pretty gallery, and a high, conical, white roof, surmounted by a falcon with a serpent in its beak, sculptured in stone.

A beautiful white clematis twines gracefully round the corner of the "*Deval,*" and a rampant brake of hemp, nettles and balsams, encircles the picturesque group of buildings; wild fig-trees too,—bearing a small, dark-blue, eatable fruit,—and tall bushes of *Melia* and of *Carissa,*—among which a species of gourd, with small fruit of the brightest yellow, has wreathed its tendrils to an aspiring height,—all flourish in wild luxuriance here. Amid many more ordinary plants, my eye was caught by a solitary citron-tree, *("Nimboo")* adorned with a profusion of green fruit, about the size of one's fist.

As we started from this place for RAMPOOR, we again, for the first time since we had quitted Delhi four months before, felt the oppressive heat of the flat country. Our path, an almost unbroken descent, lay through a forest of Cheel pines, in which we crossed several small streams. At the last turn of the road, where it bends downward to a considerably lower level, Rampoor, the capital of Bissahir, situated on a projecting eminence on the banks of the Sutlej, was pointed out to us in the distance. The country through which that river rolls on its rapid current, is, in this part, extremely pleasant; the banks indeed are yet steep, but they no longer present those gigantic mural precipices which we had seen at Rogee, or at Cheenee; and the lowest terrace,—to which the water rises at its full flood in spring,—is clothed with the succulent and brilliant verdure of luxuriant pasturage.

We followed the course of the Sutlej, from Rampoor, along easy and well-made roads, on the 30th of August; till, quitting the river-glen, we struck off in a south-westerly direction, towards KOTGHUR, where we celebrated the termination of our mountain wanderings in a most solemnizing manner at the home of two German missionaries, Messrs Rudolph and Prochnow.*

These very amiable and excellent men,—the first a native of Berlin, the second of Pomerania,—have done wisely to settle in this paradise of Kotghur, where they have erected very neat and pretty dwellings, surrounded by a charming park, and have established a large school for the Hindoos, who appear also to flock in numbers to the Church. Thus a foundation seems to be laid for forming a Christian Church in Kotghur; for the

* Agents of the Church of England Missionary Society. The Himalaya Mission, of which Kotghur is still considered the centre, was established at the request and with the assistance of some of the British residents at Simla and elsewhere, in the year 1843, since which time the gospel has been preached in the villages of the district and at the annual *melas*, or fairs; Thibetian and Hindui tracts have been distributed; medical and surgical advice and assistance given by the missionaries; orphan institutions opened; and day-schools established: in 1844 the boys' school, under the charge of Mr Rudolph, numbered from thirty to forty; while Mrs Prochnow had a school of ten or twelve girls, whom she taught to sew and knit, to read and write. Since then, the war in the Punjaub has caused some interruption to the labours of the missionaries, who were obliged to remove for a time to Simla; but from the latter part of 1845, Kotghur has again been their head-quarters, and their operations are carried on with uninterrupted activity, and not without evidences of that blessing which alone can give success. Another step has been taken in the extension of the mission towards Thibet, by the establishment of a new school at Kepoo, between Kotghur and Rampoor; and another school has been opened at Theog, between Kotghur and Simla. Mr Prochnow mentions that many people from the adjacent villages, and travellers from a distance come in, and with the children of the schools and the native servants from the plains, listen attentively not only to the services on the Lord's day, but to the daily family worship, at which he has read and explained the Scriptures, particularly the Parables, the Sermon on the Mount, and the History of the Death and Resurrection of our Lord. He had met on the road between Kotghur and Simla a wandering Lama from Chinese Tartary, who had one of the Thibetian Christian tracts which he had received from a travelling Zemindar, who told him that a *Sahib* had distributed many of them at the Rampoor fair the year before: in other instances these tracts having been distributed in Lower Kunawur and Bissahir have been met with and found to be read and highly valued in Chinese Tartary: so that these silent and unobtrusive messengers of the Gospel, clad in no foreign garb, have found their way into the Celestial Empire itself, across that very barrier which has been found so impassable for Europeans. —Tr.

mountaineers, though they themselves indeed come apparently only from curiosity to the Church, send their children to the school; not one of them however has been baptised as yet, but the boys are admirably well instructed, have learned English very quickly, and can read the Bible both in English and in Hindui, and intelligently explain what they read. In Germany, these two missionaries would doubtless be mere "candidates," whereas here, they are already beginning to gather a family circle around them. Herr Rudolph yesterday announced to us an addition to his, requesting the Prince at the same time to stand godfather to his child.

We heard a Hindui sermon, and afterwards a German one, which was very excellent, although Herr Prochnow has not spoken a word of German for three years. I am bringing home with me a Hindui Bible, which I received from him.

On the 1st of September, we enjoyed, at our early departure, a farewell view of the lovely valley of the Sutlej, bounded on either side by undulating hills; then, turning our back upon its charms, we traversed, in a southwesterly direction, the hemp-fields of Kotghur. Unfortunately, owing to a hurt on my foot, I was obliged to avail myself of a horse which the Prince had ordered for me. Quite unexpectedly we found ourselves in a forest of "*Kil*" firs *(Pinus longifolia)* and of "*Mohroo*" and "*Bhansh*" oaks, and as we penetrated into its deep recesses, matted with a thick underwood of beard-trees, bramble-bushes, balsams and ferns, we seemed suddenly transported from the burning zone to a region of everlasting spring. Many sweet and smiling hamlets, surrounded by fields of amaranth, are scattered through the wood. At one place, where the path winds round a river-glen somewhat wider than the others, we caught a glimpse of the hill of HATOO, crowned by the fort of PURANA KILLA, and soon afterwards we reached, after the ascent of a ridge some two thousand feet in height, the beautiful bungalow of NAGKANDA.

On the 4th of September, we arrived at Simla, the English Convalescent station, where there is a crowd of English officers, who have resorted hither with their families in quest of health. The place lies on the same level as at Nainethal, but there is this difference between them, that the latter is just springing into existence,—scarce twenty Englishmen are there, and no ladies except the daughters of Mr Wilson,—whereas at Simla, some hundred and fifty officers reside, half of that number being married, and provided with daughters or female relatives besides; in addition to which, many widows are settled here, and not a few solitary matrons, who console themselves at balls and varied festivities for the absence of their lords.

At the end of our long and wild Himalayan peregrinations, we arrived at the new and handsome English hotel in a somewhat barbarian costume; instead of a coat was substituted something between a cloak and a coat of mail, formed of coarse woollen stuff,—in the broad belt confining it at the waist was stuck the cutlas; feet shod with sandals by way of shoes, long hair combed back over the top of the head, and a rough and shaggy beard, completed our grotesque appearance. The whole skin of my face had peeled off twice from the reflected glare of the snow, and that which had now succeeded it was of a dark brown hue.

Now,—we draw French kid gloves over our sun-burnt hands; force our feet, broadened by exercise, into delicate dancing-boots; and never dream of appearing otherwise than in dress-coats and white waistcoats; for the most rigid etiquette is here observed. How strange does it still seem to me when I awake in the morning to find myself, not in the dripping tent, but in a comfortable bed-room furnished with all manner of luxuries. The lack of pedestrian activity too is an unwonted slavery; for our limbs, accustomed to scaling mountains and to scrambling down precipices, are now exerted only to pay morning visits, or to dance polkas at a ball!

There are, at Simla, three great Bazaars, i. e. streets consisting only of shops and warehouses, occupied chiefly by Cashmere merchants. A great number of native artisans also live in this place. Here is to be seen an infinite variety of costumes; those of the mountains mingling with those of the plains; Sikhs with the high, pointed turban, on which they generally wear an iron ring with a sharp polished edge,—a dangerous missile; Affghans with the red caftan and the noble, flowing beard; and Cashmerians, never failing to display upon their persons their beautiful shawls. The latter people are usually merchants or tailors, but the goods they sell are not suited to my purse. To complete the picturesque effect of the varied throng, there are the gay and motley uniforms of the Indian troops.

Every evening, after five o'clock, according to Oriental custom, the most stirring and animated scene begins; especially in the broad street in which our hotel is situated, the so-called "course."

No one ventures to make his appearance there who is not mounted on a handsome horse; or who cannot sport the whitest linen, the most stylish cut of coat or showy uniform, and white kid gloves: for one must needs make special toilet here, in order to enjoy the open air. Every creature is on horseback; even the fair sex dash along on fine, spirited, Arab coursers; and many an English lady may be seen galloping down the street, followed by a train of three or four elegantly equipped officers, while others of sedater age, are carried about in "*Jampans.*" The "*jampan*" is a sort of machine, in form resembling an arm-chair, suspended at either side, by means of straps, to a short pole, and borne on the shoulders of bearers in gay and varied liveries; twelve of these harlequin-like fellows running behind. You may thus form some estimate of the immense number of domestics constituting the train of a single lady; for these bearers never move hand or foot in any other employment than the carrying of the "*jampan.*" Another set of servants is kept for sending round notes, that being their only avocation; then there are some whose whole duty it is to beat the clothes, some to sweep the rooms, others to lay the table; with shoe-blacks, lamp-lighters, dog-boys (a most important post), horse-keepers, waiters and porters besides,—each office having its own peculiar name, all which it costs no small trouble to learn.

Since the arrival of our tardy steeds, we regularly join in the promenade on the "course;" I indeed only for the sake of swelling the number of the Prince's suite; for I should much prefer rambling about on foot, and shooting birds, this being precisely the season at which the yellow *Loxia* (Grosbeak) and the still almost unknown, beautiful red Cuckoo, make their appearance. I seldom accomplish rescuing the morning hours for any such excursion, as we can scarcely ever return home at night before two o'clock. A custom, you must know, reigns in this place, of never sitting down to dinner before eight or nine o'clock in the evening. If a ball is appended to the entertainment, then a second repast,—called "*Supper*,"—follows at about one in the morning. Our own dinner hour was unalterably fixed at four o'clock, but then unfortunately, we scarcely ever dine at home.

We have now for a long time been enjoying the ease and liberty of an hotel, of which, throughout the East Indies, as far as the mountains, we were always deprived, as we passed on from one Governor or public official to another, each of whom indeed placed half his house, or at least his best suite of apartments, at the Prince's disposal, but among whose brilliant and friendly hospitalities we were never free to lay aside the white neckcloth, or the French kid gloves. Here, an hotel has recently been set up for the accommodation of strangers, a thing utterly unheard of in the plains of Hindostan. A Frenchman is at the head of the establishment, and we find ourselves very well off in his house; at least I, so long inured to sleeping on the moist ground, am unconscious of, and proof against, any wetness of the walls or dampness of the floors. Moreover, a couple of old piano-fortes is to be found here; I have, after trying them, selected the best of the two, and have tuned it for the sake of playing some old favourite now and then in the evening, or accompanying a duet.

The town of Simla, when seen from a distance, has a most singular effect: it consists almost entirely of a multitude of detached pavilions; the bazaars only, lying in terraces one above another, on the face of a pretty steep hill, have a somewhat more connected appearance, and might be mistaken, at first sight, for a village or small town. The country-houses, many of them on a large scale and very handsome, surrounded by extensive "parks" or pleasure-grounds, are scattered here and there through the forest, amid the deep shades of huge cedars and firs. The above-mentioned "course" leads on one side between these villas, sweeping round the foot of a hill, to the distance of some miles, while, on the other, it extends about as far in a straight line. The distance from one country-house to another is therefore quite extraordinary, and, except on horseback, paying a round of visits would be out of the question.

The immense extent of the place seems at first astounding, for, in circumference, it is scarcely inferior to Calcutta: but soon one begins to discover that the forest, in which the whole is built, and behind which it would be natural to imagine a multitude of houses, does, in fact, not conceal any; all the dwellings being situated close to the few roads, which run along the base of the mountain ridge.

During our evening rides, we enjoyed most glorious views of our old friends, the snowy mountains, whose varied labyrinth of peaks and summits forms, when seen from this point, a single, long-drawn line in the horizon. We can scarcely now persuade ourselves, as we gaze at their majestic outline, that we were actually, but a little while since, in their very midst.

Gay balls and splendid festivities rapidly succeeded each other, and a bal masqué was also got up. To my great relief, I received a dispensation from the necessity of appearing in costume; and the idea of disguising me as a mountain lady was also relinquished, in consequence of my positively refusing to have my beard cut off. Besides, it would have been no easy matter to supply the want of the woolly tuft and of the long mazes of plaited hair. It was a bright and merry party; for there are here a great many sprightly old ladies, who, loaded with perfect gardens of flowers, rush about in the polka with most incredible zeal. They did not however appear, as I had heard they were to do, as Dianas or the Graces, but on the contrary, in remarkably pretty antiquated costumes, hoop petticoats and stiff brocades; the elderly gentlemen being equipped to correspond. The fancy dresses were all very successful, and selected with much taste. The Oriental masked travesties were also very numerous, and natural to a degree which doubtless could never have been attained in any other part of the world; for you may easily imagine, considering the generosity with which all Eastern Princes delight in lavishing presents to the right and left, that the British officers, many of them newly arrived from the remotest parts of the East Indies, having been ordered, now to the Punjaub, now to Scinde or Affghanistan, are richly supplied with costly stuffs, which they can turn to account only on occasions such as this.

There was, however, by no means a lack of young ladies; for the kind and thoughtful relatives at Simla never fail to bring up from the plains every thing in the shape of young and marriageable nieces or cousins; and here, where so many agreeable officers are stationed for pleasure's sake alone, many a youthful pair are thrown together, and many a match is made. In the course of last week only, two weddings were solemnized; no great festivities take place here at such events, any more than in England. The marriage ceremony is performed in a small and miserable church, to which we are obliged to go an hour before public worship begins, in order to be sure of finding seats. I have certainly never carried away much of edification from the service; a number of psalms is read, but the manner of it is, that the clergyman reads the first verse, the people the second, and so alternately throughout:* it is not till the very end of the service,—which is long, and in which the same thing is repeated two or three times over,—that the Epistle and Gospel are read, with a few remarks appended to them, instead of a sermon. I have however silently resolved not to enter the place again, having observed a large crack in the vaulted ceiling, which threatens to fall in before long.

* The reader will remember not only that, in joining in the service of the Church of England, our author was listening to a foreign language, but that in his own country he was accustomed to a non-liturgical mode of worship. —Tr.

SUPPLEMENT TO THE TWELFTH LETTER.

17th October 1845.

We are to start from this place, on our further journeyings, next week, our time having slipped away amid numberless balls, fetes and dinner-parties, given in honour of the Prince by the Commander-in-Chief, by General Sir Harry Smith, and by the officers. The finale was an exceedingly brilliant fête, arranged and given by Prince Waldemar himself, in which the whole beau monde of Simla took part. It was a kind of *fête champêtre* in the depth of a lovely valley, beneath giant cedars, which, as evening closed in, were lighted by many hundred lamps suspended to every branch and twig, forming altogether a magnificent saloon with a magic illumination. The fine figures and picturesque costumes,—marking many an Oriental race,—among the countless spectators gathered together from far and near, who, in scattered groups, had ranged themselves amphitheatrically on the surrounding hills, produced an effect so striking that Fancy could hardly picture a more beautiful or wondrous scene. On a large floor, laid with cloth, which had been put up in the centre of the lawn, before three spacious tents hung with elegant drapery, dancing was carried on, and the collation,—the so-called "*tiffin*,"—was served in the middle tent. The splendour of this fête has won a great and far-spread fame, which indeed it well deserves.

We are to proceed in a westerly direction from Simla, through the burning plains, which, after our long residence among the cool and beautiful forests of the mountain regions, will be most distasteful to us: our first point is to be Ferozepoor; where next we shall go after that, yet remains undecided.

THIRTEENTH LETTER.

CAMPAIGN AGAINST THE SIKHS—DEPARTURE OF THE PRINCE AND HIS SUITE FROM FEROZEPOOR FOR LOODIANA—THE BRITISH ARMY—BATTLE OF MOODKEE—THE WOUNDED—DANGEROUS RETURN TO THE CAMP—BATTLE OF FEROZESHAH—CONCLUDING REMARKS OF THE EDITOR—DEATH OF DR W. HOFFMEISTER.

In all probability, an abundance of reports, true and false, on the subject of the campaign against the Sikhs,—in which, by a strange concatenation of circumstances, I find myself involved,—will spread rapidly through all the public journals in Europe; there seems therefore to be no reason for my suffering you to remain any longer in suspense and anxiety concerning me.

The state of the case is as follows,—the Sikhs, with a force of thirty-six thousand men, have crossed the Sutlej not far from Ferozepoor, which place, with its feeble garrison, they thus keep encompassed on every side. The news of their invading the British territory caused orders to be given,—which had not been expected so soon,—for the departure of all the regiments from Loodiana; these orders were given so suddenly, that even the officers of several of the regiments were only informed of the position of affairs six hours before. We had ourselves started from Ferozepoor on the 22d of November, in spite of its being rumoured that the Sikhs were in motion; and we had returned without delay to Loodiana, intending to proceed to Umbala, where our camels and tents had been ordered to meet us. The road from Ferozepoor to Loodiana is very desolate, and the villages are poor and thinly peopled, so that we were forced to perform our palanquin journey, two at a time, on three successive evenings; the great heat making it impossible to travel except by night. We arrived in safety, — without having seen any Sikhs, — at Loodiana, where we heard of the movement, and remained, statu quo, for a fortnight, until the British army marched against the aggressors.

ATCHERIKO, *17th of December.*

I can add only a few words, to beg that you will not distress yourself on my account. The first days of the Sikh campaign are over,—weary and bitter days for me! One must be a practised horseman indeed, to maintain a good seat amidst such a tumult.

Yesterday, the first Sikh fort, WUDNEE, was taken by storm, but the artillery being too weak, the destruction of the citadel was deferred until the arrival of reinforcements.

The Sikh force is great and formidable, but the British army, mustering at this place for the first time today, is the largest ever collected in India. To-morrow some twenty regiments at least will be assembled here. The noise and tumult,—caused by the many thousand camels, the countless elephants, the numerous train of women and children accompanying the native troops, and the vast multitude of servants and horse-keepers,—baffle all description. There are at least fifty thousand men already crowded together here!

The Sikh army, shut in between FEROZEPOOR and ATCHERIKO, are cut off from the only ford, and it is impossible for them either to advance or to retreat.

MOODKEE, *20th of December*.

On the morning of the 18th, after a forced march of three days, with the British troops,—consisting of thirteen regiments of infantry, five regiments of cavalry, and seven batteries,—we arrived at the village of MOODKEE.

Shortly before the army marched into that place, it became known that the Sikhs were on the move; several shots were heard; but the irregular light cavalry repulsed the enemy's detachments, so that the British took undisputed possession of the village. The tents were quickly pitched; but the immense loads of baggage, transported on thousands of camels and elephants, and in waggons drawn by bullocks, had not yet come up, when suddenly, the officers, to a man, were hurried from their hastily snatched morsel of food, to re-mount their scarce unsaddled steeds; and the dead-tired soldiers, who had performed on two successive days marches of twenty English miles each, were roused from beside their boiling kettles by the cry, "The Sikhs are on the march!" The British troops advanced at a double quick step. I was left in the camp, my horse being completely knocked up. At a few minutes before four, the Sikh batteries opened a murderous fire of grape-shot, and the battle was begun. The air was thick and sultry; the smoke of gunpowder and the fearful dust wrapped all in one mysterious gloom; not a foe was to be seen; the lightning of the artillery alone marked his position. For two hours this cannonade continued, after which the Sikh infantry charged at the point of the bayonet, but thrice they were repulsed. Not until the blackest night had overspread the scene, did the enemy quit their position. One solitary Sikh has been taken prisoner; seventeen of the enemy's guns and three standards are taken; but the loss on the side of the British, both in killed and wounded, is very great.

Several regiments were left on the battle-field, to cover the removal of the wounded, among whom were many officers. To my unspeakable joy, the Prince and the two Counts returned without a single wound, although they had been in the hottest of the fire. Some one had alarmed me by the dreadful intelligence that one of them had fallen. Three of my dear and excellent friends have been laid in the dust this day; among them was one of the most talented medical men on the British staff. Another army surgeon has had both his legs shot off.

Yesterday morning, after a night of watching, I set out, with a detachment of troops, for the field of battle, to render some assistance in bringing in such of the wounded as were still lying there. Unfortunately, I was under the necessity of leaving my horse in the camp. We had scarcely reached the battle-field, when we were met by numerous bodies of troops, who had received orders to return to the British quarters with all possible speed, the Sikh cavalry being on the march. Notwithstanding this, the officer in command of our detachment advanced fully half a mile further. Suddenly, just as we were giving drink to the first few of the unhappy sufferers, and preparing to convey them to the camp, there appeared, in the horizon, a cloud of dust, and several random shots were fired. The commanding officer gave orders to form the line,—but the native panic for the Sikhs was too great, the Sepoys one and all broke the ranks and fled, and that with such swiftness that I could not attempt to keep up with them. I followed the road which I supposed to be the best, running at a quick pace for some two miles or so; after which, the ground became so sandy, that exhausted by the difficulty of the way, my strength failed, and I felt, to my consternation, the impossibility of traversing the remaining three miles with the same desperate speed.

The shots were approaching nearer and nearer, and with them the thick cloud of dust that concealed the foe. With great difficulty, I pushed on for another half mile; I could then scarcely muster sufficient strength to persuade the driver of an elephant laden with the slain, to make a halt and to carry me forward with the dead. He dragged me up; immediately I became insensible, and with returning consciousness I found myself in the camp. A sound sleep soon restored me.

This morning, a corpse was brought into our tent, with an open note, expressing regret and condolence on Count von O——— having been killed in the engagement of the 18th: The slain was, however, a Roman Catholic priest, who had accompanied the Irish regiments. I had seen the body lying on the battle-field, and now recognized him by his long, black beard, which had given rise to the mistake. He was actually hewn in pieces with sabre cuts.

To-day, some of the unfortunate wounded have at last arrived, after lying for two days and nights on the bloody field,—the very individuals for whom I was yesterday helping to search. Not far from the place from which I was so suddenly forced to retreat, a slightly wounded private had both his hands cut off. God be praised! mine are yet safe and sound; and right actively must I exert them, for there is a lamentable deficiency of medical attendance in the hospital.

To-morrow the army is to advance towards Ferozepoor, and I cherish a confident hope that we shall get through successfully, fresh reinforcements having now arrived. Farewell;—may we soon meet again!

The goal appointed him was other than his Fatherland!

The ardent desire, cherished from early childhood, had been fulfilled in a manner the most comprehensive, and under circumstances the most propitious. It had been his favoured lot, to traverse, in his journeyings beside the Prince, a great part of the eastern world, to understand by personal acquaintance, and to appreciate with enthusiasm, the varied wonders and the rich luxuriance of nature in the East Indies: from all the perils of his long wanderings he had escaped unscathed; neither the burning heat of a tropical clime, nor the icy cold of the Himalayan mountains had impaired his vigorous frame; neither the chasms and precipices of the rocky paths, nor the billows of the wild ocean had jeoparded his life; from amid the enjoyment of scientific pursuit, in the living brightness of blooming youth, he was called hence by an unthought-of death, and one so sudden that it may almost be called painless.

The Editor is guided, in his short notice of the immediate circumstances of his death, by the narrative contained in the letters of His Royal Highness Prince Waldemar, and in those of Count von der Gröben.

On the 21st of December, the British army advanced towards Ferozepoor, and encountered the Sikh forces at Ferozeshah, their main body being drawn up in a thick jungle. A bloody battle ensued. The British troops, marching in close array, attacked the enemy; but the murderous fire of artillery and grape-shot brought them to a stand. At this critical juncture, the Governor-General, Lord Hardinge, himself rode along the front ranks, encouraging them to the onset. Prince Waldemar accompanied him, surrounded by his fellow-travellers. While riding close beside the Prince, whom, in this moment of extreme danger, he refused to quit, Dr Hoffmeister was struck by a grape-shot, which entered his temple. He fell forward to the ground. The Prince instantly sprang from his horse, and raised him; but the vital spark had already fled; at the same moment, the advance of the forces rendered it necessary to move on. The slain were unavoidably left on the field of battle. Not until two days had elapsed, was it possible to inter them.

He was laid in the same tomb with several of his friends who fell on that bloody day; and a simple monument in the burial-ground at Ferozepoor, erected by the Prince to the memory of his faithful physician and beloved companion, records his tragic fate, and marks his journey's utmost bourn.

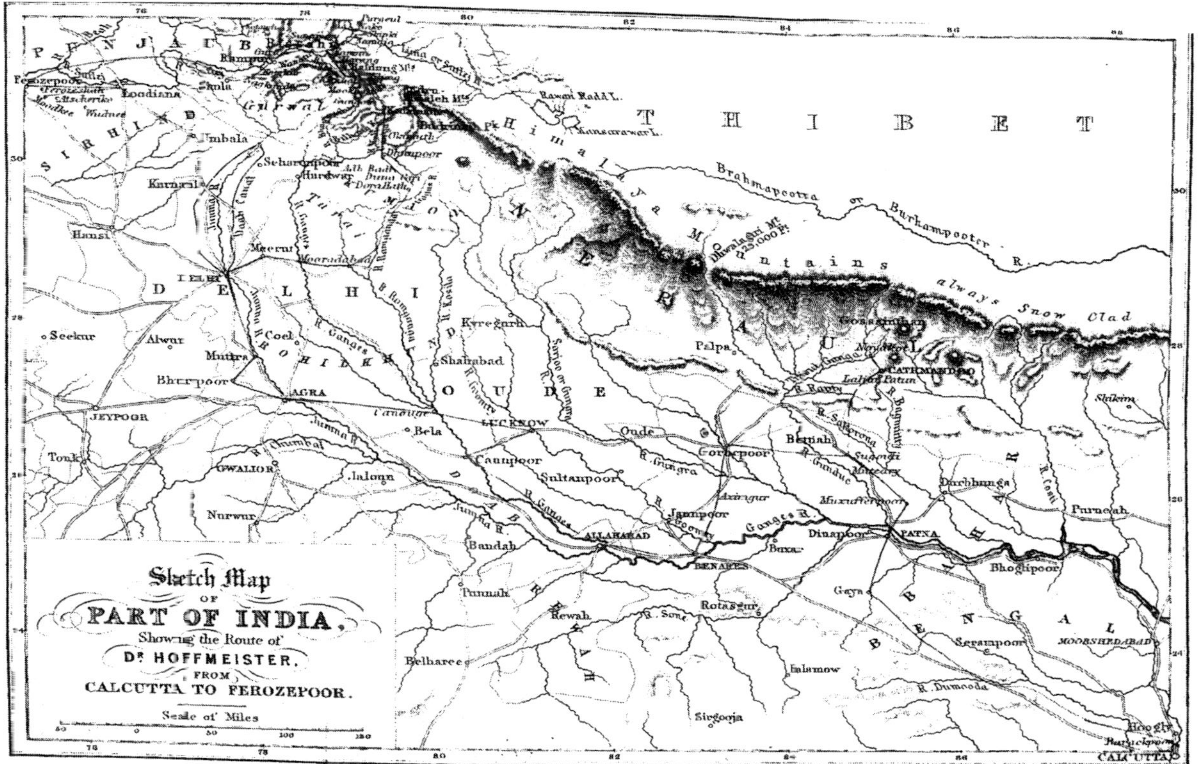
Sketch Map
OF
PART OF INDIA,
Showing the Route of
Dr. HOFFMEISTER,
FROM
CALCUTTA TO FEROZEPOOR.
Scale of Miles
T H I B E T
Himalaya Mountains always Snow Clad
Brahmapootra or Burhampooter R.
N E P A U L
P U N J A U B
S I R H I N D
D E L H I
R O H I L K H U N D
O U D E
B E N G A L
B A H A R
R E W A H
DELHI
AGRA
LUCKNOW
ALLAHABAD
BENARES
PATNA
CALCUTTA
CATHMANDOO
Ferozepoor
Loodiana
Umbala
Kurnaul
Meerut
Seharunpoor
Hurdwar
Simla
Hansi
Seekur
Alwur
Muttra
Bhurtpoor
JEYPOOR
Tonk
GWALIOR
Nurwur
Jaloun
Bela
Cawnpoor
Sultanpoor
Jaunpoor
Oude
Gorruckpoor
Bettiah
Durbhunga
Purneah
Bhogulpoor
Moorshedabad
Hoogly
Barrackpoor
Serampoor
Gaya
Rotasgur
Palamow
Sirgooja
Buxar
Dinapoor
Rewah
Punnah
Bandah
Belharee
Shahabad
Kyregarh
Palpa
Shikim
Coel
R. Ganges
R. Gangra
R. Sone
R. Jumna
R. Coosi
Dwalagiri Mt 28,000 Ft.

APPENDIX.

APPENDIX I.

ON THE GEOGRAPHICAL DISTRIBUTION OF THE CONIFERÆ, ON THE HIMALAYAN MOUNTAINS.

(FROM A M.S. ADDRESSED TO BARON VON HUMBOLDT.)

SIMLA, *15th of October*, 1845.

Amid materials so copious and varied as those which now lie before me, it is no easy task to select such as may be right and suitable, to prove to you that I have not passed with closed eyes through this most interesting portion of our travels. In this view alone, not with the idea of imparting to you any thing new, I now undertake to write down for your perusal, a few short notices on the Coniferæ of the Himalayas, and especially on their geographical distribution. Much has been done of late towards the definite arrangement of the various species; and accurate and minute descriptions have been published,—among the rest by my amiable and accomplished friend, Captain Madden, in the Quarterly Medical and Literary Journal, Delhi, 1845; pp. 34—118,—with which you are probably already familiar. The subject of their geographical distribution has, however, as far as I have observed, been hitherto left, to a great degree, in uncertainty; few of the English botanists having enjoyed an opportunity of seeing, at one view, so great a part of the Himalayan region.

The number of the different species of Coniferæ which I have seen amounts to eleven or twelve, viz :—

Three Pines : *Pinus longifolia*,........ LAMBERT,
P. excelsa,................LAMBERT,
P. Gerardiana,...........LAMBERT;

One Spruce Fir: *Picea Morinda*,.........LINK,
or *Abies Smithiana*,........LOUDON.
Two Silver Firs: *Abies Pindrow*,.........ROYLE,
A. Webbiana,........PINETUM WOBURNENSE.
One Cedar: *Cedrus Deodara*,............LOUDON.
One Cypress, or perhaps two: *Cupressus torulosa*,...LAMBERT.
Two Junipers: *Juniperus excelsa*,.........BIEBERSTEIN.
J. squamosa, ...DON.
One Yew: *Taxus baccata?*

The Southernmost point from which our mountain wanderings began, was NAINETHAL, situated on the lake of the same name, at a height of 6500 feet above the level of the sea; Long. 81° 48′, Lat. 39° 22′. At this place, there is a highly interesting forest of *Cupressus torulosa;* containing trees of forty feet in height on the Northern acclivities, and extending to an elevation of 8,500 feet on the summit of the CHOONAR mountain. The Southern acclivities, on the other hand, are clothed with *Pinus longifolia*,—trees of from 50 to 80 feet in height. The latter is a very beautiful pine; its leaves are generally grass green, and grow three in one sheath. This tree is distinguished from the *Pinus excelsa*,—a species very closely allied to it,—both by the colour of the leaves, those of the *excelsa* being always of a somewhat greyish green, and by the cones, those of the latter being from 16 to 20 inches in length. The *Pinus longifolia* continued for a long time the only tree of the Fir-tribe along our path, which lay in a direction almost due Northward; it clothes the Northern and Western slopes of the mountains on the KOSILA GUNGA, 6000—6500 feet above the sea,—the mountain ridges from BOJAN to DIULI,—the lofty crests, 7000—8000 feet high, on either side of the PONDUAKHAL PASS,—and all the declivities, near the route North-North-Westward, from DWARA *(Dora)* HATH, to the RAMGUNGA, the outliers of the DUNAGHIRA mountains. In these forests of *Pinus longifolia*, I never saw trees above from 40 to 50 feet in height, the custom of burning down the grass and the underwood having done great damage everywhere. At SUNIANI, the "*Chooloo*" Pine, as the *Pinus longifolia* is there called, grows,—together with *Quercus lanata* and *Myrica sapida*,—at an elevation of from 5600 to 6000 feet. Beyond that point, some few detached woods of pine only,—of what species I was unable to distinguish,—appear above ADH BADRI. Single pines are also met with in the neighbourhood of the Fort of CHANDPOOR; but all the surrounding summits are bare. The glens of the KURSALEE NUDDY or BANGALEE NUDDY lie at too great a depth. Even the passes in GANDIAL,—the KHONKALA KAL and the PILLEKANI (*Tillekanni*) KAL, (from 7500 to 8000 feet above the sea) have not one specimen of *Coniferæ* on their Southern sides; and the Northern slopes afford nourishment only for a scanty growth of *Taxus*. The copper mountain at DHUNPOOR is perfectly naked on its higher ridges; the deep hollows are adorned with thick woods of umbrageous trees. In the valley of the DUDEGAON, at an elevation of 6800 feet, I again met with a tolerably thick forest of *Pinus longifolia*, and it is very remarkable that the *Chamærops Martiana*, (WALLICH) is here in immediate contact with it, some tall stems of that Palm being even scattered in among the pines. The *Coniferæ* cease at a level of about 1000 feet above the channel of the ALACANANDA, and re-appear somewhat lower, at an elevation of about 1500 feet, on the right bank; from which point they extend for a distance of five or six miles, on both sides of the small river KUNEGAR, reaching as high as the summit of the ridge which separates the GANDEREGAND NUDDY from the KUNEGAR. Beyond that, there are no more *Coniferæ;* the copper-mine hills of POKRI, doubtless above 6500 feet high, bear only oak. I first met with the pine again, in crossing the pass KHALE KAL, climbing the rugged spurs of the TUNGNATH PEAK. Here, at a height of from 7800 to 8500 feet, appeared for the first time, the wonderfully beautiful *Abies Pindrow*, perfectly pyramidal, of immense height, and with very short branches. The long, flat, dark-green leaves of this tree caused it at first to be mistaken for a *Taxus* (WALLICH). At this pass, it is called "*Kooloo*," but the names vary with every glen, with the exception of the *Pinus longifolia* and *P. excelsa*, which, throughout the Western Himalayas, bear the common name of "*Cheer*" or "*Cheel*." The KHONKALA KAL also marks the beginning of the beautiful Silver Fir, *Abies Webbiana*, a tree which attains a height of some eighty feet, with short, but very white leaves. Both species of *Abies* may probably be reckoned to have the latitude of this pass,—30° 30′,—for their Southern limit. On the descent from TUNGNATH, at an elevation of 6500 feet, I also observed the "*Roi*" Fir, *Picea Morinda*, which bears a great resemblance to our *Abies*, being distinguished chiefly by its brighter foliage, and more pointed leaves. This appears to be the Southernmost point of geographical distribution with this tree also. The defile of the AGAS GUNGA,—4000 feet above the sea,—and that of the MUNDAGRI GUNGA, with the ridges, 7500 feet high, which lie between them, are clothed, on their loftiest points, with oak alone. In like manner, there is a total absence of *Coniferæ* on both banks of the MUNDAGRI GUNGA, until it receives the waters of the wild KALI GUNGA. At that place, below the level of the forests of *Pavia*, *Juglans*, and *Acer*, I found, beside the village of PHATA, a solitary *Deodara Cedar*, the first that I had seen: it is of great size, and I have no doubt has been cultivated. The path up the right bank of the MUNDAGRI to GAURICUND never rises above the region of the *Amentaceæ*. About two or three miles above GAURICUND, the attention is first arrested by the tall and majestic form of the *Abies Pindrow* peering high on the left bank, at an altitude of some 2000 feet above the bed of the stream. Not one specimen of the Fir tribe is to be seen on the way to KEDARNATH. A dense Oak forest extends as far as BHIM ODIAR, above which place, at a height of 9000 feet, the trees cease one by one, in the following order: *Quercus lanata*, *Corylus*, *Cornus*, *Rhododendron arboreum*, *Syringa*, *Salix*. On the opposite summits, on the left bank, the genus *Pinus* yet appears, even at this height, but whether the *excelsa* or the *longifolia*, I was unable to decide. From TIRJOUGEE NARAIN, 5200 feet above the sea, and situated in the heart of the Oak forest, we crossed right over six or eight trackless mountains, some higher, some lower, but all spurs of the BUDRINATH cluster, until we came down upon the GANGES (*Bhagirathi*) nearly opposite to REITHAL. The first pass, that of TSORI KAL, is about 9600 feet high; the limit of arboreous vegetation, at an elevation of 8500 feet, is marked by *Alnus*, *Betula*, and

Populus; Coniferæ are to be seen only in a hollow, at a depth of about 8000 feet,—apparently the *Abies Webbiana*. Our pathless way led on, for full four hours' march, at an elevation of from 8500 to 9000 feet. In the descent upon PAWALI DANDA, we did not come in contact with any *Coniferæ*, but threaded our way through dense and uninterrupted forests of Oak, inhabited by multitudes of the *Moschus moschiferus*, while the gorgeous *Lophophorus*, disturbed now for the first time, was perched on many a bough. In the glen of the BILLANG river, as far as the village of GOWANNA, there is still nothing but oak (three different species) to be seen. The next lofty pass, separating this river-glen from the valley of KATHURA, rises to a height,—according to my own measurement by the thermometer,—of 10,580 feet. Nevertheless, even here, the forest ends with *Quercus* and *Rhododendron arboreum*,—with a thick underwood of *Bambusa*, reaching up to an elevation of 9000 feet. On all these heights, wherever a gentler slope or a surface of table-land permits, immense prairies of herbaceous plants are to be found; *Polygonum*, *Rumex*, tall *Potentillæ*, *Arum*, and *Sonchus* of from 3 to 5 feet in height and such thickness that it is a matter of great difficulty to force one's way through. This peculiarity,—which I have never met with before or since,—characterizes all the lateral spurs of the BUDRINATH group of mountains. The ridge between the valley of KATHURA and the two BHALEGUNGA streams,—scarcely inferior in height to the last, being 10,400 feet above the sea, —is clothed with a vegetation similar in kind, yet even more gigantic: there are, at a level of 9000 feet, several very interesting lakes. The next pass, beyond the BHALEGUNGA, is exceedingly steep; its south-eastern side is destitute of all *Coniferæ;* but, on the other hand, descending from the culminating point which is 10,700 feet high, at an elevation of 8500 feet on the north-west slope, begins one of the most splendid forests of *Coniferæ* I ever saw: the deep gorge of the PELANG NUDDY, in particular, is rich with the loftiest specimens of the *Abies Pindrow*, certainly exceeding 200 feet in height, and measuring from 15 to 20 in circumference,—*Abies Webbiana* shooting up to 150 feet,—and *Picea Morinda* scarcely inferior to it. The *Pindrow* is here called "*Morin*," "*Morind*," and "*Moorinda*;" the name given to the Red Fir or *Picea Morinda* is "*Roi*." In the glen of the PILLGAON, the oak reigns alone, with a thick jungle of bamboo. The last pass before entering the valley of the GANGES is steep to the greatest degree, although its elevation does not exceed 9700 feet. The highest summits are still clothed with forests, and oak forests too; but very near the crest of the ridge, on the descent of the north-western side, begins an extensive fir wood,—first *Abies Pindrow*, then *Abies Webbiana*, then, from a level of 8000 feet down to one of 6500, the *Picea Morinda*. At the latter altitude, the *Pinus excelsa* also occurs, but few and far between. Some specimens of the *Pindrow* here measure from 30 to 40 feet in circumference; those of the "*Roi*" Fir (*Picea Morinda*,) from 15 to 20 feet. It is a giant forest, and among its majestic trees are the tallest specimens of *Coniferæ* that I have seen among the Himalayas. On the left bank of the Ganges, above REITHAL, at a height of 800 feet above the stream, begins a thin wood of *Pinus excelsa*, extending to a distance of about eight or nine miles. This tree is most unworthy of its name, for specimens of more than from 40 to 50 feet in height are great rarities. Near the FALLS OF THE GANGES, not much above the level of the stream, the *Pinus excelsa* occurs on the left bank, together with the *P. longifolia*. The *Roi* Fir ascends on either side of the river, but only a solitary tree here and there. At DANGOOL, on the left bank, at an elevation of 7500 feet, there is a forest of *Hippophaë*, *Populus*, *Morus*, and *Grewia*, with a few *Roi* Firs scattered singly through it. From DANGOOL to SOOKHEE, the rocks are nearly bare. The latter place lies amid forests of *Pavia* and *Juglans*, and not a tree of the Fir tribe is near it, though its level is 1000 feet above the stream. It is not till near the successive confluences of the three rivers, the SHEAN-GADH, the HERSILE, and the GOOMTY, with the GANGES, that, on the right bank of that river, not far from the village of JALLA, the CEDAR FOREST begins; it soon appears on the left bank also, and stretches, in vast masses, from the margin of the here shallow stream to a height of 1000 feet, extending above the level of DHERALEE on the left, and of MOOKBA on the right bank, and above BHAIRAMGATTEE on the JAHNEVI GUNGA, and continuing along the BHAGIRATHI itself, almost without interruption, as far as GUNGOTRI, and even a day's march beyond that place. It is found in its greatest perfection between DHERALEE and BHAIRAMGATTEE, although even near GUNGOTRI single trees of from 10 to 12 feet in circumference, and from 50 to 80 in height, occur. On the HERSILE and the GOOMTY, the *Cedrus Deodara* also extends to a considerable distance, but reaching only a height of some 800 feet above their respective channels. Thus the latitude of 31° 3′ appears to be the southern limit of the *Deodara Cedar*, which nearly corresponds with the elevation of SIMLA, where it occurs very frequently, although not in great perfection.

On the mountains above MOOKBA, at an elevation of 11,000 feet, a very dwarf *Cypress* is met with, covering large tracts. Above the course of the HERSILE the *Cedar* ceases; the *Pinus excelsa*, together with the *Picea Morinda*, ascends, though but thinly scattered and not wide-spread, about 200 feet higher; after which, among the meadow-glens of the numerous fountains of waters,—the sources and confluents of the GOOMTY,—arboreous vegetation finally terminates with a wood of *Corylus* and *Betula*, at the level of FOOLAL DAROO, 11,500 feet above the sea. The *Juniperus squamosa* ceases simultaneously with the *Betula*. Beyond the snowy pass of the LAMA KAGA, 16,000 feet in height, appears, among the sources of the BUSPA, a *Cypress* of very low growth, which supplied us with fuel. I believe this to be a new species of *Cupressus*, distinct from the *C. torulosa*. It grows at an elevation of from 14,000 to 15,000 feet, and also occurs again at the point where the bed of the BUSPA assumes its contracted and rocky character, a day's march and a half lower down, where it is clearly recognized as different from the *Juniperus*, by the inhabitants of CHETKOOL, who find it of no use in the preparation of Juniper-brandy. The genus *Pinus* first begins again, long after the *Betula*, on the left bank of the BUSPA, about six miles above CHETKOOL. Apparently it is the *Pinus excelsa*, growing at a height of 11,500 feet. Not until CHETKOOL do forests of *P. excelsa* appear upon the right bank also; that tree is there called the "*Linna.*" The "*Roi*"

Fir, (*Picea Morinda*) here known by the name of "*Marin*," begins, simultaneously with the genus *Populus*, at the altitude of RAGSAM, 9000 feet, and on either bank of the river. Far below Ragsam, at the confluence of the BERSEN NUDDY on the right bank of the BUSPA, the *Cedar*,—here called "*Kjelmáng*," —reappears; and at SUNGLA it is met with in great perfection, together with the *Pinus excelsa*, particularly on the less cultivated left bank, at a height of 800 feet above the stream. The entire slope of the HARUNG PASS towards the south-south-east, is destitute of all wood. On the other hand, upon the north-west side, the *Coniferæ* present themselves in large masses, extending from the summit down to the level of the Sutlej. This seems to be a general focus for all the pines of the Himalayas; they are all found here. First appears the *Pinus excelsa*, conjointly with the *Rhododendron campanulatum*, immediately below the summit, at a height of 10,600 feet. Some 600 feet lower down begins the *Abies Webbiana*, here called "*Koorooz*;" almost immediately after it, the *Picea Morinda*, and next to it again, 500 feet lower down, the *Abies Pindrow*, but only singly. All these four continue down to MEBUR (*Mebbar*) a level of 9500 feet: close below this place the *Cedrus Deodara* begins to predominate exclusively: singly, it occurs higher up.

Above the village of BARUNG, 8400 feet high, I met with the first "*Neoza pine*" (*Pinus Gerardiana*), a tree peculiar to the SUTLEJ. It continues in a beautiful and uninterrupted forest down to POOAREE, a level of 5800 feet. On the right bank of the SUTLEJ, at the elevation of CHEENEE, 9600 feet, where the culture of the vine ceases, the *Cedar* occurs in specimens of immense size,—36 feet in circumference,—intermingled with the *Pinus Gerardiana* and the *P. excelsa*. Ascending the river, as far as PANGEE, there is, on both of its banks, at an elevation of from 1000 to 3000 feet above its channel, a tolerably thick forest of *Cedrus Deodara*, varied with occasional "*Roi*" Firs (*Picea Morinda*) and bordered by "*Neoza pines*." The same forest extends up the SUTLEJ on both sides, as far as the pass of ERRENG KHAL, after which it continues to a great distance on the left alone; it is very dense, and the *Cedar* predominates in it more and more. On the other side of the ERRENG pass, above LIPPA, the wood is exceedingly thin : a stripe of miserable *Cedars* and *Neoza-Pines* runs along the rugged mountains covered with débris, as far as the heights above KANUM, where trees of every sort gradually become stunted, and the vegetation of the Thibetian steppes begins. The ERRENG PASS is remarkable, from the fact that on its southern slope the *Juniperus excelsa* occurs simultaneously with the *Cupressus*. Both being in fruit, they could not be confounded. The *Juniperus excelsa* I first saw at CHETKOOL, in a specimen 40 feet in height; beyond KANUM, on the UPPER SUTLEJ, it is the only arborescent plant. At the village of KHAB only, a few scattered *Neoza pines*, of great beauty occur. At SHIPKEE and at NAMGIAH (*Namdja*), the *Juniperus* prevails alone, as also in the valley of the LEE, and upon the mountains of NAKO, LEEO, and HANG, all of which are bare beyond description. Along the course of the LOWER SUTLEJ the *Cedar Forest* extends on both sides of the river, at an elevation of 2000 feet above its channel, for the distance of several days' journey, as far as TRANDA, where it is met with in great perfection. Not far from GURA, on the way to RAMPOOR, occurs, as a curiosity, a forest of *Pinus longifolia*, many miles in length, at an altitude of 1000 feet above the river. This tree is here called "*Kil.*" Above KOTGHUR begins a beautiful forest of *Picea Morinda, Abies Webbiana*, and *Pinus excelsa*, trees not seen before on or near the LOWER SUTLEJ. At NAGKANDA, the forests of *Cedrus Deodara* also begin; here again they are intermingled with *Abies Webbiana* and *Abies Pindrow;* the *Neoza* is wanting. The mountain-tops are clothed with woods of Fir, sometimes thicker, sometimes again more scanty, reaching even to the loftiest summits. Very noble stems of *Abies Pindrow*, and of *Picea Morinda*, are met with, a day's march above SIMLA, at PHAGOO. Immediately above that station there is also an isolated wood of *Taxus*.

The most beautiful of the *Coniferæ*, beyond all doubt, are the "*Morinda*" Fir (*Abies Pindrow*) and the "*Neoza*" pine (*Pinus Gerardiana*). The latter I have never found exceeding 50 feet in height; the stem is never straight, but bends in a most graceful curve, and is covered with an epidermis invariably smooth, and of a beautiful silver grey. The form of its huge cones is also extremely elegant, and the colour of its leaves a vivid grass-green, so that the tree must be ranked among the chief ornaments of the Himalayan mountains. Its fruit, moreover, which ripens in November, has a very fine flavour. The distribution of the *Neoza* corresponds almost exactly to that of the *grape-vine* in the valley of the SUTLEJ. The mountains above KANUM, where a dwarf form of this tree exists, form the sole exception to the general rule.

But I am forgetting that I have already far exceeded the bounds of a short notice.

SUPPLEMENT.

The following is a synopsis of the species, &c., mentioned in the foregoing sketch :—

I. PINUS LONGIFOLIA. LAMBERT, *Pinus*. t. 26, 27. ROYLE, Illustrations of the Botany of the Himalayan Mountains, Vol. II. t. 85, fig. I.—LINK, in SCHLECHTEND. Linnœa, Vol. XV., p. 507. The "*Tchil' Pine*, "*Cheloo*," "*Cheer*," or "*Cheel*," (according to ROYLE, Vol. I., p. 349, called "*cheer*," "*sullah*," and "*thansa*)," on the Sutlej, bearing the name of "*Kil*."* *Growth*, from 50 to 80 feet in height. *Geographical distribution*, from 29° 25′ to 32°. *Vegetational Limit*, from 5000 to 8000 feet above the level of the sea. Most widely distributed of all the *Coniferæ* in the Himalayas.

II. PINUS EXCELSA. LAMBERT, l. c. 33. WALLICH,—Plantæ Asiaticæ Rariores, 201. LINK, l. c., page 515. The "*Kuel*" of the natives of SIRMORE and of GURWAL; frequently designated by English travellers, on account

* "*Kil*," Sanscrit, according to Wilson, "*a species of pine*."—W. HOFFMEISTER.

of its thin drooping branches, "*the weeping fir;*" the "*Linna*" pine. *Growth*, at the highest, from 40 to 50 feet. *Geographical distribution*, from 30° 30′ to 32°. *Vegetational limit*, from 7000 to 10,600 feet above the sea. Less generally distributed, but occasionally forming forest tracts of great extent.

III. PINUS GERARDIANA. LAMBERT, l. c. — t. 79. ROYLE, l. c.—Vol. II., t. 85, fig. 2. The "*Neoza*" Pine. *Growth*, as high as 50 feet, never quite straight. *Geographical Distribution*, from 31° 15′ to 31° 45′. *Vegetational limit*, from 5800 to 9400 feet above the sea. Grows on the Sutlej only.

IV. PICEA MORINDA.—LINK, l. c., page 522. *Abies Smithiana*, LOUDON, Arb. Brit., 4, 2317. PINETUM WOBURNENSE, t. 30. *Pinus Khutrow*, ROYLE, l. c.—t. 84, fig. 1. The "*Roi*" Fir: at Chetkool, "*Marin.*" *Growth*, to 150 feet in height, and to 20 in circumference. *Geographical distribution*, from 30° 45′ to 32°. *Vegetational limit*, from 6500 to 10,000 feet above the sea. Bears more resemblance than any other to our *Abies*.

V. ABIES PINDROW.—ROYLE. l. c. Vol. I., page 354, II. t. 86. The "*Kooloo*" Silver Fir. "*Morin*," or "*Moorinda*," "*Morindaun.*" *Growth*, to 200 feet in height, and 20 in circumference. *Geographical distribution*, from 30° 30′ to 32°. *Vegetational limit*, from 8000 to 9500 feet above the sea. Perfectly pyramidal, with short branches. The constant accompaniment of vine-culture in the valley of the Sutlej.

VI. ABIES WEBBIANA.—PINETUM WOBURNENSE, tab. 41. LINK, l. c., page 532. *Pinus Webbiana* and *P. spectabilis*, LAMBERT, tab. 44, and t. 2. The "*Kuruz*," "*Chilrow*," "*Gobrea*," "*Sallar*," and "*Oonum*," Silver Fir. *Growth*, to 80 feet in height. *Geographical dis-*

tribution, from 30° 30′ to 32°. *Vegetational limit*, from 6500 to 10,000 feet above the sea. One of the rarer species.

VII. CEDRUS DEODARA. LOUDON, Arboretum Britannicum, 4,—2428. Pinetum Woburnense, tab. 48, 49. LINK, l. c., page 538. The "*Deodar*,"* or "*Kelon*" Cedar. On the Buspa it is called "*Kjelmang*."† *Growth*, to 150 feet in height, and 36 in circumference. *Geographical distribution*, from 31° 3′ to 31° 50′. *Vegetational limit*, from 8000 to 11,000 feet above the sea. The crowning glory of the Himalayas. Occasionally cultivated in situations beyond its natural habitat. Individual specimens above 40 feet in circumference.

VIII. CUPRESSUS TORULOSA.—LAMBERT. *Growth*, as high as 40 feet. *Geographical distribution*, from 29° 22′ to 32°. *Vegetational limit*, from 5500 to 8500 feet above the sea. Even to a greater elevation in a dwarf form.

IX. CUPRESSUS,—NOVA SPECIES.—*Growth*, shrubby, sociable, covering large tracts. *Geographical distribution*, from 31° 0′ to 31° 20′. *Vegetational limit*, from 11,000 to 16,000 feet above the sea. At the sources of the Goomty and the Buspa.

X. JUNIPERUS EXCELSA.—BIEBERSTEIN! *Growth*, as high as 40 feet. *Geographical distribution*, from 31° 30′ to 32°. *Vegetational limit*, from 8000 to 12,000 feet above the sea. Frequently met with in company with the *Cupressus torulosa*; extends to a more elevated habitat than any of the other *Coniferæ*; on the Upper Sutlej is the only tree, as also on the declivities sloping to-

* "*Déva-dáru*," Sanscrit, *i. e.* "*Fir of the Gods.*" "*Dâru*" is also used alone to designate the same tree.—W. HOFFMEISTER.

† "*Kilima*," Sanscrit, according to Wilson, "*a species of pine.*"—W. HOFFMEISTER.

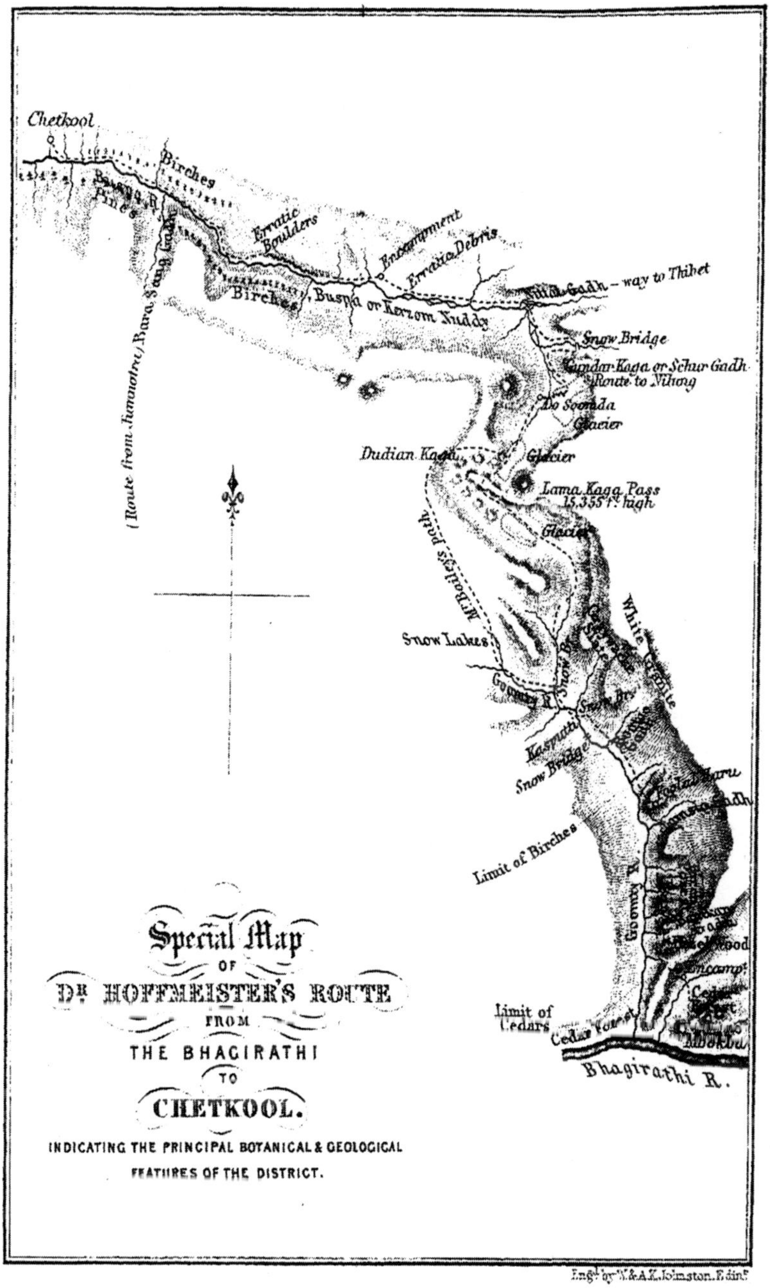

Special Map
of
Dr. HOFFMEISTER'S ROUTE
FROM
THE BHAGIRATHI
TO
CHETKOOL.
INDICATING THE PRINCIPAL BOTANICAL & GEOLOGICAL FEATURES OF THE DISTRICT.

Engd. by W. & A.K. Johnston, Edinr.

wards the table-land at Shipkee, where, however, it becomes shrubby.

XI. JUNIPERUS SQUAMOSA,—Don. *Growth*, low. *Geographical distribution*, from 31° 30′ to 32°. *Vegetational limit*, from 9000 to 11,500 feet above the sea. Occurs in company with dwarf species of the genera *Corylus* and *Betula*: ceases simultaneously with the latter tree at the above-mentioned elevation.

XII. TAXUS BACCATA? (A yew).—*Growth*, arborescent in the more favourable situations; dwarf on the heights. *Geographical distribution*, from 30° to 32°. *Vegetational limit*, from 5000 to 8000 feet above the sea. Occasionally forms forests of small extent; *e. g.* at Phagoo.

APPENDIX II.

VEGETATION OF THE HIMALAYAN MOUNTAINS.

I.—FROM NAINETHAL TO THE RAMGUNGA.

GLENS OF THE KOSILA AND USIGAKA NUDDY.

1.—*Lower Forest region.*

Phœnix humilis.—Melia.—Ficus.—Phœnix sylvestris.—Bombax.—Bassia butyracea.—Vitex.—Laurus. — Platanus.—Bauhinia. — Vitis.— Punica. — Deutzia. — Indigofera.—Cactus.—Androsace.—Fragaria Indica.—Urtica.

2.—*Upper Forest region.*

Rhododendron.—Betula.—Cerasus.—Acer.—Quercus.—Pinus longifolia.—Berberis.—Rosa.—Rubus.—Arbutus.—Carissa sepiaria.

3.—*River Glens.*

Laurus.—Berberis.—Daphne.—Hedera Helix.—Ipomæa.—Mazus.—Cyperus.—Gnaphalium.—Primula.—Adiantum.—Campanula.—Ajuga.—Impatiens.

4.—*Cultivated Plants.*

Mangifera Indica.—Triticum.

II.—VALLEY OF THE RAMGUNGA DOWN TO THE ALACANANDA.

GLENS OF THE KURSALI NUDDY AND DUDEGAON NUDDY.

1.—Lower Forest region.

Phœnix humilis.—Acacia.—Ficus.—Cassia.—Carissa.—Vitis.—Myrica sapida.—Cissus.—Pæonia.

2.—Upper Forest region.

Æsculus.—Morus.—Pyrus.—Quercus incana.—Q. semicarpifolia.—Taxus.—Pinus longifolia.—Rhododendron.—Berberis.—Rubus.—Anemone.—Aquilegia.—Cypripedium.—Fragaria Indica.—Fr. vesca.—Euphorbia.—Arum.—Lamium.

3.—River Glens.

Spiræa (veronicæfolia?) Philadelphus.—Carissa sepiaria.—Verbena officinalis.—Ajuga.—Mazus.—Agrostis.—Poa.

III.—FROM THE ALACANANDA TO KEDARNATH.

GLENS OF THE KUNEGAR AND MUNDAGRI.

1.—Lower Forest region.

Laurus.—Pterocarpus.—Phœnix humilis.—Menispermum.—Myrica.—Bambusa.—Orchis.

2.—Upper Forest region.

Quercus incana and Q. semicarpifolia.—Picea Morinda.—Pinus excelsa.—Æsculus.—Ulmus.—Acer.—Salix.—Alnus. Populus.—Taxus.—Staphylca.—Sambucus.—Cornus.—Corylus.—Vitis.—Smilax.—Cissus.—Rosa.—Arum.—Filices.

3.—Prairie Vegetation.

Arum.—Mazus.—Polygonum.—Ajuga.—Prunella.—Herminium.—Cerastium vulgatum.—Alsine media.—Myosotis.—Gnaphalium.—Juncus.—Carex (on the Lake of Durithal).

4.—*Alpine Vegetation of Kedarnath.*

Rheum.—Iris.—Fritillaria (meleagris).—Potentilla pteropoda and P. coccinea.—Primula.—Anemone *(two species)*.—Corydalis.—Myosotis.—Draba.—Pedicularis.—Gentiana.—Veratrum.—Anchusa.—Viola reniformis.—Hottonia.—Erysimum.—Nasturtium.—Caltha.—Juncus.—Carex.—Rhododendron.—Rosa.—Cotoneaster.—Salix.

IV.—FROM KEDARNATH TO THE BHAGIRETHI.

GLENS OF THE BILLANG AND BHALEGUNGA.

1.—*Forest region.*

Cornus.—Quercus ("*Mohroo*" and "*Bhansh*").—Andromeda.—Acer.—Juglans.—Alnus.—Sorbus.—Fraxinus.—Betula.—Pyrus.—Carpinus.—Taxus *(5 feet in diameter)*.—Abies Pindrow *(6 feet in diameter, and 200 in height)*.—Picea Morinda.—Corylus *(3 feet in diameter)*.—Rhododendron arboreum.—Rh. campanulatum.—Spiræa *(arborescent)*.—Xylosteum *(arborescent)*.—Berberis angustifolia.—Rhamnus.—Philadelphus.—Rubus.—Vitis.—Bambusa.—Betonica.—Urtica.—Cannabis.—Fragaria.—Impatiens.—Cheiranthus.

2.—*Tracts of Herbaceous Plants in the Forest (from 4 to 5 feet in height.)*

Rumex.—Chærophyllum.—Lamium.—Ballota.—Arum.—Sonchus.—Polygonum.—Capsella Bursa-pastoris.—Caltha Cachemiriana.—Ranunculus.

3.—*On the heights of the Passes.*

Thermopsis barbata.—Aster.—Liliaceæ and Orchideæ.

4.—*Plants under Cultivation.*

Prunus Armeniaca.—Juglans.—Amaranthus Gangeticus.—Oryza sativa.—Triticum.—Hordeum.—Panicum.

V.—GLEN OF THE BHAGIRETHI TO GUNGOTRI.

BANKS OF THE BHAGIRETHI.

1.—*Near the bed of the river.*

Berberis.—Cissus.—Rubus.—Vitis.—Aurantiaceæ.

2.—*Higher up.*

Pinus longifolia.—Pavia.—Grewia.—Betula.—Populus.—Sorbus.—Morus.—Ulmus. — Alnus. — Dryobalanus. — Salix pentandra.—Hippophaë (*"Amil"*).—Bignonia.—Caragana.—Rhamnus.—Dalbergia.—Vitis (*" Lagella"*).—Ficus (*climbing*).—Parietaria.—Rumex. —Carduus.—Pteris.—Cyperus.

3.—*Glens of tributary streams.*

Urtica (*two species*).—Cannabis.—Impatiens.—Spiræa.—Fraxinus (*coppice*).—Coriaria.—Salix.—Solanum moschatum (*at the falls of the Bhagirethi*).

4.—*Mounds of Débris.*

Saxifraga.—Cichorium.—Dianthus Barbatus.— Sempervivum. Lilium Martagon.—Epilobium.—Cucubalus.—Petasites.—Scrophularia.—Arenaria. —Myosotis.—Astragalus. — Galium.—*Higher up.*—Papaver (*blue*).—Saxifraga.—Rheum. —Sedum.—Telephium.—Primula.

5.—*First Cedar-forest, from Jalla, onward.*

Cedrus Deodara.—Fragaria.—Thlaspi.—Senecio.—Allium.—Monotropa.—Bupleurum (*at the edge of the forest*).—Indigofera.—Ribes Grossularia.

6.—*Plants under cultivation.*

Juglans.—Prunus Armeniaca.—Amygdalus Persica.—Panicum (*two species*).—Triticum.—Hordeum.

7.—*Vegetation at the Villages.*

Ribes Grossularia.—Origanum.—Thymus.—Lychnis.—Turritis.—Orobanche. — Artemisia Absinthium.—Tanacetum. —Cheiranthus.—Lonicera.

8.—*Vegetation of Bhairamgath.*

Artemisia.—Pyrethrum.—Galium.—Blitum. —Lithospermum. Soldanella.—Arenaria.—Apargia.—Asparagus acinacifolia. Scabiosa.—Pedicularis.—Origanum.—Alopecurus.—Artemisia.—Viburnum.—Indigofera.

9.—*Vegetation of Gungotri.*

Astragalus.—Athamanta.—Vicia (Cracca?)—Wiborgia.—Artemisia.—Thesium. — Epilobium. — Lilium Martagon.—Aster. — Asparagus.—Rheum. — Asperifolia.—Rumex.— —Rhododendron.—Berberis.—Philadelphus.

VI.—FROM THE BHAGIRETHI TO THE SUTLEJ.

GLENS OF THE HERSILE, THE GOOMTY, AND THE BUSPA.

1.—*Glen of the Hersile.*

Alpine Vegetation.

Papaver *(blue)*.—Anemone.—Parnassia.—Primula.—Saxifraga.—Sedum.—Telephium.—Rheum.

Forest-region.

Cedrus Deodara *(thick forest)*.—Pinus longifolia.—Picea Morinda.—Fragaria.—Cheiranthus.—Dalbergia.

2.—*Glen of the Goomty.*

Alpine Prairies.

Potentilla atropos.—Geranium (pratense?).—Rumex.—Pedicularis.—Hottonia.—Epilobium.—Centaurea.—Polemonium. — Lotus corniculatus. — Valeriana. —Campanula.—Saxifraga.—Lilium.—Astrantia.—Sagina.—Telephium.—Asperifolia.—Echium.— Polygonum. — Sedum *(two species)*. — Valeriana. — Chærophyllum. — Heracleum. —Convallaria.—Galega.—Cucubalus.—Brassica.—Arabis.—

Poa.—Alopecurus.—Briza.—Agrostis.—Carex *(three species)*.—Juncus.—Salix *(coppice)*.—Rhododendron campanulatum.—Sorbus.—Rosa Webbiana.—Artemisia.

Lama Kaga Pass.

Equisetum.—Polygonum Bistorta.—Potentilla coccinea.—Ballota.—Delphinium Cachemirianum.—Silene.—Myosotis.—Anemone (alba).—Rumex obtusifolius.—Medicago.—Musci and Lichenes.

Tracts of erratic blocks.

Rheum.—Artemisia.—Asparagus Acinacifolia.—Syringa.—Deutzia.—Berberis.—Rosa.—Alopecurus.—Phleum.—Poa.

3.—*Valley of the Buspa.*

Upper Buspa down to Chetkool.

Primula.—Potentilla.—Filago.—Astragalus *(yellow)*.—Gypsophila.—Salsola.—Pedicularis.—Gnaphalium.—Lactuca.—Geranium.—Arabis.—Nepeta.—Galium.—Tanacetum.—Senecio.—Scrophularia.—Gentiana.—Fumaria.—Delphinium *(with a fragrance of musk)*.—Silene.—Oxytropis.—Rheum.—Bellis.—Chrysanthemum *(bright rose-colour)*.—Artemisia.—Epilobium.—Veronica.—Carex *(three species)*.—Scirpus.—Poa.—Agrostis.—Tamarix.—Salix *(coppice)*.—Xylosteum.—Cupressus.—Rosa.—Umbellatæ.

Flora at Chetkool.

Pinus longifolia.—Picea Morinda.—Pedicularis *(two species)*.—Thymus.—Nepeta.—Scutellaria.—Mentha.—Chenopodium Bonus-Henricus.—Ch. album.—Blitum.—Dianthus barbatus *(white.)*—Morina Wallichiana.—Leontodon Taraxacum.—Achillea Millefolium.—Potentilla.—Apium Petroselinum.—Plantago media.—Urtica urens.—Impatiens.—Euphrasia officinalis.—Fumaria lutea.—Gnaphalium *(white)*.—Polygonum aviculare.—Myosotis *(dark-blue.)*—Artemisia.—Verbascum Thapsus.—Cucubalus.—Chenopodium *(with small round leaves)*.—Stellaria.—Galium Aparine.—Capsella Bursa-pastoris.—Rumex.—

Sagina.—Pycnocycla?—Bistorta.—Brassica.—Chærophyllum (bulbosum?)—Anthriscus.—Lamium.—Thalictrum.—Anemone discolor.—Heracleum.—Cuscuta.—Hieracium.—Medicago.—Lotus corniculatus.—Silene.—Bupleurum (falcatum?)—Arum.—Scirpus.—Phleum.—Poa.—Alopecurus.—Ribes Grossularia.

Agriculture round Chetkool.

Triticum *(two species)*.—Polygonum (fagopyrum?).—Brassica Napus.

Lower Buspa down to the Sutlej.

Populus.—Pinus longifolia.—Cedrus Deodara.—Corylus.—Syringa. — Rosa. — Indigofera.—Artemisia.—Heracleum.—Origanum.—Thalictrum.—Fragaria.—Salvia, *(2 species.)*—Linum.—Scrophularia.—Impatiens.—Dianthus.—Campanula.

At Sungla.

Prunus Armeniaca.—Amygdalus Persica.—Juglans.

Agriculture.—Polygonum fagopyrum.—Panicum.—Triticum.

VII.—VALLEY OF THE SUTLEJ FROM THE CONFLUENCE OF THE BUSPA UP TO SHIPKEE.

UPPER KUNAWUR.

1.—*From the confluence of the Buspa to the pass of Errengkhal.*

Forest.

Cedrus Deodara.—Pinus longifolia.—Picea Morinda.—Abies Webbiana.—Pinus Gerardiana.—Pyrus.—Ribes.—Helianthemum. — Geranium. — Dianthus.—Leontodon.—Artemisia Dracunculus. — Portulaca. — Medicago falcata.—Malva rotundifolia.

Glens of tributary streams.

Hoya *(rarely.)*—Myosotis.—Verbascum.—Rheum.—Senecio.—Thalictrum.—Valeriana.—Artemisia. — Thlaspi. — Nepeta.—Chenopodium *(abundant.)* — Origanum. — Impatiens.—Thymus.—Phleum.—Stipa.

Forest higher up.

Cedrus Deodara *(singly.)*—Cupressus.—Pyrus.—Viburnum. —Rosa. —Syringa. — Xylosteum. —Caragana.—Berberis. —Cotoneaster.—Spiræa Aruncus.—Sp. veronicæfolia.— Dianthus. — Orobanche.—Silene. —Eupatorium.—Erigeron.—Veronica.—Gnaphalium.—Bupleurum *(2 species.)* Rheum.—Lotus.—Blitum.—Arenaria.—Arabis. —Pedicularis.—Mentha.—Galium Aparine.—Anthriscus.—Sedum. —Cerastium.—Salvia.—Oxytropus.—Arum.—Aster.

Meadow-ground.

Salvia *(blue.)*—Polygonum laxiflorum.—Centaurea.—Heracleum.—Scabiosa (6 *feet high.*)—Epilobium.—Eupatoria. —Cichorium. —Echinops.—Leonurus.—Geranium.—Impatiens (4 *species.*)—Phleum.—Cyperus.

Flora at Cheenee.

Polygonum Hydropiper.—P. aviculare.—P. Phapur.—Pedicularis.—Orchis.—Gloxinia.—Carduus.—Gratiola.—Cannabis.—Ranunculus (arvensis ?)—Plantago major.—Mentha. —Prunella. — Lotus corniculatus. — Senecio.—Malva.— Urtica dioica.—Chenopodium album.—Ch. crispum.— Euphrasia officinalis.—Salvia (*yellow.*)—Medicago.—Impatiens (3 *species.*)—Dactylis glomerata.—Myosotis (2 *species.*)—Inula.—Spiræa Ulmaria.—Clinopodium.—Scirpus. —Agrostis.—Juncus.—Rubus.

Plants under cultivation at Cheenee.

Melia.—Populus.—Corylus.—Juglans. —Prunus Armeniacus. Amygdalus Persica.—Pyrus Malus.—Vitis.—Triticum.— Hordeum.—Polygonum.

Banks of the River.

Capparis.—Apargia.—Campanula.—Malva (2 *species.*) — Althæa.—Echinops.—Cnicus.—Carduus.—Clematis.

Flora of the Errengkhal Pass.

Cupressus.—Juniperus.—Artemisia.—Thymus. — Gnaphalium album.—Salvia.—Senecio.—Epilobium laxum.—Geranium pratense.—Pteris.—Poa laxa.—P. pratensis.—P. exilis.—

Alopecurus.—Festuca.—Carex (2 *species.*)—Morina Wallichiana.—Gypsophila.—Arenaria. —Sempervivum.—Erigeron.—Rumex scutellatus.—R. obtusifolius.—Meconopsis. — Potentilla. — Ranunculus (arvensis ?)—Polygonum laxiflorum.—P. (aviculare ?)—Sedum.—Galium Aparine. —Scrophularia purpurea.—Myosotis (2 *species.*)—Lotus corniculatus.—Leontodon Taraxacum.—Gentiana pusilla. —Gentiana.—Sagina.—Valeriana.—Aster. —Prenanthes. Senecio. — Senecillio. — Hyssopus. — Asplenium. —Aspidium.—Umbellatæ.—Astrantia (*"Lasser."*)—Cichorium. —Draba.—Campanula.—Papaver (*blue.*)—Rhododendron. —Betula (*beyond the summit of the pass.*)

2.—*From the Errengkhal Pass to Shipkee.*

Acclivities covered with debris, ramparts of the valley of the Sutlej.

Cedrus Deodara (*stunted and scanty.*)—Pinus Gerardiana (*singly and stunted.*)—Cupressus. — Caragana. — Rosa. —Ribes Grossularia. — Colutea.—Xylosteum.—Artemisia Absinthium.—Astragalus Grahamianus.—Spiræa.—Senecio. — Carduus. — Origanum. — Verbascum.—Chenopodium. — Salsola.—Zizyphus.—Thymus. — Lolium. — Poa. —Panicum.

On the heights of the Passes.

Rosa (2 *species.*)—Lonicera.—Ribes.—Caragana.—Rheum.— Delphinium Cachemirianum.—Orobanche (2 *species.*)— Geranium.—Polygonum Bistorta and P. aviculare.—Gentiana.—Veronica.—Centaurea (*white.*)—Scorzonera.—Epilobium. — Prenanthes. — Arenaria. —Avena.—Euphorbia exigua (*on the Benung Pass.*)

Glens of tributary Streams.

Beccabunga.—Mentha.—Leontodon Taraxacum.—Myosotis.— Ranunculus (bulbosus ?).—Rumex (*predominant*).—Impatiens.—Salvia (*yellow*).—Chondrilla (*blue*).—Cannabis. —Euphrasia officinalis.—Several Umbellatæ and Gramineæ.

Flora of the Villages.

Alnus.—Ribes Grossularia.—Lonicera.—Spiræa.—Clematis.—Cannabis.—Urtica.—Cuscuta.—Nepeta.—Hyoscyamus.—Salvia pratensis.—Salvia (*yellow*).—Mentha.—Adonis.—Artemisia (*two species*).—Echinops.—Poa.—Phleum.

Plants under Cultivation.

Populus alba.—Grewia.—Prunus Armeniaca.—Cerasus.—Pyrus Malus.—Tagetes.—Datura.—Althæa.—Triticum.—Hordeum (hexastichon).—Spelta.—Brassica Napus.—Brassica Rapa.—Polygonum.—Pisum.—Vicia.

VIII.—VALLEY OF THE SUTLEJ FROM THE CONFLUENCE OF THE BUSPA DOWN TO KOTGHUR.

LOWER KUNAWUR.

Mountain Forests.

Cedrus Deodara (*singly*).—Larix (*very rare*).—Pinus longifolia.—P. Gerardiana.—Picea Morinda.—Abies Pindrow.—Taxus.—Quercus ("*Mohroo*" and "*Bhansh*").—Acer.—Fraxinus.—Morus.—Grewia.—Melia.—Pyrus ("*Li*").—Amygdalus Persica.—Juglans.—Rhododendron (*last seen at Manjootee Danda*).—Alnus.—Æsculus.—Ilex.—Viburnum.—Ficus.—Philadelphus.—Dalbergia.—Carissa.—Cassia.—Dolichos.—Cucumis.—Vitis.—Clematis.—Gloxinia.—Pteris.—Impatiens.—Polygonum.

Deeper, in the river glen.

Pterocarpus.—Vitex.—Bignonia.—Volcameria.—Ficus.—Dalborgia.—Rhamnus.—Clematis.—Capparis.—Amomum.—Bambusa.—Arundo.—Gloxinia.—Nepeta.—Sedum.—Dolichos.—Convolvulus Scammonia.

Meadow-Flora.

Verbascum.—Artemisia.—Campanula.—Centaurea.—Polygala.—Gloxinia.—Nepeta.—Salvia.—Teucrium.—Pedicularis.—Epilobium laxum.—Myosotis.—Lychnis.—Aster.

—Orchis.—Androsace.—Oxalis corniculata.—Polygonum amplexicaule. — Goldfussia..— Polygonum laxiflorum. — Cnicus.—Scirpus. —Priodia.—Poa. —Festuca. —Bambusa (*small*).

Flora of the Villages.

Melia. — Ficus. —Bignonia. —Sapindus. — Carissa.—Citrus (*at Gura*).—Clematis.—Cucumis.—Cucurbita (*two species*).— Cannabis. — Urtica. — Gloxinia. — Impatiens.— Papilionaceæ.

Plants under Cultivation.

Prunus Armeniaca.—Amygdalus Persica.—Pyrus Malus.— Mangifera.—Vitis.—Dolichos.—Chenopodium.—Eleusine —Amaranthus.—Panicum (*two species*).—Triticum.—Oryza sativa (*at Kartol*).

APPENDIX III.

BIRDS OF THE HIMALAYAN MOUNTAINS.*

(Mr Hay's Collection at Simla.)

1—4. *Pyrgita,* four doubtful species.

5—6. *Pyrrhula,* two doubtful species.

7. *Enucleator.* . . . . ? *Pyrrhospiza.* A splendid bird, inhabiting only the loftiest pine forests on the borders of eternal snow.

8. *Chloris.*

9 A. *Linaria rhodochroa,* GOULD. A rare bird, found at the Buranda Pass at a height of 14,000 feet. 9 B. *Linaria rhodopepla.*—10.—11. Two new species.—N.B.—10 may perhaps be the *Erythrospiza* of PALLAS, and the female may be the *Coccothraustes roseus* of VIEILLOT.

12. *Procarduelis?* Hodgson. A rare bird, only once met with in a snow-storm on the Buranda Pass.

* The translator has not considered it necessary to burden this Appendix with the strictly technical details, interesting to the ornithologist alone, to whom, for scientific purposes, the original work is accessible. The numbers appear to refer to the arrangement in Mr Hay's collection, and are not always consecutive.—TR.

13. *Carduelis caniceps.* Frequently seen at Shipkee.

14. *Chrysomitris*, Boie. The Canary-bird of the Himalayas. Common.

15.—16. Several female birds of various species of *Linaria*, the males of which are yet unknown.

17. *Novum genus.* A dwarf form of *Coccothraustes.* Once, only, at Nagkanda, a flight of these birds was seen.—Only three male birds obtained.

18. *Coccothraustes icteroides*, Gould.—19. A new species?

20. *Euplectes philippensis?*

21.—23. *Amadina;* three unnamed species.

24. ———————— A bird resembling a Bunting.

24—26. *Emberiza;* three unnamed species.

27. ———; I saw, on the pass, before arriving at Shipkee, below Purkyul, a species of *Emberiza*, white, and apparently spurred; not in any collection.

28. *Parus monticolus.*—29. *Parus......? xanthogenys.*

30. ——— *melanolophus.*—31—32. Two unnamed species. —33. *Parus erythrocephalus.* I saw this little bird in great numbers in Nepaul.

34. A group nearly allied to the Titmouse; possibly the *Ixos.*

34 A—34 B. *Ixos;* two unnamed species.

35. *Certhia..... ? (Goodpanensis).*—36. An unnamed species. Probably the *Cinnyris Gouldiæ.* Met with at very elevated places in the mountain region, even as high as 10,657 feet above the sea; but only singly.

37—38. *Tichodroma;* two unnamed species.

39—40. *Sitta;* two unnamed species.

41. *Troglodytes;* one unnamed species.

42. *Regulus;* one unnamed species. Head not crested, but with one spot of vivid sulphur yellow, edged with black.

43. *Muscicapa melanops.*—44. *Muscicapa*, unnamed.—45—46. ———.—47. *Muscicapa Paradisea*, in all its varieties.

48. *Phœnicurus*, unnamed.—49. *Phœnicurus cœruleocephala.* —50. *Phœnicurus......? leucocephala.*—51—52. Two unnamed species.

52—57. *Saxicola;* six unnamed species.

58—66. *Sylvia;* nine unnamed species.—N.B.—58 not unlike our red-breast, but long-legged: only once met with. —60 resembling our wag-tail, but the tail short.

68. *Saxicola?*

70. *Novum Genus.* Bill very strong; in other respects resembling *Sylvia.*

71. *Enicurus......? maculatus.*—72. *Enicurus Scouleri.*—73. *Enicurus intrepidus,* nova species, discovered by Mr Hay.

74. *Motacilla alba.*—75—76, two unnamed species.—77. *Motacilla boarula.*—78, an unnamed species.

79. A long-legged bird allied to the *Motacillæ.*

80. *Phœnicornis brevirostris.*—81. *Phœnicornis princeps.*—82—85, four unnamed species.

86. *Novum Genus. Cinclosoma?*

87. Unnamed.

88. *Zosterops;* an unnamed species.

89. *Prinia,* do.

90. *Petrocincla, nova species?*—91. *Petrocincla cincloryncha.*

92. *Alcopus nigriceps.*

93. *Pastor;* an unnamed species.

94. An unnamed, Thrush-like bird.

95. *Turdus Wardii.*—96. *Turdus albicollis.*—97. *Turdus atrogularis.*—98. *Turdus erythrogaster?*—99—100, two unnamed species.—101. *Turdus poecilopterus.*—102. *Turdus viscivorus.*—103—104, two unnamed species.

105. *Turdus? Novum Genus?* Bill short, with a high ridge.

106. *Cinclosoma variegatum,* Gould.—107. *Cinclosoma erythrocephalum,* Gould. Frequently seen in Nepaul.—108. *Nova species.*

109. *Myophonus Temminkii.*

110. *Oriolus melanocephalus?*—111, an unnamed species.

112. *Pomatorhinus erythrogenys,* Gould.—113, an unnamed species.

114. *Hypsipetes psaroides,* Gould.

115. *Zoothera monticola.* Everywhere a rare bird, making its appearance in winter.

116. *Cinclus Pallasii.* Common.
117. *Upupa*, an unnamed species.
118. *Cuculus Canorus.* Tail black.—119. *Cuculus sparveroides*, GOULD.—120. *Cuculus Hymalayanus.*—121. *Nova species.*
122. *Oxylophus;* an unnamed species.
123. A nearly allied genus. Bill like that of a Cuckoo.
124. *Chalcites;* an unnamed species, only once met with.
125. *Nucifraga hemispila.* Very black; in other respects similar to our own.
126. *Picus hyperythrus*, GOULD.—127. *Picus brunnifrons*, GOULD.—128–130. *Three unnamed species.*—131. *Picus occipitalis.*—132. *Picus Shorii.*—133-134. *Two unnamed species.*—135. *Picus squamatus.*
136. *Merops;* an unnamed species.
137. *Alcedo guttatus.*—137. B. an unnamed species.
138. *Bucco grandis.*—139-141, three unnamed species.
143. *Pica vagabunda*, GOULD. All the specimens have the tail shorter than as represented in Gould's plate.—144. *Pica erythroryncha.*—145. *Pica Sinensis.*
146. *Garrulus lanceolatus.*—147. *Garrulus bispecularis.*—148 an unnamed species.—149. *Garrulus leucocephalus.*—150. *Garrulus striatus.* Rare.
149. *Dicrurus;* an unnamed species.—149 A. *Dicrurus*, also unnamed.
150. *Lamprotornis spilopterus*, GOULD. Common.
151—153. *Corvus;* three unnamed species.
154. *Pyrrhocorax;* an unnamed species.
155. *Lanius.* (*Collurio erythropterus*, GOULD.)
156. *Collurio erythronotus*, GOULD. Exactly the same as the C. Hardwickia, for the size varies in an extraordinary degree.
158—159. *Caprimulgus;* two unnamed species, the latter new.
160. *Cypselus;* an unnamed species.
162—163. *Hirundo;* two unnamed species.
166. *Psittacus schisticeps.*
170. *Columba Nepalensis.* Frequently seen on the Sutlej.—171.—*Columba leuconota.*—172. *Columba livia.* Fre-

quently seen on the Sutlej.—173. An unnamed species. Only twice seen,—in the valley of the Buspa.

174. *Vinago sphenura.*

175. *Turtur;* an unnamed species.

177. *Aquila;* an unnamed species.

178. *Gypætus barbatus.*

179. *Vultur;* an unnamed species.

180. *Astur;* an unnamed species.

181. *Buteo;* an unnamed species. A young bird.

182. A *Falco subbuteo......?*—182 B—183. Two unnamed species.—184. *Falco cenchris.*—216, an unnamed species.

185. *Circus;* an unnamed species.—187; also unnamed.

186. *Nauclerus;* an unnamed species.

188. *Pandion;* an unnamed species.

189—190. *Strix;* two unnamed species.—N.B.—189 resembling the *Uralensis.*—190 resembling the *Aluco.*

191—196. *Noctua;* six unnamed species.

197. *Scolopax monticola.*—198. *Scolopax nemoricola.*

199—200. *Tringa;* two unnamed species.—202, also unnamed.

201. *Vanellus Goensis......?*

203. *Phasianus Stocii.*—204. *Phasianus Pucrasia*—205. *Phasianus albo-cristatus.*

206. *Tetraogallus Nigellii.*

207. *Lophophorus refulgens.*

208. *Tragopan Satyrus.*

210. *Perdix francolinus.*—211. *Perdix olivaceus.*—212. *Perdix pictus.*—213; an unnamed species.

215. *Coturnix;* an unnamed species.

APPENDIX

REGISTER OF TEMPERATURE,

Date.	Morning.	Air.	Water.	Forenoon.	Air.	Water.	Afternoon.	Air.
1844		R. F.	R. F.		R. F.	R. F.		R. F.
Sept. 19	7	18°.4-73½°	17°.5-71°	”	”	”	1	23°.5-85°
24	7	20°.4-78°	”	”	”	”	”	”
25	7	20°.8-78¾°	”	10	24°.8-88°	”	”	”
26	7	21°.5-80½°	”	”	”	”	1	22°.2-82°
Oct. 2	7	18°-72½°	”	”	”	”	1	18°.4-73¼°
3	7	19°.8-76½°	”	”	”	”	1	22°.7-83°
4	7	19°-74¾°	”	”	”	”	1	26°.5-91¾°
5	7	18°.5-73½°	”	12	23°-84°	”	5	20°.2-77½°
7	7	19°-74¾°	”	”	”	”	1	23°.5-85°
9	7	19°-74¾°	”	11	25°-88½°	”	1	26°.5-91¾°
10	7	18°.8-74½°	”	10	22°.8-83¼°	”	1	26°.3-91¼
11	6	19°.5-76°	”	11	25°.3-89°	”	1	27°-93°
12	7	19°.2-75¼°	”	1	24°.8-88°	”	7	21°-79½°
27	6	21°-79½°	22°-81¾°	”	”	”	1	23¼°-84½°
28	6	20¾°-78¾°	23°.5-85°	10	23°.5-85°	23°-84°	1	24°-86¼°
29	6	24°-86¼°	23°-84°	11	25½°-89°	23¾°-85½°	1	25¼°-89°
30	6	24°-86¼°	23°.5-85°	½p11	25°-88½°	24°-86¼°	2	24¾°-87¾°
31	6	23½°-85°	23°.5-85°	½p10	23¾°-85½°	23°.5-85°	½ p.1	23°-84°
Nov. 1	6	21¾°-81°	23°-84°	½p11	23¼°-84½°	22¾°-83¼°	1	23°-84°
2	7	23°-84°	22°.5-82¾°	”	”	”	2	23½°-85°
3	6	21½°-80½°	22°.5-82¾°	½p10	22¾°-83¼°	”	1	23°-84°
4	6	21°-79½°	22°.5-82¾°	10	21°-79½°	”	2	21¼°-81°
5	6	21°-79½°	23¼°-84½°	10	21½°-80°	”	½ p.1	22¾°-83¼°
6	6	21¼°-80°	21°-79½°	10	22°-81¾°	”	do.	22°-81¾°
7	6	21°.5-80½°	21°¼-80°	11	22°-81¾°	”	do.	22¾°-83½°
8	6	21¼°-80°	21°-79½°	½p10	22°.5-82¾°	”	do.	22°.5-82¾°
9	6	20¾°-78¾°	22°-81¾°	do.	22°.5-82¾°	”	do.	23¼°-84½°
10	6	22¼°-82¼°	22°.5-82¾°	do.	23°.5-85°	”	do.	23¼°-84½°
11	6	21¼°-80°	22¾°-83¼°	do.	23°-84°	”	do.	24°-86¼°
12	6	22¼°-82¼°	22¾°-83¼°	do.	23°-84°	”	do.	22¾°-83¼°
13	”	”	”	”	”	”	”	”
14	7	22°½-82¾°	”	12	25°-88½°	”	”	”
15	7	20°-77	”	”	”	”	”	”

IV.

WEATHER, &c.

…ter.	Even-ing.	Air.	Water.	Remarks.	Place.	Height above the level of the sea.
F.		R. F.	R. F.			Feet.
"	7	19°.5-76°	"	"	Corfu.	"
"	7	22°.8-83¼°	"	"	Athens.	"
"	12	21°-79½°	"	"	"	"
"	8	18°.5-73½°	"	"	"	"
"	7	18°.4-73¼°	"	"	"	"
"	8	19°.5-76°	"	Voyage on the Mediterranean Sea.	Alexandria in the evg.	"
"	"	"	"	"	Alexandria.	"
"	9	19.5-76°	"	"	"	"
"	7	22°-81¾	"	"	Cairo.	"
"	7	23°.5-85°	"	"	"	"
"	7	22°.8-83¼°	"	"	"	"
"	7	21°.6-80¾	"	"	"	"
"	10	20°.5-78¼°	"	"	"	"
82¼°	6	22¼°-82¼°	23°.5-85°	"	Red Sea.	"
-85°	6	23¼°-84½°	22°-81¾°	Lightning in the evg.	Red Sea.	"
6¼°	6	25°-88⅓°	21°.5-80⅓°	High wind.	"	"
"	6	24°-86¼°	23°.5-85°	High wind.	"	"
-82¾°	6	23¼°-84½°	22°.5-82¾°	High wind.	Sts. of Babel Mandel.	"
-82¾°	6	22¼°-82¼°	22°.5-82¾°	"	Aden at 10 A.M.	"
-82¾°	6	22¼°-82¼	22¼°-82¼°	Rain.	Aden.	"
1¾°	¼bf.6	21°-79½°	20°.5-78¼°	High wind.	Gulf of Aden.	"
78¾°	do.	22°-81¾°	20°.5-78¼°	"	"	"
9¼°	do.	22¼°-82¼°	20¼°-77¾°	"	"	"
80°	do.	21°.5-80½°	20¾°-78¾°	"	Indian Ocean.	"
32¼°	do.	22°-81¾°	22°-81¾°	High wind.	"	"
82½°	do.	22°-81¾°	22°.5-82¾°	High wind.	"	"
32¼°	do.	22¼°-82¼°	22°.5-82¾°	Calm.	"	"
84¾°	do.	23°.2-84⅓°	24¾°-87¼°	Calm.	"	"
1¾°	do.	22½°-82¼°	24°.5-87¼°	"	"	"
	6	22°.5-82¾°	23°.5-85°	Calm.	"	"
	4	22°-81¾°	"	Lightning in the evg.	Point de Galle.	"
	5	23⅓°-84¾°	"	Rain in the afternoon.	Point de Galle.	"
	"	"	"	Rain at mid-day.	Colombo.	"

Date.	Morning.	Air.	Water.	Forenoon.	Air.	Water	Afternoon.	Air.
		R. F.	R. F.		R. F.	R. F.		R. F.
Nov. 16	7	19°.8-76½°	”	12	24°-86¼°	”	”	”
17	8	20°.8-78¾°	”	12	23°-84°	”	”	”
18	”	”	”	12	23°-84°	”	1	23°.6-85¼°
19	8	20°-77°	”	12	22°.6-83°	”	”	”
20	7	18°.5-73¼°	”	11	20°.5-78¼°	”	1	23°.8-85¾°
21	½p.7	16°.8-69¾°	”	11	18°.5-73½°	”	3	17°-70¼°
22	6	18°.5-73½°	”	11	16°.5-69°	”	3	15°-65½°
23	7	10°.8-56°	”	10	16°-67¾°	”	1	18°.5-73½
24	½p.6	14°.6-64½°	”	11	19°-74¾°	”	4	17°.8-72°
25	7	15°-65½°	”	½p10	17°.2-70½°	”	4	18°.8-74¼°
26	½p.6	19°.8-76½°	”	11	20°.5-78¼°	”	½p.2	20°.9-79°
27	½p.7	19°-74¾°	”	11	20°.2-77½°	”	4	19°.5-75¾°
28	7	18°.9-74½°	”	11	19°.2-75¼°	”	4	18°.4-73¼°
29	8	19°.8-76½°	”	”	”	”	1	20°-77°
Dec. 6	6	12°.5-60°	”	”	”	”	”	”
7	7	19°.5-75¾°	”	”	”	”	1	20°.7-78½°
8	8	19°.4-75½°	”	”	”	”	”	”
9	7	17°.5-71¼°	”	”	”	”	2	19°.2-75¼°
10	”	”	”	10	14°.3-64¾°	”	1	10°.5-55½°
11	6	8°.7-51½°	”	”	”	”	”	”
15	8	19°.5-75¾°	”	12	22°.3-82¼°	”	”	”
16	7	21°.2-80°	”	12	23°-84°	”	”	”
18	7	21°.8-81¼°	”	”	”	”	2	23°-84°
1845								
Jan. 6	7	13°.5-62¼°	”	12	19°.5-75¾°	”	2	21°.5-80½°
7	7	12°.7-60¼°	”	12	21°.5-80½°	”	5	19°.4-75½°
8	7	13°.5-62¼°	”	”	”	”	1	22°.2-82¼°
9	7	13°.8-62¾°	”	10	18°.4-73½	”	2	22°.5-82¾°
10	7	14°.2-63¾°	”	10	18°.5-73½°	”	”	”
11	7	13°.6-62½°	”	10	18°.5-73½°	”	1	23°.5-85°
12	7	12°.7-60¼°	”	”	”	”	½p.4	20°.3-87¾°
14	”	10°-54½°	”	10	17°.5-71¼°	”	4	20°-77°
22	”	”	”	1	27°-93°	”	4	22°.5-82¾°
23	7	6°.2-46°	”	10	17°.2-70¾°	”	½p.3	23°.8-85¾°
Feb. 6	7	3°-39°	”	½p.8	12°.5-60°	”	”	”
12	7	5°.5-44½°	12°-59°	12	15°.5-66¾°	”	2	20°-77°
May 3	9	23°-84°	”	11	25°-88½°	”	2	21°-79¼°
4	7	18°-72½°	”	9	23°.5-85°	”	”	”
7	6	14°.2-63¾°	”	10	18°-72½°	Lakes. 13°.8-62¾	1	22°.5-82¾°
June 2	”	”	”	12	27°-93°	”	4	26°.5-91¾°
3	”	”	”	12	23°-84°	”	2	24°.5-87½°
5	5	11°-56¾°	”	11	20°.5-78¼°	”	1	21°.2-80°
6	”	”	”	11	27°-93°	”	1	28°-95¼°
7	6	16°.5-69°	”	8	20°-77°	”	”	”
8	7	17°.5-71¼°	”	”	”	”	4	18°-72½°
9	”	”	”	10	14°-63¼°	”	4	15°.2-66°
10	6	13°.5-62¼°	”	”	”	”	½p.1	9°-52¼°
11	6	7°-48°	”	10	10°.5-55½°	”	2	24°.5-87¼°
12	6	10°.2-55°	”	9	12°.5-60°	Lake. 16°.5-69°	1	17°.2-70¾°

...r.	Evening.	Air.	Water.	Remarks.	Place.	Height above the level of the sea.
F.		R. F.	R. F.			Feet.
	5	22°-81¾°	”	Rain at mid-day.	Colombo.	”
	5	21°.6-80½°	”	Clear, bright weather.	Colombo.	”
	”	”	”	Thunder-storm.	Journey to Kandy.	”
	4	18°.2-72¾°	”	Rain.	Kandy.	”
	7	15°-65½°	”	Thunder-storm.	Pusselawa.	”
	5	15°.2-66°	”	Fog.	Rambodda.	2,000
	5	14°.3-64°	”	Sunshine.	Nuwera Ellia.	6,400
	½p.4	16°.2-68¼°	”	Rain.	Wilson Bungalow.	”
	8	15°.2-66°	”	Thunder-storm.	Badulla.	2,200
	”	”	”	Rain.	Taldenia.	1,100
	7	19°.8-76½°	”	Rain.	Galbocka.	”
	”	”	”	Rain.	Galbocka.	”
	”	”	”	Rain.	”	”
	”	”	”	Rain.	”	”
	6	18°.3-73°	”	”	Haboo Talla.	”
	½p.6	20°-77°	”	”	Ratnapoora.	”
	”	”	”	”	Ratnapoora.	”
	6	18°-72½°	”	”	Palabadoolla.	2,500
	4	9°.5-53¼°	”	Misty evening.	Adam's Peak.	7,500
	”	”	”	”	Adam's Peak.	”
	6	21°.5-80½°	”	Thunder-storm.	Colombo.	”
	6	22°.3-82¼°	”	Thunder-storm.	Colombo.	”
	7	22°-81¾°	”	”	”	”
	7	15°.5-66¾°	”	”	Calcutta.	”
	7	15°.5-66¾°	”	Mor. and evn. misty.	”	”
	”	”	”	Misty morning.	”	”
	7	16°.8-69¾°	”	Little mist.	”	”
	7	18°.2-73°	”	Cloudy sky.	”	”
	7	18°.5-73½°	”	Misty morning.	”	”
	6	11°-56¾°	”	Misty morning.	”	”
	½p.6	17°-70¼°	”	Misty morning.	”	”
	7	15°.5-66¾°	”	”	Plain near Gaya.	”
	”	”	”	”	Gaya.	”
	”	”	”	”	Forest at Bechiaco.	”
	6	14°-63¼°	”	Average temperature.	Cathmandoo.	4,500
	7	19°-74¾°	”	Thun. stor. at 2 P.M.	Delhi, to Meerut.	”
	”	”	”	”	Journey towards Mooradabad.	”
	4	18°.4-73½°	”	”	Nadnethal.	6,300
	7	23°-84°	”	”	Adh Badri.	”
	7	20°.2-77½°	”	”	”	”
	6	18°.6-73¾°	”	”	Dhunpoor.	”
	6	25°-88½°	”	”	Bamoth.	”
	”	”	”	”	Journey to Pokri.	”
	7	15°-65½°	”	”	Pokri.	”
	”	”	”	Rain.	Pokri.	”
	8	10°.5-55½°	”	Wind.	Chobeda.	”
	8	15°.5-66¾°	”	”	Durithal.	”
	6	14°-63¼°	”	Clear, bright weather.	Durithal.	”

Date.	Morning.	Air.	Water.	Forenoon.	Air.	Water.	Afternoon.	Air.
		R. F.	R. F.		R. F.	R. F.		R. F.
June 14	7	13°-61°	,,	12	24°.5-87¼°	,,	5	22°.3-82¼°
15	,,	,,	,,	12	22°-81¾°	Spring. 41°.5-125½°	4	18°.5-73½°
16	6	5°.5-44¼°	,,	,,	,,	Spring. 4°.5-42¼°	3	9°.5-53¼°
17	6	5°-43¼°	,,	11	20°.2-77½°	,,	1	18°.6-73¾°
20	,,	,,	,,	12	24°-86¼°	,,	3	16°.5-69°
21	6	8°.3-50¾°	,,	12	23°-84°	,,	,,	,,
24	,,	,,	,,	,,	,,	,,	1	12°-59°
July 8	6	14°-63¼°	,,	9	21°-79½°	,,	1	26°-90¾°
4	6	9°-52¼°	,,	,,	,,	Spring. 3°.2-39½	,,	,,
12	8	10°-54½°	,,	,,	,,	,,	½ p. 6	9°.8-54°
13	6	5°.8-45¼°	,,	,,	,,	,,	,,	,,
14	6	4°.8-43°	,,	12	5°.6-44¾°	,,	2	4°.5-42¼°
15	,,	,,	,,	,,	,,	,,	,,	,,
16	6	5°-43¼°	,,	,,	,,	,,	,,	,,
19	8	9°-52¼°	,,	,,	,,	,,	2	11°-56¾°
22	7	10°.2-55°	,,	,,	,,	,,	,,	,,
28	,,	,,	,,	,,	,,	,,	,,	,,
31	[illegible]	,,	,,	,,	,,	,,	,,	,,

Evening.	Air.	Water.	Remarks.	Place.	Height above the level of the sea.
	R. F.	R. F.			Feet.
½ p. 7	19°-74¾°	„	Rainy evening.	„	„
7	17°.5-71½°	„	„	Gauricund.	6,800
7	7°.3-48¾°	„	„	Kedarnath.	11,800
7	15°.3-66°	„	„	Journey to Gauricund.	„
„	„	„	„	Pawali Danda.	„
„	„	„	„	Gowanna.	„
„	„	„	„	Pass of Kedarakhal.	10,580
6½	17°-70¼°	„	„	Mookba.	„
6	10°.2-55°	„	„	Gungotri.	9,670
½ p. 9	8°.5-51¾°	„	„	Foolal Daroo in the Valley of the Goomty.	11,270
7	5°.2-44°	„	Misty morning.	Sources of the Goomty. Lama Kaga Pass.—	12,000
7	9°.5-53¼°	„	Snow in the aftern.	Do Soomda.	15,355
„	„	„	„	Do Soomda.	13,366
„	„	„	Wind and Rain.	Bivouac on the Buspa.	12,278
7	9°.5-53¼°	„	Rain.	Chetkool.	10,495
„	„	„	„	Ragsam.	9,756
„	„	„	„	Cheenee.	7,320
„	„	„	„	Pass of Errengkhal.	11,500